CISTERCIAN STUDIES SERIES:
NUMBER ONE HUNDRED EIGHTY-FIVE

Peter King

WESTERN MONASTICISM

CW00953527

Saint Benedict of Nursia, from an altarpiece in Rome.

CISTERCIAN STUDIES SERIES:
NUMBER ONE HUNDRED EIGHTY-FIVE

WESTERN MONASTICISM
A History of the Monastic Movement in the Latin Church

by

Peter King

CISTERCIAN PUBLICATIONS
Kalamazoo, Michigan — Spencer, Massachusetts

Cistercian Publications

Editorial Offices
The Institute of Cistercian Studies
Western Michigan University
Kalamazoo, Michigan 49008-5415
cistpub@wmich.edu

*The work of Cistercian Publications is made possible in part by support from
Western Michigan University to The Institute of Cistercian Studies.*

CISTERCIAN PUBLICATIONS BOOKS ARE AVAILABLE
AT THE FOLLOWING ADDRESSES:

The United States and Canada: Liturgical Press
Saint John's Abbey   Collegeville, MN 56321-7500
sales@litpress.org

The United Kingdom and Europe: The Columba Press
55A Spruce Avenue
Stillorgan Industrial Park
Blackrock, Co. Dublin   IRELAND
info@columba.ie

Library of Congress Cataloging-in-Publication

King, Peter, M.A.
    Western monasticism : a history of the monastic movement in the
Latin church / by Peter King.
        p. cm.—(Cistercian studies series ; no. 185)
    Includes bibliographical references (p.   ) and indexes.
    ISBN 0–87907–685–2 (alk. paper).—ISBN 0–87907–785–9
(pbk. : alk. paper)
        1. Monasticism and religious orders—Europe—History.
    2. Monasticism and religious orders—History.   I. Title.   II. Series.

BX2590.K56   1999
271—dc21   99–39500
                                                                              CIP

Typeset by BookComp, Inc.
Printed in the United States of America

FOR CHRISTINE

TABLE OF CONTENTS

PREFACE

IN HIS MONUMENTAL *Acta sanctorum ordinis sancti Benedicti*,[1] Jean Mabillon collected material for the lives of all the saints who recognised Saint Benedict as their patriarch, even though some, like the Cluniacs and the Cistercians, belonged to congregations established long after his death. Monastic saints before Saint Benedict he placed in an appendix.[2]

The present modest study, which treats of monasticism in the latin west from the beginnings to the present day, is written from the same perspective. Monasticism is here understood as a life under rule, dedicated to prayer and meditation. Other forms of religious life which developed in the west, therefore, like regular canons, friars, or regular clerks, have not been included.

I have incurred many debts. I should like to say a special word of thanks to Dr Rozanne Elder, for her friendship and encouragement over many years. Many scholars have taken time to give me advice and help: Father Hilary Costello OCSO, the Rev'd Dr Brian Halloran, Professor Peter Humfrey, Bishop Kallistos of Dioclea, Father Augustine Kelly OSB, Dr. A. J. Krailsheimer, the Rev'd Dr Adam Dunbar McCoy OHC, Dr Paul Magdalino, Father Pierdamiano Spotorno OSB, and Professor Daniel Waley.

Since this study was largely written from materials available in Scotland (otherwise I should never have finished), I owe much to Mr Neil Dumbleton and others on the staff of the University Library at Saint Andrews: Mr Martin Barkla, Mr Ken Fraser, Mrs Kate Newton, Mr Frank Storey, and Miss Jean

---

[1] Jean Mabillon, *Acta sanctorum ordinis sancti Benedicti*, 9 vols. (Paris 1668–1701).

[2] Henri Leclercq, *Mabillon* 1 (Paris 1953) 77.

Young. I was also greatly helped by Mrs Christine Gascoigne, Rare Books Librarian at Saint Andrews University Library. Dr Simone Macdougall took infinite trouble in reading the manuscript and helping it through the last stages. My son Stephen King, brilliantly transferred the text from an Amstrad to an IBM-compatible disc.

Last but not least, my dear wife Christine has read every line of this book and compiled the index. Without her love and devotion no effort would be worth while, and all achievement would be ashes.

P. K.

Saint Andrews
Feast of the Sacred Heart, 1996.

ABBREVIATIONS

For details, see the bibliography

CCM	Corpus Consuetudinum Monasticarum
DACL	Dictionnaire d'Archéologie Chrétienne et de Liturgie
DHGE	Dictionnaire d'Histoire et de Géographie Ecclésiastiques
DIP	Dizionario degli Istituti di Perfezione
DS	Dictionnaire de Spiritualité
DTC	Dictionnaire de Théologie Catholique
LM	Lexikon des Mittelalters
PL	Patrologia Latina
RB	Regula Benedicti
RM	Regula Magistri
SMBO	Studien und Mitteilungen zur Geschichte des Benediktinerordens und seiner Zweige
TRE	Theologische Realenzyklopädie

LIST OF ILLUSTRATIONS

Frontispiece. Saint Benedict, from an altarpiece in Rome. Jean Mabillon, *Museum Italicum* 1 (Paris 1687) 146.

1. Page 113. The Plan of Saint Gall.
   From Jean Mabillon, *Annales Ordinis Sancti Benedicti* 2 (Lucca 1739) 532. *Courtesy of Saint Andrews University Library.*

2. Page 132. View of the Abbey of Cluny.
   From Mabillon, *Annales Ordinis Sancti Benedicti* (Lucca 1740) 236. *Courtesy of Saint Andrews University Library.*

3. Page 180. The Cistercian Abbey of Chorin, Brandenburg (Germany)
   From W. Erdmann, *Zisterzienser-Abtei Chorin.*
   Königstein-in-Taunus 1994, page 3. Courtesy of Karl Robert Langewiesche Nachfolger, Verlag der Blauen Bücher.

4. Page 196. The Benedictine Nunnery of Malling, Kent (England).
   William Dugdale, *Monasticon Anglicanum* 3 (London 1846) 381. *Courtesy of Saint Andrews University Library.*

5. Page 241. Signorelli: Saint Benedict and Totila.
   Fresco in the Cloister of Montoliveto, near Siena (Italy). *Scala Istituto Fotografico Editoriale, Florence, Italy.*

6. Page 253. Saint Benedict's Miracle of the Raven.
   Fresco in the Cloister degli Aranci of the Badia, Florence (Italy). *Scala Istituto Fotografico Editoriale, Florence.*

7. Page 313. Choirstalls dating to 1720 in the Benedictine Abbey of Weingarten, Baden-Würtemberg (Germany). *Property of the author.*

8. Page 369. The Abbey of Einsiedeln. *Property of the author.* Saint Meinrad's Archabbey. *Courtesy of the Archabbot and Community.*

9. Page 426 The community of Our Lady of the Mississippi Abbey, Dubuque, Iowa, with Georg Müller, bishop prelate of Trondheim, on the eve of the foundation of Marienkloster Tautra (1998). *Courtesy of the Abbess and Community.*

Chapter 1
EGYPT

W ITHIN THE EARLIEST CHRISTIAN communities there were ascetics. They abstained from
marriage and sexual intercourse, adopted voluntary poverty, and dedicated themselves to a life of prayer and
good works. By the end of the first christian century they were
very numerous. The author of the Book of Revelation assigned
to them the symbolic number of 'one hundred and forty-
four thousand'. 'It is these who have not defiled themselves
with women, for they are chaste; it is these who follow the
Lamb wherever he goes.' Only they could learn the new song
which was being sung before the four living creatures and the
elders.[1] According to Athenagoras, who wrote an apology for
Christianity around 176, there were many Christians, 'both
men and women, growing old unmarried in the hope of being
united more closely with God'.[2]

There was not, and there never would be, a single mode of
life for these ascetics to follow. As late as the sixth century, some
Christians were still living as penitents within their own homes,
and their way of life was very much of their own devising. Saint
Jerome felt it necessary to warn the roman virgin Eustochium
against indulging in too much wine, luxurious foods, or visits.
He advised her to rise during the night to pray, to fast daily,
and to give time to reading. 'Read often and learn all you can.
Let sleep steal upon you with a book in your hand, and let the
sacred page catch your drooping head.' If her maids wished
to take the vow of virginity with her they should all adopt a
common life: singing psalms and receiving the Body of Christ

---

[1] Rev 14:3–5.
[2] *Athenagoras*, ed. W. R. Schoedel (Oxford 1972) 81.

together, and sharing their meals.[3] Ascetics of this kind had
a special place in the liturgy. According to Saint Augustine, a
bishop was greeted in his church by the chant of consecrated
virgins.[4]

Indirect evidence about the early ascetics is provided by
Origen, the first of the great theologians of the Church (c. 185–
c. 254). As a christian teacher in Caesarea in the 230s he
organised his pupils in a kind of religious community.[5] It was
here, no doubt, that he evolved a theory of asceticism. Origen's
experience had been shaped by the persecution of Christians.
His own father had been martyred in 202, and at the end
of his life, during the persecution of Decius, he himself was
to be tortured. His ascetic theories centred on the idea of
martyrdom in which the Christian shared most intimately in
the redemptive sufferings of Christ. Unlike certain zealots,
however, Origen did not recommend that Christians court
martyrdom. They could win the merit of the martyrs by spiritual combat—through the mortification of fasting, continual
prayer, and, above all, virginity. This final virtue was not a
mere negative abstention from sex, but a gift from God which
brought with it pure faith and the practice of Charity.[6]

Mortification, according to Origen, was also important
as a guard, preserving the purity of the ascetic against the
assaults of the senses. Clearly temptations were particularly to
be feared in the city. During the third century some christian
ascetics began to withdraw to obscure places. It has been suggested that this movement began with fugitives taking refuge
in the egyptian desert from the persecution of the Emperor
Decius (250–251). When peace returned to the Church, some
of them, having found positive value in a life of retirement,
stayed where they were.[7] Best known of these early solitaries

---

[3] *Select Letters of St. Jerome*, trans. and ed. F. A. Wright (Cambridge Mass.
1975) Ep. 22.
[4] W. H. C. Frend, *The Rise of Christianity* (London 1984) 558.
[5] Henri Crouzel, *Origen* (Edinburgh 1989) 26–27.
[6] *Ibid.* 135–144; *Dictionnaire de Spiritualité* 11: 933–961, 949–955.
[7] Frend, *Rise of Christianity*, 320–321; 422–423; D. W. Chitty, *The Desert a
City* (Crestwood, New York 1966) 6–7; 17n., 32, 33.

is Saint Anthony. The *Life of Anthony* written by his friend
Saint Athanasius, bishop of Alexandria[8] is the earliest known
biography of a christian holy man. Widely read and quickly
imitated it was responsible for many conversions, including
Augustine's.[9]

Anthony, an egyptian peasant farmer, was born around 251.
One Sunday, when he was about twenty years old, he heard in
church the words, 'If thou wilt be perfect, go and sell all thou
hast and give to the poor . . . and come, follow me'.[10] Anthony
sold the farm, keeping back a little money for his sister. Very
soon on another occasion he heard words from the Gospel: 'Do
not be anxious about tomorrow, for tomorrow will be anxious
for itself'.[11] Thereupon he gave away the rest of the money and
entrusted his sister to a 'house of virgins'.

He began his new life in a kind of shack, built on a piece
of land which had formerly belonged to him. A number of
other solitaries living in the neighbourhood gave him advice.
He provided for himself and the poor by light manual work
and was assiduous in attendance at church.

Moving to the necropolis outside the village, Anthony
wrestled with distractions from prayer and with various temptations. This spiritual combat he understood as a fight against
demons. Gradually he conquered his evil fantasies. He next
decided to cross the Nile and take up residence on the edge
of the egyptian desert. The other solitaries refused to go with
him. For twenty years he lived in an abandoned fort. Bread
was brought to him twice a year. At the end of this period his
friends, insisting on seeing him, were amazed to find him in
good health. His fame as a holy man and a miracle worker
began to spread. Others now followed his lead and took up
solitary asceticism in the desert. There was no organisation,
but they all looked to him as their adviser and leader.

---

[8] *Vie d'Antoine* ed. G. J. M. Bartelink (Paris 1994).
[9] Peter Brown, *Augustine of Hippo* (London 1990) 108–109.
[10] Mt 19:21.
[11] Mt. 6:34.

Diocletian's persecution of the Christians 303–311—the last of its kind—no doubt impelled some of these zealous Christians to flee into the desert. Anthony himself emerged from his retirement and travelled to Alexandria to give what help and comfort he could to imprisoned Christians, drawing down upon himself the wrath of the authorities. When the persecution ended, after the martyrdom of bishop Peter of Alexandria in 311, Anthony returned to his desert retreat.

The peace of the Church, established in 313, ushered in a new period. Not only was Anthony attracting more followers but he was beginning to be regarded as a christian seer whose advice was eagerly sought. He decided therefore to seek even greater seclusion on an inaccessible mountain.

After the Council of Nicaea in 325 the Church, now officially favoured by Constantine, was wracked by disputes about the doctrine of the Trinity. Athanasius, bishop of Alexandria and uncompromising champion of the Council's definitions, realised the importance of Anthony's support. In 330, shortly after ascending the See of Alexandria, he went down into the desert to consult the hermit. Anthony is said to have written to Constantine on Athanasius's behalf, and in 338 he went to Alexandria to demonstrate his support for his bishop.

When Anthony died in 356, he was over one hundred years old.[12] By this time the beginnings of monasticism as an institution can be discerned. Three centres of ascetic life were established by Anthony's disciples in the area west of the Nile Delta between Alexandria and Cairo: Nitria, settled by Ammun and his followers around 325; the Cells to which they migrated some years later in search of greater isolation; and Scete, founded by Macarius and his companions in 330.[13]

The Greek word μοναζόντες first occurs in christian papyri in 324 and 334; it was used for the solitaries and means

---

[12] Chitty (as n. 7) 1–7, 28–29.
[13] Jean Gribomont, 'Eastern Christianity', *Christian Spirituality* (London 1986) 93–94.

'those who live alone'.[14] Monks were aware, nevertheless, of the importance of contact with one another. Anthony had given them a certain unity through his teaching. Many of his disciples, in their turn, acquired fame as teachers of the spiritual life. Through the tradition of these 'elders' a kind of common rule came into being, informally and, we may assume, very gradually. Among the ascetics there came to be a distinction between the 'elders' and the 'juniors'. The 'elders' decided if and when any of the 'juniors' were to be admitted into their ranks. A 'presbyter' presided over the whole community of hermits in a certain area. Although the monks lived in their own cells, some of them remote, there were churches where they assembled for common worship on Saturdays and Sundays. The elders exercised discipline over the others, regulated the worship of the community, and distributed the alms which were sent from Alexandria and other cities. Since the monks occupied some of their time with light manual work, especially basket-weaving, the elders organised the sale of the community's produce through an officer known as the 'guardian'.[15]

The spirit of these early solitaries breathes through the collection of their sayings—the *Apophthegmata Patrum*. None of the collections now surviving dates from before the sixth century,[16] but when all allowances have been made it is generally agreed that much of the teaching of the Desert Fathers has been preserved in these texts.

> To throw yourself before God, not to measure your progress, to leave behind all self-will; these are the instruments for the work of the soul.[17]

---

[14] See E. A. Judge, 'The earliest use of *monachus* for "monk" (P. Coll. Youtie 77) and the origins of monasticism', *Jahrbuch für Antike und Christentum* 20 (1977) 2–89.

[15] Owen Chadwick, *John Cassian* (Cambridge 1968) 22–23.

[16] For a brief account see *ibid.* 1–3, and *The Sayings of the Desert Fathers*, xvii–xxi, trans. B. Ward (Kalamazoo 1975). All the quotations below are from the latter.

[17] Poemen 36.

Abba Aio questioned Abba Macarius and said: 'Give me a word.' Abba Macarius said to him: 'Flee from men, stay in your cell, weep for your sins, do not take pleasure in the conversations of men, and you will be saved.'[18]

Someone asked Abba Agathon, 'Which is better, bodily asceticism or interior vigilance?' The old man replied, ' "Man is like a tree, bodily asceticism is the foliage, interior vigilance the fruit. According to that which is written, *Every tree that bringeth not forth good fruit shall be cut down and cast into the fire* (Mt 3:10), it is clear that all our care should be directed towards the fruit, that is to say, guard of the spirit; but it needs the protection and the embellishment of the foliage, which is bodily asceticism.'[19]

The artless charity which bound these solitaries to one another is beautifully illustrated in the account of the visit of Saint Macarius to Saint Anthony:

One day Abba Macarius the Great came to Abba Anthony's dwelling on the mountain. When he knocked on the door, Anthony came out to him and said to him, 'Who are you?' " He replied, 'I am Macarius'. Then Anthony went inside and shut the door leaving him there. Later, seeing his patience, he opened the door and received Macarius with joy, saying to him, 'I have wanted to see you for a long time, having heard about you.' He rendered him all the duties of hospitality and made him rest, for he was very tired. When evening came, Abba Anthony soaked some palm-leaves for himself, and Abba Macarius said to him, 'Allow me to soak some for myself'. He replied, 'Do so'. Having made a large bundle, he soaked them. Then sitting down in the evening they spoke of the salvation of the soul, while they plaited the leaves. The rope which Macarius was making hung down through the window in the cave. Going in early, blessed Anthony saw the length of Abba Macarius' rope and said, 'Great power comes out of these hands.'[20]

---

[18] Macarius 41.
[19] Agathon 8.
[20] Macarius 4.

The monastic community spirit which can be seen in this text was the basis of the next development: the creation of communities of ascetics living together in a single establishment, with a common discipline and rhythm of life. In a very short time the word 'monastery', originally used of a cell for one or two ascetics, came to be used exclusively for a community of this kind.[21] By the fifth century Cassian, writing in Gaul, was making use of the specialised vocabulary which has been current since his time. Monks who lived together in a single community following a common rhythm of life were known as 'cenobites'. Those who lived separately, each under his own roof, he called anchorites;[22] later they were more commonly called hermits, and the distinction was made between the cenobitic and the eremitic way of life. Hermits lived in remote cells but occasionally emerged to visit one another or to take part in common worship. The name anchorite came to be reserved for solitaries who never moved from one place, like the fifth century Saint Simeon Stylites who lived for years almost immobile on top of a pillar.[23]

The origin of cenobitic monasteries is obscure. Saint Anthony at the end of the third century entrusted his sister to a 'house of virgins'.[24] It was Pachomius, however, whose successful organisation of cenobitic monasteries so changed the pattern of christian asceticism that, by the fifth century, Cassian could write of the cenobites, 'Of this kind there is the largest number of monks dwelling throughout the whole of Egypt'.[25]

Pachomius was born in the Thebaid of pagan parents, at the end of the third century.[26] In 312/313 he was impressed

[21] Chitty (as n. 7) 11.
[22] Cassian, *Conference* 18. 4, 5.
[23] On Simeon, see N. H. Baynes, *Three Byzantine Saints*, ed. E. Dawes and N. H. Baynes (Oxford 1977) 3–4; and Robert Doran, trans. *The Lives of Symeon Stylites* (Kalamazoo 1992).
[24] See above p. 17.
[25] Cassian, *Conference* 18.4.
[26] On Pachomius, see Chitty (as n. 7), 7–11, 21–28; Philip Rousseau, *Pachomius* (Berkeley 1985); A. Veilleux, *La Liturgie dans le Cénobitisme Pachômien au qua-*

into the army with other young men and marched down the banks of the Nile to take part in the civil war between Maximin and Licinius. At Luxor, where the youngsters were forced to spend the night locked in a prison, they were befriended by some Christians. Pachomius was so impressed by their charity that when the war ended he sought baptism. Within a short time he had adopted the life of an ascetic under the guidance of a solitary called Palamon. It was while he was still under the hermit's direction that he had his first vision. He had been collecting wood and wandered as far as a deserted village called Tabennesi when he heard a voice which urged him to build a monastery there and promised that many others would join him. He built himself a cabin in the place. As long as Palamon remained alive they kept in touch, but the older hermit soon died. Pachomius was then joined by his brother John, but the two quarrelled. John, the elder brother, it seems, was touchy about his seniority. Moreover he wanted to remain a solitary, whereas Pachomius wished to found a larger community. These differences continued until John's death.

Gradually Pachomius began to gather disciples, among them his favourite, Theodore. Around 320 his vocation was confirmed by another vision. His sister asked to embrace the ascetic life and not far away he established a house of women of which she became the superior. When numbers at Tabennesi had grown beyond a hundred, Pachomius established another monastery at Phbow, a few miles down the Nile. Two other monasteries already in existence asked to join the community. Around 337 Pachomius moved his headquarters to Phbow, appointing his favourite disciple Theodore superior at Tabennesi. A number of other monasteries for men and another for women were founded before Pachomius died in 346.[27]

---

trième siècle (Rome 1968). The Lives of Saint. Pachomius and other documents relating to early pachomian monasticism are collected in *Pachomian Koinonia*, 3 vols., trans. A. Veilleux (Kalamazoo 1980–1982).
[27] Chitty, 7–24; Rousseau, *Pachomius*, 57–76.

These communities were held together by Pachomius's teaching. 'They lived a cenobitic life', says one of the *Lives of Saint Pachomius:*

> So he established for them in a rule an irreproachable life-style and traditions profitable for their souls. These he took from the holy Scriptures: proper measure in clothing, equality in food, and decent sleeping arrangements.[28]

The rule which Pachomius established for his monks was conveyed through oral teaching.

> He would often sit to instruct the brothers, teaching them first of all to know blamelessly and without any ignorance the craftiness of the enemies, and to oppose them with the Lord's power. For it is written, 'In God we shall have strength'. Then he would interpret for them the words of the divine Scriptures, especially the deep and not easily comprehensible ones, and those about the Lord's incarnation, the cross, and the resurrection.[29]

A number of rules ascribed to Pachomius have survived.[30] They do not constitute an all-embracing set of enactments after the manner of the Rule of Saint Benedict, but are concerned for the most part with details of an organisation the main lines of which are always assumed.

A pachomian monastery was surrounded by a wall and contained a number of buildings used in common by the community. There was a hall for worship, a refectory, a kitchen, a bakehouse, and an infirmary. In addition there were a number of houses containing the cells of individual monks. Each house numbered about twenty to forty monks and had its own superior and second. The whole monastery was subject to a steward, who also had a second. In a later development each house was responsible for the exercise of a particular craft.[31]

---

[28] *Pachomian Koinonia*, 1: 313.
[29] *Ibid.* 236.
[30] *Pachomian Koinonia*, 2: 141–195.
[31] Chitty, 22–23.

After their evening service the monks could sleep in their cells propped up on special seats. Keeping a night-vigil was a voluntary act of private devotion. The first common service was at dawn and took place in the monastery's prayer hall. The monks took their manual work with them and worked quietly at it during the scripture readings. Penances for any fault were performed during this service. After the service the monks returned to their cells and waited for the superiors of their house to make the rounds and issue them any materials or special instructions for the day's tasks. Then they were lined up and left for work. The tasks in a pachomian monastery were varied: the sources mention husbandmen, gardeners, fullers, basketmakers, shoemakers, copyists, tailors, metalworkers, and carpenters.

The main meal of the day took place during the work period. The community ate in the refectory in complete silence. Bread and cooked vegetables formed the main items of the diet. A light evening meal followed the end of work, after which the monks returned to their houses for an evening service conducted in the special room which was set aside in each house for this purpose.[32]

At the morning office, every monk had his appointed place. All sat working quietly, while each monk in turn, beginning with the most senior, recited texts or sections of Holy Scripture. When the reader had finished, he gave a signal and all rose to their feet. They made the sign of the cross. Then, crossing their arms over their breasts, they recited the Our Father. At another signal, they repeated the sign of the cross, prostrated themselves and prayed in silence. Then yet another signal was given for them to sit down again and listen to another portion of Scripture.[33] The main feature of the evening service, which took place in the prayer room of each house, was the 'Six Prayers', the nature of which is still the subject of scholarly debate.[34]

---

[32] Rousseau (as n. 26), 77–86.

[33] Veilleux (as n. 26), 307–308.

[34] See discussion *ibid*. 309–13.

Singing the psalms was a feature of the morning service
only on Sundays. The method of chanting was 'antiphonal',
with a soloist singing the verses and a choir singing the refrain.
Each house in turn was responsible for the Sunday psalmody.
Only the head of the house could sing the verses. The other
monks of the house stood around the reading desk making the
responses.[35]

The eucharistic liturgy was the centre of the community's worship on Saturday evenings and Sunday mornings.
Pachomius did not wish any of his monks to be ordained:

> When there was a need for the Eucharist, he called in from
> the nearest churches a priest who made the celebration for
> them. For among them there was no one invested with the
> clerical office. He had deliberated on the subject and often
> told them that it was good not to ask for rank and honour,
> especially in a community, for fear this would be an occasion
> for strife, envy, jealousy, and then schisms to arise in a large
> community of monks.[36]

Some of the Pachomian communities had their own church,
but it was quite common for the monks to go to the nearest
village church for the Eucharist.[37]

The monks of the Pachomian monasteries saw themselves
as a *koinonia*—a single brotherhood. Twice a year all assembled together around their common father at Phbow. They
came together to celebrate Easter. On this occasion, according to Saint Jerome, in whose time these monasteries were
still flourishing, 'nearly fifty thousand men celebrate together
the feast of the Lord's passion'. In August they all assembled
together for a second time to render accounts and for the
appointment, if necesary, of new superiors. On this occasion
sins were forgiven and quarrels reconciled.[38]

The teachings of the desert solitaries, as later expressed
in the *Apophthegmata,* were the basis for the life of these

[35] *Ibid.*, 314–315.
[36] *Pachomian Koinonia* , 1: 314.
[37] Veilleux (as n. 26), 231–232.
[38] *Pachomian Koinonia*, 2: 143–144.

foundations. In time developed a pachomian spirituality which can be studied from its extensive literary remains. In addition to the rules attributed to Pachomius,[39] a few letters and an 'Instruction concerning a spiteful monk' have been preserved.[40] In the lives of the saint there are accounts of homilies he preached. Some of the writings of his successors Theodore and Horsiesios also survive.[41] The Testament of the latter is, in the opinion of Armand Veilleux, 'one of the most beautiful pieces of pachomian literature, and a faithful and complete expression of pachomian spirituality'.[42]

Pachomian spirituality is marked by its biblical character. The morning service, as we have seen, was based upon the reading of Scripture. On their way to the service[43] and on their way back to their cells,[44] the monks recited scriptural passages which they had learned by heart. It was Pachomius' fame as a biblical exegete which first drew Theodore, his favourite disciple, to seek him out.[45] The Testament of Horsiesios is embellished throughout with long quotations from Scripture. Every admonition to the monks is grounded upon the appropriate biblical passage.[46] Pachomius's advice to his first followers was, 'Strive, brothers, to attain to that to which you have been called: to recite psalms and teachings from other parts of the Scriptures, especially the Gospel'.[47]

Pachomian monks did not see themselves as marginal in the Church but rather as central to its life. The preface to the First Greek *Life of Saint Pachomius* begins, like the Gospel of Saint John, with the Word of God who is Truth. It continues with the promise to Abraham after the sacrifice of Isaac. There is a brief mention of Moses, and then the

---

[39] *Ibid.* 141–95.
[40] *Pachomian Koinonia*, 3: 13–89.
[41] *Ibid.* 91–224.
[42] *Ibid.* 2: 8.
[43] *Ibid.* 3: 145 (rule 3).
[44] *Ibid.* 150 (rule 28).
[45] *Ibid.* 1: 321–322.
[46] *Ibid.* 3: 171–224.
[47] *Ibid.* 312.

writer goes on to the Incarnation and the mission of the Church to preach the Gospel to all nations. There follows an account of the persecutions of the Church, with special mention of the martyrdom of Bishop Peter of Alexandria. 'From that time on there began to appear monasteries and places of ascetics honoured for their chastity and renunciation of possessions. When those who from being pagans had become monks had seen the struggles and patient endurance of the martyrs, they began to renew their life.' The life of Saint Anthony is compared to that of Elijah, Elisha, and Saint John the Baptist.Other solitaries in Egypt are mentioned by name. After the last of the persecutions, the preface continues, the number of converts to Christianity increased greatly. The career of Saint. Pachomius was a part of this new harvest of the Gospel.[48]

The first flowering of christian monasticism occurred at a critical time in the history of the Church. In 313 the so-called Edict of Milan ended the persecution of Christians once and for all. The Emperor Constantine soon began to look upon the Church as an important support of his monarchy and to grant it various privileges. Christianity soon became the new state religion. Bishops were now looked on as the emperor's advisers and held important positions at court. From having been persecuted, they became persecutors of those holding deviant opinions.

The consequent worldliness and lowering of standards did not go unnoticed. Saint. Jerome remarked that as the Church acquired princely might it became 'greater in power as measured by its wealth, but less in virtue'.[49] 'Not all bishops are true bishops', he wrote, 'You notice Peter; but mark Judas as well . . . Ecclesiastical rank does not make a man a Christian'.[50] As for christian priests, 'There are other men . . . who only seek the office of presbyter and deacon that they may be able to visit

---

[48] *Ibid.* 1: 297–299. See also the preface to the Bohairic Life, *ibid.* 23–25.
[49] Quoted in Frend, *Rise of Christianity*, 716.
[50] Ep. 14.

women freely . . . When you see these gentry, think of them rather as potential bridegrooms than as clergymen'.[51]

The monastic movement of the fourth and fifth centuries must be seen against the background of these developments. Instead of seeking influence, the monks fled the world; instead of pandering to their creature comforts, they embraced a life of asceticism. The essentially scriptural teaching of Pachomius and his successors must be understood within this context. For them Christianity demanded an immediate and literal response to the commands of the Bible and particularly of the Gospel.

The monastic movement was not generally, however, a revolt against the Church. Although Egypt was home to many religious movements, the strength of christian orthodoxy in the countryside as well as in Alexandria has recently been emphasised.[52] Pachomius was rigidly orthodox. 'The holy man gave to the orthodox bishops and successors of the apostles and of Christ himself the heed of one who sees the Lord ever presiding upon the episcopal throne in the church and teaching through it,' states one of the *Lives*.[53] In 329–330, shortly after becoming bishop of Alexandria, Athanasius visited Pachomius's community at Tabennesi.[54] One of the bishop's treatises against Arius was written 'for all those in every place who follow the monastic life'.[55] In 360 it was rumoured that the bishop, then in exile, was being hidden by the monks of Tabennesi, and the monastery was searched by imperial officers.[56] Athanasius's last visit to the pachomian communities took place in 363.[57]

Athanasius was not the only bishop to appreciate the importance of the new monastic movement. There is evidence that some pachomian monasteries were founded at the request

---

[51] Ep. 22.
[52] See discussion in Rousseau, 19–36.
[53] *Pachomian Koinonia* 1: 318.
[54] *Ibid*. 317.
[55] *Athanasius Werke*, ed. H. G. Opitz 2 (Berlin-Leipzig 1935) 181–230.
[56] *Pachomian Koinonia* 1: 395.
[57] *Ibid*. 400–402.

of local bishops. During the fourth and fifth centuries a number of monks were promoted to the egyptian episcopate. Not for the last time in christian history, it was felt that the ascetic standards of monks and hermits would benefit the Church as a whole and recall it to its original ideals.[58]

According to pachomian tradition, Anthony had thought highly of Pachomius. He even went so far as to say that the only reason why he himself had not joined a *koinonia* when he became a monk was that such a thing did not yet exist.[59] This attempt to make Pachomius' institution appear as the fulfilment of Anthony's hopes must be seen as somewhat blatant propaganda. In fact, there is evidence of polemics between cenobites and hermits. According to the latter, life in a monastery involved servitude under superiors who did not hesitate to enforce their commands with blows. A hermit senior did not demand obedience but taught by example.[60] The Pachomians countered with the argument that a hermit in his solitude did not help his fellow-Christians to carry their burdens or encourage them by his example. A cenobite who was content with the lowest place in the monastery was more meritorious than a hermit, however astonishing his ascetic practices.[61]

A far more damaging dispute arose in the last years of the fourth century and put an end to the first and most creative phase of egyptian monasticism. Christian Egypt was bilingual: Greek was the language of Alexandria and the hellenised cities; in the country the Coptic dialects were spoken. The Greek-speaking monks in the desert were greatly influenced by the erudite Origen. In the last decades of the fourth century, Evagrius Ponticus, a cosmopolitan Greek who had spent much time in Constantinople, settled in the desert and used his learning to form a systematic monastic theology. His analysis of the passions and of the demonic activity which threatened

[58] Rousseau, 158–171.
[59] *Pachomian Koinonia*, 1: 182–187.
[60] F. Ruppert, *Das pachomianische Mönchtum und die Anfänge klösterlichen Gehorsams*, (Münsterschwarzach 1971) 85–87.
[61] *Ibid.* 13–18.

the integrity of the hermit influenced all future writings on the subject.[62] For the Coptic-speaking monks, however, the concept of God held by Evagrius and other Greeks was too intellectual. They were inclined to take literally the traditional language about God: his face, his right hand, his anger, and the other human attributes applied to him in the Bible. The extent of their 'anthropomorphism' may have been exaggerated by their enemies. Theophilus, bishop of Alexandria, was himself influenced by Origen and thought highly of Evagrius. At first he was inclined to ignore complaints about intellectualism, but after the death of Evagrius in 399, he felt unable to resist mounting pressure from the Coptic monks. A synod of bishops at Alexandria condemned Origen. Monks who refused to accept the condemnation were forced to go into exile.[63]

As it turned out, the dispersal of the Greek-speaking monks had the effect of making the ideals of egyptian monasticism more widely known. The collections which eventually took the shape of the *Apophthegmata Patrum* were begun by the exiles, who also brought with them the writings of Evagrius. The exiled monk Cassian was eventually to record the teachings of the desert fathers in Latin. Saint Jerome (347–420) made a latin translation of some of the rules of Saint Pachomius, and wrote a preface in which he described the pachomian communities as they were in his day.[64] A description of a journey to Egypt in 394–395, called *Historia Monachorum in Aegypto*, exists in a Greek and a Latin version. The latter is ascribed to Jerome's contemporary Rufinus.[65] Another and even more famous description in Greek is the *Lausiac History* of Palladius.[66] Although the accuracy of some of these authors has been questioned more than once,[67] the descriptive

---

[62] *Evagrius Pontikos: The Praktikos and Chapters on Prayer*, ed. and trans., John Eudes Bamberger (Kalamazoo 1981).
[63] *Ibid.* xlviii–xlix.
[64] *Pachomian Koinonia*, 2: 141–167.
[65] Chadwick (as n. 15), 7.
[66] *Ibid.* 6–7.
[67] Palladius and Cassian are roughly treated in Veilleux (as n. 26), 138–158.

literature gave egyptian monasticism its unique and enduring reputation.

Christian asceticism did not originate in Egypt. It is as old as Christianity itself. Very early examples can be detected in various places. Nor were the hermits and cenobites of Egypt typical of christian ascetics everywhere. Developments in Syria, Cappadocia, and the West, all differed somewhat. Thanks to its brilliant propagandists, however, Egypt seized the christian imagination in the fifth century. It was the home of the first great monastic leaders. Saint Anthony and his disciples, Saint Pachomius and his successors, were organisers of genius who created the first monastic institutions. They were spiritual guides who directed their followers with wisdom and discretion, and teachers of vision who saw the relevance of the ascetic life to the Church as a whole. It is for this reason that any history of Christian monasticism, whether eastern or western, has to begin with them.

Chapter 2
THE BEGINNINGS OF MONASTICISM IN THE WEST

THE PRIEST NOVATIAN was the first ascetic in the Church of Rome who is known by name. In 249/250 he withdrew into a cell to live the life of a christian philosopher. His decision was criticised by Pope Cornelius,[1] and the resulting controversy created in the Latin Church a tradition—unknown in the East—of ecclesiastical disapproval of at least some aspects of asceticism. In the west monasticism had to justify itself. This may explain why in early latin monasticism, the literary monuments are more impressive than actual monastic establishments on the ground.

At first, information about the monastic movement came from latin translations of greek texts. One of the most influential was the Life of Anthony. A rather wooden translation into Latin was made during the lifetime of Saint Athanasius. Somewhat later a more polished latin translation by Evagrius won a wide readership and greatly influenced Saint Jerome.[2] Equally influential were the Rules of Saint Basil, translated into Latin around 396 by Rufinus of Aquileia and known in this version throughout Italy, Gaul, and Spain.[3] Basil of Caesarea in Cappadocia (330–379) had envisaged communities heavily engaged with the christian community. The *Basileiados* near his see city had buildings which housed a hospital and a poorhouse.[4] Another latin translation, also made by Rufinus of

---

[1] R. Lorenz, 'Die Anfänge des abendländischen Mönchtums im 4 Jahrhundert,' *Zeitschrift für Kirchengeschichte*, 77 (1966) 3–4.

[2] *Vie d'Antoine*, ed. G. J. M. Bartelink (Paris 1994) 95–98.

[3] *Basili Regula a Rufino Latine versa*, ed. K. Zelzer (Vienna 1986) x–xi.

[4] P. Rousseau, *Basil of Caesarea* (Berkeley 1994) 139–144.

Aquileia, which became extremely popular was the *Historia Monachorum in Aegypto.*[5]

Western readers, then, were faced with a number of contradictory accounts of fascinating developments in other parts of Christendom. An early propagandist for monasticism, who wrote in Latin for a western readership, was Saint Jerome.[6] Born around 347 in Dalmatia, he pursued his studies in Rome. Around 366 he moved to Trier, intent on a career at the imperial court. Saint Athanasius had recently lived in exile there and encouraged the beginnings of an ascetic movement. Jerome seems to have come into contact with some of its adherents. He moved to Aquileia, where Athanasius had also lived, and settled down among a small group of ascetics. Around 373 the companions set out for the East to learn about the ascetic life at first hand. After a brief stay at Antioch, Jerome settled near the city as a hermit in the desert of Chalcis. He began to learn Hebrew and to study the Bible. In 379 he was ordained a priest. Shortly afterwards he travelled to Constantinople. In 382, Pope Damasus invited him to Rome. The pope was a patron of ecclesiastical learning and encouraged Jerome to begin the new latin translation of the Bible, a project on which he continued working until his death.

In Rome Jerome was particularly associated with a group of aristocratic women who lived as ascetics in their own homes. He was soon involved in controversy. His criticisms of the roman clergy were much resented. There was an outcry after one of the penitent ladies died—from too much fasting, it was said, when she was in delicate health. About this time Jerome's patron, Pope Damasus, died and was succeeded by Siricius. The new pope was decidedly hostile to Jerome and the whole ascetic movement. So unpopular had Jerome become in Rome that he was obliged to leave. In 385 he settled in a monastery in Bethlehem and died in 419/420.

---

[5] See above p. 30.
[6] On Jerome, see Philip Rousseau, *Ascetics, Authority, and the Church* (Oxford 1978) 99–139; also Jean Gribomont in DIP 4: 1106–1107.

Jerome is one of the outstanding figures in the illustrious galaxy of the fourth century Church Fathers. His Vulgate Bible shaped the spirituality of western Christians for centuries. His methods of biblical criticism were very like those of modern scholars, though he lacked their tools. Like many a brilliant scholar, however, he was extremely quarrelsome. In his many controversies he knew no moderation. As a promoter of the monastic ideal he was an extremist. 'Though your little nephew hang on your neck,' he wrote to one aspirant to the ascetic life, 'though your mother with dishevelled hair and torn raiment show you the breasts that gave you suck, though your father fling himself upon the threshold, trample your father underfoot and go your way, fly with tearless eyes to the standard of the Cross'.[7] Some could not fail to be offended by Jerome's praise of virginity:

> It is not disparaging wedlock to prefer virginity. No one can make a comparison between two things, if one is good and the other evil. Let married women take their pride in coming next after virgins . . . Let them marry and be given in marriage who eat their bread in the sweat of their brow, whose land brings forth thorns and thistles, and whose crops are choked with brambles.[8]

In later years, Jerome came to regret his earlier vehemence.[9]

Jerome wrote three Saints' Lives which were intended to promote monasticism.[10] In the *Life of Saint Paul the First Hermit* he tried to duplicate the success of the *Life of Saint Anthony*. Paul was supposed to have been the very first Christian to live the life of a solitary in the desert, even before Saint Anthony took up the life style. Many critics, in Jerome's time and our own, have doubted whether this Paul ever actually existed. The *Life of Saint Malchus* was a monastic romance.

---

[7] *Select Letters of St. Jerome*, ed. and trans. F. A. Wright (Cambridge Mass. 1975) Ep. 14.
[8] Ep. 22.
[9] Ep. 52.
[10] Rousseau (as n. 6), 99–139.

Malchus, fired by enthusiasm for the ascetic life, abandoned his family and the prospects of a good marriage, but was disappointed by the community to which he had fled and decided to return to his relatives. On the way home he was captured by brigands and made a slave. In captivity he learned the true value of solitude and after an adventurous escape, at last embraced the ascetic life with understanding and fervour. Malchus was an historical figure whom Jerome had known, as was Hilarion who was instrumental in bringing monasticism to Palestine. The hero of Jerome's *Life of Hilarion*, was a disciple of Anthony. When Anthony began to attract crowds of followers and disciples, Hilarion returned to his native Palestine and imitated his master by living the life of a solitary in the desert. After twenty-two years he began to attract visitors. Some came for advice, some for miracle-cures, and some to join him in the ascetic life. Eventually Hilarion became alarmed at his own popularity and, accompanied by a few disciples, began a search for a more secluded retreat. First he settled at a site where Anthony himself had lived, then, after a number of other sites had proved unsatisfactory he moved to Sicily and finally considered living among the barbarians. The *Life of Hilarion*, the most mature of Jerome's biographies, opens up the possibility of development and change in the ascetic experience.[11]

A certain progression is also evident in Jerome's letters about asceticism. The early letters insist on complete separation between the solitary and persons in the world. The solitary is not to meddle with anything worldly, to avoid holding any office in the Church, and to stand aloof from controversy. When he settled in Rome, Jerome began to consider the advantages of ascetic communities in cities. He emphasised the importance of virginity, but felt that monks and virgins might influence the Church through example and exhortation. In the years immediately after his enforced departure from Rome he came to think that this had been a mistake. Ascetics

---

[11] *Ibid.* 133–9.

should leave cities and settle in the country. Towards the end of his life, however, he was once more ready to admit that ascetic life in the city was possible. He was enthusiastic about Pammachius, a widower who attended the Senate in the garb of a monk and built hospitals—the first christian politician. Nevertheless, Jerome maintained that the monastic life was lived most perfectly in solitude.[12]

Of all the early theorists who wrote about the monastic life in Latin, the most profound was John Cassian.[13] He was born in the Balkans during the second half of the fourth century. His writings give evidence that he had received an excellent education. He spoke Greek and his written Latin is fluent and elegant. In the 380s he entered a monastery in Bethlehem. After some years there he and a companion decided to go to Egypt to learn about monasticism from its most eminent practitioners. They arrived around 385 and stayed until 399. According to his own later account he travelled from hermitage to hermitage, observing the manner of life and questioning the ascetics about their teaching.

After the works of Origen had been condemned by bishop Theophilus of Alexandria,[14] Cassian was among the monks forced to leave Egypt. In 400–403 he was in Constantinople, where he was ordained deacon. In 403 he arrived at Rome. Alaric the Goth's invasion may have been the cause of his departure from Italy. He is next found in Marseille, where he founded two monasteries—one for men and one for women. Around 420, when Castor, Bishop of Apt, decided to found a monastery in his diocese, he asked Cassian for advice. This was the occasion on which Cassian wrote his *Institutes*, which described the external organisation of egyptian monasteries. Cassian realised that a thorough exposition of monastic theology was also needed, for the *Institutes* refer in several places to his intention of writing such a book. In the *Conferences*,

---

[12] *Ibid.* 99–124.
[13] What follows is based on H. Chadwick, *John Cassian* (Cambridge 1968).
[14] See above p. 30.

Cassian made a systematic arrangement of the teaching which he had absorbed from various egyptian ascetics.[15]

The accuracy of Cassian's descriptions of egyptian monasticism has recently been questioned.[16]). He claimed to describe what he himself had seen. It is clear, however, that his experience was limited to Lower Egypt, where he had lived among hermits. He also wrote about the institutions of the cenobites, though he had never visited Upper Egypt where their communities were to be found. No doubt because of the need for caution, his account of the Origenist controversy is garbled and inaccurate. The fact is that when he was writing he had been out of Egypt for twenty years. He was by then particularly concerned with the creation of a viable monastic life in Gaul, where the conditions of Egypt could not be reproduced. It should be noted, however, that he remained in touch with the other Origenist refugee monks. The same spirituality marks the Conferences and the Apophthegmata.[17]

For the benefit of monks in Gaul Cassian discussed the merits of two ways of living the monastic life—that of cenobites and that of hermits ('anchorites' in his terminology). Egyptian tradition held that the hermit's way of life was superior, though it should be remembered that the solitary did not live in literal solitude. The hermits' caves and cells were usually within walking distance of one another. The system whereby juniors were instructed by seniors was well organised. All assembled in a church for services on Sundays. By Cassian's time it

---

[15] Texts: *Jean Cassien: Conférences*, ed. E. Pichery, 3 vols. (Paris 1955–1959); *Institutions cénobitiques* ed. J. C. Guy (Paris 1965). English translations used below are from A Select Library of the Nicene and Post-Nicene Fathers of the Christian Church, 2nd series 11, ed. P. Schaff and H. Wace (rpt Grand Rapids: Eerdmans 1978) 201–290 (*Institutes*), 295–474 (*Conferences*). For modern translation of the Conferences, see *Cassian: Conferences,* [partial] translation by Colm Luibheid, introd. Owen Chadwick (New York 1985) and *Jean Cassian: The Conferences*, Ancient Christian Writers, 57, complete translation by Boniface Ramsey op (New York 1997).

[16] J. C. Guy, 'Jean Cassien, historien du monachisme égyptienne?' *Studia Patristica* 8 (1966) 363–372; Armand Veilleux, *La Liturgie dans le cénobitisme pachômien* (Rome 1968) 146–154.

[17] See discussion in Chadwick (as n. 13), 20–22.

had become customary for some egyptian ascetics to enter a cenobitic community first and then, when they had been tested, to go into the desert as hermits. In the conditions of Gaul, however, Cassian believed that monks should not be encouraged to leave the community. Few would be mature enough for a hermit's life. In a cenobitic monastery, moreover, where they were under discipline, they would have ample opportunity to practice the virtues of humility, obedience, and charity.[18]

The cenobitic monks in Egypt had been accustomed to meet twice a day for common worship—in the morning and in the evening. Cassian recommended for his monks three additional services which were taken from the monastic usages of Palestine: Terce sung at the third hour of the day, Sext at the sixth, and None at the ninth hours.[19] The regularity of these fairly short services implies that the community was living in the proximity of its church, which could be reached with ease at three-hour intervals.

Cassian's prescriptions prepared the way for the more elaborate liturgical arrangements of later western monasticism. Of the greatest importance, however, was Cassian's systematic exposition of the theoretical basis of the monastic life. For western monks it was, and remains, an indispensable and authoritative text.

First and foremost it was necessary to establish the end and purpose of monastic living. Popular descriptions of egyptian monasticism had emphasised the monks' fantastic penances and miracles. At the very beginning of the *Conferences* therefore, Cassian declared that mortifications were a means to an end.

> The final end of our profession indeed . . . is the kingdom of God or the kingdom of heaven: but the immediate aim or goal[20] is purity of heart, without which no one can gain

---

[18] *Ibid.* 50–54.
[19] *Ibid.* 71–72.
[20] Cassian uses the Greek words 'telos' and 'scopos'.

that end[21] . . . For this we must seek for solitude, for this
we know that we ought to submit to fastings, vigils, toils,
bodily nakedness, readings, and all other virtues, that through
them we may be enabled to prepare our heart and to keep it
unharmed by all evil passions, and resting on these steps to
mount to the perfection of charity.[22]

As for miracles:

It is a greater miracle to root out from one's own flesh the
incentives to wantonness than to cast out unclean spirits from
the bodies of others, and it is a grander sign to restrain the
fierce passions of anger by the virtue of patience than to
command the powers of the air.[23]

Outward practices served as a means for the inner progression of the soul towards perfect conformity with God. The
first stage was the conquest of vices; of these Cassian listed the
eight principal ones. In this fight the vices were often aided by
demons. In the course of the battle the ascetic was purified.
At first he obeys God out of fear of eternal punishment. Then
he comes to love him because he hopes for heaven. Finally he
learns to love God for God alone. The monk's prayer followed
a similar progression. Penance, intercession, and thanksgiving
were preliminary stages. The aim was the 'prayer of fire' or
'pure prayer', during which the monk lived in God alone,
having freed his mind of every image or concept.[24]

A considerable body of ascetic theology in Latin had been
built up by the middle of the fifth century. If one looks for its
practical application in the Western provinces of the Roman
Empire, the picture is desultory and unclear. When Jerome
arrived in Rome in 382 he was enthusiastic about the pious
women who were living ascetic lives in their own homes. They
had been doing this before he came, but we see them entirely
through his eyes. His letters about them are essays on the

---

[21] *Conference* 1, ch.4.
[22] *Ibid.* ch. 7.
[23] *Conference* 15 ch. 8.
[24] Chadwick (as n. 13), 82–109.

religious life, intended for the widest possible audience. Some letters describe the women's way of life in general terms in order to encourage imitators. Other letters are addressed to the women themselves. Here Jerome praises, warns, and exhorts. Amid the studied eloquence and quotations from Scripture, however, no very memorable picture of the women themselves emerges. Of Marcella, a widow who had followed a life of religious discipline for many years before Jerome came to Rome, we learn that she dressed simply, knelt on the bare ground, and sang the psalms.[25] In a panegyric written after her death, Jerome claimed that she had never gone out unless accompanied by other virgins and widows. She spent much of her time in a study of Scripture, and it was as a Scripture scholar that she particularly admired Jerome. For her the study of Scripture was always practical, 'Meditation in the law meant for her not a mere perusal of the Scriptures, as the Jewish Pharisees think, but a carrying it out in action'. Although she did not eat meat, her fasts were moderate. Of wine she drank only what was required for her health. 'She seldom appeared in public and carefully avoided the houses of ladies of rank . . . she frequently visited the churches of the apostles and martyrs for quiet prayer, avoiding the people's throng'.[26]

These traits are, in fact, largely generalities written with a didactic purpose.[27] One may surmise that many of these women were influenced by the writings of Saint Basil, and that their asceticism was marked by practical charity. Of Fabiola, another pious widow, Jerome writes, 'She preferred to break up and sell all that she could lay hands on of her property—it was a large one and suitable to her rank—and when she had turned it into money she disposed of everything for the benefit of the poor'.[28]

---

[25] Ep. 77.
[26] Ep. 127.
[27] See however J. A. McNamara, 'Muffled Voices', *Distant Echoes* Medieval Religious Women 1 (Kalamazoo 1984) 11–29.
[28] Ep. 77.

'I had the joy of seeing Rome become another Jerusalem', wrote Jerome. 'Monastic establishments for virgins were
founded in many places, and the number of monks in the city
surpassed all counting.'[29] In fact, early roman monasticism was
very ephemeral. When Jerome was obliged to leave Rome,
his most devoted disciples followed him to the Holy Land.
Although some communities of men and women remained
and were described by Saint Augustine, who visited Rome in
387,[30] they do not seem to have survived for long.

The most famous monk of the West in the fourth century
was Martin of Tours.[31] He was born in what is now Hungary,
probably around 336.[32] His parents were pagans. In spite of an
early interest in Christianity, Martin followed his father into
a military career and took part in campaigns on the frontier
of Gaul. His career in the army was later held against him
by his critics in the Church. At the age of eighteen he was
baptised, and around 356 was at last able to free himself from
the army. For a time he stayed with Saint Hilary, bishop of
Poitiers. Then he went home in an unsuccessful attempt to
convert his parents. At this time there was great sympathy with
Arianism at the imperial court and clergy like Athanasius, who
defended the strict Trinitarianism of the Council of Nicaea,
were persecuted. Hilary of Poitiers suffered in the same cause
and was driven out of his see. As a convinced Trinitarian,
Martin was eventually obliged to leave the Balkans. He went
to Italy and settled for a time in a hermitage near Milan, but
the bishop disapproved of his theological views and forced him
to leave. In 360 Martin returned to Gaul. By then Hilary had
been allowed back to his see, and Martin settled down in the
monastery of Ligugé, near Poitiers.

Some years later the see of Tours fell vacant, and the
citizens elected Martin to be their new bishop. He was conse-

---

[29] Ep. 127.
[30] Lorenz (as n. 1), 8.
[31] On Saint Martin and the problems associated with his *Vita*, see C. Stancliffe,
St. Martin and his Biographer (Oxford 1983).
[32] *Ibid.* 119–133 on the difficult chronological problems of Saint Martin's life.

crated by somewhat unwilling bishops who did not welcome
a monk as a colleague. Martin founded a monastery at Marmoutier across the Loire, some miles from Tours, and there-
after divided his time between the monastic and the pastoral
life. As a bishop he was active in fighting the last vestiges of
paganism, but his relations with his episcopal colleagues were
always poor. Occasionally he visited Trier to consult with the
emperor Maximus (383–388). He died at the very end of the
fourth century.[33]

Most of the information about Martin comes from the
pen of Sulpicius Severus, an enthusiastic admirer who began
writing when Martin was still alive. Sulpicius, a well-educated
and prosperous lawyer, some time in the 390s, after the death
of his wife, underwent a profound conversion. Somewhere
between Toulouse and Narbonne he had an estate called
Primuliacum. Here he settled down and gathered a religious
community around him. Saint Martin had a profound influence
on him. Primuliacum was modelled on Marmoutier. Sulpicius
devoted the rest of his life to defending Saint Martin against
his critics and publicising his virtues.[34]

Sulpicius did not hesitate to claim that Martin had surpassed all the saints of Egypt. 'In my secret thoughts I had
my mind turned to my friend Martin, observing on the best
of grounds that all those things which different individuals
had done separately, were easily and entirely accomplished by
that one man alone'.[35] The passage unconsciously reveals that,
whereas Egypt and Syria could provide numerous examples of
heroic asceticism, the West had as yet only one. Sulpicius, however, puts forward a view of monasticism different from that
of Egypt, one which was probably that of Martin himself. The
egyptian monks lived in solitude, he maintains, 'with heaven
only and the angels as witnesses.' Martin, on the other hand,

---

[33] *Ibid.* 112–4. See also article on Martin in DIP 5 (1978) 1034–1038.
[34] Stancliffe (as n. 31), 15–19; 30–31.
[35] Sulpicius, *Dialogues*, 1.24. English translations of Sulpicius in *A Select Library* (as n. 15) 1–122.

in the midst of crowds and intercourse with human beings—
among quarrelsome clerics and among furious bishops, while
he was harassed with almost daily scandals on all sides—
nevertheless stood absolutely firm with unconquerable virtue
against all these things, and performed such wonders as not
even those accomplished of whom we have heard that they
are, or at one time were, in the wilderness.[36]

Influenced, it may be, by Saint Basil, Martin saw no conflict
between the monastic life and service to the Church.

Sulpicius's writings are mostly concerned with Martin's
miracles. Behind the marvels the personality largely disappears and very little is revealed about the saint as monk or
abbot.[37] There is a brief description in Sulpicius's *Life of Saint
Martin*, of the community at Marmoutier.

There were altogether eighty disciples who were being disciplined after the example of the saintly master. No one
there had anything which was called his own; all things were
possessed in common. It was not allowed either to buy or sell
anything, as is the custom among most monks. No art was
practised there, except that of transcribers, and even this was
assigned to the brethren of younger years, while the elders
spent their time in prayer. Rarely did any of them go beyond
the cell, unless when they assembled at the place of prayer.
They all took their food together, after the hour of fasting was
past. No one used wine, except when illness compelled them
to do so. Most of them were clothed in garments of camels'
hair. Any dress approaching to softness was there deemed
criminal, and this must be thought the more remarkable,
because many among them were such as are deemed of
noble rank. These, though far differently brought up, had
forced themselves down to this degree of humility and patient
endurance, and we have seen numbers of these afterwards
made bishops.[38]

---

[36] Sulpicius, *Dialogues* 1. 24.
[37] Stancliffe (as n. 31), 172.
[38] Sulpicius, *Life of St. Martin*, 10.

Sharp criticism of some aspects of egyptian monasticism is audible in this passage. Egyptian monks sold their handiwork, and some of their monasteries were becoming rich. Martin clearly wanted his community to be poor. This explains the prohibition of any crafts, as well as of the buying and selling which these involved. Apart from a little copying of manuscripts, Marmoutier was to be a contemplative community devoted to prayer, and the monks were expected to remain within the precincts of the monastery. Nevertheless, there is evidence that they often accompanied Martin when he moved among his people.[39] Saint Martin's own pastoral concerns were clearly shared with his community. Marmoutier, as Sulpicius notes, was a school for future bishops.

In spite of Sulpicius Severus's enthusiasm, Saint Martin remains a shadowy figure. Saint Paulinus of Nola, on the other hand, is very real.[40] He was born in 354/355 and belonged to a gallic senatorial family in easy circumstances and christian belief. Paulinus was well educated and counted the poet Ausonius as his friend. In his youth he followed a career in government, holding administrative posts in Rome and Campania. In 384 he returned to Gaul, and then travelled to Spain, where he made an advantageous marriage to a rich heiress called Therasia.

The circumstances of Paulinus's conversion to the ascetic life are obscure. He came into contact with Saint Martin at the very end of the monk-bishop's life. There were also two family tragedies—the murder of his brother and the death of an infant son. Therasia strongly influenced her husband to adopt an ascetic life. For some years the couple lived quietly on Therasia's estate near Barcelona. In 394 Paulinus resisted an attempt by the local population to have him ordained priest. The incident induced the couple to leave Spain and make their way to Campania. On the way they called on pope Siricius in Rome, who received them coldly.[41]

---

[39] Stancliffe, 161.
[40] For what follows see W. H. C. Frend, 'Paulinus of Nola and the last century of the Western Empire,' *Journal of Roman Studies* 59(1969) 1–11.
[41] *Ibid.* 6.

During his previous stay in Campania Paulinus had conceived an affection for the shrine of Saint Felix at Nola. A local pilgrimage had grown up around the relics of Felix, a martyr of the Decian persecution in the third century. When he had been a government official in the area, Paulinus had built a road and a hostel for pilgrims to the shrine. Now he decided to settle there with his wife. Two communities, one for men and the other for women, were founded. When Therasia died in 408, Paulinus became a bishop.

From Nola Paulinus conducted a correspondence with notable ascetics and other friends throughout the Empire. His correspondents included Saint Augustine, Sulpicius Severus, and the poet Ausonius, who criticised his retirement from the active life. Paulinus justified himself in a poem:

> Not that they beggared be in mind, or brutes,
> That they have chosen their dwelling place afar
> In lonely places: but their eyes are turned
> To the high stars, the very deep of Truth.
> Freedom they seek, an emptiness apart
> From worthless hopes: din of the marketplace,
> And all the noisy crowding up of things,
> And whatsoever wars on the divine,
> At Christ's command and for his love, they hate.[42]

By Paulinus's own account, life at Nola was austere. The community cultivated poverty; food was meagre and the use of wine restricted. Yet Paulinus found opportunity to exercise his literary gifts. Every year he wrote a poem in honour of Saint Felix:

> Spring wakens the birds' voices, but for me
> My Saint's day is my spring, and in its light
> For all his happy folk the winter flowers.
> Keen frost without, midwinter, and the year
> Rigid with cold and all the country white,
> But gone the harder winter of my soul.[43]

---

[42] Translation by Helen Waddell, in *Mediaeval Latin Lyrics* (London 1948) 34–35.
[43] *Ibid.* 38–39.

It was a civilised monasticism, but the clarity of vision of the egyptian monks is notably absent. Nola hardly survived Paulinus as a monastery, though the disorders of germanic invasion in Italy may have been to blame. No more did Saint Martin's communities survive their founder.

The one long-lasting and influential community in the Latin world before the fall of the western Roman Empire was situated on the islands of Lérins. The two islands are opposite the bay of Cannes; the smaller, then called Lerina, is now named Saint-Honorat; the larger, then called Lero, is now the island of Sainte Marguerite.[44] The community was founded by Honoratus, another gallic noble who decided to abandon the conventional life natural to someone with his connections, to become a christian ascetic.

Honoratus was born between 370 and 375. He became a Christian as a young man and decided, against the wishes of his family, to go to Egypt to learn about the ascetic life. He was accompanied by his brother Venantius and by an older man who acted as guide. Venantius's death in Greece forced the other two to turn back. When they reached Fréjus in their native Gaul, the local bishop offered them the islands of Lérins as a retreat.

In its early days Lérins was undoubtedly influenced by Cassian, whose own monastery at Marseilles was not far distant. He was in touch with Lérins and dedicated the second book of the *Conferences* to Honoratus. 'Honoratus . . . presiding over a large monastery of the brethren, is hoping that his congregation, which learns a lesson from the daily sight of your saintly life, may be instructed in the precepts of those fathers'.[45] Here was a monastery in which egyptian monasticism was most perfectly adapted to the conditions of Gaul.

When he settled at Lérins, Honoratus was ordained a priest and composed the rule for the community. A church was built and buildings erected in which the monks lived the

---

[44] On Lérins, see E. Griffe, *La Gaule chrétienne a l'époque romaine*, 3 (Paris 1965) 332–41; *Les Règles des Pères*, ed. A. de Vogüé (Paris 1982), 1: 21–37.
[45] *Conferences*, Bk. 2, preface.

cenobitic life. Honoratus fully shared the life of his brethren and joined them at their meals. As in Egypt, the more advanced ascetics followed a more solitary vocation in separate cells.[46] Like many famous monasteries, Lérins was fortunate in having a line of able superiors. In 427 Honoratus left to become bishop of Arles. His successor, Maximus, was Honoratus's favourite disciple and had been chosen by him for this office. Maximus presided over Lérins for seven years, after which he too became a bishop. The next superior was Faustus, who presided over the community for twenty-six years. Faustus, a notable scholar and writer, became Bishop of Riez in 460, but maintained his connections with Lérins to the end of his life.[47]

The choice of successive superiors of Lérins to be bishops is a tribute to the high standards maintained on the islands. The proximity of Marseilles also kept the community in the public eye. From its beginning the monastery attracted recruits from every part of Gaul. It became a centre of learning. Around 420 Eucherius, the future bishop of Lyons, came there with his wife and entrusted the education of his sons to teachers from the monastery. The most famous of the scholars resident on Lérins was Vincent, author of the *Commonitorium*, a treatise showing how orthodox christian doctrine may be distinguished from heresy.[48] Although none of the later superiors of the monastery were as distinguished as the first three, the fame of Lérins lasted for almost two hundred years. At the beginning of the sixth century ascetics were still going there to learn the principles of monastic living.[49]

The surviving religious rules of Lérins give some idea of its ideals and way of life.[50] The earliest rule appears to be the work of Honoratus himself and his companions, writing under the pseudonyms of the egyptian hermits Serapion, Macarius,

---

[46] Griffe (as n. 44), 334–335.
[47] *Ibid.* 339–341.
[48] *Ibid.* 335–337.
[49] *Ibid.* 341.
[50] De Vogüé (as n. 44), 2 vols.

Paphnutius, and Macarius the Second.[51] The rule insists on the importance of the cenobitic life, since the vastness of the desert and the horror of its demons make the solitary life impossible. The brothers follow a common *horarium* and attend religious services together. Special emphasis is laid on obedience to the superior.[52]

Around 435, Romanus, formerly a monk of a community at Lyons—where the influence of Lérins was strong—left his monastery to seek greater seclusion at a place called Condat, now Saint-Claude in the Jura mountains, on the french side of the modern boundary with Switzerland, which is fifteen kilometres away. Romanus soon attracted followers who lived as much like the hermits of the egyptian desert as the severe climate of the area would allow. Other communities in the area were founded, and at Romanus's death around 460, a little *koinonia* reminiscent of Pachomius, had come into being. Lupicinus, the next superior, strengthened discipline in the communities, and Oyend, who ruled over Condat from 490–510, completed its transformation into a cenobitic community, with statutes acquired from Lérins.[53]

A unique chronicle of the first seventy-five years of the Jura communities gives an intimate picture of latin cenobite monasticism in the late fifth century.[54] Mutual charity was its hallmark. Severe though the abbots were with defaulters, they fully shared the life and hardships of the brethren. Oyend 'taught nothing by command which he had not already accomplished by his example or labour'.[55] In the harsh climate of the Jura there were many opportunities for demonstrating the virtues of the common life. 'If a brother, after being commanded to perform a particular task, had gone out in the cold weather and returned soaked by the winter storms, all the others vied with one another in stripping off some warmer or

---

[51] *Ibid.* 1: 22–26.
[52] *Ibid.* 1: 181–205.
[53] *Ibid.* 34–36; 2, 436–342, 462–395.
[54] *Vie des Pères du Jura*, ed. F. Martine (Paris 1968).
[55] *Ibid.* 422–423.

drier piece of clothing, or taking off their shoes, so as quickly to warm up and relieve the body of their brother, rather than thinking of their own'.[56]

In the Latin West monasticism was often held back by episcopal hostility, but a few bishops were among its early supporters. Around 350 bishop Eusebius of Vercelli in northern Italy made a vow of celibacy and began to live like a monk. Later he persuaded the other clerics of his see city to do the same and a kind of clerical monastery came into being.[57] Ambrose, the famous bishop of Milan, founded outside the walls of the city a monastery which was placed under the direction of a presbyter who took his instructions from the bishop himself.[58] The arrangement foreshadows the monastic establishments of Ambrose's admirer Augustine.

Saint Augustine of Hippo is the author of the oldest monastic rules surviving in Latin.[59] His conversion took place at Milan in the summer of 386. He was at the time a gregarious academic of 32 with a colourful past. The process started when he became an attentive listener to the sermons of Saint Ambrose. With some companions he took up a life of retirement, to study the Scriptures. By chance the friends were visited by Pontician, a devout Christian who, like Augustine, was a native of the roman province of Africa. He began to tell them of the life of Anthony of Egypt, of which they had never heard. They were also unaware that bishop Ambrose had founded a monastery in the outskirts of Milan. Pontician told them of this and of other monastic communities, particularly one at Trier, which some friends of his had joined. The conversation formed a turning point in Augustine's life. After Pontician had left, he went out into the garden to be alone with his thoughts. In a neighbouring garden he heard a child at some game repeating in a sing-song *Tolle, lege! Tolle, lege!* 'Take it and read!' Returning to the house Augustine took the book of the Epistles of Saint Paul,

---

[56] *Ibid.* 356–357.
[57] Lorenz (as n. 1), 9.
[58] *Ibid.* 9–10.
[59] G. Lawless, *Augustine of Hippo and his Monastic Rule* (Oxford 1987).

which he had been studying, and opened it at random. His eye fell on the words: 'Not in revelling and drunkenness, not in lust and wantonness, not in quarrels and rivalries. Rather, arm yourselves with the Lord Jesus Christ; spend no more thought on nature and nature's appetites'.[60] This was his call to a new life. A short while later he was baptised.

After resigning his professorship in Milan, Augustine retired with some companions to Cassiciacum, a villa in the Italian Alps north of Milan. Here he and some friends spent their time in prayer and study. He is next found at Rome, studying the religious communities there. In 388 he crossed to Africa, taking his friends to Thagaste, the town where he had been born. They had now had some years' experience of living together. In the house of Augustine's parents they established themselves as a monastic community.[61]

In 391 Augustine was called to Hippo by the bishop and ordained a priest. Bishop Valerius was a Greek and found difficulty in preaching in Latin. Augustine was to undertake the task of preaching regularly to the people. Some of his friends left Thagaste to follow him. The bishop set aside a garden in Hippo where they could establish a monastery, of which Augustine took charge.[62] In 395 Augustine himself became bishop of Hippo. Inevitably his life was now less secluded. The bishop's house was open to petitioners and diocesan clergy. Augustine had to leave it frequently to make pastoral visits. Nevertheless, he managed to establish some kind of community living in his household, which he himself described as a 'monastery of clerics'.[63]

The complicated critical and textual problems of the so-called 'Rule of Saint Augustine' have largely been clarified, thanks to the work of L. Verheijen over more than twenty

---

[60] Romans 13: 13. The account of Saint Augustine's conversion is in *Confessions* 8.6–12. See *St. Augustine, Confessions*, trans. and ed. R. S. Pine-Coffin (London 1961) 166–179.
[61] Lawless, *Augustine*, 29–47.
[62] *Ibid.* 62.
[63] *Ibid.*

years.[64] There need now be little doubt that Augustine himself was the author.[65] It has been shown that he wrote three
Rules, which were combined in various confusing ways in the
Middle Ages. There is a relatively short *Ordo Monasterii,* a
longer *Praeceptum,* and a short *Objurgatio* written for some
quarrelling nuns. In its original version, the *Praeceptum* was
written for monks. There is a version for nuns, in which the
male pronouns have been altered to female. The adaptation
was probably made by Augustine himself.[66]

The *Praeceptum* begins by stating that the religious life
lived in common is based on charity. Private ownership is
forbidden; all property is held in common, but individual
needs—especially those of the old, the sick, and the delicate—
are taken into account. Everyone in the community is equal.
No one is to be admired or despised because of his former
social status. Common times of prayer are to be kept by all.
Each individual is to fast and perform other penances as health
allows. The community listens to readings during common
meals. Dress is always modest and distributed from a common
wardrobe. No one is to go out of the house alone. All are to
take special care not to look at or lust after members of the
other sex. All work is to be undertaken for the good of the
community. Gifts from relatives are to be handed over to the
superior and given to the needy. The sick are to receive proper
care. Anyone needing food or clothes shall be given them
promptly, but books are to be given out only at the proper
times. The superior has the right to the loving obedience
of all, and is to show love in return. These rules were to
be read to the community every week.[67] The shorter *Ordo
monasterii* contains most of these precepts, but adds some
liturgical instructions to the community. From these it can be
seen that there were seven services: Nocturns during the night,

---

[64] Listed in Lawless, *Augustine*, 179. Verheijen's findings are conveniently
summarised ibid. 121–161.
[65] Lawless, *Augustine*, 127–135, largely based on Verheijen.
[66] Authentic text with english translations, Lawless, *Augustine*, 74–118.
[67] *Ibid*. 80–103.

Matins in the early morning, Terce, Sext, and None, a service at lamp-lighting, and another before the community retired to bed.[68]

Augustine did not believe that a specifically monastic theology was required, for the call to holiness bound all Christians. Though Augustine believed that monks and nuns had the higher vocation, he recognised the dignity of marriage and taught that 'Marriage with humility is better than virginity with pride'. As presbyter in charge of the garden monastery at Hippo, Augustine combined a life of prayer with preaching, philosophical discussions, and writing. His ideal was the apostolic community in Jerusalem.[69] In his view, monastic living generated charity and pastoral zeal.[70]

Clearly, from the beginning of the fourth century monasticism represented a new and vigorous movement in the Church, one with which all christian communities had, in the end, to come to terms. If we find it odd that not all western ecclesiastics were favourable, we must also admit that the new wave produced some disconcerting followers, in theory as well as in practice. A quantity of literature circulated to show that marriage in any form was undesirable. Tatian, the founder of a sect of heretical Christians in the second century, used and sometimes misquoted the Bible in support of this view. The same tactics were used by Tertullian, the third century apologist for Christianity who joined the heretical Montanists towards the end of his life.[71]

It is small wonder that such views encouraged eccentric practices. There were ascetics who claimed that they had so completely overcome the lusts of the flesh that men and women could live together as virgins in the same household and even sleep chastely in the same bed.[72] Since, before the

---

[68] *Ibid.* 74–75.
[69] Acts 4: 32–33.
[70] Lawless, *Augustine*, 58–62.
[71] The views expressed in the extremist literature are regaled with relish in R. L. Fox, *Pagans and Christians in the Mediterranean world from the second century A.D. to the conversion of Constantine* (London 1988) 364.
[72] *Ibid.* 369.

Lord, there was neither male nor female,[73] some men allowed
their hair to grow long like women, weighed themselves down
with chains, and went barefoot during the winter. Women, on
the other hand, cut their hair short, wore male clothing, and
tried to grow beards. Others, remembering that Christians
must be 'like children',[74] wore children's clothing and prattled
in baby-talk.[75]

Priscillianism is an example of the trouble this extremism
could cause.[76] Priscillian was a lay ascetic from the neighbourhood of Cordoba in Spain. Some time in the 370s he
began to criticise the humdrum nature of the Christianity
preached by the bishops. He emphasised the need for absolute
division between a life in God and life in the world. Christian
life and asceticism were equated; family, rank, and property,
should, in principle, be renounced at baptism. Priscillian did
not, in fact, deny that ordinary Christians living in the married
state might be saved. If they professed the orthodox faith and
gave alms to the poor, they might be forgiven. The perfect
Christian way, however, to which all should aspire, was that of
continence.

During Lent and in the weeks preceding the Epiphany,
Priscillianists withdrew from society completely and spent the
time in their houses or in the mountains, in imitation of Christ's
forty-day fast in the wilderness. The ascetic experience, they
believed, gave them prophetic powers and a special authority to interpret Scripture—a Scripture which included the
apocryphal acts of Thomas, Peter, Paul, John and Andrew,
all of which stressed the importance of virginity.[77] Priscillian
also professed a Creed in which the distinctions between the
persons of the Trinity were under-emphasised.[78]

---

[73] Gal 3: 28.
[74] Matt 18: 3.
[75] Lorenz (as n. 1), 7–8. 'Jean Moschus, dans *Le Pré spirituel*, a écrit trois cents
histoires édifiantes a faire frémir.' G. le Bras, 'Monastères et communautés,' in
G. le Bras ed., *Les Ordres Religieux* 1, Paris 1979, 14.
[76] H. Chadwick, *Priscillian of Avila* (Oxford 1976) 8–12; 70–110.
[77] *Ibid*. 77.
[78] *Ibid*. 86–91.

Some of the practices of the Priscillianists were con
demned by the spanish bishops at a Council in 380, but the
spanish Church was divided and Priscillian had many admirers. The very next year he was elected bishop of Avila and
consecrated by bishops sympathetic to him. Eventually he
and his supporters were expelled from Spain, but they began
to wander around Gaul and later Italy, gathering support.
They won the favour of the emperor Gratian, who reinstated
Priscillian in his diocese and summoned his chief opponent
in Spain to Trier for disturbing the peace of the Church.
In 383, however, Gratian was overthrown and later killed.
Maximus, his supplanter, the former governor of Britain, was
anxious to win the support of the Church and make himself
acceptable to Theodosius, the grimly orthodox emperor of the
East. Maximus summoned an ecclesiastical synod to Bordeaux.
Priscillian, believing that it would be prejudiced against him,
appealed directly to the emperor.[79]

The trial at Trier took place probably in 386.[80] It was considered improper for a secular ruler to judge a matter like heresy.
A charge of sorcery was therefore brought against Priscillian,
who was known to dabble in the occult. The accusation was
made by two spanish bishops, to the horror of Saint Martin
of Tours, who objected to bishops making a capital charge,
especially against a fellow-bishop. Priscillian was found guilty
and executed, together with two priests and three lay persons,
including a wealthy widow. Imperial officers were sent to
Spain to hunt down Priscillianists, and there were further
executions.[81]

These were the first, though not, unfortunately, the last
killings for religious reasons in the history of christian Europe. They horrified Saint Martin. Saint Ambrose of Milan
and Pope Siricius protested. Martin threatened to boycott a
forthcoming episcopal ordination, for he would not take part

---

[79] *Ibid.* 33–46; 111–148.
[80] *Ibid.* 137.
[81] *Ibid.* 144.

in a sacramental act with bloodstained bishops. The emperor persuaded him to relent, promising that if Martin took part in the consecration, the inquisition which had begun in Spain would be called off. Martin agreed to the bargain, but the memory was always painful to him. For the rest of his life he kept away from gatherings of bishops.[82]

These excesses make it not altogether surprising that monks acquired a bad reputation in some quarters. The criticisms have stuck. The monastic movement of the fourth century remains, on the whole, unpopular with historians of the period. Some forty years ago H. Lietzmann wrote that monasticism had 'nothing more than external relations with the Christian Religion'.[83] This writer considered that pachomian monks, in spite of learning long portions of the Bible by heart, had only a superficial understanding of it. The *Apophthegmata*, he thought, cited Scripture seldom and always ineptly. He noted the advice of one of the Fathers: 'If you cannot be silent, you had better talk about the sayings of the Fathers than about the Scriptures; it is not so dangerous'.[84] This, Lietzmann felt, was typical of the attitude of the monks.[85]

In fact it is a mistake to seek absolute consistency in the *Apophthegmata*, and there are plenty of passages which emphasise the importance of Scripture: 'Always have God before your eyes; whatever you do, do it according to the testimony of the holy Scriptures; in whatever place you live do not easily leave it'.[86] 'Reading the Scriptures is a great safeguard against sin'.[87] 'Ignorance of the Scriptures is a precipice and a deep abyss'.[88]

It is also a mistake to read the desert fathers as if they were medieval churchmen. At a time when the Church was troubled

---

[82] *Ibid.* 146–147.
[83] H. Lietzmann, *The Era of the Church Fathers* (New York 1951) 155.
[84] Amoun 2.
[85] Lietzmann (as n. 83) 153–154.
[86] Anthony 3.
[87] Epiphanius of Cyprus 9.
[88] Epiphanius of Cyprus 11.

with doctrinal controversies, a hermit might well have warned his pupils that discussion of the Bible in their cells could be divisive and dangerous. In fact, the monastic movement of the fourth century was deeply scriptural. The Church had won the support of the imperial government. There was no danger, and there might even be a worldly advantage in being baptised. What, then, did the profession of Christianity involve? For many Christians it seemed to demand absolute obedience to the Word of God. Anthony had found his vocation when he heard some words of the Gospel in Church. For Saint Basil, the ascetic life could be described simply as 'living according to the Gospel'.[89]

Another criticism of the monks is that they weakened roman society through their anti-social attitudes. Gibbon's strictures are famous. 'Whole legions', he writes, 'were buried in these religious sanctuaries; and the same cause which relieved the distress of individuals impaired the strength and fortitude of the empire'.[90] One may doubt whether the monastic movement seriously affected recruitment to the army, especially in the west, where the size and number of monasteries can easily be exaggerated. It is true, however, that there was a discernible bias among strict Christians against the imperial service, both civil and military. In other respects, however, monks were involved with society in new and positive ways. There is evidence, for instance, that the pachomian communities in Egypt became rich.[91] While it is not possible to write the economic history of the egyptian monasteries, it is probable that they owed their wealth to an efficient workforce which was producing goods for a ready market.

There is also ample evidence for the charitable work of monks and ascetics. In the latin version of the Rule of Saint

---

[89] Ep. 207. I am most grateful to Bishop Kallistos of Diocleia for the opportunity to discuss this problem with him, and for his illuminating comments and references.
[90] E. Gibbon, *Decline and Fall of the Roman Empire* (Everyman ed. 1910) 4, 8.
[91] P. Rousseau, *Pachomius* (Berkeley 1985) 82–84; 153–158.

Basil, the monk's duty was defined as feeding the hungry,
giving drink to the thirsty, and clothing the naked.[92] Egyptian
monks, Cassian told his readers, 'not merely refresh pilgrims
and brethren who come to visit them by means of their labours,
but actually collect an enormous store of provisions and food,
and distribute it in parts of Libya which suffer from famine
and barrenness, and also in the cities, to those who are pining
away in the squalor of prison'.[93] In Rome Fabiola founded an
infirmary for the poor and nursed them, herself bringing many
of the worst cases in from the streets.[94]

In the ancient world medicine was available for those who
could pay for it. The idea of organised charity among the poor
and disadvantaged came with Christianity and it is not the least
of the contributions of christian monks and women religious
to the civilisation of Europe.

---

[92] *Basili Regula* (as n. 3), 157.
[93] Cassian, *Institutes* Bk 10 ch. 22.
[94] Jerome Ep. 77.

Chapter 3
GAUL, SPAIN, IRELAND

WHETHER THE MONASTIC movement bears any responsibility for the eventual collapse of the Roman Empire in the west remains a matter of debate, but there can be little doubt that it became an established feature of western Christianity at the very time when imperial authority was in a state of collapse. Those drawn to the religious life naturally made for cenobitic communities. It was hardly an auspicious time for hermits. Some ecclesiastics, especially those on the iberian peninsula, went so far as to condemn the solitary life altogether.

Much of the evidence for the progress of latin monasticism comes from various religious rules which are characteristic of this time. Each of these documents is most probably a record of growth and development. Saint Caesarius of Arles' Rule for Nuns, for instance, appears to be composed in two parts. The second section begins with a short introduction:

> Since, with the aid of God, we made a rule for you at the time of the foundation of your monastery, we have frequently added some sections and cancelled others, deliberating and trying out what it would be possible for you to accomplish. Now at last, we have concluded as follows, according to what is reasonable, practicable, and conducive to holiness.[1]

Since the first draft of this rule was probably made around 512, and the final version is dated 22 June 534,[2] the rule in its present form represents over twenty years of experience

---

[1] *Césaire d'Arles, oeuvres monastiques*, ed. A. de Vogüé and J. Courreau (Paris 1988) Chapter 48. Vol. 1: 232–235

[2] *Ibid.* 272–273; W. E. Klingshirn, *Caesarius of Arles* (Cambridge 1994) 118–119.

in monastic living. Other surviving latin monastic rules of the period do not contain such clear indications of development. Their number, however, is evidence of considerable ferment and vigour.

Of the numerous rules which appeared in Gaul between the fourth and sixth centuries, that of Saint Caesarius of Arles was the most influential. Born into an aristocratic gallo-roman family around 470,[3] its author left at the age of twenty for Lérins, where he lived as a monk for some years until ill health forced him to return to the mainland. He settled at Arles where he was ordained priest and became abbot of a monastery in the suburbs. In 502 he was elected bishop of Arles, a position he held until his death in 542.[4] In his relations with the community of nuns which he founded around 512 he showed realism, honesty, and a readiness to listen. He was in no doubt about the value of the cenobitic life. 'This I urge above all,' he wrote in a letter to the nuns:

> Avoid the evil of contention like a deadly poison. Guard the sweetness of charity among yourselves. By your holy discourse, strengthen one another with spiritual medicines . . . My holy and reverend daughters, if you see anyone in doubt, console her, if you see anyone inclined to pride, apply the medicine of humility, if you see anyone given to anger, offer her the refreshing draught of patience.[5]

The rule which he wrote for the nuns emphasised the importance of a lifelong commitment. No one was to be admitted without a year's probation. The nuns were to live in obedience to an abbess elected by themselves. A number of other officers would assist her in governing the community. The community must be poor. Private property was forbidden. No one was to have a separate cell, but all were to sleep in a common dormitory. At meals the nuns must eat together in a

---

[3] On Caesarius, see Klingshirn (as above, n. 2); W. M. Daly, 'Caesarius of Arles, A Precursor of Medieval Christendom', *Traditio*, 26(1970) 1–28.

[4] Klingshirn (as n. 2), 16–32, 83–87, 260–261.

[5] *Césaire d'Arles* (as n. 1), 316 (section 6).

refectory and be silent whilst listening to reading. All were to learn to read. There was to be time set aside for study. Manual work consisted mostly of embroidery. Enclosure was strictly guarded. The nuns were never to emerge from their house, and men, above all, were to be excluded except for very special reasons. For the regular hours of prayer, the community was to follow, as far as possible, the liturgical usage of Lérins.[6]

The monastery at Arles is the first religious community known to have obtained a papal bull of exemption. It was issued by pope Hormisdas (514–523) at the request of Caesarius and decreed that no future bishop of Arles could exercise any authority in the monastery or dispose of its property. The bishop and his clergy were, however, to be allowed to visit the house for pastoral reasons.[7]

Caesarius's rule was the first in the west written explicitly for, women[8] and, as such, extremely influential. A number of sixth and seventh century monastic rules for women depended on it.[9] Cenobitic houses for women were becoming increasingly important in his time. Until then such institutions had been rare. Saint Augustine had not thought it necessary to write a rule for women; a rule for men with the pronouns changed had seemed sufficient. In his day, and for long afterwards, most dedicated women lived alone in their own houses, as recluses attached to a church, or in small groups of two or three.[10] These virgins or widows were a recognised order in the Church and set aside as dedicated to God at a special liturgical function. They might be involved in works of charity, but their chief task was to pray for the community or for individuals who asked for this service from them. They also acted, at times, as prayer-leaders.[11] They operated within an urban context. As the roman cities of Gaul declined, the traditional life of

---

[6] *Ibid.* 180–273.

[7] *Ibid.* 352–359; Klingshirn (as n. 2), 133–135.

[8] Klingshirn (as n. 2), 118.

[9] *Ibid.* 274–275.

[10] G. Muschiol, *Famula Dei* (Münster 1994) 41–42.

[11] *Ibid.* 55.

a dedicated widow or virgin became more difficult. Little is heard of them after the middle of the seventh century. A church council of 673/674 ordered all women who had taken the veil, whether widows or virgins, to live in a monastery.[12]

In 496 Clovis, the ruler of the barbarian Franks, was converted to the Catholic faith professed by his gallo-roman subjects. In an atmosphere now favourable to the Church, monasticism in Gaul made rapid strides. The extent of the involvement of the merovingian rulers is not entirely clear. In later centuries many monasteries claimed them as their founders on the strength of spurious charters of foundation. Although the more fantastic claims have long been disproved, there is good reason to believe that the kings did encourage religious foundations. Childebert I (511–558) introduced monks into the church he founded at Paris, which later became known as Saint Germain-des-Prés. A number of other foundations and benefactions as far west as Britanny and Normandy can with certainty be attributed to him. Generosity to monks and nuns was also shown by Guntram, king of Burgundy (561–593), his brother Sigbert, king of Austrasia (561–575), and Sigbert's wife Brunechildis.[13] The frankish landowners followed the example of their kings. Through royal and noble benefactions the monasteries began to acquire landed wealth.[14] By this time most of the bishops had put aside their earlier hostility to the monastic movement and favoured it with benefactions of their own.[15] Gregory, the bishop of Tours (573–593/4) played his part in raising the prestige of monks by his encouragement of the cult of Saint Martin.[16]

The career of Saint Radegund, as it was described by Gregory of Tours, Venantius Fortunatus, the nun Baudonivia, and other contemporaries, vividly illustrates the character of

---

[12] *Ibid.* 48–49.
[13] See discussion in J. Wallace-Hadrill, *The Frankish Church* (Oxford 1983) 55–58.
[14] *Ibid.* 60–62.
[15] *Ibid.* 60–61; 62.
[16] *Ibid.* 56.

merovingian monasticism.[17] Radegund was a member of the
thuringian royal family. In 531, after the Thuringians had been
defeated by Clothair, the frankish king of Soissons, Radegund
and other members of her family were carried away and around
540 she was forcibly married to her captor. After several unhappy years with her brutal husband, she escaped from him
and made her way to Noyon, where she persuaded the bishop
to ordain her a deaconess and clothe her in the religious habit.
For a time she settled on one of her estates and opened her
house to the destitute and the sick.

On her own lands she was always in danger of being
reclaimed by Clothair. Eventually she moved to the greater
security of Poitiers. Near the tomb of Saint Hilary she founded
two monasteries for nuns. One was called Saint Mary-outside-
the–Walls, and was intended as a burial place for the nuns.
In the other, also dedicated to Our Lady, Radegund lived as a
simple religious. The communities grew rapidly and eventually, according to Gregory of Tours, they numbered about 200
religious. Radegund claimed no privileges but lived in perfect obedience to the abbess Agnes. She won the admiration
of the poet Venantius Fortunatus who sent her flowers and
other gifts:

> O Queen that art so high
> Purple and gold thou passest by,
> With these poor flowers thy lover worships thee,
> Though all thy wealth thou hast flung far from thee,
> Wilt thou not hold
> The violet's purple and the crocus' gold?[18]

In exchange for his flattery the community made him gifts
of milk, cheese, eggs, vegetables, honey, and special delicacies

---

[17] H. Leclercq, 'Radegonde', DACL 14: 2044–2055; J. A. McNamara, 'Living
Sermons', S. F. Wemple, 'Female Sprituality and Mysticism in Frankish Monasticism: Radegund, Balthild, and Aldegund', *Peace Weavers*, Medieval Religious
Women 2, ed. John A. Nichols and Lillian Thomas Shank (Kalamazoo 1987)
19–37, 39–53.
[18] Trans. by Helen Waddell, *Medieval Latin Lyrics* (London 1948) 61.

from the monastery kitchen. All of these he duly acknowledged in playful verses.

Radegund was an assiduous collector of relics and her most precious acquisition was a fragment of the True Cross obtained from Constantinople. The relic was solemnly brought to Poitiers in 565. Venantius Fortunatus wrote his two finest hymns, *Vexilla Regis prodeunt*, and *Pange lingua gloriosi*—hymns still sung today—for the occasion. The dedication of Radegund's monastery was changed to the Holy Cross. The bishop of Poitiers, whom she seems in some way to have offended, stayed away from the festivities.

According to Gregory of Tours, the hostility of the bishop, which deprived her monasteries of proper direction, induced Radegund to go to Arles and adopt for her monastery the rule of Saint Caesarius. It was kept very strictly. Radegund herself performed the meanest offices in the community; serving in the kitchen and looking after the sick. So strict was the enclosure that when she died in 587 the nuns were not permitted to follow her body to the church where she was to be buried. They crowded round the windows of the towers and climbed the battlements to watch the funeral cortège. The celebrant at the obsequies was Gregory of Tours, the bishop of Poitiers having once again absented himself.[19]

In Spain there was a vigorous ascetic movement as early as the beginning of the fourth century. The fact that the Council of Elvira (300–306) went so far as to forbid bishops, priests, and deacons to abstain from marriage and the begetting of children, suggests that the clergy were particularly drawn to asceticism.[20] The power of Priscillianism later in the century is further evidence of its attraction. Orthodox christian monasticism in Spain is associated with Saint Martin of Braga. He came to Galicia 'from the east', according to Saint Isidore of Seville, and converted the swabian king Theodomir and his

---

[19] H. Leclercq (as n. 17), 1592–1594; 2044–2055.
[20] A. Linage Conde, *Los origines del monacato benedictino en la peninsula iberica*, 1 (Leon 1973) 211.

court from the Arian to the Catholic faith.[21] Martin's writings
included his own selection of the sayings of the Desert Fathers
translated into Latin. As both bishop and abbot, he ruled over
the monastery of Dumio which he founded near Braga (now
in Portugal), and from there exercised authority over his other
foundations in Spain. It was a position without precedent in
the western Church of his time. As bishop-abbot of Dumio,
Martin took part in the council of Braga in 561, and some
years later was elected as metropolitan bishop of Braga itself,
a position which he occupied until his death in 579.[22]

Spanish monasticism was given a further stimulus after the
establishment of the visigothic kingdom and the conversion of
King Recared to Catholicism in 587. From then until its conquest by the Arabs in 711, Spain was a theocratic state in which
the union of spiritual and secular authority was complete.[23] The
outstanding bishops of the period were monks. They included
bishops Martin and Fructuosus of Braga, the three brothers
Leander, Isidore, and Fulgentius, and many others.[24]

In addition to Martin of Braga's collection of the *Apophthegmata*, the writings of Cassian were known in Spain through
a compilation known as the *Regula Cassiani* made up of passages from the *Institutes*,[25] and there are numerous spanish copies of Saint Jerome's translation of the rule of Saint
Pachomius.[26] There is also evidence of the influence of the
rule of Saint Benedict on the spanish monastic rules of the
seventh century.[27]

The councils of the spanish Church underlined the role of
the bishops in maintaining monastic discipline and welded the
monasteries to the life of the Church as a whole. A council of

---

[21] J. Orlandis, *Estudios sobre instituciones monásticas medievales* (Pamplona 1971) 103–104.
[22] *Ibid.* 104, 106.
[23] See J. N. Hillgarth, 'Popular religion in Visigothic Spain', *Visigothic Spain—new approaches*, ed. E. James (Oxford 1980) 9.
[24] Linage Conde (as n. 20), 229.
[25] *Ibid.* 255–256.
[26] *Ibid.* 254.
[27] *Ibid.* 271.

546 decreed that the bishop's permission was required before the founding of a monastery, as well as for the ordination of monks as priests or clerks. Abbots had to attend the annual diocesan synods like all the other clergy.[28] In 633 the fourth council of Toledo emphasised that abbots must obey their bishops, who had the right to excommunicate them.[29] The ninth council of Toledo in 655 prescribed the procedure to be followed by a new abbot: before he was confirmed the bishop had to examine him about the rule and the tradition of the Fathers, and receive from him an oath about regular observance. Only then would the bishop hand him the abbatial staff and a book containing the rule.[30] The fourth council of Toledo also legislated about dedicated widows who did not live in communities but were clothed in a special habit and followed a life of penitence under clerical guidance, and forbade them to marry again.[31] On the other hand, the councils guaranteed the economic independence of monasteries. Bishops could not dispose of monastic estates,[32] or use monks as labourers on their own properties.[33] The council of Braga in 556 allowed monks some liturgical freedom in deciding their own method of chanting the psalms at Matins and Vespers.[34]

Within this legislative framework, the monks could set up organisations of their own. Monastic establishments were particularly numerous south of the river Minho and around Braga, as well as in the mountainous area of El Bierzo. This was the 'Thebaid' of visigothic Spain.[35] The abbots of this region met at the beginning of every month to pray for those under their government and to discuss their common concerns.[36] In 656 Saint Fructuosus, abbot of Dumio and the founder of many

---

[28] *Ibid.* 224.
[29] *Ibid.* 225.
[30] *Ibid.* 226.
[31] *Ibid.* 231.
[32] *Ibid.* 224.
[33] *Ibid.* 225.
[34] *Ibid.* 227.
[35] *Ibid.* 239–40.
[36] *Regula monastica communis* 10.2 ;PL 87: 118–119.

of the monasteries in the area, was elected bishop of Braga. The abbot-bishop of Dumio was now claiming authority over all the monasteries of the kingdom as the final court of appeal in disciplinary matters. He was the *episcopus qui sub regula vivit*, 'the bishop who lives under the rule'.[37] In him therefore episcopal authority within the Church was maintained, while the monks were subject in matters of internal discipline, to another monk.

Four religious rules have survived from the visigothic period. The oldest is that composed by Saint Leander, bishop of Seville (c.540–c.600) for his sister Florentina, abbess of a monastery of women.[38] Leander emphasised the importance of separation from the world. The sisters were to have no converse with women living in the world, still less with men, even holy ones,[39] or to have private conversations with one another. They were to spend their time reading and praying. If they did any manual work, someone was to read to them while they were thus engaged.[40] Fasting was necessary for those who were strong; abstention from meat was voluntary. Moderation was necessary in all things.[41] All private property was forbidden.[42]

The rule was insistent on the positive value of life in community. The solitary life was absolutely to be avoided.[43] Religious were exhorted to be humble and poor, and to take Our Lady as their model. They were not to lord it over servants, for these had also been called to virginity. The servants in their turn were to avoid pride. Those who had been accustomed to delicate living in the world were not to be too harshly treated, those who had been poor were to be provided with all their needs. The sick were not to be burdened. 'Let charity temper all things and draw all to the same destination of peace. Let

---

[37] Linage Conde (as n. 20), 240; Orlandis (as n. 21), 102–105.
[38] PL 72:873–894.
[39] *Ibid.* 881–883 (Ch. 1–5).
[40] *Ibid.* 883–884 (Ch. 6).
[41] *Ibid.* 884–885; 888 (Ch. 8, 15).
[42] *Ibid.* 890 (Ch. 18).
[43] *Ibid.* 890 (Ch. 17).

not her who has given up a position of power be conceited, nor her who was poor or a servant be depressed'.[44]

Leander's brother Isidore, who succeeded him as bishop of Seville around 600, wrote a rule for men which not only reveals some influence by the rule of Saint Benedict[45] but also displays the same qualities of balance and moderation.[46] An original feature is its detailed description of the plan of an ideal monastery: it must not be near a town; it must be surrounded by walls with one door leading to the outside world and another to the garden; the brothers' cells must be near the church so that they can hurry to the services; the refectory must be next to the cells to enable the servers to get there quickly. The infirmary should be placed some distance away from the other buildings so that the sick will not be disturbed. The garden must be enclosed so that the brethren can work there without having to leave the monastery.[47] The writings of Saint Isidore were widely distributed in the Carolingian Empire, and it is surely not fanciful to see in the spectacular plan of Saint Gall a pictorial interpretation of his scheme.[48]

Saint Isidore made detailed provision for the reception of postulants, who were to be kept in the monastery guesthouse for three months.[49] He regulated the liturgy for the seven traditional offices, and arranged it, and the monastic day, according to the seasons.[50] Three times a week after Terce the monks were to assemble together to listen to a sermon from one of the seniors, after which offenders were to be disciplined.[51] Light and heavy faults are listed in the rule. Punishments included flogging and excommunication for three days, or even longer if the offence was severe.[52]

---

[44] *Ibid.* 886–8 (Ch. 13–14).
[45] Linage Conde (as n. 20), 271.
[46] PL 83: 867–904.
[47] *Ibid.* 869–870 (Ch. 1).
[48] See below pp. 112–114.
[49] PL 83: 871–873 (Ch. 3).
[50] *Ibid.* 875–877 (Ch. 6).
[51] *Ibid.* 877 (Ch. 7).
[52] *Ibid.* 884–887 (Ch. 16–18).

All monks were to labour with their hands, each specialising in a particular craft. They were to be supervised by the
prior, who in turn obeyed the abbot. Manual work was to be
done in the garden. Building and agricultural labour was to be
left to servants.[53] Learning was given a place of special importance. Monks were to collect their books at the beginning of
the day and return them after Vespers. If there was something
they had not understood, they were to ask at the thrice-weekly
assembly. They could also ask the abbot after Vespers. The
explanations were to be given in the hearing of all. Books by
heretics or pagans were not to be read.[54]

Like his brother Leander, Isidore emphasised the importance of community life. Monks were forbidden the ownership
of anything. No one, unless he was old or sick, might have his
own cell. There were some who wanted to be recluses, but this
was not to be allowed. They were to remain in community,
to be cured of their faults, edify others by their virtue, and
exercise humility.[55] No one should judge himself superior to
anyone. The community should be animated, as it were, by a
single heart.[56]

The rule of Saint Fructuosus of Braga[57] resembles that of
Saint Isidore. Fructuosus became bishop of Braga in 656, after
having spent many years as a hermit and monastic founder
in the El Bierzo region. He had little in the way of spiritual
doctrine in his rule, which leaned towards strictness: Prime
was added to the traditional seven offices, and between Prime
and Terce the monks were also expected to pray during the
second hour, so that there would be no idleness.[58] Postulants
were to wait outside the monastery gate for ten days and then
to live in the guesthouse for a year under the direction of
a senior.[59]

---

[53] *Ibid.* 873–875 (Ch. 5).
[54] *Ibid.* 877–878 (Ch. 8).
[55] *Ibid.* 888–889 (Ch. 19).
[56] *Ibid.* 870–871 (Ch. 3).
[57] PL 87: 1099–1110. On Saint Fructuosus, see Orlandis (as n. 21), 71–82.
[58] PL 87: 1099–1100 (Ch. 2).
[59] *Ibid.* 1109–1110 (Ch. 21, 22).

The anonymous *Regula Communis*, probably a monastic code worked out, under the influence of Saint Fructuosus, at a meeting of visigothic abbots in northeast Spain,[60] deals with problems which affected all the monasteries of the area.[61] The first chapter condemns pseudo-monasteries. These institutions were found all over dark-age Europe. They were religious houses in name only and in fact a means of avoiding taxation. The second chapter of the *Regula Communis* is directed against priests, not themselves monks, who try to exercise authority in religious houses.[62] Another chapter attempts to standardise the procedure for the entry of postulants.[63]

In the event of whole families entering the religious life— husbands, wives, and children—the men and the women had to live apart. Parents had to yield the children absolutely into the hands of the abbot. The children could not see their parents again without permission from the prior, except in the case of the very young, who could see their mothers whenever they wished. When they were old enough they were to be sent to the monastery, whether for men or women, where they would spend the rest of their lives.[64]

Old men who entered a monastery as a retirement home were another problem. Those who turned out well were to be excused the hardest tasks on account of their age. Those who spent their time gossiping and making trouble could be warned as often as fourteen times. After that they were to be expelled.[65]

It is unlikely that any of these rules were followed to the letter. Monks considered themselves heirs to all the traditional religious rules, and each house made its own selection from them. No doubt this caused a certain ambiguity, and in Spain it became usual to define meticulously the duties of each entrant to the religious life. Saint Isidore insisted that on entering

---

[60] Linage Conde (as n. 20), 233–234; Orlandis (as n. 21), 97–123.
[61] PL 87: 1111–1127.
[62] *Ibid.* 1111–1113 (Ch. 1, 2).
[63] *Ibid.* 1113–1114 (Ch. 4).
[64] *Ibid..* 1115–1116 (Ch. 6).
[65] *Ibid..* 1116–1117 (Ch. 8).

a monastery a monk must make his promises in writing.[66]
Saint Fructuosus described the way a new monk 'receives his
pactum, which contains the whole basis of his profession'.[67]

This monastic pact was a peculiarity of visigothic monasticism. In it a monk bound himself to regular discipline. The
pact took the form of a contract and was renewed by the
whole community when a new abbot was elected.[68] The oldest
example is found at the end of the *Regula Communis*. It begins
with a statement of orthodox trinitarian doctrine. The monks
then promise to live in community under the abbot according
to the ordinances of the apostles, the rule, and the teaching of
the fathers. They will accept all the abbot's judgements, and
subject themselves to punishments for infringements of the
rule. If they leave the monastery, the abbot has the right to
pursue them. Anyone, clerical or lay, who shelters them, de-
serves excommunication. On the other hand they are assured
that the abbot will deal justly with them. His decisions will not
be made at whim, and there will be no favouritism. If he fails
in this regard, they can appeal against him to 'the bishop who
lives under the rule,' that is, the bishop of Braga.[69]

Ireland was converted to Christianity in the fifth century,
largely through the missionary efforts of Saint Patrick. He was
particularly proud of the 'sons of the Scots and the daughters of
chieftains who are known to have become monks and virgins'.
One girl, he tells us, told him a few days after he had baptised
her that she had been inspired to become a virgin of Christ.
Six days later she took the veil, undeterred by threats from her
family. Slave girls braved the wrath of their masters to embrace
the religious life.[70] Some of the women lived in small groups,
but at this early stage there seem to have been no organised
monasteries.[71]

---

[66] PL 83: 871–873.
[67] PL 87: 1110.
[68] Linage Conde (as n. 20), 291–293.
[69] PL 87: 1127–1130.
[70] *Mise Pádraig*, ed. L. MacPhilibin (Dublin 1961) 60.
[71] See J. Ryan, *Irish Monasticism* (Dublin 1931) 91–96.

The first formal religious community in Ireland dates from the very end of the missionary period. Brigid, born into a family of chieftains in the middle of the fifth century,[72] was one of the young women of noble birth whose enthusiasm for the new faith inspired her to embrace a life of asceticism. Her fame attracted a large number of followers of both sexes for whom she founded a great monastery at Kildare. Her achievements made her a national figure and she is said to have travelled around Ireland in a chariot to attend public assemblies. During one of these journeys she came across a group of pagans to whom she preached the Gospel.[73] Kildare had a community of men living side by side with the women.[74] The two communities had their own quarters and worshipped on different sides of the great church separated by a screen, but all followed the same rule.[75]

The oldest irish monastery for men appears to have been on the Aran Islands and dates from around 530.[76] Enda, its founder, had studied at Whithorn in Galloway, but since the monastic status of that church is not established, the source from which Enda derived his monasticism is not clear.[77] A stronger impulse for the monastic life came from Wales, with which Ireland was always in close contact. Around 520 there was a monastery under Saint Illtyd on the island of Caldey off the coast of Pembrokeshire.[78] Illtyd's pupil Saint David, whose monastery was at Menevia in Pembrokeshire (now Saint Davids) was a contemporary of the irish monastic founders and was said to have exercised great influence over them.[79] Through these welsh monasteries the influence of Lérins made itself felt in Ireland.[80]

---

[72] A. Gwynn and R. Hadcock, *Medieval Religious Houses: Ireland* (London 1970) 63.
[73] Ryan (as n. 71), 135–136.
[74] *Ibid.* 142–143; Gwynn and Hadcock (as n. 72), 319–320.
[75] Ryan (as n. 71), 142–143.
[76] *Ibid.* 106.
[77] *Ibid.* 105–106.
[78] *Ibid.* 110.
[79] *Ibid.* 113–114.
[80] *Ibid.* 114–116.

The sixth century was the great age of irish monastic foundations. Among the more important, Clonard in County Meath was founded by Saint Finian after his return from Britain around 520.[81] Clonmacnois, in County Offaly, one of the richest monasteries in Ireland and a great centre of learning, was founded by Finian's disciple Saint Ciaran.[82] Bangor, a famed monastery on Belfast Loch, was erected in 555 or 559 by Saint Comgall. Clonfert in Connaught was founded by Saint Brendan, who died in 577 or 583.[83] Among foundations of the early seventh century were Glendalough in County Wicklow,[84] Ferns in County Wexford,[85] and Lismore in County Waterford.[86]

By this time irish monasteries were being founded outside Ireland itself. Saint Columcille, better known as Columba, a member of the northern chieftain clan of the Ui Neill, founded the monastery of Derry around 546,[87] and Durrow in County Offaly about ten years later.[88] In 563, like many of his fellow-countrymen, he crossed the sea and migrated to Dalriada, a kingdom covering the northern coast of Antrim in Ireland, as well as Argyll, Kintyre, and the western islands of what is now Scotland. In 565 Columba settled on the island of Iona and founded a monastery which became the spiritual centre of the kingdom.[89]

Even more spectacular were the journeys of Saint Columban.[90] After spending about thirty years at the monastery of Bangor, where he won fame as a teacher, he left, some time after 593, for merovingian Gaul, accompanied by a number of

---

[81] Gwynn and Hadcock (as n.72), 63–64.
[82] *Ibid.* 64–65.
[83] *Ibid.* 64.
[84] *Ibid.* 80–81.
[85] *Ibid.* 78–79.
[86] *Ibid.* 91–92; see also L. Bieler, *Ireland, Harbinger of the Middle Ages* (London 1963) 26.
[87] Gwynn and Hadcock (as n. 72) 67–68; 168.
[88] *Ibid.* 174.
[89] On the dates see I. B. Cowan and D. E. Easson, *Medieval Religious Houses: Scotland* (London 1976) 48–49.
[90] The biographical information for the life of Saint Columban is collected together in *Sancti Columbani Opera*, ed. G. S. M. Walker (Dublin 1957) ix–xxi.

irish monks, some of whose names are known. King Childebert of Burgundy granted him Annegray, a ruined roman fort in the Vosges mountains. After a few years, the community having grown spectacularly, the king gave Columban a more spacious site at Luxeuil, where a second monastery was established. Yet a third monastery, Fontaines, had to be founded to accommodate the ever growing number of recruits.

At the height of his burgundian fame Columban was said to have ruled over two hundred twenty monks. He was unpopular with the local bishops, however, because he claimed complete exemption from them for all his monasteries. Their hostility, and a quarrel with the royal court, led to his exile in 610. An attempt to force him to return to Ireland failed and eventually, accompanied by some of his disciples, he sought refuge in the area of Bregenz, on what is now the austrian shore of Lake Constance. The hostile burgundian court could still reach him there, however. He decided to make his way across the Alps to Italy. Gall, one of his disciples who was familiar with the local language, decided to stay behind to preach to the local pagans. This was the origin of the later abbey of Saint Gall in modern Switzerland. In 612 Columban arrived in Lombardy. After a short sojourn in the court of king Agilulf, the saint was granted a solitude at Bobbio in the Appenines. There he founded a new community and there he died in 615.

There were further expansions of irish monasticism in the seventh century. In 673 Mael-ruba emigrated from Bangor to Applecross, on the scottish mainland opposite the island of Skye. The community remained in touch with Bangor until the late eighth century.[91] The irish visionary Saint Fursey, whose revelations about the afterlife are described by Bede,[92] came to England in 633 and founded a monastery at a place called Cnobehesburg, in the kingdom of the East Saxons. From there he moved to Gaul and established another monastery at Lagny near Paris. Further north the abbey of nuns at Nivelles in modern Belgium placed itself under his governance, and

[91] Cowan and Easson (as n. 89), 46.
[92] Bede, *Ecclesiastical History*, 3.19.

another monastery was founded at Fosse near Namur by his brother Foillean.[93]

These migrations created a widespread monastic movement which stretched from the Aran Islands in Galway Bay off the west coast of Ireland, to Bobbio in the mountains below Piacenza in northern Italy. All the irish communities overseas kept in contact with the mother country. The tale has often been repeated of Columba of Iona's care for a crane which was blown on to the island and lay exhausted on the shore. The monks were instructed to care for it and feed it until it was strong enough to 'return to the sweet district of Ireland from which it at first came'.[94] In the *Life of Saint Columba*, we read of a penitent, guilty of homicide and perjury, who made his way from Connaught in Ireland, to Iona, to confess his sins to Columba.[95] The saint occasionally visited Ireland to discuss ecclesiastical affairs, and was driven around in a chariot.[96] Adomnan, his successor as abbot of Iona in the seventh century attended summer synods of clergy in Ireland.[97]

The abbots of the founding houses exercised jurisdiction over houses which had been founded from theirs. Irish monasteries were thus grouped into *paruchiae* in an arrangement which somewhat foreshadows the mother-daughterhouse relationship of the later Cistercians.[98] Although in Saint Patrick's time the Church in Ireland had been governed, as everywhere else, by bishops, the monastic *paruchiae* came, in time, to replace regular diocesan government. Ireland had no cities. The monasteries were the spiritual centres of the various tribes and the abbot exercised pastoral jurisdiction in the area. It became usual for a bishop to live in the monastery to dispense those sacraments which required episcopal orders.[99]

---

[93] On Mael-ruba and Fursey, see K. Hughes, *The Church in Early Irish Society* (London 1966) 81–82.
[94] *Adomnan's Life of Columba*, ed. and trans. A. O. and M. O. Anderson (London 1961) 312–315.
[95] *Ibid.* 448–449.
[96] *Ibid.* 456–459.
[97] *Ibid.* 420–435.
[98] On the *paruchiae* see Hughes (as n. 93), 57–90.
[99] *Ibid.*

The irish monks considered their life a voluntary martyrdom, undertaken during an age when the persecution of the
Church had ceased and it was no longer possible to die for one's
faith. An ancient irish homily states that 'there are in fact three
kinds of martyrdom, which we may regard as types of cross
in human eyes: namely, white martyrdom, green martyrdom,
and red martyrdom. A person undergoes white martyrdom
when he leaves all for the sake of Christ, even though this
means fasting, hunger, and hard work. Green martyrdom is
attributed to someone who through them—that is, fasting and
work—is freed of his desires, or undergoes travail in sorrow
and penance. Red martyrdom is to be found in the sufferings
of a cross of death for Christ's sake, as was the way of the
apostles, because of the persecution of the wicked, and whilst
preaching the truths of God. These three kinds of martyrdom
are to be found in those sinful persons who are truly repentant,
who abandon their self-will and who shed their blood in fasting
and in manual labour for the sake of Christ'.[100]

Some abbots applied this doctrine in practice by imposing
a harsh rule upon their followers. 'Let the monk,' wrote Saint
Columban in his rule,

> not do as he wishes, let him eat what he is bidden, keep
> as much as he has received, complete the tale of his work,
> be subject to whom he does not like. Let him come weary
> to his bed and sleep walking, and let him be forced to rise
> while his sleep is not yet finished. Let him keep silence
> when he has suffered wrong, let him fear the superior of
> his community as a lord, love him as a father, believe that
> whatever he commands is healthful to himself and let him
> not pass judgement on the opinion of an elder.[101]

The violence of the punishments in Columban's communities,
even for minor transgressions, is disconcerting: six blows for

---

[100] U. Ó Maidín, *The Celtic Monk* (Kalamazoo 1996) 140–141.
[101] *Sancti Columbani Opera* (as n. 90), 142–143. The passage is taken from
Saint Jerome; see *Ibid.* 141 n. 2.

not saying 'Amen' to the grace at table; six for not blessing the lamp when it is lit by a junior; ten for cutting the table with a knife; twelve for forgetting the prayer before or after work; twenty-five for forgetting the chrismal (a pyx worn around the neck) when hurrying to work; fifty for speaking too loudly when there is no need, for coming late or too noisily to prayers, or for contradicting a senior. The blows were inflicted with a leather strap upon the hand.[102]

Like all western monastic legislators of the period, Columban was convinced of the value of life in community. 'Let the monk live in a community under the discipline of one father and in company with many, so that from one he may learn lowliness, from another patience.'[103] The harshness was not necessarily typical of all irish houses. A comparison of Columban's monastic Penitential with that of Cummean, compiled around the middle of the seventh century, shows that the latter prescribed much gentler punishments for the same offences.[104] Adomnan's *Life of Saint Columba* reveals a religious superior whose rule over the monks was marked by gentleness. When the saint visited the island of Hinba he ordered that the rigour of the fast be relaxed even for the penitents.[105] When a noted holy man from Ireland arrived one day at Iona, the normal Wednesday fast was similarly relaxed.[106] On another occasion Columba was distressed because the monks at Durrow were being forced to work in harsh weather on the construction of a large building.[107] At Iona, during the harvest, he was worried when the monks who had been at work in the fields came home late.[108] It would appear, then, that there was no uniformity of discipline in the irish monasteries. Indeed, a toleration of diversity was a feature of early Christianity in

---

[102] *Sancti Columbani Opera* (as n. 90), 147–51.
[103] *Ibid.* 140–141, quoting Saint Jerome.
[104] Hughes (as n. 93), 59–60.
[105] *Life of Columba* (as n. 94), 250–251.
[106] *Ibid.* 258–261.
[107] *Ibid.* 264–267.
[108] *Ibid.* 282–287. See comment in Hughes (as n. 93), 60–62.

Ireland, where even the Easter controversy aroused less heat than elsewhere.[109]

This diversity extended to liturgical matters. In his rule, Saint Columban set out the way he wanted the Office to be sung by his monks, but admitted that there were 'some Catholics' who did it differently.[110] Most irish monasteries were familiar with the six hours of Terce, Sext, None, Vespers, Nocturns, and Lauds. By the seventh century Prime was being sung in some places as an extra morning Office.[111] The liturgical day began, as with the Jews, at nightfall, with the singing of Vespers. At Iona, for instance, 'Vespers of the Lord's night' was sung on Saturday evening.[112] In the same monastery, during the seventh century, Mass was celebrated only on Sundays[113] and on a few other special solemnities, like the feast of Saint Columba.[114] On these days the monks went to church clothed in white.[115] When a number of senior priests were present, it was the custom for the most senior of all to celebrate. He entered the church to consecrate the bread and wine after the reading of the Gospel.[116] Mass was also celebrated on Iona when news was brought of the death of one of the abbots in Ireland.[117]

'Nakedness and disdain for riches', wrote Saint Columban, 'are the first perfection of monks . . . we have need of few things, according to the word of the Lord, or even of one. For few things are true necessities without which life cannot be led.'[118] Manual work in the fields was the background to the monastic life.[119] At Iona one of the monks

---

[109] Hughes, 108–110.
[110] *Sancti Columbani Opera* (as n. 90), 132–133.
[111] Ryan (as n. 71), 335–336.
[112] *Life of Columba* (as n. 94), 527. On the canonical hours at Iona, see *ibid.*, introduction, 121–122.
[113] *Ibid.* 518–519.
[114] *Ibid.* 458–459.
[115] *Ibid.* 488–489.
[116] *Ibid.* 500–501.
[117] *Ibid.* 486–489.
[118] *Sancti Columbani Opera* (as n. 90), 126–127.
[119] See e.g. *Ibid.* 149.

held the office of 'works organiser'.[120] Columba's monks built
the monastery buildings,[121] planted the fields, brought in the
harvest,[122] looked after and milked the cows. The milk churns
were brought into the monastery by a white horse, whose
particular affection for Saint Columba is recorded in a touching
passage of his *Life*.[123] There was a certain amount of specialisation in the irish communities. Saint Columban mentions
brothers who were in charge of the cooking and the serving,
and a porter.[124] At Iona there seems to have been a gang of
monks who did the heavy labour and who are referred to as
operarii fratres.[125] The later institution of lay brothers may
have originated in the irish monasteries.

Saint Columban presided over a community which was
highly stratified. In church the seniors stood in the middle of
the nave while the others were ranged to the right and left
along the sides. The novices formed yet a separate group.[126]
At the altar stood the priests and deacons.[127] The singing was
led by a first and second chanter.[128] The community also had a
number of overseers[129] with a senior overseer placed over the
rest.[130] One of these officers had charge of the guest house.[131]
In Saint Columban's monasteries the abbot was assisted by a
prior who shared some of his authority and ruled the monastery
when the abbot was away.[132] The monasteries subordinate to
Iona were ruled by priors, who were at all times obedient to
Columba's wishes.[133]

---

[120] 'Operum dispensator', *Life of Columba* (as n. 94), 284.
[121] *Ibid.* 264–265.
[122] *Ibid.* 282–287.
[123] *Ibid.* 522–523.
[124] *Sancti Columbani Opera* (as n. 90), 146–147; 150–151.
[125] *Life of Columba* (as n. 94), 516.
[126] *Sancti Columbani Opera* (as n. 90), 156–159.
[127] *Ibid.* 148–149.
[128] 'Primarius', *Ibid.* 156–157.
[129] 'Economus.'
[130] *Sancti Columbani Opera* (as n. 90), 156–157.
[131] *Ibid.* 152–153.
[132] *Ibid.* 153 n. 1.
[133] *Life of St. Columba* (as n. 94), 268–271.

From the earliest times irish monasteries were centres of intellectual activity. Dark Age learning was derivative. Scholars were aware that they were more ignorant than their predecessors under the Roman Empire. Intellectual activity consisted of finding information wherever it lay to hand. Since Ireland had never been part of the Roman Empire, all latin literature had to be imported. Some irish monks came to be intoxicated with the new learning and cultivated a deliberately obscure and pedantic latin style.[134] This form of writing produced at least one masterpiece however: the magnificent poem *Altus prosator*, attributed to Saint Columba.[135] During the seventh century, influences flowed into Ireland from Britain, Gaul, and Spain. The encyclopaedic writings of Saint Isidore of Seville were circulating in Ireland shortly after his death and provided the Irish with endless material for their own glossaries and biblical commentaries.[136] Their attitude to their sources was never slavish. Unlike other dark-age scholars, they were prepared to criticise their authorities and check their references. Copyists reacted to their materials, giving the reader their opinions of a text in many a frank marginal note.[137] The scriptoria of the irish monasteries produced illuminated manuscripts which remain among the most admired masterpieces of the Middle Ages, and their script was widely used in England and on the Continent until the twenfth century.[138]

The spirit of irish monasticism is vividly reflected in Adomnan's *Life of Saint Columba*. The author was abbot of Iona from 679–704.[139] He was writing nearly one hundred years after Columba's death and his book should not be regarded as an accurate biography.[140] Even so, it unforgettably translates the reader into an ideal irish monastery of the seventh

---

[134] See comment in L. Bieler (as n. 86), 13.
[135] *The Oxford Book of Medieval Verse*, ed. F. J. E. Raby (Oxford 1959) No. 48.
[136] K. Hughes, 'Irish Monks and Learning', *Los monjes y los estudios* (IV semaña de estudios monasticos Poblet 1963) 66–67 69–71.
[137] *Ibid.* 71–73.
[138] See Bieler (s n. 86) 15–23.
[139] *Life of St. Columba* (as n. 94) introduction, 91–98.
[140] See discussion, *Ibid.*, 18–30.

century. Columba's pastoral concern is constantly emphasised. Penitents came from Ireland to confess their sins to him and to be assigned penances.[141] Other irish visitors were questioned about their family affairs and given advice about their relatives at home.[142] Columba was equally concerned about the spiritual welfare of the Picts, and preached the Gospel to them through an interpreter.[143] On one occasion a child was brought to him for baptism by his parents and the ceremony was conducted in the open air.[144] Down to his own time, wrote Adomnan, the monasteries of Saint Columba were held in great honour both by the Picts and by the Irish in Britain.[145]

The Irish acceptance of Christianity was wholehearted, but this did not prevent a positive attitude to the pagan culture which had preceded the mission of Patrick.[146] In the land of Picts, too, Saint. Columba had words of praise for those of his pagan converts who had preserved natural goodness throughout their lives until they were baptised.[147]

The monasticism of Gaul, Spain, and Ireland during this period shows certain common characteristics. Monastic legislators were concerned with practicalities. They had little to say about theory, for they assumed the monastic spirituality of writers like Cassian, Saint Basil, and *the Apophthegmata patrum*. Although not agreed about details, most of them wanted a period of probation before anyone was admitted to a religious community. They legislated for literate communities, and made sure that time was set aside for study. They vehemently condemned private property among religious. All things must be held in common, as in the first apostolic community. Above all, they saw a cenobitic monastery as the only sure framework for the monastic life.

---

[141] *Ibid.* 253–257, 267–269.
[142] *Ibid.* 241–243.
[143] *Ibid.* 396–397.
[144] *Ibid.* 346–349.
[145] *Ibid.* 460–461.
[146] See Bieler (as n. 86), 1–2.
[147] *Life of St. Columba* (as n. 94), 274–275; 493.

Chapter 4
SAINT BENEDICT
AND SIXTH-CENTURY ITALY

THE GOTHIC INVADERS who occupied Italy and brought the western Roman Empire to an end were anxious to come to terms with their new subjects. King Theodoric (492–526) strove to win the friendship of the roman senate. Unfortunately, his adherence—and that of his followers—to the arian heresy made the creation of an integrated new state impossible. Disunity in Italy gave Justinian, the emperor at Constantinople, his opportunity. His army arrived in the peninsula in 535. Three years later, after a bloody and destructive campaign, Italy was in imperial hands. To all appearances the Roman Empire was restored, but in 541 the Goths, under their leader Totila, launched a counter-attack. Rome was twice besieged. By the time Totila had established his rule there, most of the inhabitants had died of starvation or disease. In 552 Totila was defeated and killed by an imperial army which had marched through the Balkans. In 568 the Lombards began their invasions. These fierce Germans, Arians like the Goths but lacking their respect for roman civilisation, effectively ended imperial control of Italy.

After 535, then, Italy was beset by plague, misery, and desolation. The anarchic background explains why historians of the monastic movement in this period face many problems. It was not a time favourable to meticulous record-keeping or to the preservation of archives. Basic questions of chronology and geography remain unsolved. In 1980 Benedictines celebrated the 1500th anniversary of the birth of Saint Benedict, amidst doubt whether the reputed father of latin monasticism had

actually been born in 480.[1] Altogether we know less about him
than we do about Saint Pachomius, who flourished a century
earlier. Since 1937 scholars have been studying the nearly
contemporary Rule of the Master, but after more than fifty
years of scholarly argument we are no nearer certainty about
who the Master was, what were his dates, or where he lived.[2]

The chaos was especially demoralising for those who followed older forms of monasticism. The Rule of the Master and
the Rule of Saint Benedict are particularly critical of monks
called sarabaites and gyrovagues. Sarabaites, according to the
Master, are a detestable kind of monk. He would prefer not
to call them monks at all, but for the fact that they wear the
tonsure. They live in twos or threes, are subject to no pastor,
and follow no rule. There are also hermits who indulge all
kinds of extravagances.[3] Worst of all, the Master continues,
are the gyrovagues. These so-called monks appear at the doors
of settled religious communities demanding hospitality. They
claim to be on pilgrimage or to have escaped from captivity.
They insist on being given the best food and drink. Because
they do not know the psalms, they say that they are too exhausted to attend the Night Office. When they feel that they
have outstayed their welcome they depart, beating their poor
donkey to make sure of arriving at their new destination in
good time for the next meal.[4]

Behind these unflattering portraits one can recognise the
ascetics who, since early christian times, lived, alone or in small
groups, in their own homes, following a round of penance,
prayer, and good works devised largely by themselves. Stability
had been little stressed originally. There was a tradition of
imitating the Lord who 'had nowhere to lay his head'.[5] Saint
Anthony and Saint Pachomius, had not hesitated to displace

---

[1] See discussion in *Règle de St. Benoît*, ed. E. Manning (Rochefort 1980) xxv–
xxvii.
[2] See below pp. 88–91.
[3] See *La Règle du Maître*, ed. A. de Vogüé (Paris 1964) 1:330–333. Cf. *La Règle
de St. Benoît*, ed. A. de Vogüé (Paris 1972) 1: 438–439.
[4] *La Règle du Maître*, 1:438–447.
[5] Matt 8:20; Lk 9:58.

themselves. Cassian and a companion left their monastery in Bethlehem to study the teaching of the egyptian monks. For several years they travelled from one hermitage to the other and never, in the end, returned to their own community.[6] Saint Martin's monks accompanied him on his missionary journeys.[7] Among irish monks 'exile for Christ' was a recognised form of penance.[8]

These older forms of monasticism were now regarded as out of date, but even the better organised communities in Italy were in a deplorable state by the end of the sixth century.[9] The letters of pope Saint Gregory the Great (590–604) show particular concern about the state of the monasteries. In the diocese of Sorrento monks were wandering from one house to the other as they pleased. They had withdrawn from the authority of their abbot and were acquiring private property.[10] In the diocese of Naples a certain abbot had fled from his monastery, taking some of the monks with him. The bishop was partly to blame: the man had been admitted as a monk before he had been properly tested.[11] Elsewhere the disorders were a direct result of the anarchy of the times. Owing to the destruction of their houses in barbarian raids, monks were on the move all over the island of Sicily.[12]

A number of Gregory's enactments were intended to raise monastic standards. He insisted that all who wished to enter monastic life should undergo a two-year noviciate.[13] Abbots were to be elected by their own communities.[14] No one was

---

[6] See above p. 37. Cassian also describes two kinds of unsatisfactory monks, but gyrovagues are not among them: *Conferences* 18. 7–8.

[7] Sulpicius Severus, *Life of Saint Martin* 14. 23.

[8] Ludwig Bieler, *Ireland Harbinger of the Middle Ages*, 65–67; 84; and see above pp. 73–75.

[9] See G. Jenal, 'Grégoire le Grand et la vie monastique dans l'Italie de son temps', *Colloques internationaux du CNRS: 'Grégoire le Grand* (Paris 1986) 148–149, 156.

[10] PL 77: 495–496.

[11] *Ibid.* 1082–1083.

[12] *Ibid.* 494–495.

[13] *Ibid.* 1083.

[14] *Ibid.* 918.

to become an abbess under the age of sixty.[15] Imperial officials and ex-soldiers presented a particular problem. The emperor Maurice had forbidden soldiers and those holding public office to escape from their obligations by becoming monks. Gregory ruled that if holders of public office wished to enter a monastery they must first show that the authorities had no claims against them. Ex-soldiers were to be rigorously examined. Their noviciate should last three years.[16] Elsewhere Gregory decreed that ex-soldiers could become monks only by express permission of the Holy See.[17]

Monastic endowments were particularly difficult to protect. Sometimes the heirs of a monastic founder refused to hand over properties he had bequeathed.[18] Gregory was asked to intervene on behalf of the monks of Saint Theodore near Palermo, who complained that estates they had held for forty years were seized by a greedy neighbour.[19] Bishops were sometimes unhelpful. The bishops of Cagliari in Sardinia had usually appointed a suitable manager to look after the affairs of some nuns on the island. Bishop Januarius, however, neglected to do this, with the result that the nuns had often to leave their house on business journeys.[20]

A letter from Gregory to the bishop of Ravenna about the monastery of Saint Stephen in Classe sets out the pontiff's views on the relations of monks with their bishop. No one, wrote the pope, should be allowed to damage the monastery's properties. A conflict between the monastery and the church of Ravenna must be settled by arbitrators. On the death of their abbot the community alone was to have the right to choose his successor. If there was no one suitable in the monastery they could choose an outsider. Ecclesiastics might not make lists or inventories of the monastery's estates or possessions. The

---

[15] *Ibid.* 681.
[16] *Ibid.* 909–910.
[17] *Ibid.* 1083.
[18] *Ibid.* 674–675.
[19] *Ibid.* 455–456.
[20] *Ibid.* 675–676.

abbot was to be free to visit the roman pontiff. The bishop was not to demand burdensome hospitality from the monastery; his visits should profit the house, not damage it.[21] This was not 'exemption' in the medieval sense, but Gregory clearly encouraged the view that a monastery should enjoy certain rights in relationship to the local bishop.

Calabria, in the 'toe' of Italy, was one of the few areas in the peninsula spared the chaos which made Gregory's task so difficult. Byzantine control of the province was not challenged until the eleventh century. It was in this comparatively peaceful region that Cassiodorus's monasteries of Vivarium flourished.

Cassiodorus[22] belonged to a roman senatorial family and was one of many who were prepared, after the collapse of the empire in the west, to cooperate with the new germanic rulers. He held a number of important offices under Theodoric, the ostrogothic king, and wrote eloquently on his master's behalf. After the collapse of gothic rule in Italy the political stage of Cassiodorus's career came to an end. Some time in the 540s he went to Constantinople. For about ten years he lived there, writing books and trying to influence imperial policy. In the 550s he left Constantinople and settled on his ancestral estates at Squillace in Calabria. Here he took over the direction of two monasteries which he called 'Vivarium'. It is not clear whether he actually founded them before or after his sojourn in Constantinople.[23] Most of the monks lived in a building attractively sited amidst irrigated gardens and fish-ponds. On a nearby mountain there was a hermitage for the brothers who wished to cultivate solitude.[24]

Around 536 Cassiodorus and Pope Agapetus had planned to found at Rome a Christian Academy which would rival that at Alexandria. A library had been started which was to be at the centre of this new venture. The gothic wars had

---

[21] *Ibid.* 918–919.

[22] The standard biography is J. J. O'Donnell, *Cassiodorus* (Berkeley 1979).

[23] O'Donnell, 189–193.

[24] *Ibid.* 194–198.

put an end to the project.[25] Vivarium was intended to revive
it. From Constantinople, Cassiodorus brought books for the
library. The monastery was to fulfil his hopes for establishing
a centre of christian learning.

It was once believed that Cassiodorus and his monks saved
classical literature for posterity, but in fact his view of secular learning was very limited. He thought it useful only as
an auxiliary to sacred studies.[26] The main emphasis was on
scriptural exegesis. At Vivarium he worked to establish an
accurate text of the Latin Vulgate,[27] and he composed a bibli-
ographical commentary on each book of the Bible, listing the
authors—Jerome, Ambrose, Augustine, and others—available
at Vivarium for consultation. A group of translators made latin
versions of Josephus and of important greek commentaries
on Scripture. The monks occupied themselves with copying
manuscripts.[28]

A little further north, near Naples, a somewhat older
monastic centre of learning may have been a model for Vivarium. The monastery of Castrum Lucullanum housed a refugee
community which owned an extensive library. The monks had
fled from Noricum (roughly equivalent to the modern Austria)
and settled around the tomb of Saint Severinus, the apostle of
their province. Under its abbot Eugippius, who presided over
the community in the first half of the sixth century, Castrum
Lucullanum became a centre for the copying of manuscripts.
Eugippius himself compiled an anthology of passages from
Saint Augustine.[29]

Among the monks associated with sixth-century Italy, the
most intriguing is the anonymous author of a monastic rule
cast in question and answer form; in it the replies usually begin
with the formula, 'The Lord replied through the Master'. Some

---

[25] *Ibid.* 182–185.
[26] *Ibid.* 205–206.
[27] *Ibid.* 206–207.
[28] O'Donnell (as n. 22), 215.
[29] V. Pavan, 'Eugippius', *Encyclopaedia of the Early Church* 1 (Cambridge 1992) 296; M. P. McHugh, 'Eugippius', *Encyclopaedia of Early Christianity* (Chicago 1990) 324–325.

passages in this rule also occur in the Rule of Saint Benedict. For long the scholarly consensus was that the Master's was a later compilation. Just before the Second World War, however, the theory was put forward that the Rule of the Master was in fact the older, and that Saint Benedict had borrowed great parts of it. By the 1960s most benedictine scholars had accepted the Master's priority,[30] although since then the question has been reopened once again.[31]

The Master's Rule was written for a small community. He had in mind a monastery of twenty-four monks: two groups of ten, each under the supervision of a dean, together with a cellarer and an abbot.[32] If the grounds of the monastery were more extensive each group might be under the charge of two deans making a total of twenty-six.[33] The deans were to keep their men under constant supervision, observing them at work and listening to their conversations. 'Therefore when these deans take charge of a group of ten brothers they must be solicitous for them that day or night and at any work whatever they are first of all present with them no matter what they are doing. Thus whether they are sitting, walking, or standing still, by their careful supervision and alert vigilance they must ward off from them the devil's activity.'[34] The deans were the eyes and ears of the abbot, to whom they reported any irregularities.[35]

---

[30] The controversy up to 1963 is reviewed in D. Knowles, 'The Regula Magistri and the Rule of St. Benedict', *Problems in Monastic History* (London 1963) 139–195. See also *La Règle de St. Benoît*, ed. A. de Vogüé, 7 vols. (Paris 1972), especially 1:245–314: 'Benoît dépend du Maître'.

[31] See M. Dunn, 'Mastering Benedict: Monastic Rules and their Authors in the Early Medieval West', *English Historical Review* 105 (1990) 567–594; A. de Vogüé, 'The Master and St. Benedict: A Reply to Marilyn Dunn', *Ibid.* 107 (1992) 95–103; M. Dunn, 'The Master and St. Benedict: A Rejoinder', *Ibid.* 107 (1992) 104–111.

[32] Ch. 11. In what follows the Rule of the Master is first quoted by chapter; and then by volume and page reference to *La Règle du Maître*, ed. A. de Vogüé, 2 vols., Paris 1964; in this case Ch. 11; 2: 6–33.

[33] Ch. 11; 2:12–13.

[34] *Ibid.*; 2:14–15. Translation by Luke Eberle, *The Rule of the Master* (Kalamazoo 1977) 142.

[35] Ch. 15; 2: 64–67.

The Master showed little interest in the relationship of the brothers with one another. In his view, the monastery was a school in which each monk was to be trained in ascetic discipline, and his progress marked.[36] When they were not at prayer in the oratory, the monks were to be engaged in various tasks according to their stage of spiritual development, each group being kept separate from the other: some listening to reading, youngsters learning their letters, adult illiterates also being taught to read, those who did not know the psalms learning them by heart.[37] The Master did not think agricultural work suitable for monks, since it made them too anxious about the things of the world. Hired labourers were to look after the monastery's fields.[38]

The brothers assembled in church for a night office, which was followed by Lauds. Prime was chanted at sunrise. Terce, Sext, and None were celebrated during the day. Compline was sung in the dormitory as the last service before retiring.[39] There was no priest in the monastery. The Eucharist was celebrated only on Sundays[40] and on some other special days, presumably by a priest of the diocese. The consecrated bread and wine were reserved in the monastery church and during the week the brethren received communion from the hands of the abbot (a layman) after None and immediately before their communal meal.[41]

The Master took an absolute view of the Rule he was composing. The answers to the questions asked were considered to come directly from the Lord. They were mediated to the monk through the traditional monastic sources: the Bible, the Fathers, and the Lives of the christian martyrs. The Master failed to understand the principle of legislation, which is to formulate the general principle clearly and leave the rest to

---

[36] *La Règle du Maître* (as n. 3) 1: 115–118.
[37] Ch. 50; 2:224–225.
[38] Ch. 86; 2:350–353.
[39] Ch. 33–58; 2:176–241, 258–275.
[40] Ch. 45; 2:208–209.
[41] Ch. 21; 2:102–103.

case law. He wanted to cover every eventuality. As a result, his rule is very lengthy. As an example, we note Chapter 61, where the Master discusses whether a monk, sent out of the monastery for some task and expected to return the same day, may accept an invitation to a meal, or whether he should fast through the day until his return. The answer is complicated and depends on the day of the week, the time of the day, the quality of the person issuing the invitation, and the number of times it is made.[42]

Within this rigid legislative framework, the authority of the abbot appears somewhat restricted. He may enjoin nothing which is not in accordance with the commandments of the Lord. He must consult the brothers about every major decision, though they express their opinions only at his command and the final decision lies with him.[43]

The Master left scope, however, for individual decisions. During the long nights of winter, for instance, the abbot might wish to read to the community, or individuals might wish to edify the others with some excerpt from a book. Everyone was free to listen or to read, to do some work, to study, or even to sleep a little.[44] Brothers who chose to fast more rigorously than the rest of the community during Lent were to be excused from work.[45] On Good Friday, those brothers who were unable to refrain from food for the whole day might take a meal, though their weakness was to be deplored.[46] Extra penances, however, were not to be undertaken without the abbot's permission.[47]

The most outstanding monastic personality in sixth century Italy was Saint Benedict of Nursia. Older authorities were of the opinion that he was born in 480 and died in 547.[48]

---

[42] Ch. 61; 2:278–285.
[43] Ch. 2; 1:350–353, 360–363.
[44] Ch. 44; 2:204–205.
[45] Ch. 53; 2:250–251.
[46] *Ibid.*; 2:254–255.
[47] Ch. 74; 2:312–313.
[48] These dates (with a measure of caution) are still in *Encyclopaedia of the Early Church* (as n. 29) 1:119; and in *Encyclopaedia of Early Christianity*, ed. E. Ferguson (Chicago-London 1990) 148–150.

More recent authorities have placed him rather later: c. 520–
c. 575.[49] At the end of the century Gregory the Great made
Saint Benedict's life the centrepiece of his *Dialogues*. The large
number of manuscript copies of this book are evidence of its
popularity.[50] Thanks to Gregory, Saint Benedict very rapidly
became a model for those in the latin world who embraced
the monastic life.

The *Dialogues* contain too many miracle stories for modern tastes, but Gregory was careful to quote the sources of his
information. His work provides at least some historical facts.[51]
We read that Benedict was born to a prosperous family in the
region of Nursia and that, as a young man, he was sent to Rome
to study. He was quickly disillusioned and abandoned Rome
to seek a more perfect way of life.[52] He finally settled in a cave
at Subiaco, some miles from Rome, and there lived the life
of a solitary. He was given food by a monk called Romanus,
who was at first the only one to know of his existence. Later
a local priest heard of the solitary at Subiaco and visited him
occasionally, keeping him informed of the Church's calendar,
which Benedict seemed in danger of forgetting.[53] The complete isolation of Benedict at Subiaco recalls Saint Anthony's
twenty years alone in the desert and there is no doubt that
Gregory was portraying Benedict as the Anthony of Italy.

This strict isolation ended when a local monastery, whose
superior had recently died, asked Benedict to take his place.
The experiment ended in failure. Benedict and the community were soon at loggerheads and he returned to his cave
at Subiaco.[54] His reputation, however, was now assured. He
began to gather disciples and to form a community. Other
monasteries were founded under his guidance. According
to Gregory, there were altogether twelve monasteries, each

---

[49] E. Manning in *Règle de St. Benoît*, ed. H. Rochais and E. Manning (Rochefort
1980) xxv–xxvii.
[50] *Grégoire le Grand: Dialogues* , ed. A de Vogüé, 3 vols. (Paris 1978–1980)
1:141–143.
[51] *Ibid.*
[52] *Ibid.* 2:126–127.
[53] *Ibid.* 130–139.
[54] *Grégoire. . . . Dialogues* (as n. 50) 2:140–143.

having twelve monks and one superior.[55] Benedict, however, roused the hostility of a local priest. His community was exposed to considerable harassment and he decided to leave Subiaco. A new site for his monastery was found on the summit of a mountain at Cassino, about a hundred-twenty kilometres south of Rome. Benedict had first to preach the Gospel to the local people and to destroy a temple of Apollo. Within the walls of the monastery a chapel dedicated to Saint Martin was built and a chapel to Saint John arose on the site of the pagan altar.[56]

The one event in the *Dialogues* to which an approximate date can be given is Totila's visit to Monte Cassino.[57] This must have occurred during the gothic leader's brief ascendancy between the years 541 and 552. The visit was a tribute to the saint's reputation as a miracle-worker and a seer. Benedict foretold the desolation of Rome at the end of the gothic wars[58] and the eventual destruction of Monte Cassino itself.[59] Benedict's sister Scholastica had been a dedicated virgin since her earliest youth and Gregory records a memorable visit she paid him shortly before her death.[60] Benedict himself died in the monastery chapel after receiving the *viaticum*, with the community at prayer all around him.[61]

The bare bones of the biography provided by Gregory tell us more than we know about many other figures of the period. Reasonable conjecture may add a little. It seems probable that the abbey of monks which existed in the Lateran Palace in Rome during Gregory's time was founded from Monte Cassino in Benedict's lifetime. He may have spent a great deal of time there. In some manuscripts he is described as 'abbot of Rome'. This may explain the roman character of the liturgical sections of his Rule.[62]

---

[55] *Ibid.* 148–151.
[56] *Ibid.* 160–169.
[57] *Ibid.* 180–181.
[58] *Ibid.* 184–185.
[59] *Ibid.* 192–193.
[60] *Ibid.* 230–235.
[61] *Ibid.* 242–245.
[62] E. Manning (as n. 1), xxvi.

As for the Rule itself, Gregory writes: 'He wrote a rule for monks that is remarkable for its discretion and its clarity of language. Anyone who wishes to know more about his life and character can discover in his Rule exactly what he was like as an abbot, for his life could not have differed from his teaching'.[63] Apart from the information imparted by Gregory, Benedict is known to us only from this Rule. It is worth lingering over Gregory's reference to its style. Benedict had the gift of pithy expression, so that much of the Rule is very quotable. He also showed great skill in the way he brought it to an end. It is always difficult to compose a satisfactory last paragraph. Most latin rules end abruptly after the last enactment. By comparison, Benedict's ending is all the more noteworthy. 'Whoever, therefore, you are, who are hastening to your heavenly country, fulfil first of all by the help of Christ this little Rule for beginners. And then at length, under God's protection, you shall attain those aforesaid loftier heights of wisdom and virtue.'[64] The meaning of these words has been much discussed, but their artistry should also be noted. As he brings his composition to a close, Benedict addresses the reader directly, looking back to what he has written and forward to what must yet be achieved. It is difficult to believe that so effective a stylist was inexperienced as a writer.

There had been a growing tendency among western theorists of monasticism to favour the cenobitic over the eremitical way of life. In his judicious discussion of the two, Cassian had hinted that life in community was a safer form of asceticism,[65] and the earliest rule at Lérins had made the point forcibly.[66]

---

[63] *Grégoire . . . Dialogues* (as n. 50) 2:242–243. Translation from *Life and Miracles of St. Benedict*, by Pope St. Gregory the Great, trans. and ed. O. J. Zimmermann and B. R. Avery (Collegeville 1949) 74.

[64] Ch. 73.8–9. The Rule is first quoted by chapter, and in the case of direct quotations, verse; and then by volume and page reference to *La Règle de St. Benoît*, ed. A. de Vogüé and J. Neufville, 7 vols. (Paris 1972–1977); in this case 2:674. Translations from *The Rule of St. Benedict*, ed. and trans. J. McCann (London 1952).

[65] *Conferences* 18.5–6; 19.2–9.

[66] *Les règles des saints pères*, ed. A. de Vogüé (Paris 1982) 1:182.

For Benedict there was no doubt about the superiority of the cenobitic life. In his discussion of the four kinds of monks,[67] he gives conventional praise to anchorites or hermits (he uses the two words as synonyms), though he emphasises that they should first spend time in a monastery so that they can go out 'well armed from the ranks of their community'. After dismissing sarabaites and gyrovagues, he goes on, 'Leaving them alone therefore, let us set to work by the help of God, to lay down a rule for the cenobites, that is, the strongest kind of monks (*fortissimum genus*)'. The phrase was an echo of Cassian's description of cenobites as being taken from 'the best kind of monks'(*de optimo genere monachorum*). [68]

Living in a community enabled the monk to practice the particularly christian virtue of humility. The first degree of humility, wrote Benedict, was obedience without delay. The monks, 'immediately abandoning their own affairs and forsaking their own will, dropping the work they were engaged on and, leaving it unfinished, with swift obedience follow up with their deeds the voice of him who commands them'.[69] In his chapter on humility Benedict interiorised this aspect of monastic discipline: the first degree of humility was making God a reality in one's life at all times, and this meant abandoning one's own will completely. Instant obedience, therefore, became something spontaneous and natural. The other eleven degrees of humility which Benedict described were all practical applications of this principle. The monk was to embrace willingly the hardest tasks and situations, to reveal his thoughts to his abbot at all times, to be content with the worst place in everything, actually to believe himself to be undeserving, to do nothing which was not in the Rule or recommended by his seniors, to speak little, and then only with modesty.[70]

In Chapter 72 of the Rule Benedict gave a little portrait of the ideal monastic community.

---

[67] Ch. 1; 1:436–440.
[68] *Conferences* 18.11.
[69] Ch. 5.7; 1:466–467.
[70] Ch.7; 1:472–491.

Just as there is an evil zeal of bitterness which separates from
God and leads to hell, so is there a good zeal which separates
from evil and leads to God and life everlasting. Let monks,
therefore, exercise this zeal with the most fervent love. Let
them, that is, 'give one another precedence'.[71] Let them bear
with the greatest patience one another's infirmities, whether
of body or character. Let them vie in paying obedience to
one another. Let none follow what seems good for himself,
but rather what is good for one another. Let them practice
fraternal charity with a pure love. Let them fear God. Let
them love their abbot with a sincere and humble affection.
Let them prefer nothing whatever to Christ. And may he
bring us all alike to life everlasting.[72]

The keystone of the monastic edifice was the abbot. 'Let
the abbot always remember what he is called,' wrote Benedict
twice, in so many words, in the chapter he devoted to the
superior.[73] 'He is believed to be the representative of Christ in
the monastery, and for that reason is called by a name of his,
according to the words of the Apostle: "You have received the
spirit of the adoption of sons, whereby we cry Abba, Father" '.[74]
He was not only the ruler but also the teacher of the community
and his teaching had to be absolutely in accordance with God's
law, for he would be responsible at the judgement seat of Christ
for the spiritual welfare of his charges. He must illustrate his
teaching with deeds, and on no account make any distinction of
persons within the monastery. Punishments were meted out at
his discretion,[75] though in a later chapter Benedict emphasised
that the abbot should 'study rather to be loved than feared'.[76]

Benedict's view of the abbot may look very authoritarian,
but we must remember that all ancient rulers were absolute.
The accepted maxim in the Roman Empire was, 'The will

---

[71] Rom 12:10.
[72] Ch. 72.8–12; 2:670–671.
[73] Ch. 2.1; 1:440–453: 'Meminere debet quod dicitur . . . meminere debet
semper abbas quod est, meminere quod dicitur'.
[74] Rom 8:15.
[75] Chh. 23–28; 2: 542–553.
[76] Ch. 64.15; 2:650.

of the ruler has the force of law' (*Quod principi placet legis habet vigorem*). In pagan times divine honours had been paid to the emperor, who was invoked with the gods. The most arbitrary acts, therefore, were justified. The coming of Christianity made little difference. Too many bishops haunted the imperial court and flattered the ruler. The behaviour of the emperors was in no way modified during the fourth century; the rejection of divine honours was merely formal. The emperor's representatives shared his absolutism, and complaints about the behaviour of provincial governors were particularly vigorous in the christian period. In the context of his time, Benedict's reminder that the word 'abbot' means 'father', and his insistence that the superior should strive to be loved rather than feared, was, in its way, revolutionary.

On important matters the abbot consulted the whole community. Benedict insisted that all should participate, because 'God often reveals what is better to the younger'. It was the abbot, however, who decided what matters should be discussed and who, after listening to all the opinions expressed, made the final decision. Matters of lesser importance were discussed with the seniors only.[77]

The abbot was to be freely elected by the whole community. There was to be no outside interference, unless the monks should elect someone unworthy. In that case the bishop, other abbots, or even neighbouring communities might intervene.[78]

Besides the abbot there were to be a number of other officers in the monastery. If the community was very large, one or more deans might be appointed to help the abbot with discipline.[79] The tools of the monastery were in the charge of a cellarer, who was also to take responsibility for the sick, the children, and the guests. He was also responsible for the distribution of food. If the community was large he was to be given helpers. He was warned against bad temper: 'If he

---

[77] Ch. 3; 1: 452–455.
[78] Ch. 64; 2:648–653.
[79] Ch. 21; 2:538–539.

have nothing else to give, let him give a good word in answer'.[80] Novices were to be placed under the charge of a senior 'skilled in winning souls', though Benedict did not have a title for him.[81] Near the monastery gate a porter, 'a wise old man who knows how to receive and to give a message', had his cell.[82]

Benedict was doubtful about the need for a prior. In communities where the abbot was not elected but appointed by an outside authority which also appointed a prior, there was sure to be contention. 'There are men', wrote Benedict, 'puffed up by an evil spirit of pride who regard themselves as equal to the abbot and, arrogating to themselves tyrannical power, foster troubles and dissensions in the community.' Clearly, however, there were occasions when the abbot needed a second-in-command. If such an officer was thought necessary, therefore, the abbot himself should appoint him with the advice of the community. There was to be no doubt that it was the abbot who ruled the community and if the prior stepped out of line he was to be deposed.[83]

The rhythm of monastic life was dictated by the daily services. 'Let nothing be put before the Work of God' wrote Benedict.[84] The monks rose in the night for Vigils. Matins ('Lauds' in later terminology) were sung before sunrise. The monastic day was interspersed with the shorter 'Day Hours' of Prime, Terce, Sext, and None. Vespers were sung at sunset, and Compline was the last service of the day.[85]

Benedict gave detailed directions for the distribution of the psalms at each service. They were to be so arranged that the whole psalter was sung through in a week and begun afresh every Sunday.[86] At Matins the canticles from the Old Testament were also to be sung, one for each day of the week,

---

[80] Ch. 31.13; 2:556–561.
[81] Ch. 58; 2:626–633.
[82] Ch. 66.1; 2:658–661.
[83] Ch. 65; 2:655–659.
[84] Ch. 43.3; 2:586–587.
[85] Chh. 8–19; 2:508–539.
[86] Ch. 18; 2:534–535.

arranged according to the practice of the Roman Church.[87] To provide for the celebration of the Eucharist, a member of the community could be sent to the bishop for ordination, so that the community would have its own priest.[88]

When they were not at prayer, the brothers spent their time at manual work or at reading, for which extra time was provided during Lent.[89] Manual labour could include work in the fields. Benedict remarked in a famous passage: 'But if the circumstances of the place or their poverty require them to gather the harvest themselves, let them not be discontented; for then are they truly monks when they live by the labour of their hands, like our fathers and the apostles'.[90]

The brothers were to observe the customary fasts of the Church's year, but here as elsewhere for Benedict interior disposition was more important than external observance. As one of the 'instruments of good works' early in the Rule, it is startling to find, *Jejunium amare*, 'to love fasting'.[91] During Lent each monk was encouraged, after consulting the abbot, to add something of his own to the communal observance: extra prayers, an extra fast. 'Let each one, over and above the measure prescribed for him, offer God something of his own free will in the joy of the Holy Spirit'.[92] Charity came first. Unless it was a major fast day, the abbot broke his fast when entertaining a guest.[93] Meat, however, was forbidden, except for the sick.[94]

Anyone who wished to enter the community first spent several days in the guest house, where his commitment was tested. Then he was admitted into the cell of the novices and kept under probation for two months. Only after this did the

---

[87] Ch. 13; 2:520–521.
[88] Ch. 62; 2:640–643.
[89] Ch. 48; 2:600–605.
[90] Ch. 48.8; 2:600–601.
[91] Ch. 4.13; 1:456–457.
[92] Ch. 49.6; 2: 606–607.
[93] Ch. 53; 2:612–613.
[94] Ch. 39; 2:578–579.

formal ten-month noviciate begin. Benedict gives few details, except that the novices were under the direction of a senior and were given two opportunities to withdraw. Someone who persevered then made formal profession in the oratory, where, in the presence of the whole community, the new monk made a vow of stability, conversion of life, and obedience.[95] These enactments refer to converts who made a conscious decision as adults to enter the community. In addition, Benedict accepted the common convention of his day that children might be 'offered' to the community by their parents.

According to Gregory the Great, Benedict, while he was at Subiaco, ruled over 'twelve monasteries of twelve monks each'.[96] This may strike one as a little too schematic. There is no doubt, however, that a community had gone out from Monte Cassino to settle in Terracina on the coast, and another had been established in the Lateran Palace in Rome.[97] Benedict intended his Rule for more than one monastery.[98] 'Let clothing be given to the brethren according to the nature of the locality in which they dwell and its climate, for in cold districts they will need more clothing, and in warm districts less'.[99]

Benedict was anxious to provide his monks with orthodox and uplifting spiritual teaching. He recommended that they read Cassian, the Rule of Saint Basil, and the Lives of the Fathers.[100] Most important of all was the Bible. 'What page or what utterance of the divinely inspired books of the Old and the New Testament is not a most unerring rule of human life?'[101] All the important enactments in the Rule are supported by references to Scripture. For Benedict, the life of the monk was a perfect following of the Gospel. To walk in the paths of

---

95 Ch. 58; 2:626–633.
96 See above pp. 92–93.
97 De Vogüé in *Grégoire . . . Dialogues* (as n. 50), 1:157–158.
98 *Règle de St. Benoît* (as n. 64), 1:48–49.
99 Ch. 55.1–2; 2:618–619.
100 Ch. 73; 2:672–673.
101 *Ibid.*

God and be guided by his revealed word, was the monk's sure way to Christ's kingdom.[102]

Centuries later there was much discussion about the meaning of the last chapter of the Rule.[103] Here Benedict stated that his was 'the least of rules,' and that it had been written for beginners. After observing it, he remarked, the monk might go on to the heights of perfection to be found in the writings of the Fathers. In the eleventh century publicists like Peter Damian used this chapter to argue that Benedict's ideal had really been the life of a hermit, that he had thought of the cenobitic life merely as a preparation for monastic perfection. It is, however, unlikely that this was Benedict's view. He nowhere states that the eremitical life is superior to the cenobitic. On the contrary, in the chapter in which he discusses the different kinds of monk, he is judicious in describing the life of hermits but calls cenobites the *fortissimum genus*.[104] He was, however, of the opinion that the monks in his time were rather decadent, when compared with those of the past. In arranging for the whole psalter to be sung through in one week, he pointed out that the holy fathers had done as much in a single day.[105] Wine, he remarked, ought not to be the drink of monks, but, 'in our times monks cannot be persuaded of this'.[106] The books recommended by Benedict ought to nourish the soul, but 'we slothful ill-living and negligent people must blush for shame'.[107] It seems very likely, therefore, that Benedict had in view a stricter observance: heavier fasts, longer vigils and prayers. After a long apprenticeship, these might bring the monk to the level of the Fathers.

The subsequent history of the Rule of Saint Benedict is the theme of the rest of this book. Its journey to supremacy in the latin west was slow. Eventually, however, it came to be

---

[102] Prologue, 21; 1:418–419.
[103] Quoted above p. 94.
[104] Ch. 1; 1:436–441.
[105] Ch. 18; 2:534–535.
[106] Ch. 40.6; 2:580–581.
[107] Ch. 73.7; 2:674–675.

regarded as the norm of monastic living. From the Dark Ages to the present day, Christians of the western tradition who have been drawn to life in a monastic community have judged their endeavours by its standards, and have turned to Benedict for guidance and inspiration.

Chapter 5
A SECOND BENEDICT
AND HIS PROGENY

PRIMITIVE BENEDICTINE MONASTICISM, as lived under Saint Benedict himself and in the communities directly founded by him, was short-lived. Montecassino was destroyed by the Lombards in 577. The monks took refuge in Rome and were given the monastery of Saint Pancras. This community quickly dwindled away and the monks were replaced by canons.[1] Nothing more is heard about the monks in Saint John Lateran or at Terracina. There was no continuity between these early communities and the ones which decided to live solely by the Rule of Saint Benedict in the eighth century.

Pope Saint Gregory had certainly read the Rule of Saint Benedict and gathered information about the saint from those who remembered him. His *Dialogues* emphasise Benedict's holiness and his miracles. Thanks to the popularity of this book, Benedict came to be admired as the preeminent ascetic of the west. No doubt for this reason, the seventh century northumbrian chieftain who founded the monasteries of Wearmouth and Jarrow in northern England adopted the name of Benedict Biscop.[2] It was not the Rule of Saint Benedict which the monks in these two houses followed, however, but one which had been compiled from the rules of seventeen monasteries, including Lérins.[3]

---

[1] G. Penco, *Storia del monachesimo in Italia* (Rome 1961) 88.
[2] *Encyclopaedia of the Early Church* 1:119.
[3] Bede, *The Lives of the holy Abbots of Wearmouth and Jarrow* (London 1951) 350, 352, 356.

The period c. 600–c. 750, indeed, is that of the *regulae mixtae*. Most houses had their own rules, compiled from a variety of sources. The influence of Saint Benedict can be seen particularly in the rules of the columbanian irish monasteries on the european continent.[4] The most accessible of these irish *regulae mixtae* is the *regula cuiusdam patris*,[5] which may come from Luxeuil, where, during the seventh century, the monks followed the rules of both Columban and Benedict.[6] The *regula cuiusdam patris* consists of thirty-two precepts and begins by emphasising the biblical character of monasticism. The monk is exhorted not to bend the sense of Scripture to his will, but rather to bend his will to the sense of Scripture.[7] Obedience is regarded as the supreme monastic virtue.[8] Prison looms large in this rule. Incarceration is the punishment for grumbling, arguing with superiors, and general disobedience.[9] It is assumed that the abbot will be elected by the community. Here we may see the particular influence of Saint Benedict, but the *regula cuiusdam patris* goes further and envisages as well the deposition of an unworthy abbot by the community which elected him.[10]

In the middle of the seventh century monks from Fleury on the river Loire made their way to Montecassino, then deserted, removed what they considered to be Saint Benedict's relics and took them home. Whether the remains that were enshrined at Fleury were actually those of the saint continues to be a matter of controversy.[11] In time, Fleury became a noted place of pilgrimage.[12] Saint Benedict was now associated with Gaul and his fame enhanced by miracles worked at his shrine.

---

[4] See E. John, ' "Secularium prioratus" and the Rule of Saint Benedict', *Revue Bénédictine* 75 (1965) 215–218. On Columbanus, see above pp. 73–74.
[5] PL 66:987–994.
[6] E. John (as n. 4), 218.
[7] PL 66:987.
[8] *Ibid.* 988.
[9] *Ibid.* 989.
[10] *Ibid.* 991–2.
[11] Compare the account in Penco (as n. 1), 137–138, with J. Laporte, 'Fleury', DHGE 17 (1971) 444–445.
[12] 'Fleury', DHGE 17:446.

The monks of Fleury, however, followed the mixed rule of Saint Benedict and Saint Columban.[13] There is no evidence that the acquisition of relics from Montecassino inspired any immediate change in their way of life. We may suppose that the Rule of Saint Benedict became increasingly influential in the community, but it was only in 938, under pressure from Cluny, that Fleury abandoned the last relics of the mixed rule.

The idea that the Rule of Saint Benedict alone should be normative for monks in the western Church took hold very slowly. Some of the pressure came from England, where Benedict was regarded as the preeminently roman saint. In the 740s Saint Boniface, the english missionary to Germany, was engaged in persuading monasteries of monks and nuns to follow this rule.[14] Its most single minded protagonist was Witiza, a visigothic nobleman who, like the english Biscop in the previous century, took the name 'Benedict' in religion. To historians of monasticism he is known as Benedict of Aniane, but in his own time he was *Benedictus Secundus*,[15] the renewer of latin monasticism and its second founder.

This Second Benedict was born around 750. His father was the count of Maguellonne, a stronghold on the mediterranean coast near Montpellier in modern France.[16] After spending some time at the court of Pepin the Younger and Charles the Great, he withdrew from the world. Disillusioned by the monastery he had joined, he retired to his father's estate at Aniane, about twenty-five kilometres from Montpellier. There followed some unsuccessful attempts to found a religious community. The experience persuaded him that only the Rule of Saint Benedict provided a secure basis for the cenobitic life. He decided that it should be exclusively followed by the disciples who gathered around him in the 780s.

---

[13] *Ibid.* 443–446.

[14] Mayke de Jong, 'Carolingian Monasticism: The Power of Prayer', *The New Cambridge Medieval History* 2, ed. R. McKitterick (Cambridge 1995) 629–630.

[15] On Benedict of Aniane, see CCM 1, ed. K. Hallinger (Siegburg 1963) 353, 425.

[16] On Benedict of Aniane, see TRE 5 (1980) 535–538; LM 2 (1983) 1864–1867.

Benedict of Aniane's knowledge of the benedictine life was based entirely upon reading. He knew the *Dialogues* of Saint Gregory and had studied Saint Benedict's Rule. For two hundred years no community had tried to live by it alone. The new Benedict therefore had to start from scratch. The results are described in a biography, written shortly after his death by his pupil Ardo, and in the *Memoriale Qualiter*, a brief description of life in his monasteries at the end of the eighth century.[17]

It was impossible to recreate the conditions of sixth century Italy or to imagine away the developments of the previous two hundred years.[18] Many frankish monasteries were great establishments of over a hundred monks. They had magnificent churches and lavish buildings. Large endowments in land were required to maintain them, and an elaborate organisation to administer them. They needed abbots who had the prestige to command obedience within the community and respect outside it.[19]

None of this was incompatible with the Holy Rule, but these were not the kind of communities for which the first Saint Benedict had legislated. The general attitude to monasticism had also changed. For the first Saint Benedict monastic life was a way of perfection, a 'school of the Lord's service'.[20] There is little in his Rule about the relations of the monastery to the outside world. The semi-barbarian Franks, however, were persuaded to endow monasteries generously because they believed in the efficacy of the monks' prayers. This aspect of the monastic life was therefore emphasised throughout the Dark Ages. The liturgical ideal in frankish monasteries was the *laus perennis*—an unbroken round of prayer in the monastery church, where the monks undertook relays day and night.

---

[17] CCM 1:176–282.

[18] The background to Benedict of Aniane's reforms is discussed in J. Semmler, 'Die Beschlüsse des Aachener Konzils im Jahre 816', *Zeitschrift für Kirchengeschichte* 74 (1963) 65–81.

[19] *Ibid.* 75.

[20] RB, Prologue, 45.

It did not occur to Benedict of Aniane to sweep all this away entirely, but he strove so to reshape the monastic customs of his time that they would at least be compatible with the Rule of Saint Benedict, the *una regula*, 'the one rule', as he liked to call it. Splendid buildings with a large church were begun at Aniane in 787. These provided the background to an elaborate as well as continuous liturgical life.[21] Before the Night Office the community daily recited the 'Gradual Psalms'—three rounds of five psalms, each concluding with a prayer, recited for the living both inside and outside the community and for the dead. Additional psalms were recited after Compline. There were also three solemn daily visits to the High Altar, with special ceremonies and prayers called the *Trina Oratio*.[22]

As a new and fervent community, Aniane attracted attention. In 792 Charlemagne (Charles the Great) took it under his royal protection. Monks were sent to other monasteries to promote the Rule of Saint Benedict. Benedict of Aniane carried out visitations to check on the progress of reform. His work was particularly effective in Aquitaine, where the local ruler, Charlemagne's son Louis, became his friend. According to Benedict of Aniane's biographer, 'nearly all the monasteries of Aquitaine' were persuaded to adopt the Rule of Saint Benedict. As his fame spread Benedict of Aniane was increasingly involved in the ecclesiastical affairs of the frankish state. He paid two visits to the area of the Pyrenees, where a local form of the adoptionist heresy was prevalent. He influenced the revision of liturgical books in the empire by preserving texts from the gallican and old-spanish liturgies.[23]

A benedictine revival had thus been under way for over twenty years when the carolingian monarchs intervened. Two capitularies issued in 802 by Charlemagne ordered the establishment of a proper text of the Rule of Saint Benedict

[21] TRE 5:535.
[22] Semmler (as n. 18), 73.
[23] LM 2: 1864–1865; R. E. Reynolds, 'The Organisation, Law, and Liturgy of the Western Church 700–900', *New Cambridge Medieval History* (as n. 14), 620.

and mandated its observance by all religious communities.[24] Charles the Great died in 814 and was succeeded by his son Louis 'the Pious' (814–840), the same Louis who as ruler of Aquitaine had become Benedict of Aniane's friend. As emperor, Louis inaugurated a programme of all-embracing legislation which, in the words of one authority,

> posterity cannot fail to admire. Inspired by a conception of empire and emperor rooted in theological and christian ideas, Louis and his advisers initiated a *Renovatio imperii francorum* which would embrace both the institutions of the state and the sphere of the Church.[25]

Basing himself on roman imperial practice, Louis and his advisers sought to impose uniformity throughout the empire's vast territories. In fact, these efforts are more impressive on paper than in reality. Louis' empire was wracked by civil wars, and few of the elaborate laws were observed for long.

Shortly after his accession Louis made Benedict of Aniane abbot, in quick succession, of Maursmünster in modern Alsace and of Cornelimünster near the imperial residence at Aachen. Benedict was to build the new monastery into a model for others. He was sent to inspect monasteries throughout the empire.[26] In 816 an imperial synod of abbots and some bishops met at Aachen to devise legislation which would ensure uniform monastic observance throughout the carolingian empire.[27]

There can be little doubt that the Aachen statutes were the work of Benedict of Aniane. Their purpose was to make the Rule of Saint Benedict normative for all monks in the empire and to reshape the traditional rhythm of monastic life in conformity to it. The concept of *una regula*, 'a single rule',

---

[24] Semmler (as n. 18), 22–23, and nn. 7–9.
[25] *Ibid.* 15.
[26] TRE 5:535–536; LM 2:1865.
[27] The Aachen statutes are published in CCM 1:457–468. See also the introduction by K. Hallinger, *Ibid.* xxxix–xliv, 425–428. For a systematic analysis of the legislation, see Semmler, 15–82.

was balanced by that of *una consuetudo*, 'a single custom'. The first two statutes decreed that after the synod the abbots should read the Rule of Saint Benedict aloud to their monks, and that all the monks who were able should learn it by heart. At Aachen in the following year it was decreed that a chapter of the Rule of Saint Benedict should be read in every monastery at the daily meeting of the community.[28] From this custom the meeting itself came to be called 'the chapter'.

The 816 statutes reinforced the first Saint Benedict's emphasis on the importance of manual labour. The monks were to take their turns working in the kitchen, the bakehouse, and all the other workplaces, and they were to wash their own clothes. They were not to grumble if they were sent off to collect fruit, even though this might cut short the time set aside for reading or the midday rest. Field work, however, was not considered normative. The large estates with which each abbey was endowed were worked by serfs.

The demands of the liturgy required rigorous discipline. No one was to go back to bed after the night Vigil, although a period of rest was allowed at midday after Sext, during which a monk might, if he wished, pray in the church or read. The monastic diet was to be plain. Fowl was to be eaten only by the sick in the infirmary. Monks were not allowed 'snacks'; they could eat apples and lettuce only as part of their meals. During Lent they might eat only what was sanctioned by 'the holy fathers'.[29] Wednesdays and Fridays were fast days, but on these days the monks could be given lighter tasks at the discretion of the prior.

The clothes issued to the brethren are described in detail. They were to be plain, neither shoddy nor ostentatious. As far as possible, all members of the community were to be equal and there were to be no special privileges. The table servers obviously could not take their meal at the same time as the rest, but they were to have the same food as their brothers and

---

[28] CCM 1:480.
[29] Not in all the MSS, see *Ibid.* 468.

to listen to the same reading. The abbot, above all, was not to place himself above the Rule, but to be content with the same measure of food, drink, sleep, and clothes as the rest. When reprimanded, the brothers were to accept correction with humble demeanour. Whipping was a recognised punishment, but no monk was to be stripped naked to undergo it. There was a monastic prison for serious offenders, but it was to be heated in the winter and the prisoner was to be allocated work by a superior.

Benedict of Aniane's programme was revolutionary. Every monastic custom of his time was measured against the *una regula*. It had then either to be rejected or altered. So rigorous a yardstick had never before been used. Indeed, communities which would not follow the Rule of Saint Benedict were refused the name of 'monk' and 'nun' altogether. Throughout the Dark Ages the word *monasterium* had been used loosely for any group of clerics living communally and for the buildings which housed such a group.[30] Now persons living under a rule other than that of Saint Benedict were to be known as canons or canonesses—an order of religious unknown in the early Church or in eastern Christendom.

That Benedict of Aniane's radical adaptation met with resistance is small wonder. One of the most contentious issues he raised was that of the liturgy. The Aachen statutes of 816 stated baldly that the Divine Office was to be celebrated in all monasteries in the manner laid down in the Rule of Saint Benedict. In fact, many monasteries followed the liturgy of Rome which had developed from the sixth century onward. The carolingian rulers had laid particular stress upon conformity with Roman service-books throughout the empire.[31] The bishops were particularly opposed to an enactment which endangered a generation-long striving for liturgical uniformity. After heated arguments they agreed to restrict themselves to a demand that the roman liturgy be followed on the last

---

[30] de Jong (as n. 14), 628.
[31] See Semmler (as n. 18), 23–30, 59; Reynolds (as n. 23), 617–621.

three days of Holy Week and on Easter Sunday. Even this rather modest demand met with resistance from the monastic reformers. By this compromise—more or less maintained until the Second Vatican Council—the liturgy of Rome was followed throughout Latin Christendom on Holy Thursday, Good Friday, and Holy Saturday, but monasteries reverted to their own rite on Easter Sunday.

Benedict of Aniane was obliged to sanction some departures from the *una regula*. Saint Benedict had decreed that the abbot's table should be with the guests and strangers.[32] The statutes of 816, however, directed that he must eat in the refectory with the other monks, to show them respect and demonstrate that his fare was the same as theirs. Saint Benedict had enlarged upon the disadvantages to a community of having a prior, who could easily become a rival to the abbot. Discipline in the monastery, he maintained, could most safely be entrusted to the deans.[33] In the larger and more complex monasteries of the ninth century, however, a second-in-command was absolutely necessary because the abbot might often be away. In addition, rulers and land owning nobles sometimes appointed laymen or bishops as abbots. These non-monks enjoyed the revenues of their new houses, but were not otherwise involved in the life of the community. The statutes of 816 therefore decreed that the prior should have most power in the monastery after the abbot, and that he must always be a monk.

The procedure laid down in 816 for the reception of novices departed from Saint Benedict in one matter. The Holy Rule stated that at his profession the novice could either give all his possessions to the poor or make them over to the convent. At Aachen, it was decreed that he must renounce all his property and leave it to his family. This answered complaints that abbots had lured young men into the monastic life simply for the sake of their property. It is impossible to know who

---

[32] RB 56.
[33] RB 65.

was responsible for the severe statute of 816, which deprived monasteries of an important source of income.[34]

The reforms of 816 were so thorough and so radical that their application to all the monasteries of the frankish realm was bound to be difficult. There survives a discussion by an unknown abbot of the way they should be introduced in his own house.[35] In 817, a further synod was convened at Aachen, where the reforms of the previous year were discussed and in some cases modified.[36] There was no compromise, however, with the principle that the Rule of Saint Benedict was the norm to which the customs of every house must conform.

The benedictine life which emerged from the reforms of 816 was disciplined and stately. It centred on an elaborate liturgy, in surroundings of considerable magnificence. Something of its spirit can be recaptured by a study of the 'Plan of Saint Gall', the plan of an ideal monastery probably made for Gozbert, abbot of Saint Gall in modern Switzerland, some time before 830.[37]

The most prominent feature in the plan is the monastery church, a large aisled building with an apse at either end. The altar of Saint Peter, at the east end, is the high altar and immediately below it is the tomb of Saint Gall. In the western apse is the altar of Saint Mary. In the nave are fifteen other altars. The church is preceded at the western end by an atrium, flanked by two round towers.

Along the southern flank of the church is the cloister. This is the monastic living space around which the life of the community revolves. Meetings of the community take place here.[38] Above the rooms at the east end of the cloister is the dormitory. Stretching alongside the whole southern range of the cloister is a huge refectory. West of it is the monastic kitchen.

---

[34] For a discussion of this statute see Semmler (as n. 18), 45–46.
[35] The 'Murbach statutes', CCM 1, 430–50.
[36] *Ibid.* 473–481.
[37] The plan of Saint Gall is exhaustively studied in W. Horn and E. Born, *The Plan of Saint Gall*, 3 vols. (Berkeley 1979).
[38] The Chapter House was a later development.

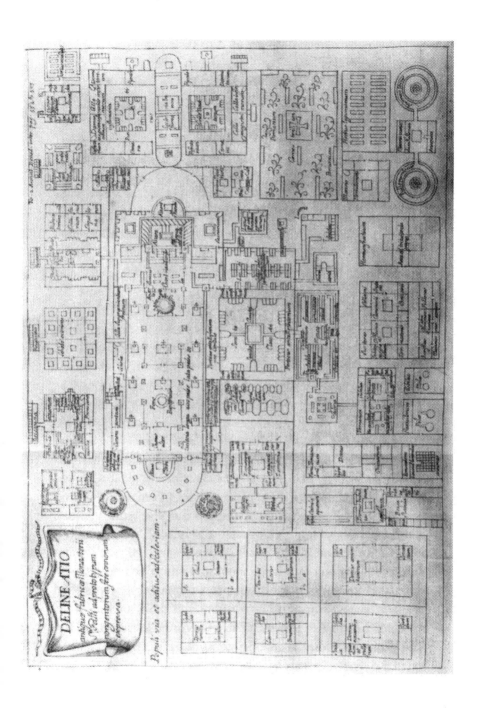

1 The Plan of Saint Gall

The novitiate and the infirmary are separate buildings to the east of the church. North of it is a separate house for the abbot; the Aachen statutes of 817 had modified those of the previous year and allowed the abbot to have separate premises.[39]

The facilities for guests are complex. Visiting monks are accommodated over the north aisle of the church. Two guest houses provide separate quarters for distinguished visitors and for paupers and pilgrims. Room is found for an external school at which youngsters not intended for the monastic life can be taught. Next to the infirmary is a house for physicians and beyond it a medical herb garden. There is also a house for blood-letting.

In the outer precincts are the workshops for curriers, turners, saddlers, shoe-makers, shield makers, sword grinders, goldsmiths, blacksmiths, fullers, coopers, and wheelwrights. There are cowsheds and poultry houses, and barns as well as bakehouses and brewhouses. The statutes of 816 supposed that the monks do all their work themselves, and the intention was clearly that all these facilities would be manned by monks, like the *fratres operarii* of Iona.[40] No doubt, in this as in other matters, the actuality often fell far short of the ideal.

Establishments of this size required a complex organisation. The Customs of Fleury, compiled in the tenth century, list twenty obedientiaries who were required for the smooth running of the house.[41] The abbot was assisted in maintaining internal discipline by a dean and a subdean. The prior was responsible for the monastery's external relations. He purchased what was necessary and supervised the work of the other obedientiaries. The precentor, together with his assistant, the succentor, intoned the chants in church. The sacristan looked after the sacred vessels and the treasures of the house. As well as caring for the books, the librarian supervised the *scriptorium*

---

[39] CCM 1:474.
[40] See above p. 79.
[41] CCM 7:9–33.

and wrote out the monastery's charters. The circator carried out inspections from time to time to make sure that no one was hiding private property or anything else improper. The cellarer was in charge of the kitchen; the chamberlain organised the alms to the poor and saw to the monks' clothing as well as their baths and shaving. Each of the two guest houses had its own supervisor. The *refectorarius* made sure that everything in the refectory was ready for the next meal and that the room was kept clean. The monastery's granaries and storehouses were under the care of the *panarius*. The infirmarian looked after the sick and the old in the infirmary. The child oblates had their own teacher. The gardener supervised the digging and planting and, as an expert horticulturalist, he had to be a man of mature age. The orchards had their own supervisor. And finally, the abbot had a personal servant who never left his side.

These, the Fleury customs stated, were only the most important obedientiaries. There was hardly anyone, in fact, who was not under obedience to perform some task or other, 'for this is the proudest boast of monks, that they are devoted to voluntary poverty and submit, not to their own will, but to that of another'.[42]

Saint Benedict allowed for the ordination of a monk to the priesthood, so that the community would need not be dependent on an outsider for the Eucharist, but he evidently did not see the need for more than one.[43] From the seventh century onwards, however, monasteries were increasingly clericalised.[44] In 784 the monastery of Saint Peter in Salzburg, in modern Austria, numbered ninety-seven monks, of whom twenty-two were priests and nine deacons. In 814 the abbey of Saint Riquier near Amiens in modern France, had thirty-two priests out of a total of three hundred monks. The monastery's statutes

---

[42] *Ibid.* 33.
[43] RB 62.
[44] Cyril Vogt, 'Deux conséquences de l'eschatologie grégorienne: la multiplication des messes privées et les moines prêtres,' *Colloques internationaux du CNRS: Grégoire le Grand* (Paris 1986) 268–276.

decreed that at least thirty masses should be celebrated at the various altars every day.[45]

The doctrine of purgatory, much emphasised by Pope Saint Gregory, had led to this increase of the clerical element in the monastic body. Patrons endowed monasteries so that they could be sure of efficacious intercession during their lifetime and especially after their death. Pope Gregory had stessed that the Mass was the most effective way of freeing the soul from the fires of purgatory. The solemn celebration of the Eucharist now became the high point of the daily monastic liturgy. In addition monk-priests celebrated private Masses at side altars for the increasing number of individuals who wanted this done for them.[46]

In these large clericalised establishments the interpretation of the Holy Rule was, of necessity, very formal. Saint Benedict, for instance, had laid down rules for a council which would aid the abbot in making major decisions. He did not even have a name for this institution, for the words *ad consilium* can mean either 'to a council' or 'to give advice.' The meeting was to take place whenever necessary, 'as often as any important matters have to be transacted in the monastery'.[47] The Aachen statutes decreed that the monks were to meet as a community every day after Prime. The assembly had a solemn character, almost like another liturgical office. First the martyrology was read, then the prescribed chapter of the Holy Rule. After these preliminaries the affairs of the house were discussed.[48]

Monastic reform and monastic learning went hand in hand. Benedict of Aniane compiled a collection of religious rules from which customs compatible with the *una regula* might be culled. In his treatise *Munimenta fidei* he outlined the pupose of monastic study. The monk must seek an understanding of the truths of the faith through a study of the Fathers, particularly Saint Jerome and Saint Gregory, in order to grow

---

[45] *Ibid.* 273.
[46] *Ibid.* 270–273.
[47] RB 3.1.
[48] CCM 1:480.

in the love of the Holy Trinity.[49] A faith based on the writings of the Fathers needed proper texts and an adequate mode of expression. Book production was therefore an important function of monasteries. The Church Latin used throughout the Middle Ages was partly a carolingian creation. Smaragdus, abbot of Saint Mihiel in Lorraine, explained that Christianity had enriched Latin with new concepts and modes of expression and had created a Christian Latin which improved on the pagan original.[50] One notable centre was the abbey of Saint Martin at Tours, at times the home of Alcuin, the preeminent sage of Charles the Great's court. Saint Denis near Paris was one of the few establishments in the West where Greek was studied and in the 830s the works of Pseudo-Dionysius were translated into Latin there.

Further east, Rabanus Maurus, abbot of Fulda in modern Germany, produced commentaries on the books of the Old and New Testaments, on the sacraments and ceremonies of the Church, on canon law, and on the spiritual life.[51] Off the southern shore of Lake Constance lay Reichenau, an island of monasteries where, at the beginning of the ninth century, Walahfrid Strabo, one of the most attractive and broad minded figures of the carolingian renaissance, wrote the first comprehensive treatise on the latin liturgy and its history.[52] The plan of Saint Gall, with its superb draughtsmanship and detailed rubrics, is, apart from its historical interest, an elegant witness to the monks' mastery of art and measurement, as well as to their comprehensive view of the nature of monasticism.

The empire of Louis the Pious, upon the stability of which the maintenance of the monastic reform depended, was constantly troubled by civil wars and broke up after his death.

[49] J. Leclercq, *The Love of Learning and the Desire for God*, translated Katherine Misrahi (New York 1982) 42–43.
[50] *Ibid.* 44–45.
[51] On Rabanus Maurus, see *Rabanus Maurus in seiner Zeit* (Mittelrheinisches Museum Mainz, 1980).
[52] On learning in the carolingian monasteries, see F. Kempf et al., *The Church in the Age of Feudalism*, Jedin and Dolan, History of the Church vol.3 (London 1980) 117–118, and bibliography.

In 843 it was divided into the segments from which Germany, France, and Italy ultimately emerged. The rulers of the successor states were usually too weak to defend their subjects from external enemies. Vikings raided from the north, Arabs from the south, and Hungarians from the east. Many monasteries were destroyed. Some communities, like those of Wearmouth and Jarrow, wandered from place to place. Others, like Fulda and Saint Gall, were plundered. Political power, where it survived, fell into the hands of magnates. Desperate for revenues to uphold their fighting men, they often seized monastic property. Communities lived in dependence on their lords protector. During this period many well-endowed churches became private property, in German, *Eigenkirchen*. In these circumstances no organisation, however well devised, could maintain a uniform monastic observance. The reforms of 816–817 had had little time to become reality, but they remained a programme towards the attainment of which zealous monks and their patrons could aim when circumstances allowed.

During the tenth century some semblance of order returned to parts of Louis' former empire. From 919 the saxon dynasty took control of Germany. In 962 Otto I was crowned emperor in Rome, and the carolingian empire was renewed. In the improved atmosphere monastic reform could once more be undertaken. The moving spirits were devout magnates and powerful bishops. The Rule of Saint Benedict was accepted as the *una regula*, but *una consuetudo* was no longer practicable. Reforms followed the spirit of the legislation of 816–817, but in each reformed monastery or group of monasteries, customs varied according to local conditions.

The most fruitful territory for monastic reform in the tenth century lay in Lorraine, Burgundy, and the Low Countries. Here various cultural impulses from north and south met and interacted. An early and influential centre of monastic renewal was Gorze, in Lorraine. The monastery there had been founded in the eighth century but had fallen on hard times.

In 934[53] bishop Adalbero of Metz handed it over to Einold, a former archdeacon of Toul, and six of his followers. Having withdrawn from the world, the archdeacon attempted, with others, to live a life of solitude and austerity. The names of his companions and their life stories were carefully preserved by a contemporary.[54] They formed a little local religious movement. In granting them an existing monastery in his diocese, the bishop bound them to observe the Rule of Saint Benedict. In time they made their monastic profession to him and elected Einold as their first abbot.[55]

In or around the year 934 two other important monastic reforms took place. On the urging of their bishop the monks of Saint Aprus in Toul accepted the rule of Saint Benedict and customs brought from Fleury. At about the same time the monks of the particularly dynamic Saint Maximin in Trier took up the full benedictine life. As early as 937 monks from there left for Magdeburg, to found a monastery on the border of the ottonian lands.[56]

In 994 abbot Ramwold of Trier was invited by the local bishop to reform the monastery of Saint Emmeran in Regensburg. Some time later the same bishop founded a monastery of nuns under abbess Uta, who had been in touch with benedictine circles in Einsiedeln. It was a short step from there to the reform of the canonesses of the upper and lower minsters in Regensburg. New communities took over, following the Rule of Saint Benedict. Those who resisted the reforms were driven out by the civil power.[57] Gorze, Toul, Saint Maximin in Trier, and houses founded from them were in touch with

[53] On the revised chronology of this reform and its consequences, see Michel Parisse, 'Introduction' and 'L'abbaye de Gorze dans le contexte politique et religieux lorrain a l'époque de Jean de Vandières (900–974)', *L'abbaye de Gorze au Xe siècle*, edd. M. Parisse and O. G. Oexle (Nancy 1993) 15–16, 62–66.
[54] P. C. Jacobsen, 'Die Vita des Johannes von Gorze', *Ibid.* 35–8.
[55] K. Hallinger, *Gorze-Kluny* 1 (Rome 1950) 51–54.
[56] *Ibid.* 59–60, 72–74; M. Parisse, 'L'abbaye de Gorze' (as n. 53), 62–63.
[57] Hallinger as (n. 55), 114–115, 136.

one another, exchanged personnel and customs, and prayed for one another's dead.[58]

Another monastic reform was based at Brogne near Namur in modern Belgium. Although the monastery there was ancient, at the beginning of the 10th century it was deserted. In 913–914 Gerard, son of its owner, Santio, decided to reestablish monastic life there. He began by rebuilding the church. From Paris he obtained relics for it, and then entered the noviciate of the famous abbey of Saint Denis near Paris. In 927, he emerged, a professed monk and a priest, and became abbot of his own foundation, of which he was also the secular lord.[59]

Brogne was never a large or a rich foundation, but in time Gerard acquired a reputation as a monastic reformer. Around 930 he was invited to restore the abbey of Saint Ghislain in Hainault, in the south of modern Belgium. The original monastery had been destroyed by the Vikings and a community of married canons now served the church. Recently the relics of Saint Ghislain had been found on the site and the canons' lifestyle was not considered sufficiently edifying for so holy a spot. Count Gislebert of Hainault decided, therefore, to bring back the monks. Some time between 931 and 934 the canons were expelled and Gerard, with some of his best monks, took their place.[60] A little later, thanks to his friendship with Arnulf, count of Flanders, Gerard was also asked to reform the abbey of Saint Peter in Ghent, as well as other monasteries in the count's dominions.[61]

These and similar centres of monastic reform in the tenth century sought to restore the benedictine life as it had been conceived by Benedict of Aniane, in so far as circumstances allowed. Each house or group of houses had its own varia-

[58] Parisse, 'Introduction', as n. 53, 16.
[59] J. Wollasch, 'Gerard von Brogne und seine Klostergründung,' *Revue Bénédictine* 70 (1960) 62–74.
[60] A. d'Haenens, 'Gerard de Brogne à l'abbaye de Saint Ghislain,' *Revue Bénédictine* 70 (1960) 101–18.
[61] J. Wollasch (as n. 59), 76. A. C. F. Koch, 'Gerard de Brogne et le maladie du comte Arnoul I de Flandre', *Revue Bénédictine* 70 (1960) 119–126.

tions on the customs of 816–817. All houses depended on
the patrons, lay or clerical, who had brought in the reformers
and supported them. The monks prayed for their benefactors
living and dead, gave them hospitality and a refuge in their
old age, accepted them or their relatives as monks if any felt
drawn to the religious life, and frequently elected members
of the founder's family as abbots. In return, the patrons gave
the monastic communities their protection, sometimes out of
a genuine zeal for religion, sometimes from selfish motives;
usually, no doubt, from a mixture of both. This close relationship with their patrons had many advantages, but it inevitably
sucked the monks into the politics of their time.

The tenth-century monastic revival in England was also
closely influenced by political circumstances.[62] Most of this
century the kings of Wessex spent recovering ground lost to
the Vikings and asserting their authority over the whole of
England. All english monasteries had been destroyed by the
Norsemen. During the reign of King Athelstan (924–940),
however, some ecclesiastics, influenced by the movements on
the Continet adopted the monastic life as a private devotion.
Around 940, Dunstan, a young nobleman from Somerset who
had taken monastic vows in private, was installed by King
Edmund of Wessex as abbot of Glastonbury, a pilgrimage site
much frequented by the Irish and once the site of a monastery.

Like other restorers of monasticism, from Benedict of
Aniane in the ninth century to Prosper Guéranger in the nineteenth, Dunstan knew the benedictine life only from books.
He had studied the Rule of Saint Benedict. No doubt some of
the monastic customaries in use on the Continent had come
his way. He had also received instruction from ecclesiastics
who were living as monks privately, some of whom may have
spent time at Fleury or some other reformed monastery. During the next ten years a group of young enthusiasts gathered
around Dunstan.

---

[62] M. David Knowles, *The Monastic Order in England* (Cambridge 1950) 35–
40.

Another leader of the english monastic restoration was Ethelwold, a native of Winchester who, in 954, was given the site of the ancient monastery of Abingdon in Berkshire. Ethelwold sent one of his followers to Fleury to study its customs, and introduced monks from the Continent to guide his young community. A third leader was Oswald, a nobleman partly of danish descent who had gone abroad to become a monk at Fleury. Recalled to England to aid the monastic revival, he founded monasteries in the east of England. In 959 Dunstan became archbishop of Canterbury. In 961 Oswald became bishop of Worcester and Ethelwold bishop of Winchester in 963.

With its three leaders on the bench of bishops, the english monastic revival made rapid progress. A large number of houses for monks and for nuns were founded. Their customs were derived from various sources: Fleury, Ghent, and the original community at Glastonbury. The lack of uniformity seems to have caused confusion and occasional acrimony.[63] At Winchester around 970 a meeting took place to unify the customs of all the english monasteries. A prime mover seems to have been King Edgar (958–975). With his encouragement, the council at Winchester drew up the *Regularis Concordia*, an english customary for all the monasteries of the realm.[64] Its elaborate liturgical directions faithfully reflect the spirit of the Aachen legislation.

The situation in politically fragmented Italy was still more confused. The site of Saint Benedict's monastery at Monte Cassino had been deserted for nearly one hundred fifty years. In 717 a brescian monk named Petronax passed with his companions through Rome on their way to the Holy Land. Pope Gregory II persuaded the group to settle instead at Monte Cassino. In 729 the young community won an important recruit in the learned Anglo-Saxon Willibald, who was returning

[63] T. Symons, 'Regularis Concordia: History and Derivation', *Tenth Century Studies*, ed. D. Parsons (Chichester 1975) 39–40.
[64] *Regularis Concordia*, ed. T. Symons (London 1953).

with some others from journeyings in the east.[65] The cassinese
monks participated fully in the carolingian renaissance and
were even persuaded, after a time, that by a process of osmosis
they were reliable guides to the mind of Saint Benedict and the
inner meaning of his Rule. A relative of Charlemagne asked
them for authoritative interpretations.[66] It was from Monte
Cassino that the emperor obtained what was considered the
authentic copy of the Holy Rule.[67] In the late ninth century,
however, the abbey found itself in the path of saracen raiders.
In 883 it was destroyed and once again abandoned. The monks
took refuge in Capua.[68]

In tenth-century Italy the renewal of monasticism was
often associated with a local religious revival in a town which
then led to the foundation of a monastery within the city
walls. Among these were the abbeys of Saint Peter in Modena,
Saint Peter in Perugia, Saint Peter in Assisi, Saint Stephen in
Genoa and many others. This close association of religious
communities with lay fervour outside the monastery walls was
a feature of the urban environment of Italy throughout the
Middle Ages[69] Many of these houses came under the influence
of the famous abbey of Cluny in Burgundy. A particular centre
of Cluniac influence was San Salvatore in Pavia, from which
other monasteries were then founded.[70]

The long period of saracen raids proved disastrous for
the many monasteries of Rome[71] Although the invaders never
penetrated the city, they laid waste the monastic estates in the
surrounding country. Deprived of most of their revenues, the
monasteries were unable to support communities of any size.
For many houses, including most of the greek monasteries, the
experience was fatal. By the beginning of the tenth century

---

[65] Penco (as n. 1), 137.
[66] Semmler (as n. 18), 26–27.
[67] Penco (as n. 1), 140.
[68] *Ibid.* 139–146.
[69] See below p. 162.
[70] Penco (as n. 1), 187–188.
[71] B. Hamilton, 'The Monastic Revival in Tenth Century Rome', *Studia Monastica* 4 (1962) 35–67.

communities of clerics had replaced monks at all the great
basilicas within the city.

Pope John X's victory over the Saracens in 915 marked
the beginning of a slow recovery which gathered pace when
the Duchy of Rome was under the rule of the devout prince
Alberic (932–954). In 936 Alberic invited Odo, abbot of Cluny,
to Rome and made him 'archimandrite' of all the roman monasteries. Odo took charge of the ancient abbey of Saint Paul's-
outside-Rome. Monks from north of the Alps were brought
into the community. A monk of Cluny, Baldwin, became its
abbot. In 942 Baldwin was made abbot of Monte Cassino,
whose community was still in exile at Capua. The next abbot
of Monte Cassino was Aligernus, who took over in 949. He
was a monk of the abbey of Saint Mary on the Aventine, a
monastery which had been founded by Prince Alberic with
Odo's encouragement. In 950 abbot Aligernus was able to take
his community back to Cassino.[72]

Odo of Cluny paid six visits to Rome altogether, [73]but his
work was cut short by his sudden death in 942. Pope Agapetus
(942–946) appealed to Einold of Gorze to continue the work[74]
but little came of this. Nevertheless Odo had given an impetus
to monasticism which was continued by Alberic and members
of the roman nobility. By the end of the tenth century fifteen
new monasteries for latin monks and nuns had been founded
in Rome, and two for greek communities.[75]

The burgundian monastery of Cluny was the preeminent
benedictine house of the tenth and eleventh centuries. Numerous attempts have been made recently to diminish its unique
importance. We are told that its customs were no different
from, and certainly not superior to, those of other reformed
monasteries, and that its attempts to supervise other houses

---

[72] Penco (as n. 1), 191–192.
[73] Hamilton (as n. 71), 47.
[74] *Ibid.* 49.
[75] *Ibid.* 63–4.

were not always disinterested.[76] There are a number of factors, however, which make this abbey unique. It was not notably dependent upon any outside support, whether lay or clerical. It was able to develop a machinery for maintaining control of many of the houses it had once reformed, so that it became the centre of something like a religious order. In addition, its influence was spread into every part of western Christendom. By the end of the eleventh century it had dependent houses in France, Spain, England, Germany, Poland, and Italy.

The abbey was founded in 909 by Duke William of Aquitaine,[77] who in the foundation charter charged that the monks were to pray for the souls of the founder and his family and to follow the Rule of Saint Benedict. The founder renounced any further power over it, nor was the local bishop of Macon to have any authority there. To ensure this the monastery was placed under the protection and authority of the Holy See.

Duke William's first choice as abbot of Cluny was Berno, abbot of Baume. Berno had been sent to reform this burgundian abbey in 886 and had insisted on the strict observance, in every detail, of the customs of Benedict of Aniane. In 890 Berno founded the abbey of Gigny in the Jura mountains. He was thus already abbot of two monasteries and Cluny became the third. Here was the germ of the later cluniac Order.

Cluny was by no means the first monastery to be commended to the protection of the pope. The decline of ottonian imperial power in the ninth century coincided with the increasing authority of popes like Nicholas I (858–867) and John VIII (872–882). The popes had the authority to excommunicate those who invaded the lands of monasteries or interfered with

---

[76] This is the message of Kassius Hallinger, *Gorze-Kluny*, 2 vols. (Rome 1950–1951).
[77] On Cluny, see Noreen Hunt, *Cluny under Saint Hugh* (London 1967); N. Hunt ed., *Cluniac Monasticism in the Central Middle Ages* (London 1971); H. E. J. Cowdrey, *The Cluniacs and the Gregorian Reform* (Oxford 1970); and the following articles: TRE 8 (1981) 126–32; LM 2 (1983) 2172–2194; J. Warrilow, 'Cluny: Silentia claustri,' in D. H. Farmer, ed., *Benedict's Disciples* (Leominster 1980) 118–138.

internal discipline.⁷⁸ In time they came to regard Cluny as a model monastery. In 931 John XI decreed that a monk of any monastery which refused reform could leave and join the community at Cluny. A monastery which asked to be reformed by Cluny could, from henceforth, be governed from there. In 998 Gregory V supported Cluny in its struggle for exemption from the authority of the bishop of Macon. In their own way, the popes were taking up Benedict of Aniane's concept of *una consuetudo*. Through Cluny, many would-be reformers hoped, the customs of all houses following the Holy Rule could be unified.⁷⁹

Cluny was fortunate in its line of able and long-lived superiors, who often nominated their successors. Berno decided to divide into two groups the monasteries over which he ruled. His nephew Guy was to take over Baume and Gigny. Cluny, the least important, was to go to Odo. Thanks to the qualities of its new superior it soon outshone the others.

Odo was abbot of Cluny from 926–942. He had been brought up at William of Aquitaine's court. He became a monk at the renowned abbey of Saint Martin in Tours. From there he went in search of a monastery where the observance was most perfect, and settled upon Baume under Berno. His spirituality was rooted in monastic tradition. He was succeeded by Aimard (942–954) and then by Maieul (954–994) who was conspicuous for gentleness and holiness. The next abbot, Odilo (994–1049), continued to spread the cluniac monastic reform in France and Italy and introduced it in Spain. Under Hugh (1049–1109) Cluny, with hundreds of dependent monasteries, reached the high point of its reputation. It was in Hugh's time that the abbey and its dependencies were organised into a kind of Order. A symbol of the importance Cluny had by then gained was the consecration in 1095 of its huge church by pope Urban II, a former monk of the abbey.

⁷⁸ Cowdrey (as n. 77) 8–15.
⁷⁹ *Ibid.* 15–22.

Cluny was often invited to undertake the reform of decayed religious houses. In 936, as we have already seen, Alberic, the ruler of Rome, invited Saint Odo to reform the monasteries of the city. Elsewhere sites were presented for cluniac settlement. Saint Flour in the Auvergne, a chapel served by canons where the relics of an alleged disciple of Jesus were venerated, was offered to abbot Odilo in 996, though it was many years before the monks were able to take possession.[80] Cluny also founded dependent priories on lands already in its possession. The more difficult task was to reform larger institutions where standards had fallen. The most famous was Fleury, to which abbot Odo was called in 930 because political anarchy in the area had led to a breakdown of discipline. The monks resisted him by force. It was only in 938 that Odo was accepted as their abbot. So inauspiciously began the most brilliant period in Fleury's history, during which it influenced the development of monasticism in England.[81]

It has been argued that some of the reforms were hardly necessary. There was an element of monastic empire-building in Cluny's expansion, and occasionally the abbey used violence and subterfuge. The abbey of Saint Bénigne in Dijon, for instance, was thoroughly reformed by an abbot from Lorraine in 985. For some reason the local bishop was dissatisfied and appealed to Cluny to complete the work. Cluny sent one of its monks, the fiery young Italian William of Volpiano, with a posse of twelve companions. At daybreak one February morning in 990 they entered the church of Saint Bénigne, took possession of the choir, and began to sing Lauds while the community was singing its own office in the crypt. The local monks came into the upper church to find an alien community in possession. All of them left in disgust. The new community was not even able to find its way around its new premises, and had no idea where the relics of Saint Bénigne were kept.[82] We should add that

---

[80] Cowdrey (as n. 77), 83–85.
[81] 'Fleury,' DHGE 17 (1971) 448.
[82] Hallinger (as n. 76), 463–465.

incidents of this kind were rare, and that there are many more examples of Cluny declining to take over an abbey offered to it.[83]

An organisation for dependent priories and reformed abbeys grew only very slowly. It began to assume recognisable shape in the eleventh century. The norm was the dependent priory, the monks of which were, strictly speaking, monks of Cluny. The abbot of Cluny appointed the prior, and the monks of the priory made their profession at the mother abbey. A monk in one of these dependent houses could be moved from one priory to another, or back to Cluny. Life in the cluniac priories was, in every particular, a reproduction of that in the mother abbey. An eloquent witness to this is the church of the priory of Paray-le-Monial (in the départment of Saône-et-Loire, France) which is a scaled-down model of the abbey church at Cluny itself.

During the tenth and eleventh centuries Cluny took over a number of abbeys which were then reduced to the rank of priory—though at a small number of very important monasteries the superior retained the title of abbot. Here the abbot of Cluny's right to appoint the superior was often resisted. There were also a number of abbeys which had been reformed by Cluny but which were subordinated to it for only a limited time. Although Cluny may be regarded as the first religious Order, the organisation was fluid and far from perfect. It has never been possible to make a satisfactory list of 'cluniac' houses.[84]

Cluny was admired most for the splendour of its liturgy. Cluniac elaboration has become almost legendary. Saint Peter Damian complained that the monks were so occupied in choir that they had scarcely half an hour in the day at their disposal.[85] On great feast days there was scarcely a break between the Night Office, which began before midnight, and High Mass, which ended the next day around noon.[86] It was in the eleventh

---

[83] Hunt, *Cluny* (as n. 77), 150–154.
[84] *Ibid.* 161–185.
[85] *Ibid.* 103.
[86] Knowles (as n. 62), 150.

century, however, after more than a century's development and elaboration, that some onlookers began to remark on it in terms of excesses. By this time the community had grown enormously, so that many liturgical functions, like the giving of Communion or processions, were greatly protracted.[87]

Four customaries from Cluny survive.[88] The oldest, compiled between 996 and 1030, contains fragments of older customaries, some of them dating from Odo's time. Around the year 1000 the abbot of Farfa in Italy asked Cluny for a copy of its customary. The answer to the request was the Farfa Customary, drawn up in the first half of the eleventh century. Around 1075 abbot Hugh asked Bernard, one of his monks, to write down the customs of Cluny in a new and official compilation. Some ten years later Ulric, another monk of the abbey, wrote down a very detailed description of the life and liturgy of Cluny for the benefit of the abbot of Hirsau in Germany.

A comparative study of all this material remains to be undertaken, but some preliminary points can be noted. The psalter constituted the normal method of prayer for clerics at this period. Most monks knew all one hundred fifty psalms by heart. 'When you are going from one place to another,' wrote Peter Damian, 'or on a journey, or about some necessary business, let your lips continually ruminate something from the Scriptures, grinding the psalms as in a mortar, so that they may ever give forth an odour as of aromatic plants.'[89] Saint Pachomius had given his monks advice in almost the same words. To the monks of Cluny it probably did not seem burdensome to recite all one hundred fifty psalms around the body of a deceased brother during the first two watches of the night or to chant the entire psalter standing barefoot in the cloister on Good Friday.[90]

---

[87] Hunt, *Cluny* (as n. 77), 104.
[88] Warrilow (as n. 77), 126–133.
[89] Quoted by Jean Leclercq in *The Spirituality of the Middle Ages* (London 1968) 98–99.
[90] Hunt, *Cluny* (as n. 77), 104.

The singing of additional offices—the 'Little Office' of Our Lady and the Office of All Saints—after some of the daily offices involved a good deal of repetition and considerably lengthened the time monks spent in choir. At the time, this was considered entirely fitting. Indeed, other groups of monks copied Cluny in this. The Cistercians—no laggards when it came to criticising Cluniacs—sang the appropriate office of Our Lady after each of the hours until the Second Vatican Council in the late twentieth century.

The great church which Saint Hugh built for the grandeur of cluniac worship remained, until its destruction during the French Revolution, one of the marvels of Christendom.[91] Within the apse a huge fresco of Christ in majesty, towering over the monks kneeling in the choir below, epitomised the essence of cluniac life and worship. A small-scale copy survives over the apse of the monks' chapel at Berze-la-Ville.[92] The glory of the Lord filled the whole house at Cluny. In his writings Saint Odo reminded his monks that their task was to make the Day of Pentecost a new reality in their lives. By spending every minute in the worship of Almighty God, they were anticipating the silence and peace of eternity and sharing the life of the angels.[93]

---

[91] On the successive buildings at Cluny, see K. J. Conant, *Carolingian and Romanesque Architecture* (London 1959) 107–125.

[92] *Ibid.* 118.

[93] Leclercq, *The Spirituality of the Middle Ages*, 106–110. See also K. Hallinger, 'The Spiritual Life of Cluny in the Early Days,' in Hunt, ed., *Cluniac Monasticism* (as n. 77), 29–55.

Chapter 6
MONASTICISM IN AN AGE OF REFORM

WESTERN EUROPE UNDERWENT profound changes in the eleventh century. The first three decades saw abundant harvests and a rise in the population. The pace of land-clearance quickened and new rural communities were founded. For the Church it was an era of expansion. Churches had to be built to serve new settlements. The ideal of having a place of worship for every centre of population, though never completely achieved, came nearer realisation. As Western Christendom became more intensely evangelised, the question of church discipline and organisation took on a new urgency.

While the 'Reformation of the eleventh century' is often associated with conflict, the many positive aspects of the quickening of church life in this era should not be forgotten. It was in the eleventh century that Christianity was firmly established in Scandinavia. The christian counter-attack against the Arabs led to the restoration of historic sees like those of Toledo, the ancient churches of Sicily, and, in 1099, Jerusalem. The bishops of the restored sees laboured to revive the dignity and traditions of their churches and encouraged research into their past.

The eleventh century was also a period of monastic restoration and expansion. Abandoned monasteries were repopulated and new ones founded. In 1008, for instance, the abbey of Fleury sent two monks, Felix and Vitalis, to restore the monasteries of Brittany, which had been destroyed by the Vikings.[1] In the North of England monastic life, so flourishing

---

[1] P. Riche and G. Devailly, 'De l'Armorique à la Bretagne', *Histoire de la Bretagne*, ed. J. Delumeau (Toulouse 1969) 138–139.

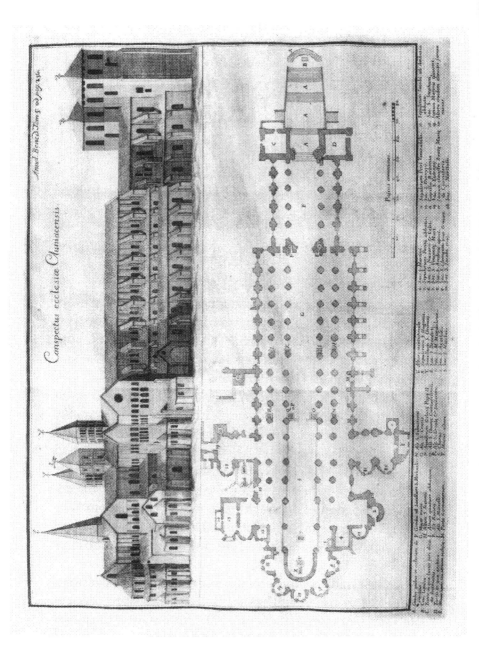

2 View of the Abbey of Cluny.

in the seventh century, had been devastated by the northern invasions. The monks who in 1073 -1074, revived the ancient monasteries of the area were inspired in part by reading Bede's *Ecclesiastical History of the English Church and People*.[2]

Monastic expansion inspired discussions about the customs to be followed by new or revived communities. Almost everywhere the monastic observances associated with Benedict of Aniane were accepted as the norm. In spite of occasional falling away in some houses and the appearance of hermit communities here and there, traditional Benedictinism was hardly challenged in the eleventh century. Monks were closely involved in the reform of the Church. On one occasion Pope Gregory VII asked Abbot Hugh of Cluny to send him the names of some of his subjects who would make suitable bishops.[3] Monks dominated the reform papacy. Frederick of Lorraine, who was elected pope as Stephen IX in 1059, had briefly been abbot of Montecassino.[4] Gregory VII himself was a monk, though to which monastery he belonged is not clear. It may have been some monastery in Rome.[5] The theory that he became a monk at Cluny during his exile in 1046–1048 has recently been revived.[6] Victor III, who succeeded him in 1086, was the former abbot Desiderius of Montecassino.[7] The next pope came from Cluny. Eudes de Chatillon was one of the monks who had been identified by abbot Hugh as suitable for promotion to the episcopate.[8] As Pope Urban II (1088–1099) he was the ablest and most effective of the popes of the reform.[9]

---

[2] David Knowles, *The Monastic Order in England* (Cambridge 1950) 166–167.

[3] G. Picasso, 'Gregorio VII e la disciplina canonica: clero e vita monastica', *Studi Gregoriani* 13 (Rome 1989) 159.

[4] Henri Bloch, *Monte Cassino in the Middle Ages* 1 (Cambridge, Massachusetts 1986) 38.

[5] See discussion in H. E. J. Cowdrey, *The Cluniacs and the Gregorian Reform* (Oxford 1970) 148 n. 4.

[6] Picasso, 'Gregorio VII' (as n. 3), 152, 159.

[7] On Desiderius as pope, see H. E. J. Cowdrey, *The Age of Abbot Desiderius* (Oxford 1983) 177–230.

[8] Picasso (as n. 3), 159.

[9] On Urban, see the study by A. Becker, *Papst Urban II* (Stuttgart 1964).

In the eleventh century then traditional benedictine monasticism occupied a central position in the life of the Church.
We have seen that under abbot Hugh (1049–1109) Cluny
reached the height of its influence and power. Gregory VII
valued Hugh's friendship and, although the two did not always
see eye to eye, the abbot was in sympathy with his aims.
Hugh's loyalty was of crucial importance during the pope's
conflict with the emperor Henry IV. On two occasions the
abbot tried to reconcile pope and king. It was through his
mediation that the two came face to face at Canossa. In 1083,
after Henry's occupation of Rome, the abbot made a fruitless
personal appeal to him on Gregory's behalf.[10]

At the same time, south of Rome, the abbey of Montecassino was experiencing its golden age under abbot Desiderius (1058–1086). The abbot belonged to the ruling house of
Benevento. As a young man he had become a hermit. Later
he joined the circle of reformers around Pope Leo IX (1048–
1054). In 1055, he became a monk of Montecassino. Three
years later, when the abbot, Frederick of Lorraine, was elected
pope, he nominated Desiderius as his successor.[11]

During his long tenure in office Desiderius built the *terra
sancti Benedicti* into a compact and manageable block of
territory.[12] The abbot's most memorable achievements were in
the field of art and learning. The rebuilding of the abbey church
began in 1066 and was completed in 1071. Pope Alexander II
came in person to consecrate it, accompanied by archdeacon
Hildebrand (the future Gregory VII), three cardinals, most
of the bishops of southern Italy, and a number of norman
princes. The early christian style in which the church was
built symbolised the programme of the Church reform. The
abbot scoured Rome for antique pillars and worked marble to
decorate the building. Thanks to his excellent relations with the

---

[10] Cowdrey, *Cluniacs* (as n. 5), 160–162.
[11] On the early life of abbot Desiderius, see Cowdrey, *Desiderius* (as n. 7),
115–117.
[12] Ibid. 2–7.

byzantine emperor Romanus IV, artists from Constantinople executed the mosaics and pavements.[13]

One of the monks at Montecassino under Desiderius was Constantinus Africanus, a converted saracen physician whose treatises made much of arabic and greek medical knowledge available in the West.[14] Alphanus of Salerno, 'the greatest poet of Italy in the eleventh',[15] was also closely associated with the abbey. A former monk of Montecassino, he became archbishop of Salerno in 1057.[16] His two poems in honour of the new church and its builder are important sources of information about Desiderius's buildings, all of which have disappeared.[17]

Some one hundred twenty-five kilometres to the north, the popes were wrestling with intractable problems. Montecassino under Desiderius must have seemed to belong to a different world. At times Gregory VII was irritated with the abbot.[18] The community at Montecassino, however, was noted for its strict observance of the Rule of Saint Benedict and in its own way was fully committed to papal policies. Abbot Desiderius was a cardinal of the Roman Church. He had a residence in Rome and occasionally joined the group of papal advisers.[19] Gregory VII's increasing difficulties at the end of his pontificate drew pope and abbot closer together. When Gregory was forced to leave Rome in May 1084, he stayed for a time at Montecassino. During the last months of the pope's life abbot Desiderius was constantly at his side.[20] He took charge of the Roman Church after Gregory's death, and was, somewhat unwillingly, elected to succeed him in 1086.[21]

---

[13] Bloch (as n. 4), 40–49; G. Carbonara, *Iussu Desiderii* (Rome 1979) 25–97.
[14] Bloch (as n. 4), 98–110.
[15] Ibid. 97.
[16] Ibid. 93–98.
[17] Ibid. 41–44.
[18] See e.g. Cowdrey, *Desiderius* (as n. 7), 135.
[19] Ibid. 61–63.
[20] Ibid. 170–176.
[21] Ibid. 185–206.

In Germany, the abbey most committed to the papal cause
was Hirsau in Swabia.[22] Originally a carolingian foundation,
it had been revived by its patron, Count Adalbert of Calw,
at the request of his uncle, Pope Leo IX. Under its able
and zealous abbot William (1069–1091) the abbey managed
to free itself from the count's control and win the right to
elect its abbot freely, as the Rule of Saint Benedict demanded.
Hirsau also secured exemption from episcopal authority. This
was particularly important because, in the struggle between
Gregory VII and Henry IV, the local bishop of Speyer was a
loyal partisan of the king.

Abbot William would also have liked to be free to choose
the abbey's *advocatus* or *vogt*. At Hirsau, however, the abbot
had to agree that the *advocatus*—who exercised an abbey's secular jurisdiction and provided the force necessary for executing
judgments, usually being paid for his pains from the abbey's
lands—would always belong to Count Adalbert's family. Abbot
William was an enthusiastic admirer of Cluny. He was encouraged by Bernard, the papal legate in Germany, himself a monk
of the great burgundian abbey. Ulrich, another former monk
of Cluny and now prior of a small monastery in the Black Forest, was also his friend. Ulrich had already made a collection
of Cluniac customs[23] and on these Abbot William based his
own *Constitutiones Hirsaugienses*. On three occasions Hirsau
monks were sent to Cluny to learn the way of life there. Abbot
Hugh of Cluny himself wrote to Hirsau, making suggestions.
Other german monasteries in turn copied the Hirsau customs.
Eventually there were one hundred-twenty associated houses.
Unlike Cluny, Hirsau made no attempt to create a centralised
organisation. The monasteries of the Hirsau family shared
the same spirit, used the same customs, and prayed for one
another's dead. As a result, they did not lack a certain collective
arrogance. 'The monastic observance,' wrote the biographer of
abbot William, 'which had almost disappeared in the german

---

[22] On Hirsau, see H. Jakobs, *Die Hirsauer* (Cologne-Graz 1961). There are also
useful articles in TRE 15(1986) 388–390; LM 5 (1991) 35–36.
[23] See above p. 129.

lands among those who presumed to call themselves monks, began, through the zeal of this holy father, to revive and recover'.

In 1075 Abbot William visited Pope Gregory VII and returned home an ardent supporter of papal policies. His monks associated themselves with the reform party in the Church. During Gregory's bitter struggle with Henry IV, and particularly after the king's excommunication in 1076, the monks of Hirsau distinguished themselves by their sermons to clergy and people in support of the pope.

In Italy and Germany the renewal of church life was not achieved without bitterness and occasionally bloodshed. Else-where the process was more peaceful. After a military defeat, for example, the chastened Count Baldwin IV of Flanders cooperated with his enemy, the bishop of Cambrai, by inviting into his dominions Richard, the young and energetic abbot of Saint Vanne in Verdun. In 1008, Richard was made abbot of Saint Vaast in the city of Arras. A zealous promotor of observant Benedictinism, the new abbot enjoyed the support of the bishop and was able, at the same time, to work on the conscience of the count. Saint Vaast became a centre of monastic reform in Flanders, bringing renewed vigour to the ancient abbey of Saint Bertin and numerous other religious houses in the area.[24] In 911 territory in north-west France was ceded to the viking leader Rollo on condition that he became a Christian. In the tenth century Normandy gradually evolved as a recognisable political unit, but the Church was little in evidence, and by the year 1000 there were only three small, struggling monasteries in the duchy.[25] The turning point came in 1001, when Duke Richard II invited the cluniac monk William of Volpiano to Normandy. William, who came from northerm Italy and had been abbot of Dijon, had reformed a large number of monasteries by encouraging them to adopt the

---

[24] D. C. Van Meter, 'Count Baldwin IV, Richard of St. Vanne, and the Inception of Monastic Reform in Eleventh-century Flanders', *Revue Bénédictine* 107 (1997) 131–148.

[25] On norman monasticism, see Knowles, *The Monastic Order* (as n. 2), 83–99.

customs of Cluny. Over these houses he continued to exercise a certain authority. He was also a noted scholar in the fields of music, medicine, mathematics, architecture, and the arts. In most of the monasteries he supervised there were schools which all who wished could attend, whether they were intent upon a clerical life or not.

In Normandy William was given the collegiate church of Fécamp, which he transformed into a monastery. From there the three existing monasteries in the duchy were reformed and new ones founded. After William's death in 1031, the pace of foundations quickened as the norman nobles began to patronise the monastic movement. By 1066, when Duke William invaded England, there were between twenty-six and twenty-eight benedictine houses in the duchy.[26] These abbeys were noted for their spacious churches. Bernay, which was under construction throughout the eleventh century, is the oldest of them still standing.[27] The most magnificent of these buildings are the two abbeys at Caen, one for women and one for men, dedicated respectively in 1066 and 1077.[28]

Many norman monasteries became in time centres of study, particularly in the fields of theology, history, and medicine. The most prominent monk in the duchy after the death of William of Volpiano was John, his successor as abbot of Fécamp. Like his predecessor he came from northern Italy. He had begun his spiritual life as a hermit and never lost his yearning for the solitary life. His writings on prayer, which in some ways foreshadow those of Saint Bernard in the next century, proved so popular that they began to be attributed to great masters like Saint Augustine, Saint Ambrose, and Saint Anselm. The originality of John was lost to view and it was left to historians of the twentieth century to rediscover him.[29]

---

[26] Ibid. 84–86.

[27] See analysis in L. Musset, *Normandie Romane* 2 (La Pierre-Qui-Vire 1975), 45–48.

[28] Ibid. 1:49–104.

[29] On John of Fécamp, see Jean Leclercq and J. P. Bonnes, *Un maître de la vie spirituelle au xie siècle* (Paris 1946); Jean Leclercq, *The Spirituality of the Middle Ages* (London 1968) 122–126.

Of all the abbeys in Normandy, Bec was the one destined to enjoy the greatest fame.[30] It was founded by a knight named Herlouin, who had been converted from the military life. Around 1034 he left the service of his lord and visited a number of monasteries, seeking guidance on how to live a more perfect christian life. The reception he was given was not always friendly. After a time he was near despair. One of the houses he visited provided the turning point. After the night office he decided to stay behind in the church in order to spend some time in solitary prayer. He noticed that one of the monks, who, like himself, thought he was alone, was doing the same. The monk prayed in his place until daybreak. Encouraged by this experience, Herlouin returned to his estate and settled down with two other companions to a life of prayer and penance. Theirs was a life of austere poverty. Herlouin's mother lived nearby and washed the clothes of the little community. After a time Herlouin himself was ordained a priest.

Slowly, the community grew. Around 1042 it was joined by its most valuable recruit. Lanfranc, a scholar from northern Italy who had already acquired some fame as a teacher before coming to Normandy, retired to Bec to live in poverty and obscurity. He found a community struggling for survival. It soon became clear that Lanfranc's skills as a teacher could save it from extinction. Within a short time the school of Bec became the most famous in Normandy. Part of its success can be attributed to the remarkable collaboration of Lanfranc and Herlouin, the former a sophisticated scholar of international renown, the latter self-taught, but evidently an able administrator and a wise judge of character who could discern promise in the young. In time Lanfranc was called from Bec to become abbot of Duke William's new abbey at Caen. After William's conquest of England Lanfranc became archbishop

[30] On Bec, see Knowles (as n. 2), 88–92; S. Vaughn, *The Abbey of Bec and the Anglo-Norman State 1034–1136* (Woodbridge 1981); C. Harper-Bill, 'Herlouin of Bec and his biographer', *Religious Motivation: Biographical and Sociological problems for the Church Historian,* Studies in Church History 15 (Oxford 1978) 15–25.

of Canterbury. Yet in the meantime Anselm of Aosta, another north-italian scholar, had joined the community at Bec. One of the most eminent of the theologians of the Middle Ages, he brought the abbey's school to the height of its fame. Eventually he succeeded Herlouin as abbot of Bec, and, in 1093, followed Lanfranc on the throne of Canterbury.Anselm's treatises approached the problems of theology in a new way. Instead of quoting a collection of authorities, he strove to demonstrate the reasonableness of faith by basing its truths, as far as possible, on rational arguments. He was, above all, an apologist for Christianity. He took note of contrary arguments, and sought to convince. To modern readers his reasoning occasionally appears specious. No doubt Anselm sometimes went too far, as Lanfranc himself was to point out, but the new method lay at the basis of scholastic philosophy, of which Anselm may be regarded the pioneer.[31]

One of the pupils at Bec, though never a monk there, was the future Pope Alexander II (1061–1073).[32] As for the monks, a memorial tablet at the abbey lists those who achieved eminence in England: three archbishops of Canterbury (Theobald, archbishop 1138–1161 was the third), four bishops of Rochester, and seven abbots. The names include the saintly Gundulf, bishop of Rochester (1077–1108) and architect of the Tower of London, and Gilbert Crispin, the learned abbot of Westminster (1085–1117).

The monks of Bec and other norman churchmen were able to gain promotion in England because of the conquest of that kingdom by Duke William of Normandy in 1066. Many of the abbots of english monasteries who had supported the national cause were slowly replaced by Normans.[33] The abbatial appointees, like the Normans who obtained bishoprics in England, were for the most part able and zealous. It was natural, perhaps, that they should be new brooms and view

---

[31] On Anselm, see R. W. Southern, *St. Anselm and his Biographer* (Cambridge 1963) especially 52–65.
[32] Knowles (as n. 2), 108.
[33] The process is described by Knowles, ibid. 102–119.

themselves as reformers. 'The monastic order, which had degenerated to the level of a lay institution, was brought back to the standard of the most observant monasteries, clerks were disciplined according to the norms of canon law, the people, after the folly of barabarous rites had been repressed, was instructed in the right forms of belief and living.'[34] Thus Gilbert Crispin, the norman abbot of Westminster, described the work of Lanfranc as archbishop of Canterbury.

The eleventh century was a period of reform and reformers had a tendency to make harsh judgements about anything that was old. We have already been seen that the monks of Hirsau thought that no proper monks existed in Germany before their time. Gilbert Crispin's remarks about english monasticism before 1066 should be treated with scepticism.[35] The new norman abbots must, however, be credited with real achievements. They initiated ambitious building works in the monasteries they ruled. Immediately after taking office Lanfranc began to build an impressive new church at Canterbury. Other abbots who followed his example were abbots Baldwin at Bury Saint Edmund's, and Scotland at Saint Augustine's Canterbury. Nothing of their work has survived, but some of the buildings undertaken by the first generation of norman superiors can still be seen at Saint Alban's, Rochester, Gloucester, Norwich, and Durham.[36] For the english communities the ambitious building programmes may have seemed disruptive. The monks at Norwich, for instance, are known to have grumbled.[37] No one likes living on a building site. In time, however, communities became accustomed to thinking of their houses on a large scale, and what was begun amidst discontent in the eleventh century was often gloriously completed with much enthusiasm in the twelfth.

---

[34] Gilbert Crispin's 'Vita domni Herluini' is printed in J. A. Robinson, *Gilbert Crispin, Abbot of Westminster* (Cambridge 1911) 100.
[35] This is not the view of Colin Platt, *The Abbeys and Priories of Medieval England* (London 1984) 1–2.
[36] Knowles (as n. 2), 120–121.
[37] Platt (as n. 34), 19–20.

With them, the new abbots brought to England their enthusiasm for learning. Many were noted collectors of books and built up the monastic libraries. Baldwin, abbot of Bury, and Faricius, abbot of Abingdon, were famed for their medical knowledge; Paul of Saint Alban's and Fulcard of Thorney were experts in music and liturgy.[38] Gilbert Crispin, abbot of Westminster, wrote on history and theology. Anselm of Aosta belongs more to Europe than to England, but at least one of his works, *Cur Deus Homo*, ('Why God was made man'), was written in 1097–1098, during his troubled time as archbishop of Canterbury and superior of the cathedral monks.[39]

The nature of norman monasticism in England is well illustrated by the Constitutions which Lanfranc compiled for the monastic community at Canterbury cathedral.[40] They were based on the customs of Cluny and other great monasteries of the time. A few communities which had close connections with Canterbury copied them, though it is unlikely that Lanfranc intended them as a code for all the monasteries of the realm.[41] For the most part they constitute a detailed liturgical directory and enable the reader to follow the monks through the elaborate ceremonial of the year, recreating for us the magnificent liturgical life of a great anglo-norman community.

Two english abbeys were untouched by the changes which followed the norman conquest. The cathedral monastery of Worcester under Saint Wulfstan[42] and the abbey of Evesham under Aethelwig[43] were ruled by superiors of such exceptional quality that the Normans dared not interfere with them. It helped that both of them had swung over to Duke William's cause in time. They were not mere time-servers, however. During the Conqueror's 'harrying of the North' in 1069–1070, when large areas of northern and western England were

---

[38] Knowles (as n. 2), 125–126.
[39] Southern (as n. 30), 77.
[40] *The Monastic Constitutions of Lanfranc*, ed. D. Knowles (London 1951).
[41] Ibid. xxi–xxii.
[42] Knowles (as n. 2), 159–161.
[43] Ibid. 161–163.

systematically ravaged, Evesham became a refugee centre. The destitute, many of them women with children, converged on the town. All the houses overflowed with homeless. Other fugitives encamped in the open air and even in the abbey cemetery. Five or six died every day. Abbot Aethelwig persuaded each of the monastery's servants and officials, and even such monks as had the means, to take in and feed one child. Prior Alfric was appointed coordinator of relief, to provide food and look after the sick.[44]

It was probably during this time of sorrow that Evesham's links with northern England were forged. The idea of reviving monastic life in the North seems first to have come to Aldwin, prior of Winchcombe. His house was at that time under the general authority of abbot Aethelwig. Aldwin had read Bede's *Ecclesiastical History*, and determined to make a pilgrimage to the northern shrines. He journeyed to Evesham to obtain Aethelwig's permission. There he was joined by two of the abbey's monks. The three of them made their way north on foot with only an ass to carry their vestments and liturgical books. Eventually they found their way to the ruins of Bede's monastery at Jarrow. They roofed the walls of the church with timber and turf and built huts for themselves. The local people knew nothing about monasticism, but were gradually won over and began to support the new community. After some years there were sufficient resources to undertake the restoration of Bede's other monastery of Wearmouth and, later on, Saint Hilda's abbey at Whitby. Recruits were not lacking for these ventures, though at first they came largely from the south. At length, in 1083, William of Saint Carilef, bishop of Durham, persuaded Aldwin and twenty-three of his monks to settle in his see city, where the shrine of Saint Cuthbert remained an important centre of local pilgrimage.

Symeon of Durham, the chronicler of these events, wrote that Aldwin 'preferred voluntary poverty and the contempt

---

[44] Ibid. 162 and n. 4; Barbara Harvey, *Living and Dying in England 1100–1540* (Oxford 1993) 19–20.

of the world to all the honours and riches of the age'.[45] At
Jarrow the companions, 'lived out their lives for Christ in
cold and hunger and utter want of all necessities, although
in the monasteries they had left behind they could have had
everything they needed'.[46] Although personally acquainted
with the pioneers,[47] Symeon belonged to a younger generation
of monks, among whom the question of monastic poverty was
becoming an important issue. We may question whether he
was able to discern accurately the motives of his predecessors
in the 1070s. We should note that Aldwin and his followers
had no hesitation about moving to Durham when they had
the opportunity. Within a short time the cathedral monastery
of Durham was the major benedictine house of northern
England, while Jarrow and Wearmouth sank to the status of
dependencies.

    The disorders and invasions which troubled much of west-
ern Europe during the eighth and ninth centuries was even
harder on hermits than on monasteries. Institutions had been
better able than isolated cells to survive random killings and the
destruction of property. The greater security of the eleventh
century, therefore, encouraged the revival of the eremitical as
well as the cenobitic life. Relations between the two kinds of
religious were normally friendly. A canon of the Council of
Trullo (692), indeed, had decreed that nobody should undertake the solitary life who had not spent at least three years in a
cenobitic community.[48] Women solitaries, who are often mentioned in the necrologies of german abbeys, were entrusted
to the spiritual care of the men's benedictine communities.
These women usually lived in a cell which had no door but
only a window through which they received their food. From
time to time a priest or monk would bring the sacraments.
Most famous of these hermitesses was Saint Wiborada, who

[45] *Symeon monachi opera omnia*, ed. T. Arnold 1, Rolls Series (London 1882)
108.
[46] Ibid. 109.
[47] On Symeon, see Knowles (as n. 2) 165 n. 1.
[48] Tomas Špidlík, 'Ermites', DHGE 15 (1963) 768.

lived near the abbey of Saint Gall in modern Switzerland, and who was martyred by the invading Hungarians in 926.[49]

In the eleventh century the island of Tombelaine, within sight of the norman abbey of Mont Saint Michel, was a place to which monks could retire to live a life of austerity and prayer. In 1054–1055 the monk Robert built himself a cell there and wrote a commentary on the Song of Songs. He corresponded with Saint Anselm, and from time to time was visited by other monks who encouraged his work. In 1065–1066, he left at the invitation of Odo of Bayeux, to take charge of a monastery on the mainland.[50] In spite of the increasing elaboration of its community life, the burgundian abbey of Cluny was also noted for the ascetics who lived in semi-retirement side-by-side with the cenobites. By the middle of the twelfth century there were some four hundred monk-hermits in the woods around the abbey.[51]

In these and many other places, the solitaries were considered a part of a conventional monastic community and, presumably, owed obedience to its abbot. This meant that they were under the direction of a cenobite. Hermits who were so isolated as to be subject to no external rule were very rare. The most famous was Meinrad, a monk and priest of the abbey of Reichenau in the ninth century. After some years as superior of a priory on the banks of Lake Zürich in modern Switzerland, he retired to the mountains and built himself a cell in which he lived for twenty-six years. In 861 he was murdered by two robbers. Other hermits settled in the place, which became known as *Meinratszelle*. A little community of hermits came into being. In the late tenth century a certain Eberhardt refashioned the community into a conventional benedictine abbey.

---

[49] H. Grundmann, 'Eremiti in Germania dal X al XII secolo: "Einsiedler" e "Klausner' ", *L'Eremitismo in occidente nei secoli xi e xii*, Miscellanea del centro di studi medioevali 4 (Milan 1962) 313–314.

[50] P. Quivy, J. Tiron, 'Robert de Tombelaine et son commentaire sur le cantique des cantiques', *Millénaire monastique de Mont Saint-Michel*, ed. R. Foreville, 2 (Paris 1967) 347–356.

[51] Giles Constable, 'The Monastic Policy of Peter the Venerable,' *Cluniac Studies* (London 1980) 131–133.

Its name, 'Einsiedeln, taken from the german word for hermit, is a reminder of its eremitical beginnings.[52] During the tenth century successive abbots of Pomposa in northern Italy retired to live as solitaries on various islands at the mouth of the Po. From there they continued to direct the policies of their abbey, leaving day-to-day affairs to vicars.[53] In this case, hermits were ruling cenobites.

It was Saint Romuald of Ravenna (c. 952–1027) who did most to raise the prestige of the eremitical life. Throughout his career he insisted on its autonomy through a discipline appropriate to it, inspired by the many witnesses to its value in the writings of the early Christians.[54] Romuald was the son of a nobleman in the Ravennate in the north east of modern Italy. He entered the monastery of Sant'Apollinare in Classe in Ravenna as a penance, because his father had killed a relative in a judicial duel. After three years he left, disillusioned by the formal life of a conventional benedictine abbey, and went north to join Marino, an austere but ignorant hermit living in the marshes of the Veneto. Both ascetics soon realised that they needed guidance. Around 978 they fell in with Guarino, abbot of Saint Michael of Cuxa in the Pyrenees, who was visiting Venice. With some companions they followed the abbot to Catalonia and formed a community of hermits near his abbey. At Cuxa Romuald found a library of early christian ascetic works which provided a systematic basis for the theology and practice of the eremitical life.[55]

Romuald returned to Italy in 988. From then on he travelled from place to place, founding hermitages and at times preaching about simony and the evils of the time. There was always something experimental about his work. His knowledge of the hermit life was derived from reading. It was no easy task to put into practice the teachings of the Desert Fathers in the

---

[52] Grundmann (as n. 48), 316.
[53] G. Tabacco, 'Romualdo di Ravenna e gli inizi dell' eremismo camaldolese', in *L'Eremitismo in occidente* (as n. 48), 108.
[54] Ibid. 73–119.
[55] Ibid. 105–107.

conditions of contemporary Italy. He attracted the attention of the visionary emperor Otto III, who wanted to unite the hermits into a school for missionaries to the Slavs and Romuald allowed two of his followers to go to Poland, where they were martyred.[56] Inevitably, Otto and Romuald failed to understand one another. After the breach between them, Romuald abandoned the adriatic coast, the scene of his labours until this time. Around 1004 he founded a community in the forests of the Appenines. Here, and in the March of Tuscany, he was to live and preach until his death in 1027. Romuald's teachings were later summarised by a disciple:[57]

> Sit in your cell as if it were Paradise. Put behind your back the memory of the world. Be cautious about your thoughts, like a skillful fisherman angling for fish. One way is through the psalms—never neglect it. If, in your youthful fervour, you cannot manage them all, meditate now one psalm now another, and strive to understand with your mind. If your thoughts wander as you read do not give up, but carry on, and correct yourself by your understanding of the text. Before all else place yourself in the presence of God with fear and trembling, like one who stands before the face of the emperor. Destroy your will totally and sit there like a mule, content with the grace of God, not knowing what to do or to eat unless your mother gives it to you.[58]

Although Romuald always resisted any suggestion that hermits be placed under the rule of a cenobite, he was aware of their need for guidance and support. Complete isolation had its dangers. He gathered his hermits, therefore, into small communities. One of these was at Camaldoli, near Arezzo. There Romuald founded a hermitage around 1012. It consisted of a church dedicated to the Saviour and five cells separated from one anothers, each inhabited by one hermit. Romuald

---

[56] On this episode, see Jean Leclercq, 'St. Romuald et le monachisme missionnaire,' *Revue Bénédictine* 72 (1962) 307–323.
[57] Bruno of Querfurt.
[58] This passage is frequently quoted, see e.g. Tabacco (as n. 52), 89 n. 66; Leclercq (as n. 55), 311–312.

appointed 'the venerable hermit Peter' to preside over the
little community. A few properties provided a modest endowment which freed the hermits from secular cares.[59] In these
hermitages the ascetics contemplated God. Before entering
the enclosure, which was to be their 'prison', they gave all
their property to the poor. Self-flagellation was the supreme
mark of lives devoted to penance.[60]

The important part Romuald played in the revival of eremitical monasticism was recognised by his contemporaries,
who recognised him as: 'The first in our time to live according
to the Conferences of the Hermit Fathers';[61] 'Our spiritual
father of pious memory, the most famous hermit Romuald';[62]
'The memorable father of hermits'.[63] Apart from one brief
summary,[64] however, no extended record of his teaching survives. His sermons, though passionate, were rare. 'He held his
tongue, but his whole life was a sermon', wrote his biographer,
Saint Peter Damian.[65]

Peter Damian, a tireless propagandist for the eremitical
life, was by contrast a compulsive writer.[66] His surviving output
comprises about one hundred and seventy letters, fifty-three
sermons, seven saints' lives, and a large number of minor
treatises, liturgical compositions, poems, and epigrams.[67] He
was born in Ravenna around 1006. Little is known for certain
about his early life, but it is clear that he received an excellent
education. After some years as a teacher in his native city,
he became dissatisfied with worldly success. He considered
entering a monastery, but the turning point in his spiritual
quest came around 1035, when he was visited by two hermits
from Fonte Avellana in the Appenines. He was so moved by

[59] Tabacco (as n. 52), 52, 73–76.
[60] Ibid. 81.
[61] Ibid. 88.
[62] Ibid. 74.
[63] Ibid. 75.
[64] See above p. 147.
[65] 'Tacente lingua predicante vita.' Quoted by Tabacco (as n. 52), 82.
[66] F. Dressler, *Petrus Damiani: Leben und Werk* (Rome 1954).
[67] *New Catholic Encyclopaedia* 11 (1967) 214–215.

their holiness that he decided to accompany them back to their remote solitude.

At Fonte Avellana Peter found himself the only educated man in a community of rustics. They seem to have been somewhat overawed by him. The prior thought that the customary year's probation could be waived in his case. Presently he was ordained priest and soon found himself in demand in other hermitages as a preacher and spiritual director. Wherever he went he made good use of the monastic library. In 1042 he began to write the *Life of Saint Romuald*. The next year he was elected prior of Fonte Avellana, a position he held until his death in 1072. From there he founded other hermitages and monasteries. In 1057 Pope Stephen IX made him a cardinal of the Roman See. He acted as papal legate in Milan, Cluny, and Florence. Though a zealous proponent of church reform, he disliked his role as a churchman and tried several times to resign. He never forgave Hildebrand, the future Gregory VII, who had persuaded the pope to call him to the curia.

Peter Damian wrote two treatises about the eremitical life: *De ordine eremitarum et facultatibus eremi Fontis Avellani* (About the order of hermits and the institutions of the hermitage of Fonte Avellana)[68] and *De suae congregationis institutis ad Stephanum monachum* (About the rules of his community, addressed to Stephen the monk).[69] Convinced that hermits needed system and rule, he based his precepts on Palladius's *Lausiac History*, Sulpicius Severus's *Life of Saint Martin of Tours*, Cassian's *Conferences*, and other early ascetic works. He quoted these works more frequently than he did the Rule of Saint Benedict. His exhortation to the hermits at Fonte Avellana lists the books he had collected in the library for the edifictation of the brethren: the Bible of the Old and New Testaments with glosses, the passions of the holy martyrs, the homilies of the holy fathers, and commentaries on Scripture

---

[68] PL 145:327–336.
[69] PL 145:335–364. The treatises are analysed by Dressler, *Petrus Damiani*, 44–65.

by Saints Gregory, Ambrose, Augustine, Jerome, Prosper of
Aquitaine, and Bede, and by Amalarius and other authorities.[70]

Peter began from the assumption that a monastery was
useful only as a preparation for life in a hermitage or as a
refuge for those from whom little progress in the spiritual life
could be expected. 'For someone striving for the summit of
perfection, a monastery can be called an encampment not an
abode, not a home but a hospice, not the goal of his journey
but a rest on the way'.[71] His letters mention a few other ways
a monastery might be useful: the hermits might occasionally
attend the services in the monastic church, the cenobites could
give useful economic help to the hermitage and look after sick
and elderly hermits.[72]

There were twenty hermits at Fonte Avellana. They were
usually priests and lived either alone or two to a cell. They
ate together on great feasts, but otherwise they kept to their
cells except when the bell rang for morning Mass or Chapter.
There were also fifteen laybrothers who did the heavy work
of the community.[73] The hermits alone had the right to elect
the prior, who had to be one of themselves and not a cenobite.
He had not, however, the absolute powers or the prestige of
a benedictine abbot.[74] Entry into the community was either
through a monastery, in which case the postulant had to renounce the follies of cenobitic observance,[75] or, in the case
of very chosen souls, directly from the world. In the latter
instance the postulant was to be introduced to the customs of
the hermits gradually, but Peter was of the opinion that such
recruits were more to be valued, since a monastery often did
more harm than good.[76]

The hermits were bound to say the daily office of the
Church. If two brethren shared a cell they were bound to recite,

---

[70] PL 145:334.
[71] PL 145:393.
[72] Dressler (as n. 65), 43.
[73] Ibid. 45–46.
[74] PL 145:360.
[75] Ibid. 362.
[76] Ibid. 361.

every day, the entire psalter twice over, once for the living and once for the dead. They added the *Te Deum*, the *Nunc Dimittis*, the Nicene and Athanasian creeds, the *Gloria in excelsis Deo*, the Our Father, the Litany of the Saints with appropriate prayers, and the prayers attributed to Saint Romuald. A hermit who did not share his cell needed to say only one complete psalter and half of a second for the dead, unless he had the strength to complete it.[77]

Peter demanded heavy fasts from the brethren.[78] Their clothes were to be threadbare.[79] The long severe winters of the Apennines notwithstanding, they were allowed neither shoes nor socks.[80] There was to be little time for sleep.[81] They were to discipline themselves with flagellation,[82] which came to be so much a part of Peter's system that some believed that he had invented it.[83] In all this there was a tendency to measure spiritual progress by the quantity and severity of penances undertaken. Harsh though the practices he imposed were, Peter was ready with suggestions on how they could be exceeded.[84]

It is no small tribute to Cluny that in 1063, when Peter visited the abbey as papal legate, he was impressed by what he found.[85] He noted that the community contained 'many Pauls and not a few Anthonys'.[86] He was always devoted to Saint Benedict, as the hymn he wrote in honour of the saint shows.[87] His concentrated reading of the early monuments of monasticism, however, had made clear to him that the conventional interpretation of Saint Benedict's Rule was not necessarily the authentic, or the only one possible.

---

[77] Ibid. 343–344.
[78] Ibid. 331–332, 340.
[79] Ibid. 353.
[80] Ibid. 332, 343.
[81] Ibid. 332.
[82] Ibid. 331, 332.
[83] Dressler (as n. 65), 53.
[84] PL 145:346–347.
[85] De gallica profectione; PL 145:865–880.
[86] Ibid. 875.
[87] PL 145:957–958.

Peter always resented having been called out of his hermitage by the Holy See. In the troubled era of church reform
this was the fate of many a would-be recluse. Another victim
was Saint Bruno, an eminent teacher in the cathedral school of
Rheims.[88] Around 1080, he abandoned the life of the schools
and, with two companions, built a hermitage in a remote forest.
It turned out not to be remote enough. He was too well-known
to be left long in peace. To escape the crowds who sought him
out he looked for a site in Haute Savoie, in what is now the
french side of the Alps.

The community, including Bruno himself, now numbered
seven. In Savoy they found themselves in the diocese of Hugh,
bishop of Grenoble, one of the most attractive of the protagonists of church reform. Through his influence the companions found a refuge on the mountain known as La Grande
Chartreuse. The bishop supervised the building of a simple
hermitage and church, which he consecrated in 1084. It was
not the only time that Saint Hugh climbed the steep slopes and
found his way along remote tracks to visit a site which even
today, after nine hundred years, is almost inaccessible.

In 1088, however, Eudes de Chatillon, a former student
of Bruno at Rheims, was elected pope and took the name
Urban II. The situation of the Holy See was precarious and
the pope needed able assistants. In 1089 he summoned Bruno
to Italy. Bruno spent the rest of his life in the papal service
and died in 1101, without ever seeing La Grande Chartreuse
again. His departure almost spelled the end of the community.
The original owner of the mountain claimed it back, and the
hermits were obliged to abandon it for a time.

In southern Italy Bruno founded a hermitage where, in
between his official duties, he was allowed to live. His surviving letters betray a lyricism unknown to Peter Damian. He
could appreciate the landscape where his new hermitage was
situated.

---

[88] On Saint Bruno, see B. Bligny, *L'Église et les ordres religieux dans le royaume
de Bourgogne aux XI et XII siècles* (Grenoble 1960) 256–267.

What shall I say about the beauty of the site, its pure and healthy air, or the wide and hospitable plain, stretched out between the mountains? How can I adequately describe the green fields and pastures decked with flowers? How may I do justice to the distant views of hills rising gently all around, the hidden and shady valleys and the abundance of rivers, streams, and fountains?[89]

This loveliness provided all the relaxation an ascetic would need.

The divine joy which the solitude and silence of the hermitage provides its followers however, only they can know who have experienced it. Here the strong may enter into themselves whenever they wish and live alone, constantly nursing the seeds of goodness and nourished by the fruits of paradise. Here you may find that look whose keen glance lights upon the divine spouse, and which, through its clarity and purity makes God visible. Here leisure itself is functional and strength comes from inaction.[90]

The abrasive writings of Peter Damian,[91] might well give the impression that there was a 'hermit movement' critical of benedictine monasticism. In fact, the eremitic and cenobitic were parallel vocations and mutual hostility was very unusual. The hermits and solitaries, for instance, who frequented the woods and wetlands of Hainault, on either side of the modern border between France and Belgium, enjoyed friendly relations with their benedictine neighbours.[92] A good example is Aibert, who was born around 1065 near Tournai in modern Belgium.[93] After some years as a hermit, he was asked to accompany a local abbot on a journey to Rome. At the

---

[89] *Lettres des premiers chartreux*, ed. par un chartreux (Paris 1967) 68–69. The editor points out the general resemblance of this passage to one by Saint John Chrysostom, but adds that Bruno's is far more specific.

[90] Ibid. 70–71.

[91] See above p. 150.

[92] C. Dereine, 'Ermites, reclus et recluses dans l'ancien diocèse de Cambrai entre Scarpe et Haine,' *Revue Bénédictine* 97 (1987) 289–313.

[93] On Aibert, see ibid. 302–304.

monastery of Vallombrosa in Tuscany, one of the party became ill and Aibert stayed behind to look after him. Vallombrosa was a new and austere community.[94] Aibert was sufficiently impressed by it to decide, on his return to Hainault, to become a benedictine monk. After some years, during which he was entrusted with various monastic offices, he decided to return to the wilderness. In 1115 he constructed himself a hermitage in the valley of the river Haine. He was ordained, and given authority to hear confessions and impose penances. By the time of his death in 1140 he had become a popular preacher and confessor, as well as a noted advocate of church reform.

For a while it was thought that the revival of eremitic monasticism in the West was stimulated by greek ascetics, especially the numerous greek hermits and monks of southern Italy. This view has recently come under heavy criticism.[95] It is well to remember, however, that East and West did not exist in separate compartments. There was always contact, and before the crusading era it was not necessarily hostile. While a more modest view of the greek contribution to the rediscovery of the hermit life is in order, the part played by greek monks in the very early days of western church reform is well attested.

During the tenth century saracen raids on southern Italy, and particularly on Calabria, created a flood of refugee monks, some of whom eventually settled in the Holy Roman Empire. For a time the abbeys of Burtscheid, near Aachen, and Nonantola, near Modena, had greek abbots.[96] Greek monks

---

[94] See below pp. 161–166.

[95] M. Dunne, 'Eastern influences on western monasticism in the eleventh and twelfth centuries', *Byzantium and the West*: Proceedings of the 18th Spring Symposium of Byzantine Studies, Oxford 1984 (Amsterdam 1988) 245–259, with references to all the older literature. The article is critical of Bernard Hamilton and Patricia McNulty, 'Orientale lumen et magistra latinitas—Greek Influences on Western Monasticism (900–1100)', *Le millénaire de Mont Athos 963–1963* (Chevetogne) 191–216, in which the greek contribution to western monasticism in the tenth and eleventh centuries is given special prominence.

[96] A. Bayer, 'Griechen in Westen im 10 und 11 Jahrhundert: Simeon von Trier und Simeon von Reichenau', *Kaiserin Theophanu* ed. A. von Eeuw and P. Schreiner, 1 (Cologne 1991) 340.

are known to have found a haven at Gorze and Reichenau.[97] The cult of a certain Simeon of Achaia, believed to have been a monk at Reichenau, enjoyed some local popularity, though it is more likely that he is a fiction invented to account for the presence, among the abbey's relics, of one of the jars from the marriage feast at Cana.[98]

Another Greek called Simeon is better attested. He was born around 970 and brought up in Constantinople. As a young man he made a pilgrimage to the Holy Land. For many years he acted as a guide to pilgrims, helped by his knowledge of languages, especially Latin. His *Vita* reads like a novel. The endless journeys he made between east and west, braving pirates and dangerous sea crossings, must make him the patron saint of tourism. On his travels he made a number of eminent friends: Richard, abbot of Saint Vanne; Eberwin, abbot of Saint Martin in Trier; and Poppo, archbishop of Trier. It was the archbishop who finally found him a home. In 1032 Simeon was enclosed in the ruins of the majestic Porta Nigra at Trier and there he died three years later.[99] He is still remembered at Trier, but in that city of monasteries none showed any sign of greek influence, not even the community which eventually tended his shrine. As for the refugee monks elsewhere in the Empire, no doubt they accommodated themselves, as best they could, to the life around them.

The saracen raids on southern Italy where there was a considerable *indigenous greek population,[100] obliged a number of greek monks and hermits to seek security in Campania and Latium. Among the most famous of the refugees was Saint Nilus the Young.[101] Born in Rossano around 910, he acquired a reputation as the most admired abbot and holy man in southern

[97] Ibid. 337–338, 340.
[98] Ibid. 337–339.
[99] Ibid. 35–37.
[100] A. Guillon, 'Il monachesimo greco in Italia meridionale e in Sicilia nel medioevo,' *L'Eremitismo in Occidente* (as n. 48), 355–379, especially 360–361.
[101] On Saint Nilus, see ibid. 372–373; V. von Falkenhausen, 'Il monachesimo Italo-Greco e i suoi rapporti con il monachesimo Benedettino,' *L'Esperienza monastica e la Puglia* ed. C. D. Fonseca (Bari 1983) 1:127–129; J. M. Whale,

Italy. In the early 980s, his monastery near Rossano had to be abandoned. At Constantinople he was too much admired, says his biographer, and he therefore made for the latin regions of the north where his desire for obscurity could be satisfied.[102] Still too much honoured at Capua, he pressed on until he came with his followers to Montecassino.Abbot Aligernus offered him Vallelucio, one of the abbey's properties, and here Nilus and his community lived for fifteen years.[103]

Abbot Aligernus made sure that the Greeks were treated with consideration. Even so, with two communities with different linguistic and liturgical traditions living in close proximity, tensions were unavoidable.[104] After the abbot's death in 984, Nilus and his followers felt obliged to move, first to Serperi, near Gaeta, and then, after some years, to the ruins of a roman villa near the gates of Rome. Here, at Grottaferrata, the community was finally to settle, but Nilus died in September 1005, before actually reaching it.

However much he might shun publicity, Nilus was too eminent to remain in obscurity. At Montecassino the monks consulted him about the meaning of the monastic life, the interpretation of Scripture and the differences between Greeks and Latins.[105] In 998 he interceded in vain on behalf of John Philagathos, a Greek who had briefly driven Pope Gregory V from Rome and usurped the papal see. After a military campaign led by the Emperor Otto III to restore *status quo,* John was caught, cruelly mutilated, and imprisoned.[106] In the face of Nilus's pleas, pope and emperor were inexorable. The pope died soon afterwards. Some months later a repentant emperor visited Nilus. According to Nilus's biographer, Otto placed his crown in the saint's hand. In 1002 the emperor

'St. Bartholomew of Grottaferrata,' *Eastern Churches Quarterly* 11 (1956) 202–214.
[102] Βίος καί πολιτεία τοῦ ὁσίου πατρός ἡμῶν Νείλου τοῦ νέου, ed. G. Giovanelli (Grottaferrata 1972) 112.
[103] Ibid. 112–113; Von Falkenhausen (as n. 100), 128–129.
[104] Giovanelli (as n. 102), 113–117.
[105] Ibid. 114–117.
[106] Ibid. 126–128.

died and his ambitious plans for imperial government in Italy collapsed.[107]

The author of Nilus' biography was almost certainly Bartholomew, who took over the rule of Grottaferrata in 1012.[108] The abbot was often involved in the affairs of the papacy and of central Italy during this period.[109] Among the witnesses to a papal document of 1044, Bartholomew is the only one of eleven abbots described as *venerabilis*.[110] In 1048 it was he who persuaded Pope Benedict IX to resign to make way for the line of popes who championed the church reform.[111]

The speeches and sentiments attributed to Nilus by his biographer often have an eleventh-century flavour. Nilus's decision to leave Vallelucio is described this way:

> The number of the brethren had increased and there was a superabundance of all they needed. The monastery had become large and famous for its achievements, which had not been the case formerly. He saw that the brethren were no longer as intent upon spiritual combat and exact observance as they had once been. They had chosen the broad way, and contended with one another which was the greater. . . . When the holy man had seen all this, knowing that an increase in wealth is for many the cause of corruption and of the complete abandonment of religious discipline, he rose up and departed from there, seeking a retired spot which would provide the necessities of the body only after much labour, so that, nourished by penury alone, they might be coerced to the discipline of the ascetic life as by a bit.[112]

A little further north Peter Damian was saying much the same. Was Bartholomew himself influenced by the hermit movements of central Italy? Whatever may be the case, it

---

[107] Ibid. 129.
[108] Whale (as n. 101), 208. On Bartholomew's authorship of Nilus's *Vita*, see Giovanelli (as n. 102) 12–24.
[109] Details in Whale (as n. 101), 211–213.
[110] PL 141:1365.
[111] Whale (as n. 101), 213.
[112] Giovanelli (as n. 102), 123.

is most probable that the impact of the Greeks was local. Discussions about the nature of monasticism were a feature of the times and they very likely took place among the roman abbots. Here the local Greeks would have had a contribution to make, as the speeches put into Nilus's mouth show.[113]

---

[113] Ibid. 113–115.

Chapter 7
WHITE MONKS, BLACK MONKS

THE CHURCH REFORM of the eleventh century was in part a popular movement, bringing into the centre of church life people who had until then been on the margins. The general excitement during a six-year struggle to rid Florence of its simoniac bishop (1062–1068) is almost palpable in a contemporary account of the affair.[1] It was easy for the founders of new monastic movements, who were often deeply committed to reform, to identify with the poor. From this it was a short step to reject the wealth and elaboration associated with the great religious houses of the period.

The criticisms directed at traditional benedictine houses have persuaded some scholars that a crisis in western monasticism occurred at this time. In fact, this interpretation of developments during the eleventh century is difficult to prove. There was such a variety of religious movements that no single explanation will cover them all. There is no doubt that traditional benedictine houses were closely associated with the ruling classes. However austere the lives of individual monks, monastic chroniclers praised abbots who increased the properties of the house and constructed magnificent buildings. Good order in a monastery and prosperity were generally considered to go together; material and spiritual well-being were linked.[2] Two customs associated with this view were later to cause offense to the founders of strict communities: dowries and oblature. One was the offering of a gift when a

---

[1] P. di Re ed., *Biografie di Giovanni Gualberto al confronto* (Rome 1974) 63–66.
[2] John van Engen, 'The "Crisis of Monasticism" Reconsidered: Benedictine Monasticism in the Years 1050–1150', *Speculum* 61 (1986) 269–304, and especially 285–292.

person entered a monastery. Until the eleventh century this was regarded as perfectly normal and justifiable. It increased the monastery's endowments and prevented the new entrant from being a burden on the community. Once the church reform was under way, however, it was often condemned as 'simony'—the purchase of spiritual gifts. The other custom repudiated by later reformers was the offering of children (also accompanied by a gift) to monasteries. Child oblates are frequently mentioned by Saint Benedict, who saw nothing wrong with them. By the twelfth century, however, many monks saw them as an obstacle to good order, and monastic reformers usually insisted on recruits of mature age.[3]

Aside from these, there is no evidence for widespread decadence in traditional benedictinism during this period. It is true that Saint Peter Damian wrote a book condemning homosexuality among monks.[4] Occasional protests were voiced about the involvement of certain abbots in simony. Nevertheless, during the eleventh century, as we have seen, benedictine abbeys were at the height of their spiritual development. This was the age of Abbot Desiderius, Hugh of Cluny, William of Hirsau, John of Fécamp, and Anselm of Aosta. The pioneers of radical monasticism were not really faced with a decline in standards. The intolerance of innovators must not be forgotten. The Cluniacs themselves had looked down on monks whose customs differed from their own.[5] Norman monks in England thought the natives monks were not monks at all. So it is not surprising that Peter Damian should describe the conventional monasticism of his time as 'useless'.

Many of the leaders of the church reform combined popular agitation with learning. A general interest in the early documents of Christianity was reflected in monastic circles by a study of the beginnings of christian monasticism. Some, like Saints Romuald, Peter Damian, and Bruno, were inspired by

---

[3] J. H. Lynch, *Simoniacal Entry into Religious Life 1000–1260* (Columbus, Ohio 1976) 3–105.

[4] *Petri Damiani Liber Gomorrhianus;* PL 145: 159–190.

[5] See above p. 127.

pre-benedictine ideals. Others did not go so far. They accepted the Rule of Saint Benedict as the basis for the monastic life but interpreted it more literally than had become usual. Instead of great abbeys and elaborate liturgies, they preferred smaller houses, set away from centres of population. Instead of owning numerous estates, partly worked by serfs, they wanted monks to work the land themselves. Some communities lived this way by choice, others through force of circumstances. The monks of Evesham who lived in straitened circumstances in the revived monasteries of Wearmouth and Jarrow, for instance, do not seem to have been committed to poverty for they had no objection to accepting a more favourable site when it was offered by the bishop of Durham.[6]

Western monastic history during the eleventh century is best viewed as a period of vigorous experiment during which the great venture begun by Benedict of Aniane two centuries earlier was developing in various directions, not all of them compatible with one another. The excitement and controversy of the church reform movement encouraged boldness and radicalism.

One of the earliest of the more austere benedictine communities was at Vallombrosa in Tuscany, Italy. John Gualbert, its founder, was probably born in the•very last years of the tenth century.[7] Against the wishes of his family he became a monk at the abbey of San Miniato in Florence some time after 1025.[8] He was still very young[9] and, like a number of his contemporaries in Florence, was ardently committed to church reform. In 1035 he left San Miniato with a companion because its abbot had been involved in simony, and began to search for a community which would answer to his ideals.[10] Their first stop was at Camaldoli. Saint Romuald was not long

---

[6] See above p. 144.

[7] P. di Re, *Giovanni Gualberto nelle fonti dei secoli XI–XII* (Rome 1974) 19–24.

[8] Ibid. 27–28.

[9] 'Iuventute floridus', Di Re (as n. 1), 22.

[10] Ibid. 31–32. For the chronology of John's life, see ibid. 17, and Di Re (as n. 7), 7–8.

dead and life there was sufficiently austere, but John's vocation
was for 'the cenobitic life as the Rule of blessed Benedict describes it'.[11] John and his companion therefore left Camaldoli.
In the spring of 1036 they arrived at a remote place called
Vallombrosa, where two hermits, former monks of the abbey
of Settimo, were living with the permission of their abbot.
Here John settled and founded a new community.[12]

News of the foundation of Vallombrosa caused a schism
at San Miniato, some of whose monks left to join the new
community.[13] John was encouraged and protected by Guarino,
abbot of Settimo, a vigorous champion of church reform.[14] An
early benefactor was Itta, abbess of Saint Ilario, who was the
actual owner of the land on which the new monastery was
built.[15] In 1038 Rudolf, bishop of Padeborn, who had accompanied the Emperor Conrad's expedition to Italy, consecrated
the high altar of the monastery church.[16] In early documents
John was called 'Provost' of the community. His formal election
as abbot took place around 1050, and in 1058 the completed
monastery church was consecrated by a roman cardinal.[17]

In the course of time John founded and reformed other
monasteries in the area. He was a tireless champion of church
reform and at times his monks went around the diocese of
Florence preaching inflammatory sermons. Pope Alexander II
and his cardinals, who needed the support of Count Godfrey
of Tuscany, were far from pleased. At one point Peter Damian
called John Gualbert and his monks 'locusts who ravage the
green fields of Holy Church. Let the south wind arise and blow
them into the Red Sea!'[18]

In the midst of violence and controversy, then, Vallombrosa
became the centre of a little confederation of monasteries. At

---

[11] Di Re (as n. 1), 28–29.
[12] Di Re (as n. 7), 39.
[13] Di Re (as n. 1), 30.
[14] Di Re (as n. 7), 39.
[15] Ibid. 43.
[16] Ibid. 43.
[17] Ibid. 43–45.
[18] Di Re (as n. 1), 59.

the time of John Gualbert's death in 1073, it numbered nine houses, including Vallombrosa itself. John carried out frequent visitations.[19] During his thirty-seven years as a religious superior he shaped the development of the young institute.

John insisted on a very literal and strict interpretation of the Rule of Saint Benedict. With his first companions at Vallombrosa he 'chose to live not just according to the cenobite custom of monasteries, but to observe the law of the holy fathers, that is, of the apostles, of Saint Basil, and especially of Saint Benedict, about inexpensive clothing, humbleness of mind, and an exemplary way of life'. In this passage from the biography of John written by an anonymous disciple,[20] a distinction is drawn between the *consuetudo* (custom) of most cenobite monasteries and the *norma* (inviolable law) laid down by the holy fathers, especially Saint Benedict.

Poverty was an essential ingredient of vallombrosan monasticism. Once on a visit to the abbey of Moscheta John observed that the community had erected buildings which he thought too sumptuous. 'Have you constructed palaces in this place for your pleasure?' he asked the abbot. He left Moscheta in anger and soon after his departure, we are told, the nearby river rose and swept the buildings away.[21] John wanted his communities to support themselves through agricultural labour and to provide all that they needed for themselves. The monks' habits were woven from the wool of their own flocks and were grey instead of the conventional black. They ate their plain meals off bare tables without a tablecloth.[22]

For John the adoption of monastic poverty involved identification with the poor. During a time of famine he sold the copes in the church to raise money for those in distress. He encouraged the building of bridges and hostels for travellers. He involved himself, as we have seen, in the struggle for church

---

[19] Di Re (as n. 7), 49–53. On John as visitor see D. R. Duvernay, 'Cîteaux, Vallombreuse et Étienne Harding', *Analecta SOC* 8 (1952) 438–440.
[20] Di Re (as n. 1), 31.
[21] Ibid. 43–44.
[22] Ibid. 34–35.

reform. This meant not only a campaign against its opponents, but also the encouragement of the common life among clerics, and the restoration of ruined churches.[23]

Involvement with society created problems, particularly about monastic enclosure. John solved the difficulty by recruiting laymen or *conversi* (converts), who would be subject to monastic discipline and observe the same austerities as the monks, but who were not bound by the monks' strict discipline of silence. They could therefore be sent to markets and deal with business matters outside the precincts of the monastery.[24] Although Vallombrosa was not the first monastery to recruit lay brothers to do work not allowed to monks, it seems to have been the first whose economy depended on them so heavily.[25]

As long as he lived John personally directed the abbots of his dependent monasteries. He had appointed them all.[26] In 1073, as he lay dying, he was concerned about the survival of his congregation and its ideals. It seemed a simple matter. Charity had been the guiding principle of the little institute. 'To preserve it for ever,' he wrote in his testament,

> That fraternal unity which comes from obliging ourselves to accept the direction of one person is the most effective . . . And so, to make sure that charity remains among you always, it is my wish that after my death your concerns and policies should be guided by Father Rodolfo, as, during my life, they were by myself.[27]

Rodolfo, the former abbot of Moscheta, duly succeeded him.[28] The abbots present at John Gualbert's death may be said to have gone through a form of election. The new abbot of Vallombrosa held office for only three years (1073–1076),

---

[23] Ibid. 38–39.
[24] Ibid. 35.
[25] On the customs and organisation of Vallombrosa, see Duvernay (as n. 19), 379–493. On lay brothers, ibid. 415–423.
[26] E.g. abbot Rodolfo *ab illo ibi ordinatus fuerat abbas*, Di Re (as n. 1), 44.
[27] For the full text of John's letter, see ibid. 71–72.
[28] Ibid. 73.

but he introduced an important innovation. Every year he held a meeting of all the dependent abbots and some of the monks. The proceedings seem to have been fairly informal. The participants edified one another with incidents from Scripture, the lives of the fathers, or the life of John Gualbert.[29] No doubt problems common to them all were discussed as well. By the end of the eleventh century these meetings consisted of abbots only. 'They meet once a year,' wrote a biographer of Saint John Gualbert,

> always remembering the goodness, holiness, and precepts of their saintly first father. They make available to one another whatever they have under their care, their persons namely, and their properties, according to the decisions of the abbot of Vallombrosa, whom they have elected to rule over themselves in the place of John their first abbot'.[30]

The Vallombrosans provide the earliest example of a religious Order of the kind which was to become common. It was a confederation of monasteries each of which was engaged in agriculture. As well as monks who were bound to recite the offices in choir, the Vallombrosans recruited lay brothers who provided the backbone of the workforce and were not bound by strict monastic enclosure. There was a senior abbey, whose abbot shared the government with the other abbots. An annual meeting of all the abbots was the supreme authority of the order.

These arrangements are exactly like those of the Cistercians a generation later. It is natural to ask whether some knowledge of vallombrosan institutions had influenced the later Order. It would seem likely that this was so. Although vallombrosan houses were to be found mainly in central and northern Italy, there were, for a time, two small houses in France.[31] The only thorough investigation of this

---

[29] Ibid. 70.
[30] Ibid. 74.
[31] Duvernay (as n. 19), 455–456.

question, however, undertaken over forty years ago, ended inconclusively.[32]

In the generation after the death of John Gualbert, austere monasticism spread north of the Alps. The forests of Maine, on the border between the duchies of Normandy and Britanny in northern France, were home to numerous hermits. Four of them became famous. The oldest was Robert of Arbrissel, a breton priest who will be discussed in the next chapter. The others were Raoul de la Futaye, another Breton closely associated with Robert; Vitalis, a norman clerk who had given up a rich benefice; and Bernard, who had come to the forest from a conventional benedictine monastery. These men were priests who could dispense the sacraments and give spiritual advice and leadership to the other hermits in the area. They undertook preaching tours in which they castigated the evils of their time, particularly the sins of the rich and the corruption of the Church. From time to time the four leaders held conferences at which the problems of Church and society were discussed.[33]

Eventually each of the four leaders founded religious houses. Apart from Robert of Arbrissel, they adopted in the end the Rule of Saint Benedict interpreted in the light of their hermit experience. Some time before 1124 Raoul de la Futaye returned to his native Britanny and there founded for his followers the monastery of Saint Sulpice-la-Forêt, where a community of monks was assisted by some lay brothers.[34] In 1113 Vitalis, after lengthy negotiations, obtained land for a monastery in the norman forest of Savigny. In the years which followed, a monastery of women was attached. Almost nothing is known about the customs of the new community, except that the monks wore undyed robes instead of black, as reformed religious tended to do.[35] Such was the reputation of Savigny

---

[32] Ibid. 451–490.
[33] J. van Moolenbroek, *Vital l'ermite prédicateur itinérant, fondateur de l'abbaye normande de Savigny* (Maastricht 1990) 159–173.
[34] Ibid. 160, 364 n. 7.
[35] Ibid. 191.

that, after Vitalis's death in 1122, monasteries in subjection to it were founded in Normandy and England, forming a small 'Savignac' Order.[36]

Bernard had also originally settled in the forest of Savigny.[37] The proximity of Vitalis made a move necessary. In 1109 Bernard was granted land at Tiron on the properties of the church of Chartres. Bernard's hermit followers had been earning their keep by maintaining the crafts they had practised in the world. This craft tradition was maintained at Tiron.[38] In 1117, just before Bernard died, David, earl of Huntingdon and future king of Scotland, came to visit him and brought a group of monks back to his native land, settling them at Selkirk, near the border with England.[39] In 1128 the monks of Selkirk moved to Kelso and there began to build a magnificent monastery. Another royal abbey, Arbroath, was founded in 1178. Altogether the Tironensians had eight houses in Scotland.[40] Theirs was the first of the reformed benedictine orders to spread internationally.

Around 1100 Bishop Hugh of Grenoble, in the mountainous east of modern France, gave his estate at Chalais to a hermit also called Bernard. La Grande Chartreuse was not far away, but the bishop wanted Bernard and his followers to follow the Rule of Saint Benedict. Another monastery affiliated to Chalais was founded in 1140. Further foundations followed. The chalaisian monks lived on the slopes of remote mountains in the Dauphiné and Provence, and followed the life of woodmen and shepherds. Their Order flourished for

---

[36] Ibid. 180–199.

[37] On Bernard of Tiron, see L. Raison and R. Niderst, 'Le mouvement érémitique dans l'ouest de la France à la fin du XIe siècle et au début du XIIe', *Annales de Bretagne* 55 (1948) 2–45; DHGE 8 (1935) 754–755; *Dictionnaire de biographie française* 6 (1954) 90–91; J. de Bascher, 'La "Vita" de saint Bernard d'Abbeville, abbé de saint-Cyprien de Poitiers et de Tiron', *Revue Mabillion* 59 (1979) 411–416.

[38] Moolenbroek (as n. 33), 181.

[39] G. W. S. Barrow, *The Kingdom of the Scots* (London 1973) 174–176.

[40] J. B. Cowan and D. E. Easson, *Medieval Religious Houses: Scotland* (London 1976) 66–71.

about a century before being absorbed by the Carthusians and Cistercians.[41]

Reformed benedictine monasticism might have developed a pattern of local congregations spread all over western Europe. In fact, it came to be dominated by a great Order which had the leaders of genius, the organisation, the sense of purpose and, it must be said, the ruthlessness, to eclipse and sometimes to absorb the smaller groupings, and to become in itself the embodiment of all the new monastic ideals: the Cistercians.[42]

The history of the Cistercian Order begins with the turbulent career of Saint Robert of Molesme.[43] He belonged to a family of minor landowners in Champagne, in modern France. As a young man he became a monk in a benedictine abbey near the city of Troyes and rose to be prior. His reputation was such that he was elected abbot of a neighbouring house, but after a short time he returned to Troyes. From there he was called to be the superior of another monastery, but was again unsuccessful. In 1074 he joined a group of hermits in the forest of Collan, and in the next year obtained a site at Molesme in the burgundian diocese of Langres, where he could live with his followers.

Saint Robert favoured an austere interpretation of the Rule of Saint Benedict. The new foundation at Molesme attracted many recruits who were dissatisfied with monasticism of the cluniac variety. Soon the question of how their rigorous ideals were to be put into practice gave rise to passionate debates. In 1090 Robert himself left the abbey to join a group of hermits,

---

[41] B. Bligny, *L'Église et les ordres religieux dans le royaume de Bourgogne aux XIe et XIIe siècles* (Grenoble 1960) 395–440.

[42] From the vast bibliography on cistercian history the following are the most useful surveys: J. B. Mahn, *L'ordre cistercien et son gouvernement des origines au milieu du XIIIe siècle* (Paris 1951); J. M. Canivez, 'Cîteaux (ordre)', DHGE 12 (1951) 852–997; Ambrosius Schneider ed., *Die Cistercienser: Geschichte, Geist, Kunst* (Cologne 1974); L. J. Lekai, *The Cistercians: Ideals and Reality* (Kent, Ohio: Kent University Press 1977); J. B. Auberger, *L'unanimité cistercienne primitive* (Achel 1986).

[43] For what follows, see especially Lekai (as n. 42), 11–17.

but after some months he returned. The same year saw the temporary departure of four of his closest followers, including Alberic and Stephen, who were soon to play an important part in the cistercian movement. They returned after some months, but in 1096–1097 they led another group of protesters who settled at Aulps (Alps) in the diocese of Geneva.

Towards the end of 1097 Robert and his closest followers, including Alberic and Stephen, decided to break with Molesme once and for all. With the permission of Archbishop Hugh of Die, the papal legate in the region, they formed a new community. A benefactor granted them a remote site in the woods to the south of Dijon. The place was called Cîteaux, although in the early days the foundation was usually called simply the 'New Monastery'. Here Robert and his companions hoped that they could live out their ideals undisturbed. By rumours of their departure, however, the reputation of Molesme had been gravely compromised. The monks demanded that their abbot return and appealed to pope Urban II. In 1099 Archbishop Hugh of Die presided over a synod at which it was agreed that Robert should return to Molesme, taking with him those who found life at the New Monastery uncongenial.

Robert of Molesme's personality does not stand out clearly in the documents. He may have found it difficult to translate his ideals into practice. The experience of his erratic leadership could explain why his successors at Cîteaux tried to define their aims in writing. He seems eventually to have exasperated Archbishop Hugh of Die. The settlement of 1099 referred to Robert's 'usual instability'.[44] Archbishop Hugh was noted as an uncompromising reformer, 'more Catholic,' as the French say, 'than God himself.' Even so, it was unusual to put so personal a remark into an official document.

Most of Robert's followers seem to have gone back to Molesme with him, leaving the New Monastery struggling for survival. According to one authority only eight monks

---

[44] *Les plus anciens textes de Cîteaux*, ed. J. C. Bouton and J. B. van Damme (Achel 1974) 65.

remained.[45] It was left to his prior and the new abbot, Alberic, to guide the community through its darkest days. In 1100 he obtained a papal privilege, which confirmed the arrangements with Molesme made by Archbishop Hugh and encouraged the monks of this small reformed community to persevere.[46]

The early days at Cîteaux were hard. The site was difficult to cultivate.[47] The area was badly drained, and streams, ponds, and marshland abounded. The name Cîteaux is thought to come from *cistelli*, the latin word for reeds. Encroachment upon the ubiquitous forest had already begun before the monks arrived. In the clearings and on the edges of the woods were human settlements with the inhabitants of which the monks of the New Monastery had to come to terms. A much larger estate than the one originally granted was required to ensure religious solitude. To obtain this it was necessary to win the good will of the local lords. It was only in 1110–1111 that the New Monastery acquired the endowments which ensured its future as a viable religious house.

By this time Alberic had been succeeded as abbot by the Englishman Stephen Harding.[48] Stephen had once been an oblate of the benedictine abbey of Sherborne in Dorset, England, and had left, probably as a result of the disturbances following the norman conquest of England in 1066.[49] He had gone first to Scotland and then to northern France, where he studied at one of the schools. Then, accompanied by another exiled Englishman, he journeyed to Rome. On their return to France the two men became monks at Molesme. Both were associated with the reforming party which gathered around Abbot Robert and they followed him to Cîteaux. After the

---

[45] Lekai (as n. 42), 15.

[46] *Les plus anciens textes* (as n. 44), 74–75.

[47] On the physical geography of Cîteaux and the early history of the abbey's estates, see A. Saint-Denis, 'L'évolution du paysage autour de l'abbaye—de la naissance à l'apogée: 1098–1250', *Pour une histoire monumentale de l'abbaye de Cîteaux*, ed. M. Plouvier and A. Saint-Denis (Dijon-Vitreux 1998) 43–65.

[48] H. E. J. Cowdrey, 'Quidam frater Stephanus nomine, anglicus natione', *Revue Bénédictine* 101 (1991) 322–340.

[49] Ibid. 328.

settlement of 1099 Stephen remained in the New Monastery, while his friend accompanied Robert back to Molesme. Even so, the friendship between the two persisted.

Saint Stephen was a man of energy and he had a more than local reputation. He managed to attract to the New Monastery the endowments which ensured its survival.[50] A man of learning, he shared the contemporary interest in original sources. Uninfluenced by the prevailing antisemitism of his time, he did not hesitate to involve jewish rabbis in a gigantic work of standardising the Vulgate text of the Bible.[51] He tried to regulate the chant used by his monks by returning to what he considered to be the authentic hymns written by Saint Ambrose. These and no others were to be used at the New Monastery.[52] With his encouragement fine manuscripts were produced for Cîteaux.[53]

There is ample evidence that Stephen was a firm, even authoritarian, superior.[54] He gave his followers a sense of purpose. Soon there were enough recruits at Cîteaux to make possible the foundation of colonies. The first group of monks was sent out in 1113 to La Ferté, some fifty kilometres to the south of Cîteaux.[55] The next followed in 1114 to settle at Pontigny about a hundred kilometres to the north east, near the ancient city of Auxerre.[56] With three houses at some distance from one another, Stephen was concerned that the austere interpretation of the Rule of Saint Benedict which he had encouraged at Cîteaux should be maintained by all his followers. Bishop Humbald of Auxerre and his chapter were consulted. According to a reliable twelfth-century source, 'The

[50] J. Marilier, *Chartes et documents concernant l'abbaye de Cîteaux* (Rome 1961) 57–92.
[51] Ibid. 56 (No. 32).
[52] Ibid. 55 (No. 31). See Chrysogonus Waddell, *The Twelfth Century Cistercian Hymnal* (Gethsemani Abbey/Cistercian Publications 1984) 1:18–22; 2:12.
[53] On manuscript production at Cîteaux under Stephen Harding, see Auberger (as n. 42), 190–204.
[54] Cowdrey (as n. 47), 324–325.
[55] Marilier (as n. 50), 65–66 (No. 42).
[56] Ibid. 66 (No. 43).

bishop and the chapter of canons gave their full agreement
to a charter of charity and unanimity, which was drawn up
and approved between the New Monastery and the abbeys
founded from it'.[57]

This earliest text of the *Carta Caritatis*, the fundamental
constitution of the Cistercian Order, has not survived. It is
clear that the document underwent many revisions. The oldest
version which now survives dates from 1119, the year in which
Pope Calixtus II confirmed it.[58] Frequent revisions of the text
were made necessary by the rapid expansion of the Order.[59]
There were twelve abbeys by 1119.[60] In 1120 the first cistercian
community was founded in Italy. The Cistercians appeared in
Germany in 1123 and in England in 1129.[61]

Saint Stephen resigned as abbot of Cîteaux in 1133 and
died the next year.[62] By this time the Cistercian Order had
spread all over western christendom. In his last years Stephen's
reputation was overshadowed and his Order dominated by the
most famous abbot in its history—Saint Bernard of Clairvaux.[63]

---

[57] Ibid. 66 (No. 43).

[58] Auberger (as n. 42), 32–33; 35.

[59] J. B. van Damme, 'Les textes cisterciennes de 1119', *Cîteaux* 34 (1983) 92–110.

[60] See charts in F. van der Meer, *Atlas de l'ordre cistercien* (Paris-Brussels 1965) i–vii.

[61] Lekai (as n. 42), 36–38.

[62] On the resignation, see Cowdrey (as n. 47), 336.

[63] There is, as yet, no adequate modern biography of Saint Bernard. The standard work remains E. Vacandard, *Vie de St. Bernard* (1910). In English there is Watkin Williams, *St. Bernard of Clairvaux* (Manchester 1935). See also Etienne Gilson, *The Mystical Theology of St. Bernard* (London 1955-rpt. Kalamazoo 1990); Jean Leclercq, *Saint Bernard of Clairvaux and the Cistercian Spirit* (Kalamazoo 1976); Benedicta Ward ed., *The Influence of Saint Bernard: Anglican Essays* (Oxford 1976); Basil Pennington ed., *Saint Bernard of Clairvaux: Studies Commemorating the Eighth Centenary of his Canonisation* (Kalamazoo 1977); G. R. Evans, *The Mind of St. Bernard of Clairvaux* (Oxford 1983); John R. Sommerfeldt ed., *Bernardus Magister* (Kalamazoo 1990).
The standard edition of the writings of Saint Bernard is *Sancti Bernardi Opera*, edd. J. Leclercq, C. H. Talbot, and H. M. Rochais, 8 vols. (Rome 1957–1978). In this study quotations from treatises are from *Sancti Bernardi Opera Omnia* ed. J. Mabillon (Paris 1839). Letters are quoted from the translation by Bruno Scott James, *The Letters of St. Bernard of Clairvaux* (London 1953-rpt Stroud-Kalamazoo 1998).

Bernard was born around 1090 near Dijon. His father was a knight. Both his parents were devout Christians. He received a good education in the local schools. As a young man he felt drawn to the monastic life and particularly to Cîteaux, which was acquiring a considerable reputation under Saint Stephen Harding. In 1113 he joined the community, having persuaded thirty friends and relatives to do the same. Two years later Saint Stephen sent him with a party of others to Clairvaux in Champagne, to the north of Cîteaux. Here a new community under Bernard as its abbot attracted so many recruits that it was able to found its first colony as early as 1118.

The success of the 'new monasticism' caused doubt and contention in more traditional houses. It was only a matter of time before differences of interpretation became a matter of dispute within Cluny itself.[64] Bernard involved himself in the controversy about monastic observance with an open letter[65] and a treatise.[66] In the years after 1118, the earliest of his writings on the spiritual life were also beginning to circulate.[67] He was already, therefore, one of the better known and more articulate spokesmen for the new ideas when a papal schism in 1130 thrust him into the heart of the affairs of Christendom.

On the death of Pope Honorius II, the Roman See was disputed between Cardinal Gregory of Sant'Angelo, who took the title Innocent II, and Cardinal Peter Leonis of Santa Maria in Trastevere, who took the title Anacletus II.[68] It was once believed that the papal court was split between the supporters of the old monasticism and the new, the party of Anacletus

---

[64] See A. Bredero, 'Cluny et Cîteaux au XIIe siècle; les origines de la controverse', *Studi Medievali* ser. 3, 12 (1971) 135–175.

[65] Ep. 1; trans. Bruno Scott James (as n. 63), 1ff.

[66] Apologia ad Guillelmum, *Opera* ed. Mabillon as n. 63, 2, 1220–1246.

[67] On the chronology of Saint Bernard's earliest writings, see C. J. Holdsworth, 'The Early Writings of Bernard of Clairvaux', *Cîteaux* 45 (1994) 21–61, especially the chronological table, pp. 58–60.

[68] On the events of the election, see H. Bloch, *Monte Cassino in the Middle Ages,* 2 (Cambridge Mass. 1986) 943–960.

representing the old, and that of Innocent its critics.[69] The election of Innocent had been engineered by Cardinal Haimeric, chancellor of the Roman See, who certainly had connections with Bernard and other leaders of reformed monasticism. Among Innocent's supporters, however, were Peter the Venerable, abbot of Cluny, and the cluniac cardinal Matthew of Albano, an uncompromising advocate of the old monasticism.

When Innocent II was driven from Rome, he took refuge across the Alps. Bernard supported his cause with energy and enthusiasm. 'The Church supports him with good reason,' he wrote, 'for it has learned that his reputation is more fair and his election more sound'.[70] History has confirmed neither assertion. In any case, Bernard knew only one of the candidates and had no means of judging the circumstances of the election. The only concrete fact available was Anacletus' jewish descent through his great-grandfather. 'It is to the injury of Christ,' wrote Bernard, 'that a man of jewish race has seized for himself the See of Peter'.[71]

In 1138–39, after military intervention by the Emperor Lothar, Innocent's cause eventually triumphed. The pope owed much to Bernard's brilliant advocacy, and the Cistercians were rewarded with support and privileges. Bernard's attempts to curb Innocent's vindictiveness eventually lost him favour at the papal court.[72] The situation changed in 1145, when a cistercian monk, a former pupil of Bernard, was elected pope as Eugenius III. It was a measure of the importance of the Cistercian Order and of the abbot of Clairvaux that the pontiff himself presided over the Chaper General in 1147. On this occasion the Order of Savigny, with its twenty-nine houses, and the smaller Orders of Obazine and Cadouin were incorporated into the Cistercian Order.[73] By the middle of the

---

[69] H. Klewitz, 'Das Ende des Reformpapstums', *Deutsches Archiv* 3 (1939) 372–412.

[70] Ep. 125; Scott James 128.

[71] Ep. 139; Scott James 142.

[72] Ep. 213; Scott James 283.

[73] J. M. Canivez, *Statuta Capitulorum Generalium ordinis Cisterciensis*, 1 (Louvain 1933) s.a. 1147; Lekai (as n. 42), 36.

twelfth century the Order numbered around three hundred fifty houses for men.[74]

It was natural that the rhetorically brilliant Bernard should be asked to preach the Second Crusade, called to relieve the Christians in the Holy Land. He threw himself into the work with his customary zeal. When popular excitement gave rise to anti-jewish riots, he forgot his former antisemitism and defended the victims.[75] The Crusade's miserable failure greatly damaged his prestige. He was not spared the recriminations which attend any fiasco, as we can see from the agonised *apologia* in his treatise *On Consideration*.[76] The clouds had not yet cleared at the time of his death 1153. For a time, especially in the pontificate of Adrian IV (1154–1159) there was a reaction against his influence and that of his Order.

Bernard's greatness lies in his theology. He realised that the greater austerity of the new monasticism required a corresponding deepening of a monk's spirituality. He investigated and, as far as he could, described the Christian's incorporation into the life of the Godhead. Here, and in his discussions of the monastic life, he displayed a prudence and balance often lacking in his public activities. As with every genius his work astonishes not only by its quality but also by its quantity. During the thirteenth century his writings became unfashionable, but they enjoyed a revival in the late Middle Ages and never again lost their place among the masterpieces of western spirituality. Bernard was not only a great theologian, but also a magnificent stylist. He condemned the unnecessary decoration of monastic churches,[77] but neglected no device to embellish his own prose. The beauty of his Latin defies translation.

In the Western Church the eleventh and twelfth centuries were a time of mass movements in religion. Peter the Hermit persuaded thousands to join his ill-considered crusade to the east. Contemporaries spoke of vast numbers of monks: five

---

[74] Lekai (as n. 42), 34.
[75] Ep. 365; Scott James 393.
[76] *De consideratione* 2.1; *Opera*, ed. Mabillon (as n. 63), 2:1022–1024.
[77] *Apologia* 12.28–29; *Opera*, ed. Mabillon (as n. 63), 2:1242–1243.

hundred at Clairvaux under Saint Bernard, eight hundred at Rievaulx in Yorkshire in the time of his contemporary Saint Aelred.[78] Many medieval writers had difficulties expressing large numbers with precision and we may therefore suspect that figures are exaggerated, but the impression of great multitudes is inescapable. In an atmosphere of popular excitement, leaders were more important than documents. By his preaching, Bernard made a profound impression on his contemporaries. The Cistercian Order of his time contained other recruits of quality: Guerric of Igny, Isaac of Stella (l'Étoile), Aelred of Rievaulx, and many others. Their teaching and example gave the Order its dynamism.

At all times, the written documents of the cistercian reform were subordinate to the oral teaching and leadership of its abbots. In fact, the text of the *Carta Caritatis* was easily changed. We can distinguish four stages. First came the original text of 1114. It has not survived, but is presumably embedded in the expanded text which was confirmed by Pope Paschal II in 1119—the text now known to scholars as the *Carta Caritatis Prior*.[79] It was in force during the lifetime of Saint Bernard. After his death there was another revision, known to scholars as the *Carta Caritatis Posterior*.[80] Finally the prologue to the document was extensively revised in 1316.[81]

In its earlier form the *Carta Caritatis* was composed by Saint Stephen Harding and the wording of some sections reflect his imperious will.[82] The aim was to maintain the original ideals intact. Abbot Stephen stated that he wished to retain 'cure of souls' of the abbots of houses founded from Cîteaux, 'So that if ever they try to deviate, even a little, from their holy resolution and the observance of the Holy Rule,

---

[78] Lekai (as n. 42), 44.

[79] For the text of the *Carta Caritatis Prior*, see *Les plus anciens textes* (as n. 44), 89–102.

[80] *Les plus anciens textes* (as n. 44), 132–142. English translation in Lekai (as n. 42), 461–466.

[81] J. B. van Damme, 'Le prologue de la charte de charite', *Cîteaux* 36 (1985), 115–128.

[82] Cowdrey (as n. 47), 324–325.

which God forbid, they may return to true observance through our vigilance'.[83] For this reason the abbots were to assemble annually for a chapter at Cîteaux and submit themselves to abbot Stephen and his community for the correction of faults, showing themselves obedient in all matters which concerned the observance of the Rule and the discipline of their order. They could also come to the aid of any abbey which was in financial or other difficulties.[84]

Discipline was also to be maintained by a system of visitations. Every abbot was to visit annually all the houses which his monastery had founded.[85] Thus the 'filiations' characteristic of the Cistercian Order came into being: each abbey had a mother house stretching back in line to the original community at Cîteaux. A mother house could not, however, hold a separate annual chapter with the houses it had founded.[86] To emphasize the superiority of Cîteaux, it was decreed that the Rule of Saint Benedict should be everywhere interpreted as it was in the New Monastery. Throughout the Order all the service books were to conform to those of the common mother house.[87]

The election of a cistercian abbot was to take place in the presence and with the advice of the abbot of the mother house (the 'father abbot'). The election of an abbot of Cîteaux was to be supervised by as many cistercian abbots as could be assembled within fifteen days.[88] An errant abbot was to warned to amend by the abbot of Cîteaux. If he refused, the bishop of the diocese and his canons were to be asked to depose him. Only if the diocesan authorities were negligent could the abbot of Cîteaux, associating other abbots with him, depose the culprit or, if his whole community condoned his conduct, proceed to expel the house from the Order. An errant abbot of Cîteaux was to be warned by the abbots of La Ferté, Pontigny,

---

[83] *Les plus anciens textes* (as n. 44), 91.
[84] Ibid. 95, 96.
[85] Ibid. 94.
[86] Ibid. 96.
[87] Ibid. 92–93.
[88] Ibid. 101–102.

and Clairvaux. If he was defiant they were to follow a similar procedure, associating with themselves all the daughter houses of Cîteaux.[89]

When the *Carta Caritatis Prior* was composed the Order still consisted of houses in Burgundy and Champagne. In the years which followed it spread throughout western Christendom. For twenty years the dominant figure had been the abbot of Clairvaux. These circumstances are reflected in the *Carta Caritatis Posterior.* According to this revision, the abbey of Cîteaux was to undergo an annual visitation from the four senior abbots of the order: La Ferté, Pontigny, Clairvaux, and Morimond.[90] In the annual chapter of abbots, now known as the Chapter General, the abbot of Cîteaux had no special powers. The chapter itself was the supreme authority. Attendance every year was obligatory for all abbots except those who lived in remote areas; with them the chapter could make special arrangements.[91] Elections of abbots were to be supervised by father abbots or, in the case of Cîteaux, the abbots of the mother house's four senior daughters.[92] Father abbots, or, in the case of Cîteaux, these four senior abbots, were responsible for deposing errant abbots. The local bishop and his clergy were no longer to be involved.[93]

In his *Apologia to Abbot William*, written around 1124.[94] Bernard tried to distinguish the chief characteristics of cistercian monasticism: 'A diet that is lean and unlovely. . . . the well known cheapness and roughness of our clothes, the sweat of daily toil, our continual fasts and vigils'.[95] These ideals were embodied in the legislation of the Chapter General, particularly

---

[89] Ibid. 97–98.
[90] Ibid. 134.
[91] Ibid. 135–136.
[92] Ibid. 137.
[93] Ibid. 140–142.
[94] *Apologia ad Guillelmum* (as n. 66).
[95] Ibid. 1220. *Opera*, ed. Mabillon (as n. 63) 2:1220. Translation by Michael Casey ocso, *Bernard of Clairvaux, Treatises* 1 (Spencer-Kalamazoo-Shannon 1970) 34; rpt as *Cistercians and Cluniacs: The Case for Citeaux. The Apologia to Abbot William* (Kalamazoo) 34.

in the collection of statutes known as the *Instituta Capituli Generalis*.[96] The Cistercians wanted recruits genuinely called to monastic life and renounced the child-oblates allowed in the Rule of Saint Benedict. No one under fifteen years of age was to enter the novitiate.[97] The extra articles of clothing and bedding allowed to the Benedictines by the Aachen legislation were also rejected. There were strict regulations about simplicity in worship. The altar cloths and vestments were to be of plain material and only the priest's stole and maniple could be of silk. The altar vessels were to be neither of gold or silver nor decorated with jewels, except for one chalice and the tube with which the communion wine was sucked up—these might be of silver and could be gilded.[98] Gold, to the use of which in monastic churches Saint Bernard had strenuously objected,[99] was to be completely excluded from the sanctuary. Chasubles were to be of one colour.[100] The Cistercians also rejected most of the extra processions and ceremonies which had become a feature of traditional benedictine life. They returned, in principle, to the seven traditional services, retaining from the additions to the Rule only the daily conventual mass, the daily chapter, and occasional masses for the dead.[101]

All abbeys were to be dedicated to the Virgin Mary[102] and were to be situated in the country 'far from the haunts of men'.[103] Cistercians were to reject such sources of revenue as income or tithes from parish churches, rents, manors, villeins, or profits from furnaces or mills.[104] They were to live by the fruits of their own labour, tilling the soil and tending flocks or vines, so long as these activities were conducted

---

[96] Canivez, *Statuta* (as n. 73), s.a. 1134.
[97] Ibid. 1134, 78.
[98] Ibid. 1134, 4, 10.
[99] *Apologia* 12.2; *Opera*, ed. Mabillon (as n. 63), 2:1242–1243.
[100] Canivez, *Statuta*, 1134, 10.
[101] *Les 'Ecclesiastica Officia' cisterciens du XIIe siecle*, ed. D. Choisselet and P. Vernet (Reiningue 1989) 32–35, 192–245.
[102] Canivez, *Statuta*, 1134, 18.
[103] Ibid. 1134, 1.
[104] Ibid. 1134, 9.

3 The Cistercian Abbey of Chorin

in remote areas.[105] On outlying estates, farmhouses known as granges were erected as subordinate centres of economic activity. Choir monks who were sent there had to return to their monastery as soon as possible.[106]

The necessary continuity of work on the land, especially in outlying properties, could not be combined with the monks' duties in choir. The introduction of lay brothers who would bear the main burden of labour in the fields is attributed to abbot Alberic.

> Thereupon they decided to admit with the permission of their bishop, bearded lay-brothers and to treat them in life and death as their equals, excepting only the status as monks; and to admit also hired workers.[107] For they realized that without the help of these men they would be unable to observe fully the precepts of the Rule by day and by night. . . . And while they established granges for the practice of agriculture in a number of places, they decreed that the aforementioned lay brothers, and not the monks, should manage those houses, because according to the Rule the dwelling place of monks ought to be within their cloister.[108]

The attribution to Alberic of this innovation unknown to the the Rule is more than likely. After most of the monks who had followed Robert had returned with him to Molesme, the eight who remained to cultivate an unpromising terrain had their work cut out.[109]

In the twelfth and thirteenth centuries lay brothers were essential to every cistercian abbey. They dominated the granges. Their prayers were simple. Instead of reciting the Divine Office, they attended a daily Mass and recited a prescribed number of 'Our Fathers' in the fields. Their fasts were less rigorous than those of the monks. In the early

---

[105] Ibid. 1134, 5.
[106] Ibid. 1134, 59.
[107] The Latin is equally awkward.
[108] *Les plus anciens textes* (as n. 44), 78. Translation in Lekai (as n. 42), 459.
[109] Auberger (as n. 42), 167–168.

years the laybrotherhood proved attractive to knights, but it was soon reserved for the unlettered lower classes, who here, for the first time, found an opportunity to enter the religious life.[110]

The contrast between the Order's legislation and its actual practice, between 'ideals and reality' has often been stressed. In 1178, for instance, Sambor, prince of Pomerania endowed the abbey of Oliwa, near Gdansk in modern Poland, with the land on which the abbey stood and also with seven villages, the tithes of the market booths by the castle of Gdansk, a tithe of the prince's toll and of his cattle, a tithe from the local fisheries, free fishing of sea and river fish, and freedom from tax for all its ships, its goods, and its men.[111]

The fact is that the rules were always subordinate to the inspiration of the leaders on the spot. The monk's most visible source of authority was his abbot. In his treatise, *De praecepto et dispensatione*, Saint Bernard discussed the abbot's dispensatory power. Bernard distinguished between the law of God— such as 'Thou shalt not kill, thou shalt not commit fornication', which was valid for all people and from which there could be no dispensation[112]—and the Rule of Saint Benedict—which was no more than an exhortation, except for monks who had sworn to observe it.[113] In the latter case, a dispensation from a particular observance could be granted from necessity. The guiding principle was charity.[114] Moreover, the abbot must always bear in mind the spiritual principles upon which the Rule was based. These must never be violated. The abbot was not above the Rule. The regular life was subject, not to his will, but to his discretion.[115] A distinction was also made between the more and the less important precepts of the Rule.[116]

[110] Lekai (as n. 42), 334–346.
[111] G. Nitschke, *Die Kathedrale zu Oliva* (Hildesheim 1963) 4–5.
[112] *De praecepto et dispensatione* 1.1–3.8; Mabillon, *Opera* (as n. 63), 2:1175–1179.
[113] Ibid. 1175–1176.
[114] Ibid. 1177.
[115] Ibid. 1179–1181
[116] Ibid. 1183–1185.

Saint Bernard, of course, was writing about the Rule of Saint Benedict and not the statutes of the Chapter General. One might assume, then, that if dispensations from the Rule were possible, this would be even more true of the order's legislation. In any case, the coherent picture presented by the *Instituta Capituli Generalis* is probably misleading. These Institutes are traditionally dated to 1134 because a seventeenth-century cistercian scholar placed them under the year Saint Stephen Harding died.[117] Recent research implies that, while some of the statutes are very early, others could have been incorporated at any time during the first half of the twelfth century. There are, moreover, manuscripts in which some statutes have been scratched out and others added.[118] It is clear that the Order's legislation grew piecemeal, with a great deal of trial and error.

In such circumstances there would always have been room for disagreement. Modern scholarship emphasises disunity in the Order rather than unity. In the light of experience Saint Stephen Harding seems to have modified some of the radicalism of the early days. The line followed at Clairvaux under Saint Bernard was more rigid. In the generation after Stephen Harding's death the leading abbots of the Order, including the abbot of Cîteaux, were all former monks of Clairvaux. Saint Bernard's influence was paramount, and the Order was pulled back from compromise.[119]

According to the *Carta Caritatis posterior*, abbots from distant regions could attend the Chapter General less often than once a year.[120] When they did come, then, they were 'outsiders'; unfamiliar with the procedures or the inner tensions. Those who came annually could dominate the proceedings. The contrast between the Order's legislation and reality on the ground must have been partly geographical.

---

[117] A. Manrique, *Annales Cistercienses*, 1 (Lyons 1642) 272–282.
[118] Auberger (as n. 42), 61–62.
[119] Ibid. 314–315.
[120] See above n. 91.

In the early twelfth century monastic exemptions from
episcopal authority had alienated the bishops. The privileges
of the ancient benedictine abbeys had earned them powerful
enemies. To reform-minded prelates, the early Cistercians,
with their insistence on humility, seemed more acceptable.
Saint Bernard was opposed to exemptions of any kind in the
Church, 'whereby bishops become more insolent, and monks
more dissolute'.[121] Even in his day, however, the situation was
changing. In 1132 Innocent II exempted cistercian abbots
from attendance at diocesan synods. In 1152 Eugenius III
allowed them to continue to hold services even in territories
under interdict. In 1169 Pope Alexander III conceded that
if a local bishop refused to bless a new cistercian abbot, the
elect could receive his benediction from any catholic bishop.
In addition, no bishop could threaten a cistercian abbey with
ecclesiastical sanctions. All these privileges were confirmed by
a bull of Lucius III in 1184.

The greatest ill feeling, however, was caused by cistercian
exemption from tithes. In theory every piece of cultivated land
was subject to a tax of a tenth from all profits for the support
of the Church The payments were made to the parish priest
who divided them into four portions: one part each for the
bishop, the priest, the church fabric, and the poor. In the
eleventh century many churches, and their attached tithes,
were acquired by monasteries.

The Cistercians felt that monasteries should not be endowed in this way. Tithes were among the properties they
renounced. They concluded , therefore, that they should not
pay tithes from their own lands. Where they had cleared land
themselves this created no problems. The difficulties arose
when they acquired land on which tithes had previously been
paid. In 1132 Innocent II declared that they should not pay
tithe for any land they owned. In the 1150s some churches
and monasteries began to suffer as Cistercians acquired land
which had previously been subject to the tithes. In 1156 pope

---

[121] *De consideratione* 4.16; Mabillon, *Opera* (as n. 63), 2:1050.

Adrian IV made a distinction between land cleared by the monks themselves and land already in cultivation. The former was to be free from tithes; the latter should continue to pay.

In 1159 there was another papal schism. Alexander III, the candidate favoured by the church reformers, took refuge for a time in France. He was loyally supported by the Cistercians. The situation of 1130–1138 was repeated. In the matter of tithes the grateful pope was ready to return to the position before 1156, but the unpopularity of the Cistercians increased until the Chapter General grew alarmed and tried to hold further acquisitions of tithed land in check. The matter was finally settled at the Fourth Lateran Council of 1215. All cistercian land acquired before 1215 was judged exempt, but tithes were liable from everything acquired afterwards, whether it was newly cleared or not.[122]

By the end of the twelfth century their exemptions and privileges had made the Cistercians many enemies, but the Order had been dogged by controversy since its foundation. The exodus of 1099 involved criticism of Molesme, 'a laxer monastery' as the papal confirmation of 1100 had put it.[123] More serious was Saint Bernard's involvement with the internal tensions of the abbey of Cluny.[124]

The appearance of so many religious communities following the 'new monasticism' had an unsettling effect. The bitter controversy which had led to the original schism at Molesme was repeated, probably many times, in monasteries of the traditional type. In 1132–1133, for example, there were two parties in the abbey of Saint Mary at York, England, bitterly divided about the observance of the Rule of Saint Benedict. In the end, the monks of the stricter party, with the encouragement of Saint Bernard, left the abbey and settled in a remote yorkshire valley which they called Fountains.[125]

---

[122] Lekai (as n. 42), 65–68.

[123] *Les plus anciens textes* (as n. 44), 75.

[124] Bredero (as n. 64), 135–175.

[125] David Knowles, *The Monastic Order in England* (Cambridge 1950) 231–237.

It can be a matter of no surprise therefore, that Cluny itself was affected by the general disquiet. After the death of its great abbot Hugh, various problems surfaced. During his last years the abbot had been too ill to visit more distant dependent priories. Novices had been accepted and eventually professed without proper supervision. Since the monks in the priories were officially monks of Cluny, the great abbey was burdened, in the first decades of the twelfth century, with unsuitable subjects.[126] It has been suggested that Abbot Pons of Melgueil, who succeeded Hugh in 1109, wanted a thorough reform of the monastic life of Cluny, somewhat on the lines of the 'new monasticism'. At Cluny, however, the ancient way of life, not unsurprisingly, had its ardent supporters.[127] Pope Calixtus II, himself a benedictine monk and former archbishop of Vienne, was personally acquainted with the protagonists and at first protected Pons, but he could not ignore the complaints of bishops about monastic exemptions. In the earlier phase of the struggle for church reform, the popes had favoured monastic exemption, because the bishops had not everywhere been reliable. By the early twelfth century, however, there was a new generation of bishops, loyal to the papacy, enthusiastic for church reform, and favourable to the 'new monasticism'.[128]

When Abbot Pons went to Rome in 1122 he was given little sympathy and was persuaded to resign. From Rome Pons went on pilgrimage to Jerusalem. In 1126, perhaps at the prompting of some of his supporters, he returned to Cluny and attempted to reclaim his office. The attempted *coup d'état* failed. There was rioting among Cluny's servants and the abbey was pillaged.[129] Pons had caused a major scandal in the Church. He was summoned to Rome and died in prison.[130]

---

[126] Bredero (as n. 64), 159.
[127] Ibid. 161.
[128] Ibid. 161–162.
[129] Ibid. 158.
[130] For an account of this affair against a wider background, see H. Jedin ed. *Handbuch der Kirchengeschichte*, 3 (Freiburg im Br. 1973) 9.

The abbot whom Pons tried to displace in 1126 was Peter the Venerable, who stood for traditional cluniac monasticism. While he made less impact on his contemporaries than Bernard of Clairvaux, he fought an impressive rearguard action on behalf of his abbey and was able to avert, for a time, its total decline. His election in 1122 was a setback for reformed monasticism at Cluny.

Was Bernard involved in some way in this affair? Much depends upon the dating of his controversial writings. Over twenty years ago it was suggested that Bernard's first broadside came in 1124, in a letter to his nephew Robert, a former monk of Clairvaux who had been persuaded to leave and become a monk at Cluny,[131] and that his *Apologia*, which appeared some time later, was intended to appeal directly to the party in Cluny which favoured abbot Pons.[132] A more recent study[133] has dated the two works to a period between 1121 and 1125, and suggested that they might be dated nearer to the ealier year than to the later. If this is true, there is no necessary connection with the troubles at Cluny. The matter, however, remains far from settled.[134]

Bernard's letter to Robert drew unflattering comparisons between the two monasteries. It appears that Robert had complained publicly about Bernard's harshness, for Bernard half admits the charge. If he was too hard, he wrote, he would now be gentle. The behaviour of Cluny, however, had been dastardly. While Bernard was absent, its Grand Prior had come to Clairvaux to persuade Robert to leave. 'He preached a new Gospel. He commended feasting and condemned fasting. He called voluntary poverty wretched and poured scorn upon fasts, vigils, silence, and manual labour'.[135]

---

[131] See below, n. 135.

[132] The argument is set out in Adriaan Bredero, 'Cluny et Cîteaux' (as n. 64).

[133] Holdsworth (as n. 67).

[134] Adriaan Bredero, *Bernard of Clairvaux between Cult and History* (Grand Rapids: Eerdmans 1996) 121 n. 72 and 218, does not accept Holdsworth's arguments.

[135] Ep. 1; Scott James 1.

Bernard's *Apologia,* which followed soon after the letter
to Robert, was a more systematic criticism of conservative
monasticism.[136] Bernard began by expressing his esteem for
the Cluniacs. He had never tried to dissuade anyone from
joining them, or (a telling point) to inveigle one of their monks
into becoming a Cistercian.[137] The variety of different religious
Orders should not destroy the charity between them.[138] The
trouble was that because the admirable fathers of Cluny had
relaxed some rigours in the Rule, certain monks had taken
advantage of their kindness. 'Laxity is labelled discretion, ex-
travagance generosity, talkativeness sociability, and laughter
joy. Fine clothes and costly caparisons are regarded as mere
respectability, and being fussy about bedding is hygiene'.[139]
Bernard repeated in detail complaints that the Cluniacs ate
and drank more than the Rule allowed. This would certainly
not be what their saints—Odo, Maieul, Odilo, and Hugh—
had in mind, to say nothing about the ancient fathers.[140] The
Cluniacs' clothes were too luxurious, and their abbots went
about like great lords. 'I am lying if I did not see an abbot
accompanied by sixty horses and more'.[141] Too much money
was spent on ostentatious church building, golden ornaments
in the sanctuary, and curious carvings in the cloisters.[142]

We do not know whether the Cluniacs replied to the
Apologia, but some years later[143] Peter the Venerable wrote
a long letter in defense of cluniac monasticism.[144] It was a
reply to a detailed criticism of Cluny made, either orally or in
writing, by some cistercian abbots[145] with which Saint Bernard

[136] For contradictory views on the dating of the *Apologia*, see Bredero (as n. 64), 141, 148, and Holdsworth (as n. 67) 39–52.
[137] *Apologia* 2.4; *Opera,* ed. Mabillon (as n. 63), 2:1224–1225.
[138] Ibid., 3, 5–6.12; Mabillon (as n. 63), 2:1226–1234.
[139] Ibid. 8.16; Mabillon (as n. 63) 2:1234–1236. Translation (as n. 95), 53.
[140] Ibid., 9.23; Mabillon (as n. 63), 2:1239.
[141] Ibid. 11.27; Mabillon (as n. 63), 2:1241.
[142] Ibid., 12.28–29; Mabillon (as n. 63), 2:1242–1243.
[143] *The Letters of Peter the Venerable,* ed. Giles Constable, 2 (Cambridge Mass. 1967) 270–274.
[144] Ep. 28; Constable (as n. 143) 1:52–104.
[145] *Quidam vestrorum,* Letter 28; Constable 1:53

had associated himself.[146] Peter listed the charges and dealt with them one by one. As far as manual labour was concerned, he contended, the spirit was more important than the letter of the Rule. Cluniac monks were not idle, and in any case agricultural work was unsuitable for choir-monks.[147] In defense of his monks' warm clothing he quoted Saint Benedict who had allowed that the local climate should be taken into account.[148]

More important than the details was Peter's contention that charity lay at the basis of the Rule. If a superior took account of local conditions or difficulties, it was because of the Gospel's insistence on this virtue before all others.[149] In drawing a distinction between the laws of God which must be held to the letter and religious rules from which monks can be dispensed in the name of charity.[150] Peter's position was the same as Saint Bernard's in *De praecepto et dispensatione*.[151] The two abbots even used the same quotation from Saint Leo.[152]

More telling was Peter's complaint about cistercian pharisaism. 'O new race of pharisees brought back to the world, dividing themselves from others, preferring themselves to all the rest!'[153] Peter was particularly critical of the white robes of the Cistercians.[154] In fact, the Vallombrosans and, generally, all reformed monks had refrained, for reasons of economy, from dyeing their robes black.[155] It was the Cistercians, however, who were particularly associated with white robes and came to be known as the 'white monks'. It was a small matter, but Peter was right to see symbolism in the change of colour from

---

[146] The letter is addressed to Saint Bernard.
[147] Letter 28; Constable 1:70–85.
[148] Ibid. pp. 62–64.
[149] See particularly pp. 88–101.
[150] Ibid.
[151] Compare Peter's letter (Constable, pp. 88–101), with *De praecepto et dispensatione* 1.1–3.8 (Mabillon, as n. 63, 2:1177–1179).
[152] Letter 28, p. 61; De praecepto et dispensatione, 1178.
[153] Letter 28, p. 57.
[154] Ibid.
[155] *Letters of Peter the Venerable* (as n. 143), 2:116.

the traditional black. In no more spectacular way could the Cistercians emphasise that they were different.

In time Peter met some of the criticisms of Cluny by issuing reforming statutes for his subjects. He did this at Chapters General of cluniac priors which met—clearly in imitation of the cistercian institution—at Cluny in 1132, 1140, and 1150.[156] Towards the end of his life his statutes were collected together.[157] They are remarkable because Peter gives a reason for each one. Many were concerned with the proper celebration of the liturgy, and, because its length and elaboration at Cluny was a subject of criticism, Peter suggested a few cuts.[158] There were regulations enforcing more rigorous fasting and abstinence.[159] The prohibition of meat in the Rule was emphasised.[160] Manual labour was restored to its proper place in the monastic day, although, it should be noted, this referred to domestic tasks inside the abbey and not to work in the fields.[161] There was a renewed insistence on silence in the monastery[162] and simplicity in clothing.[163] Peter's reforms were resisted and the statutes were not strictly observed.[164]

There were other attempts by black monks to reform their way of life after the model of the new Orders. In 1132 Pope Innocent II, exiled from Rome by his rival, was at Rheims, presiding over a council. In preparation for it some benedictine abbots in the province had met and decided upon a programme of reforms on the lines of the 'new monasticism'. Among other innovations they decided to meet annually, as did the Cistercians in their General Chapter. These policies were bitterly opposed by the highly respected but intransigent Matthew,

---

[156] Consuetudines Benedictinae Variae ed. Giles Constable, *Corpus Consuetudinum Monasticarum*, 6 (Siegburg 1975) 22–23.
[157] Ibid. 39–40. The statutes are printed on pp. 40–106.
[158] Statute 31.
[159] Statutes 10, 11, 14, 15, 27.
[160] Statute 12.
[161] Statute 39.
[162] Statutes 19, 20, 21, 22, 42.
[163] Statutes 17, 18.
[164] Consuetudines Benedictinae (as n. 156), 23–24.

the former Grand Prior of Cluny, now cardinal bishop of Albano. His criticism of the abbots of the province of Rheims included a long and passionate defence of the ancient cluniac monasticism.[165] The abbots, however, held their ground. At one of the first of their annual meetings they replied to the cardinal with a letter—very likely written by Saint Bernard's friend, William of Saint Thierry—in which they defended their actions and corrected some of the legate's misrepresentations.

With these controversies Saint Bernard did not concern himself. The argument with Peter the Venerable had left a bitter taste. After 1130 both abbots were ardent partisans of Innocent II and put aside their differences in the common cause. In later years Bernard's relations with Peter were correct but distant.[166] Bernard also discouraged cistercian monks from attacking the Cluniacs.[167] After his death the floodgates were opened and the controversy between black and white monks plumbed new depths.[168]

Reform during the eleventh and twelfth centuries was not limited to monasteries. Determined attempts were made to recall the secular clergy to the apostolic life. The council of Aachen of 817 had allowed the priests or canons attached to large churches to divide the revenues into individual lots or prebends. Strict churchmen in the period of reform wanted them to return to the common life. Councils held in Rome in 1059 and 1063 put together legislation derived from various

---

[165] On Matthew of Albano, see U. Berlière, 'Le cardinal Matthieu d'Albano', *Revue Bénédictine* 18 (1901) 113–140. On the cardinal's defence of cluniac customs, ibid. pp. 281–303. On the Synod of Rheims, its aftermath, and the part played by William of Saint Thierry, see Stanley Ceglar, The Chapter of Soissons (autumn 1132) and the authorship of the Reply of the Benedictine Abbots to Cardinal Matthew', *Studies in Medieval Cistercian History* 2, ed. John R. Sommerfeldt (Kalamazoo: Cistercian Publications 1976) 92–105; and S. Ceglar, 'William of Saint Thierry and his Leading Role at the First Chapters of the Benedictine Abbots', *William Abbot of Saint Thierry* (Kalamazoo 1987) 34–49.
[166] A. Bredero, 'St. Bernard in his Relations with Peter the Venerable', *Bernardus Magister* (as note 63), 315–347.
[167] A. Bredero, 'Le dialogus duorum monachorum,' *Studi Medievali* ser. 3, 22:2 (1981) 555.
[168] Ibid. 501–585.

sources, among which Saint Augustine's monastic rule held pride of place. Canons were now expected to devote themselves to an elaborate liturgy, to observe the fasts, to cut down on the consumption of meat, and to obey a superior. The way of life prescribed in the roman documents was later known as the *Ordo Antiquus*, for in the twelfth century an *Ordo Novus* for canons came to the fore which insisted on more fasting, greater austerity, and communities situated in solitary places. The foremost advocate of this stricter *Ordo* was Saint Norbert of Xanten (1085–1134) an itinerant preacher who was persuaded to settle with his followers in northern France at Prémontré, which presently became the centre of a new Premonstratensian Order.[169]

The influence of monasticism, both traditional and new, upon houses of canons is obvious. Canons were not monks. They did not take the three traditional monastic vows, but usually swore a simple oath, promising to obey their superior and observe the customs of their house.[170] Their history, therefore, falls outside the scope of this study.

In the twelfth century western monasticism became specialised. There were hermit monks, monks devoted to elaborate liturgy, and monks living austerely in the country. They all had their own spirituality, their liturgical customs, privileges, history, saints, separate uniforms, and, sometimes, their own organisation. They formed identifiable communities within the Church, with their own interests to further at the papal court and before kings and bishops.

This development must be seen against the background of the Church reform. The search for a pure and authentic Christianity encouraged outstanding holiness, heroism, and insight on the one hand; bigotry, harshness, and formalism on

---

[169] On the beginnings and development of regular canons, see Bligny (as n. 41), 198–208; 'Norberto', DIP 6 (1980) 322–325; 'Premostratensi', ibid. 7 (1983) 720–746.

[170] For a disscussion of the difference between monks and canons, see J. Dubois, 'Les ordres religieux au xiie siècle, selon la curie romaine', *Revue Bénédictine* 78 (1968) 283–309.

the other. It was in this era that the great divisions which have so damaged Christianity first appeared: West against East, popes against emperors, clergy against laity, white monks against black. No one more dramatically embodies these paradoxes in his character and writings than Saint Bernard of Clairvaux.

Chapter 8
RELIGIOUS WOMEN IN
THE HIGH MIDDLE AGES

U NTIL THE MIDDLE of the tenth century monasteries for women were comparatively rare. For the most part they were elaborate institutions, often founded by widowed queens or princesses. These prestigious ladies and their successors presided over religious houses with spacious precincts enclosing numerous churches and impressive domestic buildings. A large body of clerks was attached to the community to celebrate Mass and administer the sacraments. An army of serfs provided labour for the estates. Holy Cross in Poitiers in the time of Saint Radegund was an abbey of this kind.[1] So were Nivelles in modern Belgium, founded in 647–650 by Itta, widow of Pepin the Elder and her daughter Gertrude,[2] and Whitby in Yorkshire, England, founded around 657 by Hilda, grandaughter of Edwin, king of Northumbria.[3]

By the time of the church reforms, many of these institutions had become decadent. They were, in any case, too few and too exclusive to accommodate the many women who were now inspired to adopt the monastic life. The new religious movements, however, had been started by men and directed towards their particular requirements. It does not appear, for instance, that Saint Romuald and Saint Peter Damian ever seriously considered the needs of religious women. The arrangements for women, therefore, often had something provisional about them. The division of monks into religious orders, which was a feature of western monasticism by the end of the twelfth

---

[1] See above pp. 62–64.
[2] P. Schmitz, *Histoire de l'ordre de Saint Benoît*, 7 (Maredsous 1956) 19.
[3] Ibid. 24–26. On monasteries for women in the Dark Ages, see ibid. 3–44.

4 The Benedictine Nunnery of Malling, Kent.

century, fulfilled the needs of the men. Throughout the Middle Ages there were houses for female religious which could not be fitted into any Order. The priory of Clerkenwell near London, for instance, was sometimes described as augustinian and sometimes as benedictine.[4]

Many women who were drawn to the religious life simply settled near a benedictine monastery, accepted the direction of the men, and adopted a more or less monastic life. In southern Germany it was not uncommon for communities of women to live side by side with the monks, depending on them for spiritual direction and the sacraments and sharing some of the revenues of the monastery. At Benediktbeuern in Bavaria, for instance, there was such a community of women until the late thirteenth century.[5] Attached to the abbey of Admont in modern Austria, a famous house of nuns, founded in 1116–1120, lasted until the sixteenth century.[6] At Melk, overlooking the Danube south of Vienna, there was a house of women which lasted from the eleventh century until the fourteenth.[7] Most prestigious were the 'Ladies of Saint Peter' (*Petersfrauen*) attached to the ancient abbey of Saint Peter in Salzburg, modern Austria, a community which probably came into being in the early twelfth century. Its buildings were adjacent to the abbey. The nuns worshipped in the parish church, where their gallery jutted into the nave. Here they recited their office, which was timed so as not to interfere with the parish Masses.[8]

Arrangements of this kind were often the result of spontaneous religious movements among the women. In the early years of the twelfth century, a young woman called Christina,

---

[4] *A History of the County of Middlesex*, ed. J. S. Cockburn, H. P. F. King, K. G. T. McDonnell, 1 (Oxford 1969) 170.

[5] U. Berlière, 'Les monastères doubles aux xiie et xiiie siècles', *Académie royale de Belgique, classe des lettres et des sciences morales et politiques*, 18/3 (1923) 13.

[6] Ibid. 15.

[7] Ibid. 17.

[8] H. Dopsch, 'Die Petersfrauen', *St. Peter in Salzburg*: Dommuseum zu Salzburg, Sonderschein 7 (Salzburg 1982) 85–90.

who wished to live the life of a virgin against the wishes of
her parents, hid in the cell of a hermit at Markyate, near Saint
Albans Abbey in England. On the hermit's death she inherited
the cell and there, with other devout women, lived a penitential life. They were under the direction of Geoffrey, abbot
of Saint Albans, who eventually persuaded them to adopt the
Benedictine Rule and submit to the government of the monks.
At about the same time Abbot Geoffrey also persuaded some
hermitesses living at Sopwell near Saint Albans to become
Benedictines.[9]

The term 'double monastery', often applied by historians to
arrangements under which monastic men and women lived in
close proximity, in fact covers a great variety of situations. Since
women depended for the sacraments and spiritual guidance
upon a male priesthood it was obviously an advantage if monks
and nuns were within easy reach of one another. Even today
in the departement Nord, France, the abbey of Sainte Cécile,
founded in 1866 for benedictine nuns, can be seen below the
horizon from the windows of the famous abbey of Solesmes.

During the course of the Middle Ages, however, the double
monasteries came under pressure and the women usually
ended up being moved to a more distant site. Sometimes the
relocation was motivated by economic reasons, sometimes by
the fear of scandal, real or imagined.[10] Misogyny no doubt also
had a part to play. In 1344, when Saint Bridget [Birgitta] of
Sweden settled in a cell by the walls of the cistercian abbey of
Alvastra, one of the monks grumbled, 'Why does this lady live
here in a monastery of monks, against our Rule, introducing
an unheard-of custom?'[11]

During the church reform, therefore, some houses were

---

[9] Sharon K. Elkins, *Holy Women of Twelfth Century England* (Chapel Hill,
North Carolina 1988) 17–38, 46–47; Sally Thompson, *Women Religious: The
Founding of English Nunneries after the Conquest* (Oxford 1991) 56–57;
D. Knowles, R. N. Hadcock, *Medieval Religious Houses: England and Wales*
(London 1971) 74–75.
[10] Schmitz (as n. 2), 50–51.
[11] *Den heliga Birgittas Revelaciones extravagantes*, ed. L. Hollman, Svenska
Fornskriftssällskapets samlingar 2:5 (Uppsala 1956) 176.

founded which, from the start, were for women only. The abbey of Cluny was particularly concerned to foster the Benedictine Rule, as it was lived in the great abbey, among women. In the time of Abbot Odilo,[12] Cluny was visited by Ada, abbess of Saint Maur in Verdun. During her visit she was present at a meeting of the chapter and, on the Sunday, walked in the monastic procession.[13]

For women, an important house was Marcigny, founded in 1056 by abbot Hugh and originally intended for the wives of those who had become monks at Cluny. Abbot Hugh's brother Geoffrey provided the land, and religious life began there in 1061. A twelfth-century *Ordo* from Marcigny shows that the life of the nuns was centred on an elaborate liturgical life, like that at Cluny. The priests came from a little priory of twelve monks which Hugh established in the neighbourhood. Like cluniac monks, the nuns made their profession to the abbot of Cluny or his deputy. They were famed for the strictness with which they observed their enclosure. Peter the Venerable tells us that during a fire at Marcigny, even the risk of death could not induce the nuns to leave the building. A miracle was required to save them from being burned alive.[14]

Abbot Hugh wanted mature women at Marcigny, and no children. The minimum age for admittance was twenty and postulants were to show that they had a genuine vocation. The number of nuns was limited to ninety-nine—the hundredth place was reserved for the Blessed Virgin, who was the abbess. Her deputy at Marcigny was the prioress.[15] The nuns belonged to the most illustrious families of Europe. They included at various times a daughter of King Malcolm Canmore of Scotland, the widow of King Stephen of England, her sister, and her daughter.[16]

---

[12] See above p. 126.
[13] Schmitz (as n. 2), 71.
[14] Ibid. 71–75.
[15] J. Verdon, 'Les moniales dans la France de l'ouest au xie et xiie siècles: étude d'histoire sociale', *Cahiers de civilisation médiévale* 19 (1976) 254.
[16] Schmitz (as n. 2), 73–74.

Marcigny was only one of the numerous monasteries for women which were founded in the tenth and eleventh centuries, and which followed the Benedictine Rule as far as possible.[17] At the head of each house was an abbess, who was usually elected by the community, although, as in abbeys for men, outsiders sometimes interfered. After her election she was blessed by the bishop, and her authority was absolute, as the Rule demanded. She was aided by a number of obedientiaries. At Ronceray in Anjou, they were the dean, the sacristess, the almoness, the cellaress, and the treasuress. A small group of priests provided the sacraments. At Ronceray they numbered four and had their own house and endowments, and served in the church day and night.[18]

A number of monastic theologians interested themselves in the spirituality of nuns. John of Fécamp[19] wrote of Jesus as their spouse. The *Speculum Virginum* composed in the Rhine area provided a complete guide to the monastic life for women. There is evidence of high culture among the nuns themselves. Cecilia, abbess of Holy Trinity Caen, a daughter of William the Conqueror, King of England, had been carefully educated in the various sciences. The abbey of Ronceray ran a successful 'extern' school for girls who did not themselves intend to become nuns.[20]

All these provide examples of a way of life originally conceived for men being adapted, more or less successfully, for nuns. There was , however, a small number of pioneers who tried to map out a manner of monastic living which took ac-

---

[17] See Mary Skinner, 'Benedictine Life for Women in Central France—A Feminist Revival', *Distant Echoes*, Medieval Religious Women, 1 (Kalamazoo 1984) 87–113; Verdon, 'Les moniales . . .' (as n. 15); Verdon, 'Recherches sur les monastères féminins dans la France de sud aux ixe—xie siècles', *Annales du Midi*, 88 (1976) 117–138.

[18] Verdon, 'Les moniales . . .' (as n. 15), 255–257.

[19] See above p. 138.

[20] Verdon, 'Les moniales . . .' (as n. 15), 259–261.

count, first, of the needs of the women. Of these the most spectacular, if not the most successful, was Robert of Arbrissel.[21]

Robert was born in Brittany in humble circumstances
around the middle of the eleventh century. He was in his
thirties when, after a largely misspent youth, he began his
studies at Paris. Here he acquired an enthusiasm for the church
reform, then in its first fervour, which never left him.After
some time he was invited to Rennes in his native Britanny
to help Bishop Sylvester reform the diocese. Robert's efforts
succeeded only in hardening the opposition. After Bishop
Sylvester's death in 1093 he was forced to leave. He settled
in Angers, a middle-aged and hitherto unsuccessful priest, to
continue his studies.[22]

Around 1095 he felt a call to leave everything and settle in
the 'desert'. The wilderness in this case was the forest of Craon
on the borders of Anjou and Brittany. Here Robert was in touch
with other hermits—Raoul de la Futaye, Vitalis of Savigny, and
Bernard of Tiron. They met for occasional conferences and,
since Robert was the oldest and had studied in the schools,
he was informally recognised as their leader.[23] He became a
renowned preacher, drawing crowds to hear his denunciations
of the evils of his time—greed, sexual permissiveness, and
corruption in the Church. In 1096 Pope Urban II, passing
through the area to win support for the Crusade, gave him
papal authority to preach wherever he wished.[24]

It was not long before he had disciples. He formed them
into a house of canons regular, but the life of a conventional
religious superior did not suit him, and he took to the roads
to continue his preaching. Once again a band of admirers
gathered round him, men and women, drawn from all classes,

---

[21] On Robert of Arbrissel, see J. M. Bienvenu, *L'étonnant fondateur de Fontrevaud, Robert d'Arbrissel* (Paris 1981); J. Dalarun, *L'impossible sainteté: la vie
retrouvé de Robert d'Arbrissel* (Paris 1985); J. Dalarun, *Robert d'Arbrissel,
fondateur de Fontrevaud* (Paris 1986).
[22] Bienvenu. *L'étonnant fondateur* (as above, n. 21), 15–26.
[23] See above p. 166; Bienvenu (as n. 21), 39–40.
[24] Bienvenu (as n. 21), 41–47.

including former prostitutes. This second phase of Robert's preaching vocation coincided with political chaos in Anjou and a severe famine. He and his followers were not the only ones on the road, and he seems to have chosen this way of life deliberately to show his solidarity with the homeless.[25]

As well as admirers Robert had severe critics, among whom was Marbod, the bishop of Rennes. The bishop objected to Robert's appearance. Unkempt, unshaved, dressed in rags, he was certainly no credit to the priesthood. His followers were no better. Vehement condemnations of corruption in the Church, argued the bishop, could be misunderstood. Such things should not be proclaimed indiscriminately to the laity. Above all, Robert practised a bizarre form of penance. To test his resistance to the allurements of sex, it was his habit to sleep throughout the night in the company of women. This extreme ascesis, known as *syneisactism,* was known in the early Church and frequently condemned by the Fathers. In spite of numerous admonishments Robert persisted with it throughout his life.[26]

Robert's way of shocking conventional opinion is well illustrated by an incident which probably took place in these years. He arrived at Menat in the Auvergne, intending to preach in the abbey church. The monks had a rule (not unknown elsewhere) that no woman could enter their church and it was believed that any woman who did so would immediately drop dead. Without hesitation Robert entered, accompanied by his female followers. The porters were horrified and began to pray to their patron saint to strike the women dead. 'Enough, foolish people,' exclaimed Robert.

'Stop making these stupid and vain prayers! Let me tell you that the saints are not the enemies of the spouses of Jesus Christ. What you are saying is quite absurd, and the purity of the catholic faith teaches us the very opposite. The Gospel tells of that blessed sinner who kissed the feet of the

---

[25] Ibid. 52–57.
[26] Ibid. 62–71.

Redeemer, bathed them with her tears, dried them with her hair, and poured ointment on his holy head. Who, then, will dare to say that there is any church which it is not lawful for a woman to enter, unless she is prohibited because of her sins and guilt? What is greater, the material temple of God, or the spiritual temple in which God dwells? If a woman can take and eat the body and blood of Jesus Christ, imagine what folly it is to believe that she cannot enter a church!'

The porters were shamed into silence and the local taboo was abandoned from that day.[27]

The complaints against Robert came to a head at a council at Poitiers, presided over by two papal legates, in November 1100. Robert's followers were by now so numerous that their wanderings led to disorders. Among them were women who had left their husbands. In spite of threats, Robert refused to hand them back.

Marriages at this time were property deals and the consent of those involved was not asked. The Church was doubtful about many of these unions, especially since some women were brutally treated after they had married. Later in the twelfth century canon lawyers devised minimum safeguards for a proper christian marriage. At the Council of Poitiers Robert was vindicated. Some time later, most probably in 1101, he was given property at Fontrevaud in Anjou and there he settled with his followers.[28] It is probable that the legates at the Council had insisted that he organise his community into a regular religious house.

His male and female followers were now strictly segregated. Chaplains were to come from the ranks of the men, and there were also brothers to do the heavy physical labour. The male members of the community were to be for ever subject to the rule of the female members. The educated women sang in the choir and, after 1115, followed the Rule of Saint Benedict. The illiterate women acted as servants in the house. No one

---

[27] Quoted in Dalarun, *Robert d'Arbrissel* (as n. 21), 128–130.
[28] Bienvenu (as n. 21), 68–74.

was to be turned away. There was a place for all, according to the aptitudes of each.

This was Robert's vision. Until his death he enjoyed the title of 'Master' of Fontrevaud. His preaching in the church drew large crowds and had lost none of its asperity. Administration and the clear statement of an ideal, however, were not among his gifts. Before long Fontrevaud was richly endowed by the angevin aristocracy. Noble ladies entered the community in large numbers and soon took control. Calling themselves 'ladies of the choir' they asserted their ascendancy over the rest, including the men, by their social superiority. They fretted under the harsh discipline imposed by Robert. An ambitious building programme was begun. Fontrevaud remains one of the most impressive of the romanesque abbeys in France.[29]

The first abbess was Hersende, widow of a wealthy angevin nobleman. His son by an earlier marriage, who was therefore Hersende's stepson, was the original owner of the site of Fontrevaud and its chief benefactor. Hersende ruled until 1112/3, when she was succeeded by Petronilla, who had been twice married, each time to one of the leading landowners in the area. Under these ladies Fontrevaud was a strict, well-run, and much admired house, but it no longer answered to Robert's ideal. Some time in 1103–1104, therefore, he once more took to the roads. He was now a highly respected and venerated churchman. His fiery sermons continued to draw large crowds. He remained master of Fontrevaud and involved himself, from time to time, in its government. On his journeys he founded other houses, so that Fontrevaud became the mother house of an Order. When he died at one of his foundations in 1116,[30] the nuns of Fontrevaud gave him a splendid funeral in their church, and then systematically obliterated his memory.[31]

A less colourful but ultimately more successful guide for

---

[29] Ibid. 75–78.
[30] Ibid. 87–89, 93–157.
[31] Ibid. 157–169.

women religious was the Englishman Gilbert of Sempringham.[32] He was born around 1089 in Lincolnshire. Here his
father had a small estate. Gilbert suffered from some physical
disability which made him unfit for the life of a knight and
eventually he was sent to the schools in Normandy. He returned in minor orders and was made rector of the churches of
Sempringham and West Torrington of which his father was the
patron. Next he went to Lincoln and joined the bishop's household. After some years he was ordained a priest. He impressed
two successive bishops of Lincoln and a brilliant ecclesiastical
career might have been his. He preferred, however, to return
to Sempringham and to pastoral work among simple people.

Among his flock were seven young women who wished to
adopt the life of hermits. He built them a shelter against the
north side of the parish church. Through a window they com-
municated with some hand-picked local women who provided
for their needs. The little community's endowments came from
Gilbert's two churches.

The women helpers turned out to be prone to gossip, and
on the advice of some local cistercian monks, Gilbert organised
them into a lay sisterhood. Some land was given to the new
community, and it became necessary to recruit men to work it.
These were enrolled as lay brothers. Around 1139 the whole
community moved away from the parish church to new buildings nearby. In time Gilbert's fame spread and endowments
came in for a second community in Lincolnshire. In 1147,
feeling that he was not sufficiently experienced to guide a
growing religious movement, Gilbert travelled to Cîteaux to
ask the cistercian Chapter General to take his communities
into the Cistercian Order.[33]

It is more than likely that local Cistercians, who had already
given him advice and support, encouraged him to look towards
their Order. He must have travelled to the Chapter General in

---

[32] On Gilbert and his Order, see the introduction to Raymonde Foreville and
Gillian Keir edd., *The Book of Saint Gilbert* (Oxford 1987); and Brian Golding,
Gilbert of Sempringham and the Gilbertine Order (Oxford 1995).
[33] Golding (as n. 32), 20–25.

the company of english cistercian abbots. News that the Order of Savigny, which had houses in England, was to be absorbed into the Cistercians, must also have reached him. The 1147 chapter was, indeed, an important one in cistercian history. Pope Eugenius III, himself a Cistercian, presided over it in person. The Cistercians agreed to absorb the Order of Savigny, and the two smaller Orders of Obazine and Cadouin. Gilbert and his followers, however, were not accepted. The official excuse was that 'monks of their order [the Cistercian] were not permitted authority over the religious life of others, least of all that of nuns'.[34]

In fact, both Savigny and Obazine had houses of nuns. Savigny, however, was a well established Order of twenty-nnine houses. Stephen of Obazine was personally known to, and recommended by the pope. Gilbert's Order, on the other hand, numbered only two small houses. There were, as yet, no statutes for them.[35] The recommendation of his bishop and the support, which must be assumed, of local cistercian abbots were not sufficient to sway the Chapter General.

Pope Eugenius III, however, encouraged Gilbert and con-firmed him as 'master' of his little Order. Kind words came from Saint Bernard. Gilbert stayed on at Cîteaux after the Chapter General had closed and later travelled to Clairvaux to study the cistercian statutes and way of life. Saint Bernard, who was often away from Clairvaux at that time, is unlikely to have been very closely involved.[36] In the years following his return to England Gilbert set up communities of canons following the Rule of Saint Augustine to minister to the sisters and brothers in the new Order of Sempringham.[37]

It grew rapidly. Most of its houses had been founded by 1150. It remained a Lincolnshire order, with very few houses outside the county. This compactness, at a time when communications were slow and difficult accounts, to some

---

[34] *The Book of Saint Gilbert* (as n. 32), xx, 43.
[35] Golding (as n. 32), 26–28.
[36] Ibid. 28–31.
[37] Ibid. 31–33.

extent, for its ability to surmount the inevitable early crises, and to maintain high standards until its suppression in the sixteenth century. Lincolnshire was a poor county, and the endowments of the Order consisted largely of small parcels of land given by peasants. It is likely that the nuns themselves had fairly modest backgrounds.[38]

Gilbert's statutes evolved slowly. They have survived only in their final form. Each gilbertine community had four elements: the choir nuns, the lay sisters, the canons, and the lay brothers. The sexes were strictly separated. A wall even ran down the middle of the church so that they could not see each other. The nuns followed the Rule of Saint Benedict as interpreted by the Cistercians; the priests were canons following the Rule of Saint Augustine.[39] Supreme authority in the Order was exercised by a chapter general, which was attended by nuns as well as monks. The nuns took part in visitations and in the election of the master who was the head of the Order. At the beginning the Order was specifically designed to meet the religious needs of women, as the various foundation charters of gilbertine houses emphasise. The men were auxiliaries.[40]

Gilbert and his Order were not spared trials and disappointments. In the quarrel which broke out between King Henry II and Archbishop Thomas Becket in 1164, Gilbert took the archbishop's side. Becket hid in a number of gilbertine houses before slipping abroad. As a result Gilbert was brought before royal justices and questioned several times.[41] Some time in the 1160s a passionate affair between a nun and a brother at the gilbertine house of Watton in Yorkshire developed into a lurid scandal which was to haunt Gilbert for the rest of his life.[42] Worst of all, a revolt was staged by gilbertine lay brothers. Three ringleaders went abroad and brought complaints about

---

[38] Ibid. 147–148.
[39] *The Book of Saint Gilbert* (as n. 32), xx–xxii.
[40] Ibid. xxii, xlv–lii.
[41] Ibid. xxiii–lxii.
[42] Giles Constable, 'Aelred of Rievaulx and the Nun of Watton', *Medieval Women*, ed. D. Baker (Oxford 1978) 205–226; Golding (as n. 32), 33–38.

the Order of Sempringham to the exiled archbishop and Pope
Alexander III. The Watton scandal provided pefect ammuni-
tion. The Becket controversy, thanks to which communications
between the pope and England were, at times, interrupted,
dragged out the gilbertine dispute, which was not settled until
the visit to England of two papal legates in 1176. The legates
vindicated Gilbert completely.[43] Indeed, all the letters written
about the affair. by the pope, the exiled archbishop, and various
english bishops, take Gilbert's side. The arguments on the
other side have not survived. It is worth noting that the life
of the laybrothers was very harsh. Many of them were serfs
brought up on the gilbertine estates. They did all the heavy
work, while the decisions were made by others. Gilbert himself
was noted for his austere rule. In 1186, at the very end of his
life, he was persuaded by Bishop Hugh of Lincoln to temper
the rigorous constitutions of the Order as far as the lay brothers
were concerned, and to allow them a more generous measure
of food and clothing.[44]

It was natural that women, as well as men, should take
the initiative in providing for the religious needs of their
sex. In northern France, the area now known as Belgium
and parts of north-west Germany, devout women scattered
around the cities were living in their own homes or with their
parents, observing the counsels of perfection, visiting the sick
and distressed, and earning their own living by spinning or
handiwork.[45] Though usually associated with some monastery,
they did not take vows, and could pass easily to another form
of life. These women were sometimes called *beguines*, a name
of very obscure origin. They were also known as *mulieres
religiosae* (women living a religious life), or *conversae a saeculo*
(women converted from the world). Around 1200 some of
them were being encouraged to live together in a particular
part of the town. They would then elect a mistress and place

---

[43] Golding (as n.32), 40–51.
[44] Ibid. 51.
[45] For the classic account of beguines, see E. W. McDonnell, *The Beguines and
Beghards in Medieval Culture* (New Brunswick, NJ 1954).

themselves under the guidance of sympathetic clergy.[46] They had critics who accused them of heresy, but they found an ardent champion in Jacques de Vitry, an augustinian canon of Oignies, in modern Belgium, who became successively bishop of Acre in the Holy Land and cardinal of the Roman See. In 1216 Jacques persuaded Pope Honorius III to approve their way of life.[47]

These women did not live a monastic life and their further history is outside the scope of this study. It is necessary to mention them, however, because in the thirteenth century many of them passed into the Cistercian Order. Moreover, the beguines and the cistercian nuns had a common spirituality, based on a very personal relationship to Jesus as their spouse, a particular devotion to the Eucharist, and an ardent pastoral concern.

Jacques de Vitry eloquently described the influx of women into the Cistercian Order in his day. Noble matrons abandoned their properties, young girls—to the anger of their parents—spurned advantageous marriages, in order to follow Christ by embracing poverty. In his time seven abbeys for women had been founded in the diocese of Liége alone, and the movement had spread as far as the christian east.[48]

Jacques de Vitry was astonished that the frail sex could take on all the austerities of the cistercian life.[49] The founders of the Cistercian Order also had their doubts and at the beginning avoided taking responsibility for women religious. As we have already seen, the Chapter General made this an excuse for not accepting Gilbert of Sempringham's foundations into the Order.[50] What some saw as the problem of women religious indeed, had presented itself as early as 1113. In that year, when

---

[46] Ibid. 5–7.
[47] Ibid. 6. See also Herbert Grundmann, *Religiöse Bewegungen im Mittelalter* (Berlin 1935) 170. Translated into English as *Religious Movements in the Middle Ages* by Steven Rowan (Notre Dame-London 1995) 139.
[48] *The Historia Occidentalis of Jacques de Vitry*, ed. J. F. Hinnebusch (Fribourg 1972) 116–118.
[49] Ibid. 116–117.
[50] See above p. 206.

Bernard entered Cîteaux with thirty friends and relatives, a number of the women closest to the young postulants felt the urge to enter religion as well. They were directed to apply to Molesme, where some devout women were already living close to the abbey. Molesme possessed a parish church at Jully, in the diocese of Langres. The castle there belonged to a relative of Bernard. After some negotiations Molesme acquired it, and the women already attached to the abbey, as well as those inspired by Bernard and his followers, were transferred there.

According to the customs of Jully, the nuns dressed plainly and worked their own lands. They renounced churches and tithes, abstained from meat and observed strict enclosure. The community was not to exceed seventy choir nuns and four lay sisters, along with four priests from Molesme who were to dispense the sacraments. The head of the community was the prioress.[51]

After a while more houses for women were founded from Jully and looked to it as their mother house. Even so, although some of its customs had been framed after advice from cistercian abbots, including Bernard of Clairvaux,[52] it cannot be called a cistercian house. Molesme, which took responsibility for it, might enjoy friendly relations with the Cistercians, but it remained a house of traditional Benedictines. As for Jully, the house which most closely resembled it was Marcigny.

A certain ambiguity is also apparent in the early history of the abbey of Tart. A little over three miles from Cîteaux, it was founded some time between 1120 and 1125. Its rich endowments were presented to Stephen Harding, abbot of Cîteaux, through whose hands they were passed on to the nuns. The responsibility of the abbey of Cîteaux for this house of religious women was thus emphasised.[53] A later document stated that abbot Stephen had established an abbey for nuns living according to the customs of the Cistercian Order. The

---

[51] J. Bouton ed., *Les moniales cisterciennes*, 1 (Aiguebelle 1986) 41–42.
[52] Ibid. 42.
[53] Ibid. 43–45.

abbot of Cîteaux was to enjoy full powers of supervision at Tart, with the right to carry out visitations. He could nominate and depose the abbess. He was to have the same rights in the houses founded from Tart. Once a year, on 29 September the abbesses of this filiation were to meet in a general chapter under the supervision of the abbot of Cîteaux or his deputy. It is known that these chapters general met throughout the thirteenth century.[54]

Tart and its daughters, then, would appear to have been houses for cistercian nuns. A closer inspection of the documents, however, raises a doubt. The affairs of this group of houses were not, as far as can be seen, ever discussed by the Chapters General at Cîteaux. Tart and its daughter houses observed cistercian customs more exactly than did Jully. It appears, however, that they were under the personal jurisdiction of the abbot of Cîteaux, and not of the Cistercian Order as a whole.[55]

At the end of the twelfth century a rather similar grouping of houses for nuns developed in Spain.[56] In 1187 King Alfonso of Castile decided to make over to the Cistercian Order the monastery of Las Huelgas, which he and his wife had founded for nuns near their capital city of Burgos. A letter was sent to the Chapter General at Cîteaux, asking that the abbess of Las Huelgas be allowed, in future, to hold a chapter general of all the abbesses of Castile and Leon. In deference to the wishes of the king, the chapter fathers at Cîteaux agreed to the request, extended the privileges of the Cistercian Order to Las Huelgas, and allowed the abbess to choose one or two neighbouring cistercian abbots to act as visitors to her house.

A chapter general was duly held at Las Huelgas in April 1189, attended by several bishops and cistercian abbots, as well as by seven abbesses from Castile and Leon. The abbesses of Perales and Gradefes, however, came most unwillingly. Their

---

[54] Ibid. 47–51.
[55] Ibid. 49.
[56] P. Feige, 'Filiation und Landeshoheit—die Entstehung der Zisterzienserkongregationen auf der iberischen Halbinsel', *Zisterzienser Studien* 1 (1975) 37–77.

abbeys were much older than Las Huelgas—an upstart with nothing but royal favour to commend it. The two abbesses maintained that they must first consult their mother house in Navarre. After their mother abbess had declared herself satisfied with the arrangements in the neighbouring kingdom, the general chapter at Las Huelgas was reconvened. All now swore obedience to the abbess of Las Huelgas, who was to be to them what the abbot of Cîteaux was to the abbots of the Cistercian Order. A general chapter of abbesses was to be held every year on Saint Martin's day (11 November).

Only two years later King Alfonso complained to the Chapter General at Cîteaux that three abbesses (Cana had joined Perales and Gradefes) were refusing to attend the chapter at Las Huelgas. The fathers at Cîteaux replied that they could only advise, not force, the abbesses to go. In 1199 the abbot of Cîteaux was himself in Castile. King Alfonso confirmed the privileges of Las Huelgas and declared that it would be the burial place of his dynasty. It does not appear, however, that the disciplinary problems of Las Huelgas were solved, and in the thirteenth century its relations with Cîteaux were unhappy.[57]

It has sometimes been suggested that the attitude of the Cistercians to religious women was coloured by antifeminism.[58] In fact, the Order's policy was far from consistent, and it is likely that opinions were divided. The women who were persuaded to settle at Jully had, as we have seen, no further contact with the Cistercian Order. In 1147 Gilbert of Sempringham was advised that cistercian policy was not to take responsibility for women religious. On the other hand, Saint Bernard and other senior abbots supported the initiatives at Jully and Sempringham. At Tart Stephen Harding took full responsibility for an abbey which was within easy reach of Cîteaux. At Las Huelgas the Cistercians, dealing with a

[57] Ibid. 38–46.
[58] Sally Thompson, 'The Problem of Cistercian Nuns in the Twelfth and Early Thirteenth Centuries', in Barker, ed., *Medieval Women* (as n. 42), 227–252.

determined and exceptionally generous king, were ready to go at least part of the way with him.

There is evidence here of some undecisiveness, but not of any hostility to women. The Cistercians were always encouraging where women religious were concerned, though they preferred to avoid close involvement. There were sound reasons for their caution. An abbot who made himself responsible for a monastery of women was obliged to send them suitable chaplains. One such priest was not enough; there would have to be a minimum of two. Walter of Utrecht, abbot of Villers (1214–1221) and himself a great supporter of women religious, explained the difficulties. After he had founded ten monasteries for women, he found that he had sent so many of his best men out as chaplains that there were not enough left to teach his novices.[59] If we remember that houses of women eventually far outnumbered those for men—in the area of modern Belgium probably amounting to a ratio of four to one[60]—the hesitations of the Cistercians are easily explained. As for the chaplains, their lives were not always easy. In a house of women they were isolated and often did not have enough to do to fill the day.[61]

No consistent policy about religious women can be discerned from the legislation of the Cistercian Chapter General in the thirteenth century. A statute of 1220 forbade further incorporations of nuns into the Order. Five years later the Chapter General relented a little—new foundations by existing communities were allowed. In 1228 this concession was abrogated, though any abbey of women might, if it wished, follow cistercian customs, provided it did not claim to belong to the Order. In 1235 new foundations of women were once

[59] J. M. Canivez, *L'ordre de Cîteaux en Belgique* (Scourmont 1926) 14, 90. On manpower problems when monasteries had to supply priests for women religious, see Penelope D. Johnson, *Equal in Monastic Profession* (Chicago 1991) 92.
[60] Roger DeGanck, *Beatrice of Nazareth in her Context* (Kalamazoo 1991) 18–20.
[61] Canivez (as n. 59), 14.

again allowed. In 1244 they were made more difficult because the Order demanded that any new cistercian house of nuns must have a written statement from the local bishop confirming its exemption from his jurisdiction. In the following year the Chapter General stated that a sealed letter from the local cathedral chapter would also be required.[62]

Irrespective of these enactments, the thirteenth-century statutes of the Cistercian Chapter General record the incorporation of houses for women into the Order practically every year. In 1227, for instance, the Chapter General incorporated an abbey of nuns in Moravia at the request of the bishop of Olomouc. Santa Maria della Piana in modern Italy was admitted in 1230 at the petition of the pope. In 1237 ten abbeys for nuns were admitted: four in modern France, three in modern Belgium (including the famous house of Nazareth), one in Germany, one in Italy, and one in Spain.[63]

When the cistercian statutes were codified in 1237 and 1257, the Chapter General's legislation about nuns was arranged into a coherent whole. The prohibition of founding new houses for women was repeated. Each community of women was to be under the jurisdiction of the abbot of a men's community. In person or through a deputy, this 'father abbot' was to carry out regular visitations. If the house had been founded by another house of nuns, its abbess was not to be present at the visitation, though she might visit her daughter house on another occasion and make suggestions, provided they did not conflict with the decrees of the father abbot. In more recently founded houses enclosure was to be strictly observed; in the older ones the abbess and obedientiaries might leave the precincts to transact important business with permission of the father abbot. Apart from the visitor, only highly respected persons were to enter the enclosure. Except where the visitor was concerned, confessions were to be made

---

[62] DeGanck (as n. 60), 14–16.
[63] For a fuller history of incorporations by the Order, see Bouton (as n. 51), 69–82.

through a window. Necessary communications with the outside world had to be through a grille. The nuns' chaplains and
the brothers sent to do the heavy work were to swear fidelity
to the abbess and could be disciplined by her.[64]

A study of cistercian legislation in this matter, then, shows
considerable uncertainty and, no doubt, a sharp division of
opinion in the Order. While the Chapter General at times
displayed a certain caution, abbots in the area now known
as Belgium were enthusiastically encouraging a remarkable
feminine religious movement.

In the early decades of the twelfth century many women
who longed for life in a religious community had been welcomed by the Premonstratensian Order. Its founder, Saint
Norbert, was sympathetic to their needs. All the major premonstratensian houses were 'double monasteries'. By the middle of the twelfth century one chronicler estimated the number
of women attached to the Order at ten thousand.[65] After one
or two scandals, however,[66] it was decided to move the women
a greater distance away from the communities of men. The
burden of providing pastoral care soon turned the canons
against a mission to women altogether. In the later twelfth
and throughout the thirteenth centuries the premonstratensian chapters general legislated ever more strictly against the
reception of women into the Order.[67]

Since premonstratensian doors were closed, Jacques de
Vitry explains, the women turned to the Cistercians.[68] The
number of houses for cistercian nuns founded in the first
half of the thirteenth century is astonishing—one hundred-
fifty in Germany and sixty-six in the small area of modern
Belgium.[69] Attempts have been made to find social or political
explanations. Wars and crusades had created many widows, it

---

[64] *Les codifications cisterciennes de 1237 et de 1257*, ed. B. Lucet (Paris 1977)
191–196, 349–357.
[65] U. Berlière, 'Les monasteres doubles' (as n. 5), 22–23.
[66] Saint Bernard Ep. 79; Scott James No. 81.
[67] U. Berlière, 'Les monasteres doubles' (as n. 5), 23–26.
[68] *Historia Occidentalis* (as n. 48), 117.
[69] DeGanck (as n. 60), 17.

has been claimed, and a shortage of eligible husbands.[70] Many of the nuns belonged to noble or rich bourgeois families. In the lower ranks of society, indeed, there was no lack of professions open to women: they could be spinners and weavers, for instance. Women salted and packed herrings, sold produce at markets, and owned taverns. Others went into domestic service. None of these outlets were open to the daughters of nobles or merchants. For them the only alternative to marriage was a monastery.[71]

It would be foolish, nevertheless, to underrate the importance of religious motivation, to which all the sources bear witness. There were at hand, after all, monasteries for women which made few demands on their members. Entering a cistercian house involved a particular commitment to voluntary poverty and a life of penance.[72] It was precisely to find greater austerity and poverty that Lutgard and Juliana of Cornillon, two well-known holy women of this period, left the more traditional houses at which they had begun their lives as religious.[73]

A number of the women who embraced the religious life during this period were outstanding for sanctity. Beatrice, prioress of the cistercian house of Nazareth near Lierre in modern Belgium (1202/4–1268), wrote a treatise entitled *Van seven manieren van heileger minnen* ('Of the seven ways of holy loving') and an autobiography, which is now lost.[74] Lutgard (1182–1246), who entered the cistercian house of Aywières from a less austere benedictine establishment, came to be known for her charity to the sick, her devotion to the souls in Purgatory, and her strict asceticism.[75] Juliana of Cornillon (1193–1258) was prioress of an augustinian house which she

[70] Canivez (as n. 59), 11.
[71] McDonnell (as n. 45), 85.
[72] On motivation, see Grundmann, *Religiöse Bewegungen*, (as n. 47), 191–197.
[73] McDonnell (as n. 45), 301–305. Juliana took refuge with the Cistercians but did not actually enter the Order; see below. On Lutgard, see Canivez (as n. 59), 180–181.
[74] Roger DeGanck, ed. and trans., *The Life of Beatrice of Nazareth* (Kalamazoo 1991) xix, xxiv.
[75] Canivez (as n. 59), 180–185.

tried to reform. In the end she was forced to leave and found refuge with Cistercians, though she never formally joined the Order. She was noted for her devotion to the Eucharist, and urged the institution of a feast in its honour. Largely through her efforts the feast of Corpus Christi was first celebrated in Liége in 1246; it was extended to the whole church by Pope Urban IV in 1265.[76]

These women, and famous beguines like Hadewijch and Mary of Oignies, were strongly influenced by Saint Bernard. Juliana of Cornillion is said to have known by heart twenty of his sermons on the Song of Songs.[77] Love was the central theme of Bernard's spirituality. The women were inspired to express their love for Jesus in language which was lyrical and very personal. Their insights often came to them through visions. It has been suggested that there was a difference between male and female spirituality. Monks had left behind a mother, sister, or fiancée. For them Our Lady was a substitute—they sublimated their love of the feminine in their devotion to her. The women, however, saw Christ as their divine spouse. He represented for them the earthly love they had renounced.[78] Be that as it may, the writings of the religious women of this period were enormously influential. The affective language they used appears in vernacular prayers composed for the laity throughout the Middle Ages. Until the Second Vatican Council, every Catholic book of devotion contained prayers which echoed their spirituality.[79]

Whatever the misgivings of the cistercian Chapter General about female religious, the cistercian abbots of the southern Low Countries enthusiastically supported them. The abbey of Villers in Brabant was particularly notable in this respect. The community stood out as a centre of religious fervour. In

---

[76] McDonnell (as n. 45), 299–315.

[77] Ibid. 300; Canivez (as n. 59), 91.

[78] Simone Roisin, *L'hagiographie cistercienne dans le diocese de Liège au xiiie siècle* (Louvain 1947) 115–116.

[79] For an introduction to this subject, see S. Axters, *The Spirituality of the Old Low Countries* (London 1954) and De Ganck (as n. 60).

the seventeenth century the monks composed a 'Litany of the Saints of Villers' which contained sixty names. Because of the miracles worked at the tomb of one of the brothers, the abbey petitioned for his canonisation. Pope Gregory IX was not averse, but the Chapter General refused to support the cause, 'in case saints are cheapened in the Order because of their profusion'.

A succession of abbots—Charles de Seyne (1197–1209), Conrad of Urach (1209–1214; later abbot of Clairvaux and finally a cardinal), Walter of Utrecht (1214–1221), William of Brussels (1221–1237), and Jacques de Bonal (1276–1283)—defended female religious from accusations of heresy, gave advice and encouragement to prospective founders of abbeys for women, and took over their pastoral care. Villers extended its ministry beyond the Cistercian Order. Juliana of Cornillon, exiled from her own religious house, received advice and support there, and asked to be buried in the abbey church.[80] Impoverished beguines received regular pensions from Villers, as its account books show.[81]

The cistercian nuns also owed a great deal to the generosity of the ducal house of Brabant. In 1201 Henry I, duke of Brabant, and his wife, gave land for the foundation of La Cambre, now at the end of the Avenue Louise in Brussels. This was one of the houses under the pastoral care of Villers. So was Valduc, generously endowed by Duke Henry II in 1231.[82]

In England, Saint Hilda's Whitby did not survive the viking ravages of the ninth century, but nine monasteries of nuns were in existence in the kingdom at the time of its conquest by William of Normandy. Most of them had close connections with the old english royal family and remained centres of english sentiment long after the abbeys for men had swung to the Normans. They were also notable centres of learning. The poetess Marie de France was abbess of Shaftesbury. Latin

---

[80] Canivez (as n. 59), 86–92.
[81] McDonnell (as n. 45), 336–338.
[82] Canivez (as n. 59), 149–156, 198–202.

poetry of high quality was produced at Amesbury, Wilton, and the nuns' minster at Winchester. Girls of noble families were often sent to these abbeys to be educated,[83] and the letters of Saint Anselm bear witness to their high standard of observance.

On the other hand, the outburst of religious fervour among women in the southern Low Countries found no echoes across the Channel, in spite of England's close economic and cultural ties with this area. Indeed, the only english nun venerated as a saint after the Norman Conquest was Christina of Markyate.[84] Although a large number of religious houses for women were founded in England after 1066, none of them achieved any eminence.[85]

Throughout the Middle Ages the ethos of religious houses, whether for men or for women, was the same. In an observant community the day was dominated by the liturgy, from the night office in the small hours to Compline in the evening, after which the religious observed the 'great silence' until the morning. The worship of God was a sufficient end in itself, but the prayers of religious were also considered to be of value to society and to individuals. The foundation charters of houses for nuns show that the prayers of the women were appreciated no less than those of the men.[86] As patrons increasingly demanded Masses, however, the women were at a disadvantage. In an abbey for men, where all the choir monks were priests, the desired Masses could easily be provided. Nuns, on the other hand, had to pay chaplains to cope with the demand. This was necessary even where small communities of priests were attached. A house of women, therefore, had additional expenses which the men were spared.[87]

The quality and variety of feminine religious life during the High Middle Ages can be gauged from the study of three remarkable women. The best known nun of the period is also,

---

[83] D. Knowles, *The Monastic Order in England* (Cambridge 1950) 136–139.
[84] See above pp. 197–198.
[85] See the thorough study by S. Thompson (above n. 9).
[86] Johnson (as n. 59), 59, 233–236.
[87] Ibid. 137–138.

perhaps, the most problematical. Heloïse was born around the year 1090.[88] From an early age she gave evidence of a remarkable intelligence and aptitude for letters. She was first sent to be educated by the benedictine nuns of Argenteuil, north of Paris. Later her uncle Fulbert, a canon of Paris, took her into his own house and engaged Abelard, another canon of the cathedral and a renowned teacher, to tutor her privately. The two young people became lovers and presently Heloïse gave birth to a boy. After some bargaining with her family Abelard and Heloïse were married, but by this time (it was around the year 1117) church reformers were making progress with their demand that the clergy should be celibate. Although there were still many married clergymen, the position of a cleric's wife was becoming uncomfortable. This may lie behind Heloïse's later assertion that she would have preferred to be Abelard's whore.

Fulbert bided his time, waiting for an opportunity to take his revenge for the insult to his family. One night hired ruffians attacked Abelard and emasculated him. He felt obliged to become a monk and chose to enter the prestigious abbey of Saint Denis near Paris. Heloïse returned to Argenteuil where she had been educated and, at his insistence, became a nun there. When, around 1131, she and the other nuns were expelled for alleged immorality they took refuge at the Paraclete, a property in Champagne which belonged to Abelard and to which he had retired to take up a hermit's life after disagreements with the monks of Saint Denis. In 1135 Heloïse was elected abbess of the Paraclete.

As a religious superior she was highly regarded in the monastic circles of her time. Bernard of Clairvaux visited the Paraclete and preached to the nuns, who listened with rapt

[88] On Heloïse see H. Silvestre, DHGE 23 (1990) 946–958, with bibliography. The most recent study of the relationship between Heloïse and Abelard is to be found in Michael Clanchy, *Abelard: A Medieval Life* (Oxford 1997). There is an english translation of Heloïse's statutes for the Paraclete: Institutiones Nostrae: *The Paraclete Statutes*, ed, and trans. C. Waddell (Gethsemani-Kalamazoo 1987).

attention ' as to an angel'.[89] Peter the Venerable compared Heloïse to Deborah and other heroines, adding that it would be a joy to him if she settled at Marcigny.[90] Abelard's influence always remained paramount. In a series of letters, he tried to spiritualise their former relationship, addressing her as 'Handmaid of the Lord, once dear to me in the world, now most dear in Christ, once wife in the flesh, now sister in the spirit, and sharing the same profession with me'.[91] He answered her questions about difficult passages in Holy Scripture, composed a set of hymns for her community, and dedicated a number of treatises to her. Heloise never repudiated her past. Her letters to Abelard were written with passion. She claims that it was entirely at his request that she entered religion and does not fall in with his spiritualising of their relationship.

Heloïse was able to obtain numerous privileges for her house from successive popes and kings of France, as well as from bishops and nobles. She compiled a set of customs for her community: *Institutiones Nostrae*, ('our institutions'). She thus joined, in a modest way, the ranks of monastic legislators of this period. All in all, however, we may ask whether her religious vocation was genuine and to what extent her achievements as an abbess were, for her, only the second best option.

Peter the Venerable did not doubt her love for Abelard and showed a delicate understanding for her feelings. In 1140, after the Council of Sens had condemned Abelard as a heretic and the sentence had been confirmed by the pope, Peter gave the aging philosopher refuge at Cluny. In a letter to Heloïse he subsequently described Abelard's last days. Later he brought the body to the Paraclete for burial. Heloïse herself died, a highly respected and influential abbess, in 1164. The admiration in which, in spite of her lurid past, she was held by the leading churchmen of her day is a tribute to her remarkable gifts,

---

[89] Clanchy (as n. 88), 152, maintains that Bernard came 'nosing around' the Paraclete and that Heloise got round him by flattery. But is it likely that Bernard would have preached there uninvited?
[90] Schmitz (as n. 2), 89–90.
[91] DHGE 23:949.

and sheds an unexpectedly pleasant light upon ecclesiastical society at the time.

Hildegard of Bingen was her exact contemporary. She was born in 1098.[92] Her parents belonged to the rhenish franconian aristocracy. The nobility in this area had exercised authority and responsibility since roman times. From her family background Hildegard derived her imperiousness, and her fearlessness in the face of emperors and prelates.

Already as a small child she saw visions. 'From the moment I was formed,' she wrote in an autobiography which has survived in part, 'when with a breath of life God created me in my mother's womb, he blazed this vision on my soul. When I was three years old I received enough illumination to set me trembling, but because of my youth I could not speak of it'.[93] When she was eight years old her parents entrusted her to Jutta, a recluse who was 'mistress' of a small community of female hermits attached to the abbey of Disibodenberg near the Rhine. From the start of her religious life, therefore, Hildegard imbibed the ideals of the new reformed monasticism. In 1136 Jutta died, and Hildegard was elected to succeed her.

In 1141 she began to write her visions down. They attracted attention and the inevitable charges of heresy. She appealed to Saint Bernard, who wrote to her encouragingly. In 1147–1148, Pope Eugenius III came to Germany to preach the Crusade, accompanied by the abbot of Clairvaux. A synod was held at Trier at which, with Bernard's support, she was vindicated. Around this time Hildegard decided to move her community to a more central location. She obtained land at Rupertsberg, near Bingen on the Rhine. By 1150 all her nuns were settled there. It is probable that they here began to observe the Benedictine Rule. The move was not welcome to the monks of Disibodenberg, among others. Hildegard had consulted no one . Always adept at gaining the support of the right people,

---

[92] On Hildegard, see DS 7/1 (1968) 505–521; LM 5 (1991) 13–15.
[93] Quoted DS 7/1:508.

she rode out the storm with the help of her friend Henry, the archbishop of Mainz.

Because the emperors were so often at loggerheads with the popes, the church reforms met with the greatest opposition in Germany. Rupertsberg became an important centre of the papal party. Hildegard gathered about her a group of able propagandists, some of whose names are known: her secretary the monk Volmar, for instance, and his successor Guibert of Gembloux. Some three hundred of her own letters have survived.

In 1159 there was a papal schism at Rome. Victor IV was supported by the emperor Frederick Barbarossa, while the party of church reformers recognised Alexander III. Because of the crisis in the Church Hildegard undertook four preaching tours. Her first journey in 1160 took her south to Mainz and then to the area of modern Bavaria. Later in the year she went west to Trier and the area of Lorraine on the borders with France. A few years later she went by ship down the Rhine to Cologne and the towns along the river banks. The purpose of this journey was to combat the cathar heresy. A final journey took her to Swabia. Here the emperor exercised great influence, but the cause of Pope Alexander was supported by the great abbeys. Wherever Hildegard went she drew vast crowds. She preached about the schism and also about the christian life. The vices of the clergy and laity she condemned, and she took the opportunity to visit monasteries and to support reform.

Essential to Hildegard's thought was the idea that the visible and material world could only be understood by reference to the reality behind it. She was conscious of the cosmic importance of all moral conflicts. The battle between good and evil within an individual was of significance for the whole world. The person—the microcosm—reflects the conflicts of the universe—the macrocosm. She illustrated these themes by the use of images. Some she borrowed from the Bible, the liturgy, or popular mythology; some she invented herself—the city, the tower, the throne, the man in the sea, and many others.

The extraordinary miniatures which illustrate one of her books were probably worked out under her direction.

Hildegard's intention was to restore the divine and cosmic harmony which had been destroyed by sin. Bad health she took as a sign of disharmony and interested herself in medicine on which she wrote a treatise. Music was a sign of the harmony which God intended. Seventy-seven of Hildegard's musical compositions survive, as well as a musical morality play, the *Ordo Virtutum* ('the ordering of the virtues').

In 1177 Rupertsberg was placed under interdict, on a pretext, by the chapter of Mainz. The real reasons are obscure, but no doubt Hildegard's propaganda during the recently healed schism had caused much bitterness. The archbishop was away in Italy and Hildegard had to wait until his return in 1179 for the sentence to be lifted. She died a few months later.

Like Hildegard, Gertrude the Great joined a religious community at a very early age, but here the resemblance ends. Gertrude was born in 1256. She entered the monastery of Helfta in Saxony at the age of five, and her whole development took place within its walls.[94] She was known to a number of learned friars in the neighbourhood,[95] but her writings attracted little attention. Only in the sixteenth century, when her works were printed, did she shoot into fame as one of the luminaries of the Roman Catholic Church.[96]

The community to which she belonged was truly remarkable.[97] It was founded in 1229 by Count Burchard of Mansfeld and his wife for some 'grey sisters' from Halberstadt. The sisters settled on the Mansfeld estates and the founders stipulated that they were to live according to the cistercian observances. The house was never officially incorporated into the Order, however. It was one of the many monasteries for

---

[94] On Gertrude, see DS 6 (1967) 331–339; *Les moniales cisterciennes* (as n. 51), vol. 4:133–138; *Gertrude d'Helfta: Oeuvres Spirituelles*, 1 (Paris 1967) 7–38; M. J. Finnegan, *The Women of Helfta* (Athens, Georgia 1991).

[95] *Oeuvres spirituelles* (as n. 94), 2:104–105.

[96] See discussion in *Oeuvres* (as n. 94), 1:16–38.

[97] On Helfta, see DHGE 23 (1990) 894–896.

women where the cistercian way of life was adopted, without the Cistercian Order taking any responsibility for it. The community remained subject to the bishop of Halberstadt, and dominican friars acted as chaplains.

The site on the Mansfeld estate proved inconvenient. In 1234 the community moved to Rodarsdorf, some miles south. In 1258 shortage of water made another move necessary. This time the nuns settled at Helfta. In 1284 the monastery was sacked during some local disturbances, and in 1296, during a vacancy of the diocese, placed under an interdict by the canons of Halberstadt. In 1342 the house was burned down in the course of more civil disorders. The nuns moved some miles away to a new site at Neu-Helfta, where they remained until their house was suppressed at the Reformation. In spite of these occasional reverses of fortune, the monastery was well endowed and patronised by noble familes in the region. The standard of observance was high. Around 1270 the beguine Mechtild of Magdeburg settled at Helfta, without joining the community. Her influence, and that of the abbess, Gertrude of Hackeborn (1251–1291/2), laid the foundations for the remarkable flowering of theology and mysticism, which made Helfta one of the most creative monasteries of the Middle Ages.[98]

The most formative influence on the future Gertrude the Great was that of the novice-mistress Mechtild the Younger (1241–1299—not to be confused with her namesake of Magdeburg). Mechtild the Younger's revelations and spiritual experiences were later recorded by an anonymous nun who was most probably Gertrude herself. Gertrude's own way of life and the nature of her experiences were later described in detail by another anonymous nun. Helfta, then, is unique for the line of spiritual writers associated with it, each building on the work of her predecessor, but retaining her own individuality.

Gertrude herself was a talented young woman and at all times an observant nun, but it was only in 1281, when she

---

[98] Finnegan (as n. 92), 1–5.

was twenty-five, that she underwent a true conversion. Her writings must date from after that time. She had learned the affective spirituality of the beguines, probably from the older Mechtild, but there were other influences: the Benedictine Rule lived out with cistercian simplicity, the fathers, Saint Bernard, and the Bible, parts of which she translated.[99]

Gertrude's theology was based on a direct confrontation with God, expressed through visions and revelations. There was a certain tension in her view of the Godhead; she saw God sometimes as a majestic king and judge and at others as a tender lover.[100] Intimacy, however, predominated. Her anthropology was optimistic. She did not emphasise the contrast between the perfection of the Divinity and the corruption of the flesh, but insisted that what was human could be absorbed into the divine. 'O my love, you do not only enlighten but deify. . . .'[101] 'O beloved Jesus, by that love which drew you, my God, to be made man, so that you might seek and save that which was lost, come now into me, O my well-beloved, and enable me to penetrate even into your own self'.[102] She concludes a meditation on the Transfiguration of Christ by assuring her readers that, by his grace, both the soul and the body can be transfigured into his glory.[103]

'When necessity required,' her anonymous admirer tells us, 'she often abandoned the sweetness of contemplation, because there was need to help someone in temptation, console

---

[99] *The Herald*, 1.7.1–4; *Oeuvres* (as n. 94) 2:152–159. On Gertrude's spirituality, see Finnegan (as n. 94), 113–130. [English translation by Alexandra Barratt is *The Herald of God's Loving-Kindness*, Books 1–2 (Kalamazoo 1991) pp. 57–60—ed.]

[100] On the contradictions in Gertrude, see *Les moniales cisterciennes* (as n. 51), vol. 4: 133–134.

[101] *O amor non lucifer sed deifer*, *Exercises*, 5; *Oeuvres* (as n. 94), 1: 160–161. [English translation by Gertrud Jaron Lewis and Jack Lewis, *Gertrud the Great of Helfta; Spiritual Exercises* (Kalamazoo 1989) 74, line 38: 'O love, not light-bearing but God-bearing'—ed.]

[102] *Exercises*, 2; *Oeuvres* (as n. 94), 1:84–85; [ET (as n. 101), 36—ed.]

[103] *The Herald*, 3.12.2; *Oeuvres* (as n. 94) 3:54–55 [English translation by Alexandra Barratt, *The Herald of God's Loving Kindness*, Book 3 (Kalamazoo 1999) 53—ed.]

someone in despair, or aid someone in need.'[104] If any member of the community was in need of correction, Gertrude was tireless, even when told by others that she was wasting her time. Outside Helfta she supported a general reform of the religious life. The rest of her time she spent writing treatises and commentaries,[105] distributing copies where she thought they would do good.[106]

She was well aware of the conventional view of the frailty of women, and at times shared it.

> Proportion my strength to the enterprises I must undertake for love of you . . . grant to my feebler sex that manly courage which may give me the right to enter one day into the mystic chamber where the union of the soul with yourself is made perfect.[107]

At other times she did not hesitate to advise the scrupulous whether they should go to Communion or not.[108] She was sure that she had divine sanction:

> Then the Lord breathed on her and bestowed on her the Holy Spirit saying, 'Receive the Holy Spirit within you,[109] whose sins you shall remit they are remitted'. Then she replied, 'Lord, how can this be, when this power of binding and loosing is given only to priests?' The Lord answered, 'If by my Spirit you judge that there is no guilt in the case of some person, be sure that he will be held guiltless before me. If in someone's case you judge there is guilt, he will be held guilty before me, for I speak through your mouth.[110]

The sixteenth-century editors of Gertrude's writings confused her with her namesake and contemporary, the abbess

---

[104] *The Herald* 1.4.2; *Oeuvres* 2:142–144 [*The Herald* . . . Bk. 1 (as n. 99) 51—ed.]

[105] *The Herald* 1.7.1–4; *Oeuvres* 2:152–159 [ET(as n. 99), 57–60—ed.]

[106] *The Herald* 1.4.2; *Oeuvres* 2:142–144 [ET (as n. 99), 50–51—ed.]

[107] *Exercises*, 5; *Oeuvres* (as n. 94), 1:186–187; [ET (as n. 101), 87—ed.]

[108] *The Herald* 1.14.1–2; *Oeuvres* (as n. 94), 2:196–199 [ET (as n. 99), 82–83—ed.].

[109] Plural.

[110] *The Herald*, 4. 32.1; *Oeuvres* (as n. 94). 2:281.

Gertrude of Hackeborn. Our Gertrude thus became 'Saint
Gertrude, Virgin and Abbess'. Her cognomen, 'The Great',
though well deserved, also made her appear formidable. In
fact, it should never be forgotten that when she died in 1301/
1302 she was around forty-five. Her writings still breathe the
ardour of youth, and some of the tensions are unresolved. The
lyrical quality of her Latin makes it easy to overlook her ability
to absorb and synthesise the many influences upon her. The
beauty is almost painful:

> O Jesus, one and only Love of my heart, O my beloved
> overflowing with tenderness, loved, loved, loved far above
> all that has ever been loved, my heart sighs and languishes
> with desire of you. You are for it like a spring-day, instinct
> with quickening life, and fragrant with the balmy sweetness
> of countless flowers. May this most intimate union with you
> be effected in me, true and living Sun that you are! Then shall
> your genial influence make my soul bud flowers and fruits of
> a growth in holiness not unworthy of you. With breathless
> eagerness I await your coming.[111]

---

[111] *Exercises* 3; *Oeuvres* (as n. 94), 1:96–97; [ET (as n. 101), 40–41—ed.]

Chapter 9
DECAY AND RENEWAL:
THE LATE MIDDLE AGES

THE MORAL DECADENCE of monks and nuns is a familiar theme in the literature of the late Middle Ages.. For Giovanni Boccaccio, monks are hypocrites who will miss no opportunity to indulge their sexual lusts provided they can do so in secret.[1] In Chaucer's *Canterbury Tales* we meet a monk who lives like a country gentleman and loves hunting:

> He did not rate that text a plucked hen
> Which says that hunters are not holy men
> And that a monk uncloistered is a mere
> Fish out of water, flapping on the pier,
> That is to say, a monk out of his cloister.
> That was a text he held not worth an oyster.[2]

Western Monasticism was suffering from its very success. In Saint Bernard's time the reformed monasteries had to struggle for survival. Hard work and discipline brought them prosperity and even wealth. Already by the end of the twelfth century they were rich, and, as such, subject to bitter criticism.[3] In the early thirteenth century the white monks were upstaged by the friars, who were providing new and heroic models of poverty. A profound analysis of the decline of the old monastic orders can be found in the writings of an anonymous early Franciscan:

---

[1] *The Decameron*, 1st Day, 4th story.
[2] *Geoffrey Chaucer: The Canterbury Tales*, translated by N. Coghill (London 1985) 23–24.
[3] See L. J. Lekai, *The Cistercians, Ideals and Reality* (Kent, Ohio 1977) 299–303.

But once they were walking in such great fervour of love for Christ, Avarice, taking the name of Discretion, began to say to them: 'Do not show yourselves so unbending before men and do not despise in this way the honour they show you; but show yourselves affable to them and do not outwardly spurn the glory they offer you, but do so at most inwardly. It is good to have the friendship of kings, acquaintance with princes, and familiarity with the great, for when they thus honour and revere you, when they rise and come to meet you, many who see this will be the more easily turned to God by their example.' They indeed, seeing the advantage of this, accepted the proffered counsel; but not guarding themselves against the snare set for them along the way, they at length embraced glory and honour with all their heart.[4]

There is a notable lack of confidence in the religious life in the writings of many late medieval holy men and women. Saint Bridget of Sweden compared the religious orders of her time to a vineyard, where weeds had so corrupted the vines that they were hardly able to bear fruit.[5] In Raymund of Capua's Life of Saint Catherine of Siena, the saint is depicted as a lonely figure, in spite of belonging to a religious community. Her sisters appear as obstacles to her spiritual progress. 'Take my word for it,' comments her biographer, himself a friar, 'it is precisely in spiritual and religious minded people—unless self-love be altogether dead in them—that envy often holds sway in its deadliest form; and it is lashed into uncontrollable fury when they witness others performing feats which they know themselves incapable of'.[6]

Because of their wealth religious houses came to be valued more as profitable concerns than as centres of spirituality. By the twelfth century the abbots of great benedictine houses had become powerful feudal lords. This made frequent contact with seculars necessary, and it was found that a community's

---

[4] 'Sacrum Commercium', translated by P. Hermann ofm, *St. Francis of Assisi: Writings and Biographies*, ed. M. A. Habig, (London 1979–Chicago 1983) 1578.
[5] *Sancta Birgitta, Opera Minora* 1, ed. S. Eklund (Stockholm 1975) 102–103.
[6] *The Life of St. Catherine of Siena by Raymond of Capua*, trans. and ed. C. Kerans op (Dublin 1980) 165.

monastic peace would best be preserved if the abbot lived in a separate establishment, with his own household and with revenues to uphold it.[7] The reformed Orders held out against such arrangements, but by the thirteenth century they too had succumbed. Increasingly the office of abbot was regarded as a source of income. From the fourteenth century the Avignon popes made abbatial appointments regardless of the wishes of the community. Eventually, for political or family reasons, a secular clerk or even a layman might be appointed 'commendatory abbot' of a religious house. The interest he took in his office was usually purely financial.[8] Nothing was more effective than the system of *commendam* in destroying the discipline of religious houses.

As the standard of comfort within religious houses rose, the common life was gradually abandoned. A study of the monasteries in the area of the Lower Rhine during the thirteenth and fourteenth centuries[9] shows that most monks had ceased to observe the Rule in the matter of private property. Monasteries limited the number of monks they would admit, so that the properties of the house could be divided into portions from which each monk enjoyed a personal income.[10] Communities had a common meal together only on special feast days; otherwise each monk ate in his own cell, waited upon by one or more servants. Enclosure was ignored, and the habit seldom worn. One monastery had an official whose task it was to reward with special payments those monks who were present at one of the daily offices. The author of a recent study of the abbey of Westminster in England during the late Middle Ages,[11] remarks that by the fifteenth century the

---

[7] For the process as it developed in England, see D. Knowles, *The Monastic Order in England* (Cambridge 1950) 404–406.

[8] Philibert Schmitz, *Histoire de l'ordre de Saint Benoît*, 3 (Maredsous 1948) 5.

[9] E. Wisplinghoff, 'Die Benediktinerkloster des Niederrheins', *Festschrift H. Heimpel*, Veröffentlichungen des Max-Planck-Instituts für Geschichte, 36/2 (Göttingen 1972) 277–291.

[10] For the development of private property in English monasteries at this period see Knowles, *The Religious Orders in England*, 2 (Cambridge 1955) 240–245.

[11] Barbara Harvey, *Living and Dying in England 1100–1540: The Monastic Experience* (Oxford 1993).

common life was, for most Benedictines, a thing of the past. Regular attendance at the liturgical hours and the partaking of common meals were obligations from which the more senior monks were freed. Monks belonged to the upper classes and expected to be as well housed and fed as their social equals.[12] Saint Benedict's prohibition of flesh meat was circumvented by allowing meat to be eaten outside the refectory. On any given day more than half the community would be eating in the *misericord*, a 'mercy' room originally intended for the sick, where dishes not allowed by the Rule could be consumed.[13] The early Cistercians had insisted on a strictly vegetarian diet, but in the thirteenth century the white monks, too, began to weaken until, in 1475, they obtained from Pope Sixtus IV a general dispensation allowing them to eat meat.[14]

Wealth, then, led to the abandonment of the common life and this, paradoxically, often led to the eventual loss of wealth itself. When each individual monk enjoyed his own personal share of the revenues, there was less reason to treat the common property of the house with respect. In the late thirteenth and early fourteenth centuries the monasteries of the Lower Rhine were crippled by debts which coherent economic policies could easily have avoided. This was happening at a time of general prosperity, when the landowners round about were doing well.[15] Among perceptive monks at this period it was noted that 'the religious life breeds wealth, wealth destroys the religious life, after which the wealth goes too'.[16]

Contemporaries were more interested in the complete breakdown of discipline in some houses and evidence of immorality. Then as now, people delighted to hear of scandals among those who were supposed to be exemplars of virtue. No doubt these tales lost nothing in the telling. Research, however,

---

[12] Ibid. 1–2.
[13] Ibid. 9–14.
[14] G. Müller, 'Der Fleischgenuss im Orden', *Cistercienser Chronik* 18 (1906) *passim.*
[15] Wisplinghoff (as n. 9), 277–291.
[16] Quoted P. Engelbert, 'Die Bursfelder Benediktinerkongregation', *Historisches Jahrbuch* 103 (1983) 41.

disconcertingly confirms much of the moral criticism. Some bulls of Pope Benedict XII make uncomfortable reading. In 1335 he ordered his legate to investigate the religious houses in the ecclesiastical provinces of Narbonne and Arles.[17] The state of the monasteries, wrote the pope, was deplorable. Monks were guilty of immorality and luxury. They left their enclosure to go hunting. Superiors involved themselves in business transactions and dissipated monastic property. Monks were known to leave church before the service was over. Not infrequently they absented themselves from the canonical hours altogether, preferring instead to listen to secular music. They seldom wore the monastic habit. Many were unfaithful to their vow of chastity, caring little for the disrepute their conduct brought the religious life. Since the pope lived at Avignon, and these provinces were on his doorstep, he would have been well informed about conditions there.

The most striking impression given by these papal documents is that there was a whole region in which not a single edifying religious house was to be found. This wholesale decadence of the religious life can be observed everywhere in the late Middle Ages.. In the county of Lancaster in England, a rather poor area, there were nine religious houses (not counting the friaries): three benedictine priories, two cistercian abbeys, three augustinian priories and one premonstratensian abbey. In the first half of the fourteenth century each of them was involved in at least one lawsuit about property.[18] Some of these disputes involved the participants in violence.[19] Religious discipline suffered accordingly. In 1334 it was found that a former prior of the benedictine house at Upholland was living like a private gentleman on one of the abbey's estates, making no effort to observe the Rule.[20] In 1347 the augustinian prior of Burclough was accused of being involved in the criminal

---

[17] *Benoît XII, lettres closes et patentes intéressant les pays autres que la France*, ed. J. M. Vidal et G. Mollat (Paris 1950) Nos. 493, 494.
[18] *The Victoria History of the County of Lancaster*, 2, ed. W. Farrer and J. Brownhill (London 1908) 102–161.
[19] See e.g. ibid. 108, 170–171.
[20] Ibid. 111.

abduction of a widow. In the course of this affair two persons were killed.[21] At the premonstratensian abbey of Cockersand, one canon was murdered by another in 1327. Twenty years later the abbot of Cockersand, accompanied by four of his canons and a band of armed men, assaulted and badly wounded a knight in the town of Lancaster.[22]

One can easily gain the impression that there was not a single observant religious house in the late Middle Ages. In fact, among the ancient and famous monasteries were quite a few in which a high standard was maintained. Moreover, even a decayed religious house could be revived by a dedicated superior. For much of the fifteenth century, for example, the cistercian house of Kinloss in Scotland was noted for laxity and immorality. Then, in 1500, the monks elected a new abbot, Thomas Chrystall. Already as a novice Chrystall had been an example of traditional monastic piety. As superior he inaugurated an ambitious building programme. The abbey church was re-roofed and redecorated. A new library was built and stocked with the works of the Fathers. There was a renewed emphasis on the restoration of regular discipline. The revived house attracted recruits. When he was elected, there were fourteen monks at Kinloss. When he retired in 1528, there were twenty. [23] His achievement, on the very eve of the Reformation, was indeed remarkable.

The fact remains, however, that although there were outstanding centres of monastic excellence in the late Middle Ages, regular observance in the majority of houses left much to be desired. Most religious communities were perfectly respectable, and incidents of vice, though spectacular, were not typical. There can be no doubt, however, that in general life in a religious house was comfortable, that individualism had triumphed over the common life, and that the Divine Office was no longer given the priority which Saint Benedict

---

[21] Ibid. 150.

[22] Ibid. 155.

[23] *Ferrerii Historia Abbatum de Kynloss una cum vita Thomae Chrystalli abbatis*, ed. J. P. Muirhead (Edinburgh 1839).

had assigned to it. No historian familiar with the sources can ignore the cumulative evidence of a widespread decline in standards which appears in papal and episcopal registers, visitation records, conciliar decrees, wills, narrative sources, archaeological evidence, and the strictures of holy men and women.

The Church was well aware of the need for reform. The specialisation of the religious life and its expression through numerous orders, often competing with one another, the proliferation of every kind of religious house, were now seen as considerable obstacles to the maintenance of discipline. Already in 1215 the Fourth Lateran Council forbade the foundation of any new religious order, 'lest too great a variety . . . lead to grave confusion in God's Church'. In 1274 the Second Council of Lyons renewed this prohibition which, it was stated, had not been properly observed.[24] At the Council of Vienne in 1311 there was a concerted attack on the religious orders and their privileges.[25] The bishop of Angers said that there were too many small religious houses. They should be amalgamated, because a larger community was more likely to be disciplined.[26] The Fourth Lateran Council had been more positive when it decreed that in every province or kingdom abbots who were not accustomed to meeting in chapters general (that is to say, the black monks) should in future assemble regularly to discuss the reform of their order and the observance of the Rule. They should meet 'in the manner of Cistercians', and at the beginning some Cistercians might be asked to attend, in order to guide them about procedure.[27]

During the twelfth century the popes had protected religious movements when asked to do so, approved their legislation, and granted them exemptions and privileges. They had not otherwise interfered in the internal affairs of the new

---

[24] *Decrees of the Ecumenical Councils*, 1, ed. N. P. Tanner, (Georgetown 1990) 242 (Lateran); 326–327 (II Lyons).
[25] J. Lecler, *Vienne*, Histoire des conciles écuméniques, 8 (Paris 1964) 120–127.
[26] Ibid. 126.
[27] Tanner (as n. 24), 240–241.

orders. In the thirteenth century, however, the popes involved themselves far more intimately in the affairs of religious. A landmark was the decision by Gregory IX, in 1230, that the Testament of Saint Francis was not literally binding on the Franciscans.[28] Some thirty years later the problems of the Cistercians preoccupied the papacy. The powers of the five senior abbots over the Order as a whole were ill-defined. The abbot of Cîteaux was at loggerheads with the four others. Clement IV's bull *Parvus Fons* of 1265 effectively replaced the *Carta Caritatis*. The composition of the *Diffinitorium*, an inner steering committee of the Chapter General which in fact managed its business, had become a bone of contention. The bull ensured that each of the five senior abbots should have equal representation upon it. The bull also limited the powers of father abbots and of visitors. In future, except in very routine cases, they could not depose an abbot without the approval of the Chapter General.[29] These interventions by the papacy in the internal affairs of monks, for which there was no precedent in earlier practice, were justified by the then prevailing doctrine of the pope as 'universal ordinary', according to which he was the immediate superior of every Christian.

The most thoroughgoing papal legislation about the religious life was initiated by pope Benedict XII (1334–1342).[30] The bulls he issued about monastic indiscipline in southern France date from the beginning of his pontificate. His legate was ordered to investigate and reform all religious houses of whatever Order, as well as cathedrals and collegiate churches. This wholesale attitude to the religious life was also a feature of

---

[28] J. R. H. Moorman, *A History of the Franciscan Order* (Oxford 1968) 89–91.
[29] Text of the bull, Canivez, *Statuta* 1265 pp. 22–30. For the background see Lekai (as n. 3), 69–72.
[30] On Pope Benedict's reforms, see G. Mollat, *The Popes at Avignon* (London 1949) 29–33; J. B. Mahn, *Le pape Benoît XII et les cisterciens,* Bibliothèque de l'école des hautes études fasc. 295 (Paris 1949); Bernhard Schimmelpfennig, 'Zisterzienserideal und Kirchenreform–Benedikt XII (1334–42) als Reformpapst', *Zisterzienserstudien* 3 (1976) 11–43; B. Schimmelpfennig, 'Das Papstum und die Reform des Zisterzienserordens im späten Mittelalter', in K. Elm ed., *Reformbemühungen und Observanzbestrebungen im spätmittelalterlichen Ordenswesen* (Berlin 1989) 399–430.

the time. To disregard the separate traditions and privileges of the different orders seemed to contemporaries to be the only way to effect reform. It is noteworthy that Pope Benedict, a Cistercian sincerely attached to his own Order,[31] shared this view. This brutal attempt to bring in reform from the outside, however, was bound to provoke fierce opposition. One friar wrote of the pope, ' One can say of him that the best thing he ever did was to die'.[32]

It was natural that Benedict should first attempt to reform his own Cistercian Order. His advisers were the abbots of Cîteaux, La Ferté, Clairvaux, and Morimond.[33] They managed to soften some of the pope's more radical suggestions, alleging no less than forty objections to his proposal (borrowed from the Dominicans) that one monk elected from each community should sit with the abbots at the Chapter General.[34] In the end, Benedict's bull *Fulgens sicut stella* (1334) was little more than an appendix to *Parvus Fons*, dealing with matters not touched upon in the earlier document. The ancient rules about attendance at the Chapter General, meat-eating, and sleeping in the common dormitory were reinforced. There were detailed provisions about proper financial management in each house and in the Order as a whole. More innovative were its provisions about study. Each abbey was to send a certain number of monks to university, the cleverest to Paris, others to local *studia* like Oxford or Salamanca. They were to study theology, but not law.[35]

Benedict's bull *Summi Magistri* (1336), directed at the Benedictines, built on the work of the Fourth Lateran Council. It was composed with the advice of the abbot of Cluny and five other abbots from eastern and southern France. The black monks were grouped into thirty-six specially created provinces.

---

[31] See introduction to the bull *Fulgens sicut stella*, Canivez, *Statuta* 1335, pp. 410–411.
[32] Quoted, Schimmelpfennig, 'Zisterzienserideal' (as n. 30), 31.
[33] Schimmelpfennig (as above), 32.
[34] Mahn (as n. 30), 90–116.
[35] Schimmelpfennig, 'Zisterzienserideal' (as n. 30), 32–33. For the text of *Fulgens*, see *Statuta* (as n. 29), pp. 410–436.

The abbots of each were to meet every three years for a provincial chapter. In every monastery a master was to teach grammar, logic, and philosophy, and a number of monks from each house were to be sent to the principal universities to study theology, scripture, or canon law.[36] Pope Benedict also issued bulls for the augustinian canons and the franciscan friars, though his attempts to legislate for the Dominicans failed. The long term results of the pope's efforts were meagre. The statutes of the cistercian chapters general often cited *Fulgens sicut stella*.[37] Not even this modest success could be claimed for the benedictine reforms. There the system of provincial chapters and visitations arising from them never really got off the ground.[38]

For this there were a number of reasons. Benedict's advisers came from the area of modern France. For *Fulgens* he chose four of the five senior cistercian abbots; for *Summi Magistri* 'some cardinals', and the abbots of Cluny, La Chaise Dieu, Marseille, Psalmody, Montolieu, and Issoire.[39] This was limited and rather regional counsel for the reform of an Order which covered the whole of western Christendom, from Spain to Poland, from Scandinavia to southern Italy. Moreover, Benedict was pope for only eight years and was succeeeded by a pontiff whose aims and policies were very different. In any case, the fourteenth-century papacy lacked the spiritual vitality to initiate a real religious revival. Its residence in southern France since 1305 made it the target of bitter criticism, whilst its return to Rome in 1378 was the direct cause of a damaging schism.

In the monasteries themselves, senior figures felt that decline could be halted if monks were better educated. The friars, especially the Dominicans, shone in the new scholastic disciplines. Monks, by comparison, seemed ignorant and rustic. The best recruits were joining the new mendicant Orders. One

[36] Schmitz (as n. 8), 66–72.
[37] Schimmelpfennig, 'Das Papstum' (as n. 30), 404–406.
[38] Schmitz (as n. 8), 71–72.
[39] Schimmelpfennig, 'Zisterzienserideal' (as n. 30), 32.

abbot who felt strongly about intellectual standards among monks was the Cistercian Stephen of Lexington, successively abbot of Stanley in England (1223), Savigny in Normandy (1229), and Clairvaux (1243).[40] Thanks to his initiative the cistercian College of Saint Bernard at the university of Paris came into being around 1246, and other cistercian colleges followed at Montpellier, Oxford, Salamanca, Bologna, and elsewhere.[41] At Paris the cistercian college acquired a high reputation.[42] Jean de Mirecourt, who taught there in the 1340s, won wide repute as an extreme exponent of the nominalist school of philosophy. Another renowned cistercian scholar was the German Conrad of Ebrach. After teaching for some years at Bologna he went to Paris in 1370. From 1376–1384 he was teaching in Prague. In the latter year he moved to Vienna where he helped to organise the faculty of theology in the newly founded university there.[43]

The Benedictines followed hard on the heels of their cistercian brethren in bringing their monks to the universities. At Paris the earliest college for Benedictines was the college of Fleury. It was projected for monks of that ancient abbey in 1247, although it was another ten years before it actually got off the ground. More prestigious was the college of Cluny. The cluniac Chapter General agreed on the foundation in 1260 and the college was fully operative in 1269. Throughout the thirteenth century the Benedictines founded colleges in the universities of Christendom.[44] Almost everywhere the Cistercians were ahead of them. At Oxford, for instance, the white monks came first with the abbey of Rewley, founded in 1281 just outside the city walls. From here the student monks

---

[40] On Stephen of Lexington and cistercian university studies, see Lekai (as n. 3), 78–86.
[41] Ibid. 78–86.
[42] Ibid. 82.
[43] *Dictionnaire des auteurs cisterciens*, ed. E. Brouette, A. Dimier, et E. Manning (Rochefort 1975–1978), 184, 411.
[44] U. Berlière, 'Les collèges bénédictins aux universités du moyen âge', RB 10 (1893) 145–158. On the college of Cluny, see Beaunier, *Receuil des abbayes et prieurés de l'ancienne France* 1 (Paris 1905) 104.

could walk into town to attend lectures and disputations in the schools. The English Benedictines planned a house of studies at Oxford in 1277, but it was a reality only in the very last years of the thirteenth century.[45]

Something more than university education was required for a real reform of monastic life. For that, spiritual renewal was essential. During the fourteenth and fifteenth centuries a number of small but fervent movements became the leaven which eventually was to revitalise the monastic mass. One of the earliest was centred upon the monastery of Montoliveto near Siena in modern Italy.[46] Its founder, Giovanni di Mino de' Tolomei, belonged to one of the ruling families of the city. He was of a studious disposition, and, after studying civil law at the city university, had stayed there to continue his studies and to teach. In 1313 he retired with two companions to Mount Accona, a family property near Siena. Others of like mind soon joined the new community. These pioneers of the Olivetan movement were moved to return to the very origin of monasticism, as a later historian of the congregation pointed out: 'The intention was to cultivate solitude and simplicity, obey the rules of austerity, and together send praises up to heaven. From a study of their origins you might say that the founders of our movement were hermits, not monks'.[47]

By now, however, the ecclesiastical authorities had come to view spontaneous religious movements with suspicion. A century earlier, the Fourth Lateran Council had forbidden new religious orders. The hermits on Mount Accona were therefore under pressure to choose from one of the existing rules. Some influences came from the Cistercians who were highly regarded in Siena. The companions on Mount Accona wore white robes, and Giovanni Tolomei, their leader, chose

[45] Knowles, *The Religious Orders* (as n. 10) 1:25–27; 2:25.
[46] On Montoliveto and the Olivetans, see P. Lugano, 'Inizi e primi sviluppi dell' istituzione di Monte Oliveto 131–48', *Benedictina* 1 (1947) 43–81; G. M. Picasso, 'Aspetti e problemi della storia della congregazione benedittina do Monte Oliveto', *Studia Monastica*, 3 (1961) 383–408.
[47] Quoted Picasso (as above), 384 n. 3.

5 Luca Signorelli (1441–1523). Saint Benedict and Totila. Fresco in the
Cloister of Monte Oliveto, Siena (Italy).

Bernard as his name in religion. In the end, however, the community chose to become Benedictines. In 1318–1319 they sought approval from the bishop of Arezzo, in whose diocese Mount Accona was situated. He clothed them in their habits and agreed, for the time being, to act as their visitor. The name of Mount Accona was changed to Mount Olivet (Montoliveto).

It is unlikely that Bernard Tolomei originally planned to found a religious institute. Montoliveto was simply a fervent benedictine house. The bishop, however, had given the monks the right to make their own statutes. Bernard persuaded his companions to elect their abbot for one year only. The idea that a superior should hold office for a limited period was borrowed from the friars, and here for the first time applied to a monastic house. It was a convenient way of avoiding the *commendam*. Bernard, who suffered from very poor eyesight, insisted that he should not himself be reelected, but in 1321 the community persuaded him to change his mind. After that, he was reelected year after year until his death in 1348.

Montoliveto came under threat for some years because Bishop Tarlati of Arezzo, its first patron, fell foul of the Holy See and was excommunicated in 1320. After anxious negotiations with Avignon, Pope John XXII confirmed the rights of the abbey in 1324 and 1325. The fame of the community spread, as did that of its founder. Pope Benedict XII, who saw Montoliveto as an ideal monastery, was conspicuous in his support. During his reign, monks from Montoliveto founded houses elsewhere: the abbey's town property in Siena, a church in Arezzo, and a property in Florence were enlarged into monasteries. By 1344, when a bull of privileges was issued by Pope Clement VI, Montoliveto stood at the head of a small congregation of ten houses. This first period of expansion ended in 1348 with the Black Death. Bernard Tolomei was called to Siena to minister to the plague victims. He and a number of his fellow monks died there. The Olivetan movement began to expand again, at a slower rate, in the 1360s and 1370s.

The Olivetans never claimed to be an Order. Theirs was a 'congregation'—a group of observant benedictine monasteries

bound together by shared customs and a common organisation. In his bull of 1344 Pope Clement VI had forbidden
the Olivetans to spread beyond the Alps. The annual Chapter
General, therefore, was a gathering of monks from central and
northern Italy. This concentration in one geographical area
was an advantage. Long distances did not hinder attendance
or effective visitation.

Except at Montoliveto itself, olivetan superiors had the
title of 'prior'. These priors were appointed by the abbot of
Montoliveto and held office for one year only. They alone,
together with four representatives from Montoliveto, elected
the abbot of the mother house. After 1351 it was decreed
that he should hold office for three years. The congregation's
highest authority was the Chapter General. It was attended
by all the priors and one or two representatives from each
house. It decided on new foundations or on the expulsion of
a house from the congregation. It made final decisions about
discipline. It alone had the power to accept postulants and it
could move monks from one house to the other.

Although Montoliveto itself was in a remote spot in the
country, many olivetan houses were in or near towns. Bishops
often had pastoral reasons for inviting the reformed monks into
their dioceses. In 1348, when the Olivetans took possession
of a site near the walls of Foligno, they received a ringing
commendation from the local bishop:

> The bishop knows from experience that the abbot and broth-
> ers of the monastery of Our Lady of Montoliveto . . . are
> religious of strict observance and of holy life and conversation.
> Through them the people can be taught virtue, and the clergy
> encouraged, by their word and example, to live more holy
> lives, and to embrace reform.[48]

Because most of Bernard Tolomei's letters have been lost,
it is impossible to trace the influence of the Olivetans in
detail. There can be no doubt, however, that they were at the

---

[48] Lugano (as n. 46), 64 n.

centre of monastic renewal in the Italy of the fourteenth and fifteenth centuries. It is no coincidence that other reformed congregations copied their organisation.

The monks who enjoyed the highest prestige in the later Middle Ages were the Carthusians. In no way does the history of their Order follow the pattern of the others. Only in a modest way did it share in the expansion of monasticism during the twelfth century. While some of its houses were much admired, they remained few. During the fourteenth and fifteenth centuries, however, when the religious orders of western Christendom were in disarray, the Carthusians enjoyed two centuries of expansion. One hundred and five charterhouses were founded in the fourteenth century, no fewer than six in the year 1328 alone.[49] The Black Death slowed the trend but did not stop it. All classes were united in encouraging the Order. Pope John XXII, together with a number of cardinals, founded two charterhouses near Avignon,[50] King John of Bohemia founded one near Prague,[51] and King James I of Scotland one at Perth.[52] The charterhouse of Florence was founded by Niccolo Acciajoli, a rich citizen.[53] The charterhouse at Bruges came into being after a collection among the citizens and had no particular founder.[54]

The carthusian expansion was not a massive monastic movement like those of the twelfth century. The number of monks in a charterhouse was usually small. Sixteen monks and sixteen laybrothers was the norm, which was seldom exceeded.[55] It is worth noting, however, that the Carthusians never lacked vocations in the late Middle Ages, and some explanation for the popularity of their Order is necessary.

---

[49] Figures in DIP 2 (1973) 788; for foundations in 1328, see C. Le Couteulx, *Annales ordinis Cartusiensis*, 5 (Montreuil 1889) 228.

[50] *Annales Ordinis Cartusiensis* (as above), 80, 109.

[51] Ibid. 417.

[52] W. N. M. Beckett, 'The Perth Charterhouse before 1500', *Analecta Cartusiana* 128 (1988) 1–74.

[53] *Annales Ordinis Cartusiensis* (as n. 49), 409.

[54] Ibid. 115.

[55] G. Le Bras, ed., *Les ordres réligieux*, 1 (Paris 1979) 587.

The general interest in the solitary life may be one reason. Carthusians were hermits living in community. They were also admired for their austerity, and for the fact that their Order had never needed to be reformed—'never reformed because never deformed' was their proud boast.[56] They were regarded as something of a spiritual élite, and thus served as an example to other religious. The reformed congregations of the late Middle Ages often borrowed enactments from carthusian statutes.[57] Not a few monks left their own monasteries to enter a charterhouse.[58] The Carthusians also occasionally involved themselves more actively in monastic reform. In the fifteenth century a number of tracts on the subject were written by monks of the Order.[59] Carthusians were occasionally asked to act as visitors in the houses of other religious Orders,[60] and at least on one occasion a carthusian prior was chosen as abbot of a benedictine house which was in need of reform.[61]

Among thoughtful Christians, however, the charterhouses were particularly noted as centres of spirituality. Many of the new foundations were near towns. It is half an hour's walk from the centre of Dijon to the famous Chartreuse de Champmol, and anyone who climbs the hill to visit the former charterhouse of Florence sees the city spread out in a panorama below. The monks were available to those who wanted to consult them, and outsiders were sometimes allowed to share the life of the community. Baldwin of Luxembourg, archbishop of Trier, for instance, founded a charterhouse near his see city in 1331. Every now and then he went there on retreat, living the austere life of a brother for a few days.[62]

The Carthusians did not develop a distinctive theology of their own. Rather, they sought to make widely available the

---

[56] See discussion in H. Rüthing, 'Die Karthäuser und die spätmittelalterlichen Ordensreformen', in *Reformbemühungen* (as n. 30), 35–40.
[57] Ibid. 41–42.
[58] Ibid. 44.
[59] Ibid. 45–50.
[60] Ibid. 50–4.
[61] Ibid. 54, and see below p. 257.
[62] *Annales ordinis Cartusiensis* (as n. 49), 308.

best authors of the past and of their own time. They copied and promulgated devout books like the anonymous *Cloud of Unknowing.*[63] Their own writers were conservative. They repudiated scholasticism, basing their work on Scripture, the Church Fathers, and Saint Bernard. They addressed themselves to all Christians, and were emphatic that a life of contemplation was necessary and within the reach of everyone. Ludolph of Saxony, the most influential of the carthusian authors of the late Middle Ages, aimed to reach the widest possible audience. He had begun religious life as a dominican friar, and throughout his writings he emphasised the importance of the apostolic life and of preaching the word of God.[64] He entered the Carthusian Order around 1340 and died at the charterhouse of Strasbourg in 1377/1378. His *Vita Jesu Christi* was a long meditation on the life of Christ in which every stage was a subject for reflection leading to prayer. Ludolph's immense learning and use of authorities, not all of which have been identified, have led commentators to refer to the book as a *Summa Evangelica.* The reader was expected, first of all, to make the scenes in the life of Jesus really present. 'Although many facts are here related as if they happened in the past,' wrote Ludolph, 'you must meditate upon them all as if they are happening in the present'.[65] By conforming to his divine exemplar, the reader could make the Word-made-flesh present in himself and thus, through love, repair the image of God broken by the Fall.

The spirituality of the Carthusians directly influenced the *Devotio Moderna.* Gerard Groot, the father of the movement, was a learned and rather worldly dutch prelate who was familiar with the schools of Paris and the latest intellectual fashions.[66] Around 1378 after a conversation with a carthusian

---

[63] J. P. H. Clark, 'The *Cloud of Unknowing* and the Contemplative Life', *Die Kartäuser und ihre Welt* (Salzburg 1993) 45–46; P. Hodgson ed., *The Cloud of Unknowing and Related Treatises* (Salzburg 1982) xi–xii.

[64] On Ludolph, see M. I. Bodenstedt, *The Vita Christi of Ludolphus the Carthusian* (Washington D.C. 1944); DS 9 (1975–1976) 1130–1138.

[65] Quoted DS (as above), 1136.

[66] On the *Devotio Moderna*, see E. F. Jacob, 'Gerard Groote and the Beginnings of the "New Devotion" in the Low Countries', *Journal of Ecclesiastical History* 3 (1952) 40–57; R. R. Post, *The Modern Devotion.* Leiden 1968.

prior, he withdrew to a charterhouse to spend some time in retreat. He emerged committed to the life of a wandering preacher. At first he had the support of the bishop of Utrecht, but his unsparing condemnation of the vices of the clergy made him enemies, and eventually the bishop forbade him to speak in public. He appealed to the pope, but died in 1384 before he could be rehabilitated.

Gerard had encouraged pious laymen to come together in associations, bound together by common charity but without formal vows. 'The Brothers or Sisters of the Common Life' eventually spread all over the Netherlands and Germany. In 1387 the augustinian priory of Windesheim was founded as a spiritual centre for the new movement.

Windesheim and its associated religious houses, as well as the brothers and sisters of the Common Life, were bound together by a common spirituality. Special revelations, visions, and theological speculation were discouraged. The *Devotio Moderna* encouraged affective prayer based on the traditional sources recommended by Ludolph of Saxony and the carthusian authors. The keynotes were sobriety and moderation, the virtues emphasised were essentially social—obedience, humility, and charity. For this reason the *Devotio Moderna* was particularly suited to the reform of religious houses. 'It is a great gift from God to have knowledge of the scriptures,' wrote Thomas à Kempis, one of the best known of the movement's writers, 'but to maintain the discipline of one's Order is far preferable'.[67] The movement's devotional masterpiece, the much-read *Imitation of Christ* often appealed to religious directly.

> It is not easy to live in a religious community and remain there without fault, persevering faithfully until death. Blessed is he who has thus lived happily and well to the end . . . Be content to be accounted a fool for Christ's sake if you wish to be a religious. The habit and tonsure by themselves are of small

---

[67] *Thomae Hemerken a Kempis. . . . Opera Omnia* ed. M. J. Pohl, 2: *Libellus de Disciplina Claustralium*, 269.

significance; it is the transformation of one's way of life and the complete mortification of the passions that make a true religious.[68]

A religious who earnestly and devoutly contemplates the most holy life and passion of Our Lord will find it in an abundance of all things profitable and needful to him, nor need he seek any other model than Jesus. Oh, if Jesus crucified would come into our hearts, how quickly and fully we would be instructed! . . . Observe how many behave, who live strictly under the monastic discipline. They seldom go out, they live retired, they eat the poorest food; they work hard, they talk little, they keep long watches; they rise early, they spend much time in prayer, they study much, and always guard themselves with discipline. Consider the Carthusians, the Cistercians, and the monks and nuns of the various Orders, how they rise each night to sing the praises of Our Lord.[69]

The late fourteenth century also witnessed the Great Schism. Since 1305 the popes had lived in the south of what is today France, eventually settling at Avignon. Calls to return to Rome were fiercely resisted by the cardinals, who were mostly french. They were deeply unhappy about the return to Rome in 1378. The election of a south Italian as pope in that year, perhaps as a result of undue pressure from the roman mob, was a signal for the malcontents to elect a rival who returned to Avignon. A 'roman' and an 'avignon' obedience thus came into being. In 1409 the Council of Pisa tried to solve the problem by deposing the rival popes and making a new election. Both the 'roman' and 'avignon' popes, however, refused to resign, so there was now a third, 'pisan' pope as well. At last, in 1417, the council of Constance managed to elect a pope recognised by all of Christendom.

Many dioceses, and all the religious Orders were split during this schism. It hardly needs to be said that the Church

---

[68] Ibid.: *De Imitatione Christi* 28–29. English translation, *Thomas à Kempis: The Imitation of Christ*, trans.L. Sherley-Price (London: Penguin Classics, 1952) 45. On the influence of Ludolph of Saxony on the *Imitation*, see Bodenstedt (as n. 64), 57.

[69] *De Imitatione Christi* (as n. 67) 54–55; English translation (as n. 68), 64–65.

suffered greatly and that in many places ecclesiastical discipline broke down. On the other hand, the avignon papacy,
with its enormous bureaucracy, had stifled initiative. During
the schisms the rival popes could not afford to lose supporters.
New ideas, which had had no chance of acceptance, could now
spread. Devout groups of laypeople living without vows, like
the brothers and sisters of the Common Life, were anath-
ema to the old papal bureaucrats. During the period of the
schism, however, they could flourish and even receive eventual
approval from one of the schism popes. In this atmosphere,
the *Devotio Moderna* spread quickly outside the confines of
the Low Countries. Copies of the *Imitation of Christ* were
available in Italy in the early fifteenth century. The book played
no small part in the spiritual development of a young venetian
nobleman called Ludovico Barbo.[70]

Ludovico belonged to a rich venetian family. At the age
of fifteen or sixteen he became the commendatory prior of
San Giorgio in Alga, a decayed house of augustinian friars. He
studied law at the university of Padua and some time in 1403
he underwent a conversion. On his own initiative he seems
to have taken religious vows, joining the augustinian friars to
whom his priory belonged.

Around this time he came into contact with a group of
earnest venetian clerics concerned about the reform of the
Church and the religious life. The group included two future
popes: Angelo Correr who, elected as Pope Gregory XII in
1406, was the last pope of the 'roman' line; and Gabriele
Condulmer, who in 1431 became Pope Eugenius IV of a
reunited Christendom. In 1400 these men, clearly influenced
by the brothers of the Common Life, together with a number
of other devout clerics, decided to form an association. At first

---

[70] On Ludovico Barbo and the benedictine observance in Italy, see I. Tasso,
Ludovico Barbo (1381–1443) (Rome 1952); A. Pratesi, 'Ludovico Barbo', *Dizio-
nario biografico degli Italiani*, 6 (Rome 1964) 244–249; A. Pantoni, 'Con-
gregazione benedettina Cassinese', DIP 2:1477–1485; R. Pepi, 'Sta Giustina',
DIP 8:693–702; D. M. Lunn, 'Benedictine Reform Movements in the Later
Middle Ages', *Downside Review* 91 (1973) 275–297.

they met in Venice. In 1404 Ludovico Barbo offered them San Giorgio. Here, without taking vows of any kind, the friends lived the common life, observed the liturgical hours, and gave time to reading and private prayer. Their superiors held office for one year only. Ludovico Barbo was living at San Giorgio also, without being a part of the community. He observed the vows of the augustinian friars, but took part in the common exercises.

Like many other spontaneous religious associations of the period, the community at San Giorgio seemed to go back to the very origins of christian monasticism. The revival of monastic observance at the abbey of Santa Giustina in Padua followed a similar pattern. The ancient abbey had fallen upon very bad times. The buildings were in ruin, the properties had been usurped, and the community consisted of three monks. Pope Gregory XII was anxious to bring the monastery back to life. An attempt to introduce a community of Olivetans failed. The pope and the curia then decided to call in Ludovico Barbo. In February 1409 he made his profession as a monk of Saint Benedict and received the abbatial blessing.

The composition of the new community was not, at first, very promising. Abbot Ludovico Barbo was twenty-six years old. He had only just changed from the Augustinian to the Benedictine Rule. He had under him the three monks of the abbey, two priests from San Giorgio (who soon left), and two camaldolese hermits 'lent' by a sympathetic abbot of the neighbourhood. The first two years were miserable, but from 1411 recruits began to come, particularly from the university of Padua. After that there was a rapid increase in vocations— in ten years there are said to have been two hundred recruits. With the abbey buildings in ruins there was nowhere to put them. Abbot Ludovico therefore took over ruined monasteries elsewhere. He soon found it impossible to govern them all. In this way a new benedictine congregation came into being. In 1419, with the approval of Pope Martin V, Santa Giustina and three other monasteries were joined together in the small congregation *De Unitate* (Of Unity).

As it grew, the congregation changed its name. After 1433 it was known as the congregation of monks of the observance, or of Santa Giustina. In 1504, when Montecassino, the cradle of benedictine monasticism was incorporated, the name was changed to the Cassinese congregation, by which it has been known ever since. Its centralised constitution was similar to that of the Olivetans. An annual Chapter General exercised supreme authority. It consisted of abbots, priors, and elected representatives from each house. Its first task was to elect visitors and a president. All these officials held office for one year only. The abbot of Santa Giustina enjoyed no particular precedence. Abbots originally held office for life, according to the ancient benedictine tradition. In 1432, however, it was decided that abbots should be appointed by the Chapter General for one year only. They might be reelected, but not indefinitely. By the end of the fifteenth century the congregation's monasteries enjoyed security, the admiration of contemporaries, and wealth. Learning flourished in their houses, particularly theology, based on a renewed study of the Fathers.[71]

The reformed Benedictines of Italy came to a new understanding of Saint Benedict. In Saint Gregory's biography he is an awesome figure—an ascetic, miracle worker, and seer. Gregory had also written, however, that 'Anyone who wishes to know more about his life and character can discover from his rule exactly what he was like'.[72] The gentle, wise Benedict of early Italian Renaissance art owes much to the observant monks who had been stimulated, it may be, by Gregory's hint. This Benedict greets the visitor to Montoliveto who looks up at the relief by Della Robbia over the monastery gate. We see him again in the frescoes by Signorelli and Sodoma in the Grand Cloister. Here we see no despotic abbot, living away from his community. The frescoes show Benedict surrounded by his brethren. He is dressed in the white olivetan habit; he has no

[71] See B. Collett, *Italian Benedictine Scholars and the Reformation* (Oxford 1985).
[72] *Life and Miracles of Saint Benedict* by Pope Saint Gregory the Great, trans. and ed. O. J. Zimmermann and B. R. Avery (Collegeville 1949) 74.

halo and wears no special insignia of office. He is recognisable
only by his white beard and dignified bearing.

The fresco-cycle in the 'cloister of the orange trees' at the
Badia in Florence is similar in spirit. One scene is particularly
striking. Saint Benedict is giving his pet raven the poisoned
loaf sent him by an enemy and instructing the bird to fly away
with it. Saint Gregory did not place this incident anywhere
in particular in the monastery,[73] but tradition located it in the
refectory, during the community meal. The artist in Florence
depicts Benedict leaning over the table to talk to the bird. The
other monks sit quietly in their places. The bare walls of the
room, the long table with its white tablecloth, the black robes
of the brethren, give an impression of simplicity and peace.
Here we see Benedict as the ideal superior of an observant
house. The frescoes at Florence were most probably painted
during the lifetime of Ludovico Barbo.

From Italy reformed benedictine monasticism spread to
Germany. The key monastery was Subiaco, not far from
Rome.[74] Here, at the 'Sacro Speco' Saint Benedict had spent
three years in strict seclusion, but the monastery there had
ceased to exist in the ninth century. In 1358, after an earlier
revival had collapsed, the site was visited by the bishop of Todi.
An energetic reform was now undertaken. In 1364 a new abbot
brought in learned monks from Germany and Austria. Subiaco
thus became a somewhat exotic expatriate community, and so
it remained until the end of the fifteenth century. In time
it took over the neighbouring abbey of Santa Scholastica as
a subordinate house, but, for the rest, it stood outside the
mainstream of italian monastic reform.

The customs of Subiaco, compiled around 1400, were
the earliest systematic formulation of the ideals of observant
monasticism.[75] They insisted upon the full restoration of the

---

[73] Ibid. 160–163.
[74] Bruno Albers, 'Une nouvelle édition des *consuetudines Sublacenses*', *Revue Bénédictine* 19 (1902) 183–204; I. Tasso, *Ludovico Tasso* (as n. 70), 32.
[75] *Consuetudines Monasticae*, ed. Bruno Albers, 2 (Monte Cassino 1905) 119–226.

6 Saint Benedict's Miracle of the Raven.
Fresco in the Cloister degli Aranci, Badia, Florentina, Florence, Italy.

benedictine *horarium*. The tasks of the various obedientiaries were defined and the eating of meat outside the infirmary forbidden. Manual labour was to consist of work in the kitchen and in the garden. The importance of study and book production was emphasised. No novices were to be received under the age of eighteen.

> Although the Rule mentions boys, in the conditions of the world as we know them today this is in every way unsuitable, as experience has taught all religious of the Observance in modern times.[76]

The customs also allowed partitions between the beds in the common dormitory. Each carrel was to have a window for reading and writing, as well as a table and chair.[77]

Little detail is known about the early expatriate community, but no doubt the foreign monks kept in touch with their homelands. In 1403 a group of students and scholars in the university of Vienna gave up their studies to become monks at Subiaco. Among them was Nicholas Seyringer, the university's rector, and Peter von Rosenheim, a prominent academic.[78] The newcomers had sufficient influence at Subiaco for Nicholas Seyringer to become prior in 1410 and abbot in 1412. After only a short period of office, however, Nicholas and his companions were driven out by an intruder who was trying to gain control of the monastery and its revenues. The refugees made their way to Constance, where the council which was to end the papal schism was in progress. Martin V, the pope of a reunited Chrstendom, was particularly interested in the reform of the religious orders. In 1418 he gave Nicholas Seyringer and some of his fellow monks wide powers to reform the monasteries of Austria and Bavaria.

---

[76] Ibid. 223.
[77] Ibid. 125.
[78] On the reform of Melk, see F. X. Thoma, 'Petrus von Rosenheim osb', SMBO 45 (1927) 94–222; J. Angerer, 'Die liturgisch-musikalische Erneuerung der Melker Reform', *Österreichische Akademie der Wissenschaften: Philosophisch-Historische Klasse* 287 (1974). There is a short history of the reform of Melk on pp. 29–75.

Nicholas Seyringer had made powerful friends at the Council of Constance. Dukes Albrecht of Austria and William of Bavaria provided the support of the secular arm without which, at this period, nothing could have been accomplished. Papal legates and reforming bishops were also involved. As early as 1418 the reformers were able to take over the abbey of Melk on the Danube, some miles downriver from Vienna. The elderly abbot resigned and Nicholas Seyringer took his place. The customs of Subiaco, adapted to austrian circumstances, were introduced. As the customs of Melk, they were the central document of the reform.

Pope Martin had given the visitors wide powers. In the monasteries they visited they usually deposed the superior and most of the obedientiaries. These and 'irreformable' monks were encouraged to leave and live in retirement. A new community was then formed from those who remained, strengthened by recruits from the universities or (as the reform spread) from other reformed houses. Statutes based on the customs of Melk were introduced and a new superior elected. The support of the prince was vital because it was sometimes necessary to support reform with force. At the reform of Ederberg in Bavaria in 1427, the visitors were accompanied by the prince's councillors and forty armed men. A guard was placed at the door of the church, where the abbot and his nine monks were examined one by one.

A vivid account survives of the proceedings at the austrian abbey of Göttweig. Here one of the visitors was Leonhard, prior of the charterhouse of Gaming. It was the Carthusian who was chosen to preach to the monks. He laid bare their failings: they ate meat, they lay about in feather beds, they bathed naked, they did not observe the fasts, they did not keep silence, they broke their vows, they repudiated poverty. After the sermon the following dialogue took place:

The abbot: In all these matters I confess myself guilty.

Prior Leonhard: Are you ready to improve and to live according to the Rule of Saint Benedict?

The abbot: Venerable father, I am a weak man, but as far as I can and my strength allows, I shall willingly do so.

Prior Leonhard: Thanks be to God. I shall take some time to consider the penance to be laid upon you.

It was noted that the Carthusian visitor was far stricter than his benedictine colleagues.[79]

In the period 1418–1431, thirty-two religious houses were reformed by Melk, of which twenty were benedictine abbeys for men and three were benedictine houses for women. This was nowhere near a majority of the houses in the area, nor, with a few exceptions, did the reform touch the richest and most famous houses. No attempt was made to bind the reformed houses together by any central organisation. The customs of Melk and confraternities of prayer formed the only link among them.

At around the same time a monastic reform movement came into being based on the south bavarian abbey of Kastl.[80] It owed its success to two able and long-lived abbots: Otto Nordweiner (1378–1399), and George Kemnater (1399–1434). Both enforced claustral discipline and expertly administered the properties of the house. They were warmly supported by their prince, Ruprecht of the Palatinate, who from 1400 until his death in 1410 held, not without challenge, the title of King of the Romans.

At Kastl there was a strong influence from Bohemia. Several of the abbey's monks are known to have come from there. Abbot George was probably a graduate of Prague. This university, founded in 1348 by the emperor Charles IV, was the oldest in the empire. Until the hussite troubles in the early fifteenth century, it was an important intellectual and religious centre. A number of very sophisticated and learned men, therefore, had a hand in formulating the customs of Kastl, which seem to date, in their present form, from around 1400. These customs were

---

[79] Rüthing (as n. 56), 51–52.
[80] On the reform of Kastl, see P. Maier, 'Ursprung und Ausbreitung der Kastler Reformbewegung', SMBO 102 (1991) 75–204.

the instruments whereby various monasteries in the area of the Rhine were reformed. They were strongly influenced by the customaries of Cluny. The reform of Kastl was dignified and learned. The councils of Constance (1414–1418), and Basel (1431–1449) gave it strong support, but apart from the abbey of Saint Giles in Nürnberg, none of the houses where it was introduced was large or famous.

The Melk and Kastl reformers did not feel the need to organise their monasteries in any way. The congregation of Bursfelde, on the other hand, which was the most effective of all the german monastic reform movements, was highly organised, and this may account for its survival until 1803.[81] The initiator of the reform was Johannes Dederoth, a graduate of the university of Erfurt and a monk of Northeim, a benedictine monastery in the modern state of Lower Saxony in Germany. The house was, like so many others, riven by internal disputes. Johannes had been sent to Rome on behalf of one of the parties and had been impressed by the reformed benedictine monasteries of Italy. He found it impossible to introduce anything of the kind in his own house. In 1430, however, Duke Otto of Brunswick, who was concerned about the state of the religious houses in his dominions, sent him to reform the nearby monastery of Clus. Within three years Johannes had succeeded. In 1433 the duke sent him to Bursfelde.

This abbey was, like the others with which Johannes was concerned, in Lower Saxony. According to a later tradition, the only inhabitants were a single monk and his cow. The roof of the church was covered with thatch and the building was used as a stable. Clus was too small to provide the nucleus of a reformed community. Dederoth therefore turned for help to Johannes Rode, a former carthusian prior who had been persuaded to join the Benedictines in order to become abbot, and reform the monastery, of Saint Matthias in Trier. The abbot

---

[81] On the reform of Bursfelde, see P. Engelbert, 'Die Bursfelder Benediktinerkongregation und die spätmittelalterlichen Reformbewegungen', *Historisches Jahrbuch* 103 (1983) 35–55; P. Engelbert, 'Bursfelder Kongregation', LM 2:1108–1110.

was able to spare four of his monks. Two of these went to Clus. The other two settled at Bursfelde.

When Johannes Dederoth died of the pestilence in 1439, his work had only just begun. The reform continued under his successors. As early as 1435 the Bursfelders had been asked to reform another house in Lower Saxony. In the 1440s they were encouraged to spread their observance by papal legates as well as by the council of Basel. By the end of the fifteenth century ninety-four houses for men and over sixty for women were following their customs.

Life in houses which had been reformed by Bursfelde was spartan. One modern authority has stated that their observances were stricter than those of modern Trappists.[82] Their liturgy was austere. Organs, then becoming popular, were banned in their churches. They admired, above all, the Carthusians, copying them when they could and sharing their spirituality. The congregation of Bursfelde had a centralised constitution based on italian models. Supreme authority was vested in a Chapter General which appointed visitors to inspect every house and to ensure that the chapter's statutes were observed. Unlike the Italians, however, the Bursfelders allowed abbots to be elected for life. Until the Reformation the abbot of Bursfelde was the president of the congregation.

On the other side of Europe a congregation of reformed Benedictines came into existence in Castile.[83] In 1389 King Juan I (1379–1390) obtained a bull from Pope Clement VII, the first pope of the 'Avignon' obedience, authorising the foundation of an observant monastery of Benedictines in his kingdom. The king then decreed that the half-ruined royal castle of Valladolid should be turned into a religious house. The monks took possession in 1390. They promised to observe the Rule of Saint Benedict literally and austerely. Enclosure was strictly and almost obsessively enforced. Absolute poverty

---

[82] Engelbert, 'Die Bursfelder Benediktinerkongregation' (as above), 47.

[83] For a brief account of the congregation of Valladolid see *Historia General de España y America*, 5, ed. L. Suarez Fernandez (Madrid 1981) 216–219; Lunn (as n. 70), 285–286. On Garcia de Cisneros, see DS 2/1 (1953) 910–921.

was observed. So that the house should never become rich, the king gave no land, but only made an annual grant of bread and wine. Manual rather than intellectual work was encouraged. To preserve humility and discourage the *commendam* the superior held the rank of prior.

There was no plan, at first, to make the monastery a centre of reform. It was Pope Martin V who expressly mitigated the strict rules of enclosure so that the monks could be sent to reform other religious houses. A beginning was made in 1433 with the monastery of Saint John in Burgos. The reform of this house took three years.

Because of the papal schism, the observance at Valladolid began somewhat in isolation from centres of monastic reform elsewhere. The reunion of Christendom made possible contact with the outside world, especially Italy. In 1439 Garcia de Frias, prior of Valladolid, visited Ludovico Barbo to obtain advice about various aspects of monastic reform. The congregation of Valladolid, nevertheless, did not literally follow the italian example. It preserved many characteristics peculiar to itself. Cluny during its heyday had exercised enormous influence in the iberian peninsula. The new congregation followed its customaries closely, especially where the liturgy was concerned. An organisation developed slowly. The priors of Valladolid at first held office for life. Their term of office was cut to three years in 1466. They remained at the head of the congregation, however, and the other superiors swore obedience to them. A Chapter General met every three years and appointed visitors and other officials.

Here, as elsewhere, the inspiration of reform was the *Devotio Moderna*. In 1493 Garcia de Cisneros, who had already held various important offices in the congregation, became prior of Montserrat, a famous pilgrimage centre in Catalonia. Here he published the *Exercitatorio de la Vida Spiritual*. It was a compilation of the spiritual classics of the west, as seen from a 15th century perspective. There were extracts from Saint Bernard, William of Saint Thierry, and Saint Bonaventure, but most important were the long citations from the *Imitation of Christ* and from other writings of the same school of spirituality.

Like that of the Carthusians, the spirituality of Valladolid was based on traditional sources. Around 1500, Garcia de Cisneros, prior of Montserrat, published his *Exercitatorio de la Vida Spiritual* (Book of Exercises for the Spiritual Life). A systematic exposition of mystical prayer, it quoted Cassian, Saint Augustine, Richard of Saint Victor, Saint Bernard, and the famous fifteenth-century Paris theologian, Jean Gerson.

Monastic reform in the late Middle Ages thus had an underlying philosophy which gave it impetus and a certain unity. Its success, however, must not be exaggerated. Among monks it spread most widely among the Benedictines. Even in Italy and Germany, however, the majority of black monk houses were not affected, and reform often failed to touch the most important ones. In France, because of the strength of the *commendam*, monastic reform could make little headway. A small group of reformed benedictine houses based on Chézal-Benoît (in the modern department of Cher) came into being at the end of the fifteenth century, but embraced only a handful of houses.[84] In England an attempted reform of the black monks in 1421, piloted by king Henry V and possibly inspired by the observant movements in Germany, was a complete failure.[85] The white monks, too, were resistant to the new influences. Indeed, early in the fourteenth century their most able spokesman had claimed that the Cistercians were in no need of reform at all. Around 1317–1318 Jacques de Thérines, abbot of Chaalis, some fifty kilometres north of Paris, addressed a long memorandum about the matter to Pope John XXII.[86] Jacques began with a long description of the cistercian life. The monks, he wrote, were bound by the threefold vows pronounced by all Benedictines. They observed strict enclosure and the greatest austerity in food and drink. Outside the infirmary,

---

[84] On Chézal-Benoît, see DIP 2 (1973) 883–885 and bibliography.
[85] Knowles, *The Religious Orders in England* 2 (Cambridge 1955) 182–184.
[86] N. Valois, 'Un plaidoyer du xive siècle en faveur des cisterciens', *Bibliothèque de l'école des chartes,* 69 (1908) 352–368.

the consumption of meat was strictly forbidden. In the silence of their houses they gave themselves over to contemplation and reading. They were assiduous in prayer and attendance at the divine office. They found time during the day for manual labour.[87] They were generous in giving hospitality to those who sought it and in distributing alms to the poor. The Order was particularly anxious to encourage study and had its teachers at the major universities, especially Paris.[88]

It would be idle, Jacques continued, to claim that everything in the Order was perfect. There was, however, an adequate machinery for correcting abuses. All cistercian abbots and monks were obliged to go to confession once a week. In addition, every professed monk had to confess to his abbot once a year. In all abbeys a chapter was held every day, and once a year there was a visitation. Even the abbey of Cîteaux must submit to an annual visitation from its four immediate daughters. As for abbots, they were disciplined at the annual Chapter General.[89]

There is some evidence that the abbot of Chaalis knew little about areas distant from northern France where he lived.[90] Certainly the abbeys of southern France which horrified Benedict XII seem to have belonged to a different world. The Cistercians, however, were more resistant to carthusian influence than were the Benedictines. White monks like Jacques de Thérines no doubt sincerely believed that the Order had all the machinery necessary to enforce discipline. Outside

---

[87] Ibid. 361. 'In suis claustris. . . . celestia contemplantur, lectioni vacantes, orationibus insistentes, divinum officium sollempnissime celebrantes, interdum manibus laborantes. . . .' N. Valois, who edited this text in 1908 (see n. 85 above) translated *interdum* as 'parfois'. According to him, Jacques had written ' . . . sometimes working with their hands'. In fact, in late Latin, *interdum* can mean 'meanwhile', 'in the meantime' (see Lewis and Short, *A Latin Dictionary*). The context makes clear that the Cistercians worked with their hands *in the intervals* between study, prayer, and the office. The passage is evidence for the persistence of daily manual labour in observant cistercian houses into the fourteenth century.

[88] Ibid. 361.

[89] Ibid. 362.

[90] Peter King, *The Finances of the Cistercian Order in the Fourteenth Century* (Kalamazoo 1985) 96.

influence was fiercely resisted. In fact, the ancient constitution of the Order was working badly. The General Chapter had lost authority. Attendance figures are seldom available, but it is known that in 1356 twenty-three abbots were present, and in 1357 twenty-four, out of a total of some seven hundred.[91] The papal schism further weakened the cistercian system. Since Cîteaux was in France, the Chapter General there was attended only by abbots who recognised the 'avignon' popes. The 'roman' popes soon took action and organised rival Chapters General for their own obedience.[92]

Observant congregations of the type which developed among the black monks were rare among their white brethren. An early centre of cistercian reform was the abbey of Kamp on the Lower Rhine, near the border of modern Germany with the Netherlands.[93] In the late fourteenth century its abbot, William of Kamp (1382–1402), corresponded with Gerard Groot, the founder of the *Devotio Moderna*. Groot praised him and his community for their strict lives and occasionally sent to Kamp young men who wished to embrace the religious life.

In 1394–1395 Kamp founded a daughter house at Marienburg in the diocese of Utrecht, in the modern Netherlands. The house was colonised by twelve monks from Kamp which, as the mother house, reserved visitation rights. In 1412 six monks and three laybrothers from Marienburg settled at Warmond. In the same year a dutch community of 'good men' which for six years had been living without any particular rule at Sibculo, a remote and marshy site, asked for incorporation into the Cistercian Order. The Chapter General placed the

[91] See Peter King, 'Attendance at the Cistercian Chapter General during the 14th Century', *Festskrift til Troels Dahlerup* (Aarhus 1985) 55–63.
[92] B. Griesser, 'Statuten von Generalkapiteln ausserhalb Cîteaux: Wien 1393 und Heilsbronn 1398', *Cistercienser-Chronik* n.f. 33/4 (1955) 65–83.
[93] On Kamp and the *Colligatio* of Sibculo, see K. Elm and P. Feige, 'Reformen und Kongregationsbildungen der Zisterzienser in Spätmittelalter und früher Neuzeit', *Die Zisterzienser: Ordensleben zwischen Ideal und Wirklichkeit* ed. K. Elm et al. (Cologne 1981) 243–254. The statutes of the *Colligatio* and attendant documents are printed in *Historia sive NotitiaeEpiscopatus Daventriensis*, ed. J. Lindeborn (Cologne 1670) 399–407.

petitioners under its own jurisdiction and permitted them to choose an observant cistercian abbot as its visitor.

In 1417 these three small dutch houses petitioned the abbot of Cîteaux, who was attending the Council of Constance, to approve their association and the statutes which they had worked out among themselves and some of which went beyond traditional cistercian observance. They asked in particular to be allowed to observe perpetual enclosure 'after the manner of Carthusians'.

The abbot of Cîteaux handed the petition on to the abbots of Kamp and Menterna. The latter abbey, another noted centre of reform, was situated in the very north of the Netherlands. Under the authority of these two abbots a final draft of the statutes was agreed upon in 1418. The document insisted upon a strict return to cistercian austerity in clothing and diet. The monks were to live in isolated places in the country. Daily manual labour was to be compulsory for everyone. The liturgy was to be punctually and meticulously performed. Superiors of the three houses were to hold the title of prior, not abbot, and were to share in every way the privations of their brethren.

The association of these three dutch houses was to be called the *Colligatio Galilaeensis*, after the latin name for Sibculo. The word *colligatio*, meaning 'gathering', was chosen rather than the word *congregatio*, which would have implied an organisation within the Cistercian Order. Similarly, the word *capitulum*, 'chapter', was avoided, although the three priors and their monks agreed to come together annually for a *convocatio*, a 'meeting' or 'discussion', at which the affairs of each house were to be discussed in turn, and one of the three priors replaced. With great tact, then, susceptibilities at the cistercian Chapter General were respected and the traditional government of the Order was not challenged

The Low Countries, where the *Devotio Moderna* had originated, were ideal territory for the *Colligatio*. Its superiors were soon being asked to reform other communities in the area. In 1418 the nuns of Yesse in Friesland asked to be placed under the pastoral care of the brothers of Sibculo, and some years later they adopted the constitutions of the Gathering. In 1428 the ancient abbey of Bloemkamp received permission from Pope Martin V to join and to demote itself from an abbey to a priory. By the end of the fifteenth century the Gathering consisted of a round dozen houses for men and women, in the modern Netherlands and north-west modern Germany. It was, then, a very local growth. Here, as elsewhere, there can be no doubt that concentration in a small area generated the intensity which kept the movement healthy until it was snuffed out by the Reformation.

These dutch Cistercians never tried to withdraw from the jurisdiction of the Cistercian Order. The reformed Cistercians of Castile in modern Spain, on the other hand, seem to have placed little value on unity with Cîteaux. Martin Vargas, their leader, was a native of Andalusia who had spent many years in Italy, ending as confessor of Pope Martin V.[94] He was thus familiar with monastic reform movements in Italy. In 1420 he returned to Spain and entered the cistercian abbey of Piedra in Aragon. This was a daughter house of the great abbey of Poblet, where strict observance of the Rule and the cistercian constitutions had recently been restored.

Martin yearned to return to his native Castile. Since it was unlikely that the existing cistercian abbeys in the kingdom could be reformed, Martin and his friends planned the foundation of a new house. Here the Rule of Saint Benedict would be strictly observed, with perpetual abstinence from meat, rough habits for the community, and bedding of straw. In 1425 Martin returned to Rome to lay his project before Martin V. The pope authorised him to found two hermitages. They were to enjoy all the privileges of the Cistercian Order but be subject only to the authority of the abbot of Poblet.On his return from Rome Martin found a site for a new house in the outskirts of Toledo. He called it Montesion (*Mons Syon*).

---

[94] On Martin Vargas and the congregation of Castile, see P. Feige, 'Filiation und Landeshoheit', *Zisterzienser Studien* 1 (1975) 48–62; K. Elm and P. Feige, *Die Zisterzienser* (as n. 92), 249–252; D. Yanez, 'Los primeros usos de la congregación de Castilla', *Cîteaux* 32 (1981) 1–16.

It soon acquired numerous endowments. Martin's other foundations also attracted the generosity of the laity, so that the original ideal of poverty and an austere life proved difficult to uphold.

In 1430 Martin took over the ancient abbey of Valbuena in somewhat dubious circumstances. Abbot Fernando was an intruder who had displaced the rightful superior. Now, with the help of the king and the bishop of Palencia, Fernando was himself expelled and Martin Vargas installed in his place. Fernando appealed to the Chapter General at Cîteaux. His intrigues were largely responsible for the Cistercian Order's suspicion of, and eventual hostility to, the reform of Castile.

Martin preferred to rely on the papacy. In 1437 Pope Eugenius IV approved the foundation of a new congregation. Superiors could be called abbots, but they were to be elected for a three-year term of office. Every three years a provincial chapter, consisting of all the abbots and one procurator for each house of the congregation was to assemble. Martin was to be *reformator* for life. After his death the chapter was to elect a president who, like the other superiors in the congregation, would hold office for three years only. The provincial chapter would send one representative to the Chapter General at Cîteaux. The abbot of Cîteaux and the Chapter General retained vague powers of supervision. In spite of the protection of the papacy, however, the hostility of the Cistercian authorities was not overcome. Martin was accused of ambition and greed for money. In 1439 he was excommunicated by the Chapter General. Montesion was expelled from the Order, Martin himself died in 1446 in a cistercian prison.

Such were the tempestuous beginnings of the cistercian congregation of Castile. It is clear that the Cistercian Order would find the congregation's constitutions of 1437 unacceptable. One may ask, however, why an arrangement similar to that agreed for the Gathering of Sibculo, was not possible in Spain? Probably the answer lies in the greater discretion of the dutch observants and a certain abrasiveness in Martin

Vargas. His reliance on papal support, and his insistence upon italian examples, may have lost him valuable support at home. It proved impossible, however, to suppress the cistercian congregation of Castile. By the early sixteenth century Cîteaux had accepted realities. The congregation survived into the nineteenth century.

The monastic renewal associated with Saint Bridget of Sweden seems, at first sight, to be based on principles rather different from the movements inspired by the *Devotio Moderna*. Bridget was a swedish noblewoman who had embraced a life of seclusion and prayer after the death of her husband.[95] In 1350, accompanied by some swedish ecclesiastics, she had journeyed to Rome to take part in the celebrations of the Holy Year. It was rumoured that Pope Clement VI, who was settled in Avignon, would come in person to the Holy City to preside over the celebrations. Bridget was anxious to pass on to him the messages which she was convinced she had received from God about the reform of the Church, the return of the papacy to Rome, and the ending of the war between the kings of England and France. Clement VI did not come, however, and for Bridget and her companions, what had no doubt been planned as a visit of some months turned into a sojourn which lasted the rest of her life. In 1367 her prayers seemed to be answered. In that year Pope Urban V decided, against the advice of his cardinals, to make the return to Rome. The turbulence there and in central Italy, however, made it impossible for him to stay. In 1370 he returned to Avignon with Bridget's curses ringing in his ears.

The enormous disappointment marked a turning point in her life. She corresponded with Gregory XI, Urban's successor, but she now saw the problems of Christendom in a more supernatural light. The writings of her last years have a certain serenity, especially the visions she recorded during a pilgrim-

---

[95] For a brief biography, see Sr Patricia O.SS.S., 'Birgitta Birgersdotter', *Studies in St. Birgitta and the Brigittine Order*, ed. J. Hogg (Salzburg 1993) 1: 7–28

age to the Holy Land in 1372. She died in 1373, shortly after her return to Rome.

Bridget was aware of the decay of the religious life in her time. Long before she went to Rome she had determined to compose a new religious rule which would be the instrument whereby all the monastic orders were to be renewed and reformed.[96] Her resolve was the more remarkable since she had no personal experience of the religious life. She was a married woman who had raised a large family. Her experience as head of a large aristocratic household was certainly valuable, but it was only after she had settled in Rome that a community came into being around her.

This germ of the future Bridgettine Order was typical of the basic communities of the late Middle Ages. Bridget's Swedish companions consisted of a dominican friar who acted as superior,[97] a cistercian monk, and a secular priest. Later the group was joined by Bridget's daughter Catherine, and later still by a retired spanish bishop. They rose in the night to recite the office, adding other devotions until daybreak. The hours were completed at the end of the day.[98] The singing of the Marian hymn *Ave maris stella* ('Hail, star of the ocean') before retiring to bed, was a special feature of their devotions.[99] Absolute silence was maintained in the house, except for one hour which was spent in edifying conversation.[100] During the day the companions made pilgrimages to the various holy shrines in Rome and elsewhere.[101] Even when she was an old woman Bridget did not omit this fatiguing exercise, and one of her companions kept some sugar in his pocket to refresh

[96] *Sancta Birgitta Opera Minora* 1: Regula Salvatoris, ed. S. Eklund (Stockholm 1975) 103–104.
[97] *Acta et processus canonizacionis sancte Birgitte* ed. I. Collijn (Uppsala 1924–1931) 369, 489, 498.
[98] Ibid. 12, 13, 310–311.
[99] *Den heliga Birgittas reuelaciones extrauagantes*, ed. L. Hollman (Uppsala 1956) 121.
[100] *Acta et processus* (as n. 97) 311.
[101] Ibid. 308, 370.

her when she felt faint.[102] At times, when money from Sweden did not arrive, they found it necessary to beg at the church doors.[103] When money was available, however, it was given to the poor, though the superior of the house, who was in charge of the finances, had sometimes to curb Bridget's generosity.[104] The companions also visited the hospitals of Rome to wash and bathe the sores of the sick.[105]

Saint Bridget's *Rule of Our Saviour* and the *Revelationes Extravagantes* which are a commentary upon it, were composed over the course of about twenty years.[106] She insisted that the rule had been dictated by Christ, and it was written, as if by him, in the first person singular. Each chapter heading emphasised the point: 'Here Christ commands . . . here Christ disposes . . .' Bridget wanted a large community which would be a microcosm of the whole Church. Thus it would contain both men and women, but it was to be 'first and principally for women'.[107] The abbess was to be the head and ruler of the whole house, because, said Christ, the blessed Virgin 'was the head and queen of my apostles and disciples, after I had ascended into heaven'.[108] Nevertheless, Bridget, ever a realist, had to admit, 'It will be easy to find women who will subject themselves to the Order, but only with difficulty will men be found who will be willing to subject themselves to the rule of a woman'.[109]

A bridgettine community was to consist of eighty-five persons: sixty women, thirteen priests (representing the twelve apostles and Saint Paul), four deacons (for the four doctors of the Latin Church), and eight lay brothers. These eighty-five persons also represented the thirteen apostles and seventy-two

---

[102] Ibid. 367.
[103] Ibid. 312.
[104] Ibid. 498.
[105] Ibid. 316.
[106] R. Ellis, *Syon Abbey: The Spirituality of the English Bridgettines* (Salzburg 1984) 4–5.
[107] Regula Salvatoris (as n. 96), 105, Ch.1.
[108] Ibid. 120, Ch.14.
[109] *Extravagantes* (as n. 99), 130.

disciples.[110] There were strict rules about the separation of men and women in the house, and about contact with the outside world.[111] The sisters were to devote themselves to prayer and reading. Whatever time was left over was to be spent on manual work for the benefit of the Church and the poor.[112] The priests were to be learned men and their chief task was to provide the women with proper pastoral care. On Sundays and holy days they were to preach to the faithful in the vulgar tongue.[113]

The monastic renewals of the late Middle Ages can give a confused impression. The areas in which they occurred were widely separated, and there were certain parts of western Christendom to which they did not penetrate at all. It is therefore easy to overlook or underrate them. In fact they had a number of features in common. Most of them were inspired by the *Devotio Moderna*. They began, therefore, during the period of confusion in the medieval Church caused by the Great Schism. Their spontaneity was their strength, but also their weakness. Without a powerful papacy to back them they relied on enthusiastic bishops, papal legates, the fifteen-century councils, and, above all, secular princes.

The renewal was everywhere forwarded by university graduates. Bernardo Tolomei, founder of the Olivetans, had been a teacher at the university of Siena. The abbey of Santa Giustina found many of its early recruits at the university of Padua. The turning point at Subiaco came when Nicholas Seyringer and a group of eminent scholars from the university of Vienna threw up their studies and crossed the Alps to become Benedictines, in a dramatic gesture of renunciation which would have delighted Saint Bernard. Saint Bridget insisted that the priests in her Order should be learned men capable of explaining the scriptures to the faithful. In all observant houses novices were carefully chosen. The Subiaco customs insisted upon a minimum age and renounced the recruitment of children.

---

[110] Regula Salvatoris (as n. 96), 118, Ch.12.
[111] Ibid. 109, Ch. 7; 110, Ch. 8; 118, Ch. 12.
[112] Ibid. 128, Ch. 23.
[113] Ibid. 121, Ch.15.

The decay of so many famous religious communities encouraged radical thinking about the purpose of monasticism. There is a very basic feeling about Saint Bridget's first community in Rome, the clerks at San Giorgio in Alga, or the 'good men' of Sibculo, who had been living together for some years without any rule before deciding to become Cistercians. Particular rules and the differences between the orders were seen as matters of secondary importance. No one objected when Ludovico Barbo, who had taken vows as an augustinian friar and then lived in a community of secular clerks, was nominated abbot of a benedictine house.

Observant monks and nuns in the late Middle Ages lived out their lives in depressing circumstances. The majority of monasteries remained unaffected by any reform. The religious life continued to be held in low esteem. It required a special faith and courage to revive a way of life that was universally despised. Saint Bridget writes eloquently of the hostility of the Romans to her first endeavours.

> Some of them threatened to burn her alive, others cursed her as a heretic and a witch. The blessed Bridget herself bore all their threats and insults patiently. But she was afraid that her household, and others of her family and friends who were with her in Rome, would fall away, intimidated by hardship and hatred.[114]

The visions and prophecies of Saint Bridget had a wide circulation in late medieval Europe. Their emphasis seems, at first sight, rather different from the *Devotio Moderna* with its insistence on soberness and its suspicion of the extraordinary in religious experience. At a deeper level, however, the preoccupations of both traditions are the same. Bridget's visions at Jerusalem of the passion and crucifixion[115] are among the most touching of all her writings. The comment which she puts into

---

[114] *Extravagantes* (as n. 99), 121.
[115] *Sanctae Birgittae revelaciones lib. VII*, ed. B. Bergh (Uppsala 1967) 164–168.

the mouth of Christ is significant: 'The princes of the earth, the prelates of churches, and all classes of society, are more concerned and pleased with the delights of the earth than with my death, passion, and wounds'.[116] A return to the foundations of Christianity was a matter of urgency. 'Arise, soul devoted to Christ', wrote Ludolph of Saxony.

> Wake up, every christian soul, and faithfully study everything that is said about Jesus Christ. Meditate attentively, examine in detail, and imitate the example of your Lord. For your sake he came down to earth from his heavenly throne. For your own sake flee what is earthly and seek out what is of heaven. If the world is sweet, Christ is more so. If the world is bitter, Christ has borne it all for your sake. Stand up and walk, do not tire on the way, so that you may not lose the place reserved for you in your true home.[117]

A very simple and uncompromising return to Christ was the central theme of enlightened piety in the late Middle Ages. It prompted a few brave souls to return to the roots of christian monasticism and continued to inspire their successors in the turbulent sixteenth century.[118]

---

[116] Ibid. 169.

[117] Ludolphus de Saxonia, *Vita Jesu Christi* (Paris 1865) 6.

[118] For some general reflections on monastic reform at this period, see D. Mertens, 'Monastische Reformbewegungen des 15. Jahrhunderts: Ideen—Ziele—Resultate', in J. Hlaváchek and A. Patschovsky, edd., *Reform von Kirche und Reich zur Zeit der Konzilien von Konstanz und Basel* (Constance 1996) 157–181.

Chapter 10
CATHOLIC MONASTICISM UNDER THE COUNTER REFORMATION

WERE THERE TOO MANY monasteries in Europe on the eve of the Reformation, as one could argue? Some were wholly corrupt—gifts for satirists like Erasmus of Rotterdam. Here and there a few centres of spiritual excellence survived, especially among the Benedictines. The *Exercitatorio de la Vida Spiritual* of Garcia de Cisneros, published in 1500, was evidence of the high standards at the abbey of Montserrat where he was superior.[1] In his numerous treatises, Louis de Blois, abbot of Liessies in northern France near the modern border with Belgium (1530–66), urged upon his readers a deep and personal devotion to the life and passion of Christ.[2]

He was writing at a time of catastrophic religious change. By the end of the sixteenth century the religious life, as it had been known in western Europe for one and a half millennia, had practically ceased in England, Scandinavia, Holland, northern and much of south-western Germany, Bohemia, and Hungary. The Reformation seldom distinguished between observant and undisciplined houses. Bursfelde in Saxony, centre of a great benedictine reform movement, Vadstena in Sweden, burial place of Saint Bridget and a notable centre of piety, suffered with the rest. Most reformers were hostile to the very idea of monasticism. Martin Luther's plea that monastic buildings and endowments should be used for educational and

---

[1] On Garcia de Cisneros, see DS 2/1 (1953) 910–921.
[2] On Louis de Blois, see DS 1 (1937) 1730–1738.

charitable purposes was little regarded.[3] Monastic property was bought up cheaply or seized by princes and nobles.

Monasteries hardly fared better in the lands which remained Catholic. Princes often claimed the right to reform them and, aided by bishops, would close smaller houses on their own authority. In Italy, Spain, and Portugal, the buildings were sometimes given to the new society of Jesuits. In France monasteries suffered during the Wars of Religion (1562–1598). Protestant armies pillaged and burned religious houses, and sometimes put their inmates to the sword. The medieval section of the Metropolitan Museum of Art in New York contains architectural remains from three french abbeys which suffered in this way: Saint Guilhem, sacked by the Huguenots in 1568; Pontaut, partly destroyed in 1569; and Trie, laid waste in 1571.[4]

The council of Trent (1545–1563) succeeded in effecting a thorough reform of the Roman Catholic Church, but its decrees on the religious life were enacted during the very last session, by which time the fathers were anxious to return home. Conciliar legislation took for granted the religious life as it had existed in the Middle Ages. New institutes like those of the Jesuits or Theatines were not considered, nor were the constitutions of the older Orders reviewed. Instead the council addressed itself to certain abuses and provided a somewhat artificially uniform legislative framework for all the various forms of the religious life.[5]

The holding of private property by religious was strictly forbidden.[6] The minimum age for profession in any Order was set at sixteen, and at least a year's novitiate was enjoined

---

[3] See below Chapter 13.

[4] J. J. Rorimer, *The Cloisters: The Buildings and the Collection of Medieval Art in Fort Tryon Park* (New York 1963) 46, 63, 111.

[5] *Decrees of the Ecumenical Councils*, ed. N. P. Tanner (Georgetown 1990) 2:776–784. See also Philibert Schmitz, *Histoire de l'ordre de Saint Benoît* 4 (Maredsous 1948) 3–6.

[6] *Decrees* (as n. 5), 776–777.

beforehand.[7] Religious superiors were to be elected by secret ballot.[8] Abbesses and prioresses had normally to be at least forty years of age, and had to have been professed for at least eight.[9] One decree was to cause serious difficulty. The council strictly reinforced the law about the enclosure of nuns. After profession, no woman religious was to be allowed out of her monastery except for a very serious reason and only with the approval of the bishop.[10] The decree was levelled against some scandalous abuses and was welcome to those who wished to restore the strict monastic life for women. On the other hand, it frustrated founders like Saint Jane Frances de Chantal and Mary Ward, who wanted institutes for women to be able to engage in teaching and nursing.

As far as monks were concerned, the most important decree was the one which reinforced the enactments of Innocent III and Benedict XII about the government of exempt religious houses.[11] Such houses were to group themselves into congregations and to hold chapters general every three years. Here statutes could be made and a system of visitation organised. The unit for such congregations was to be the ecclesiastical province, but if there were not enough houses in a single province, two or three could be combined to create the congregation. The congregations which had come into being during the late Middle Ages thus provided a model for the future. In Spain, indeed, the congregation of Valladolid continued much as before.[12] Garcia de Cisneros was only one of its eminent theologians, historians, and canonists during Spain's 'Golden Age'. Around 1592 the abbey of Montserrat, where he had been abbot, established a small dependent priory in Lima in Peru, and in 1602 another in Mexico City. This expansion into

---

[7] Ibid. 781.
[8] Ibid. 778.
[9] Ibid. 778–779.
[10] Ibid. 777–778.
[11] Ibid. 779. See Schmitz (as n. 5), 4–5.
[12] Schmitz (as n. 5) 168–169.

Spanish America was modest. The task of these houses was to foster the cult of Our Lady of Montserrat and to collect offerings for the upkeep of the shrine in the mother country.[13]

The fact that in Portugal many of the major abbeys were held *in commendam*, hampered benedictine reform in that kingdom. In 1567 Pope, later Saint, Pius V finally succeeded in uniting the reformed benedictine houses into a congregation, with superiors elected for three years, and customs borrowed from Valladolid. The centre of the congregation was to be at Tibães, near Braga in northern Portugal. Eventually it embraced all the benedictine abbeys of the kingdom.[14]

In 1578 the Portuguese Benedictines were asked to make a foundation across the ocean. Land was acquired in Bahia, then the capital of the portuguese possessions in the Americas.[15] The foundation of the monastery of São Sebastian, the first benedictine monastery in the New World, came two years later.[16] Other foundations followed: São Bento de Olinda in 1586,[17] Our Lady of Montserrat in Rio de Janeiro in 1593,[18] and Our Lady of the Assumption in São Paulo in 1599.[19] Eight more monasteries were founded in Brazil during the next century.[20] There was, then, a considerable benedictine presence in Portuguese America. In time the brazilian branch of the congregation became rich in plantations and slaves.[21]

The Cassinese Congregation in Italy[22] flourished under the watchful eye of the Counter Reformation popes.[23] By the end of the sixteenth century it embraced practically all the

---

[13] *The Cambridge History of Latin America*, ed. L. Bethell, 1 (Cambridge 1984) 520.

[14] DIP 7 (1973) 131–132; Schmitz (as n. 5), 169–171.

[15] *Catalogo dos Bispos, Gerais, Provinciais, Abades e mais cargos de ordem de São Bento do Brasil 1582–1975*, ed. D. José Lohr-Endres (Salvador-Bahia 1976) 7.

[16] Ibid. 55.

[17] Ibid. 59.

[18] Ibid. 63.

[19] Ibid. 70.

[20] Ibid. 67, 74–76, 79–86, 89.

[21] *Cambridge History of Latin America* (as n. 15), 545–550.

[22] See above p. 251.

[23] Schmitz (as n. 5), 148–153.

benedictine houses of the peninsula. The congregation was noted for its scholars, many of whom became curial cardinals. During the seventeenth century unwise financial management by the Chapter General and heavy taxation in the papal state caused some difficulties. The republic of Venice would have liked its benedictine abbeys to form a society of their own and it was, perhaps, to avoid dismemberment that the congregation was divided into seven provinces in 1607. There was also a recruitment crisis because so many of the abbeys would accept novices only from noble families. On the whole, however, the Cassinese survived into the eighteenth century as the most prestigious of the benedictine congregations, constantly held up as a model to others.

The situation in Switzerland and Germany was more diffi-cult.[24] The Congregation of Bursfelde took some time to re-cover from the loss of its mother house. The reforms of Melk and Kastl lost their impetus. In many monasteries the commu-nities were demoralised and the standard of observance was deplorably low. The papal nuncios of the Counter Reforma-tion, well meaning but ignorant of local conditions, wanted to effect reform by uniting the benedictine houses of Germany into a congregation modelled on the Cassinese. To this policy there were justified objections. How could superiors hold of-fice for three years only, when some abbots were princes of the Empire? How could such abbots surrender their powers to a chapter general? As for the bishops and the secular Catholic princes, they feared monastic congregations as threats to their authority.

Monastic reform in the Holy Roman Empire, therefore, proceeded slowly. In the sixteenth century energetic superiors reformed the great abbeys of Saint Gall, Reichenau, and Ein-siedeln in Switzerland. Acceptance of novices from bourgeois families helped recruitment. These three abbeys formed the nucleus of the *Congregatio Helvetica*, which was formed with

---

[24] Ibid. 117–147; W. Seibrich, *Gegenreformation als Restauration* (Münster 1991) 17–24.

the support of an able papal nuncio in 1602 and received papal approval in the same year. By the middle of the seventeenth century it included all the benedictine abbeys of Switzerland. The congregation had a Chapter General which arranged for the annual visitation of all constituent houses, and ensured uniformity of discipline and liturgical observance.

In 1617 the archbishop of Salzburg founded a Catholic university in his see city and entrusted it to the Benedictines. An informal group of benedictine houses in south-west Germany came into being to support it financially and provide it with professors and students. In 1641 this became the Benedictine Congregation of the diocese of Salzburg, comprising seven abbeys, with its mother house at Saint Peter's in Salzburg.

The congregation of Upper Swabia, comprising abbeys in the present area of Baden-Würtemberg, was set up in 1602–1603, after birth-pangs lasting some twenty years. The organisation of the Bavarian Congregation was finalised only in 1684. Bursfelde,[25] reduced from ninety-six abbeys to thirty, took time to recover, but the reduced congregation, confined mainly to the area of Cologne and the Lower Rhine, was flourishing by the middle of the seventeenth century. The german congregations were less centralised than the Cassinese. Abbots held office for life. Monks vowed stability to a single house and not to the congregation, and individual communities retained their autonomy in matters of discipline.

There remained many abbeys which were not incorporated into any congregation. Most were in a deplorable condition. Ferdinand II's ill-conceived 'Edict of Restitution' of 1629, under which ecclesiastical property seized by Protestants was to be returned, raised hopes of a return to the past which were soon dashed. In fact, the Thirty Years' War was disastrous for the monks. Many houses were destroyed and their inhabitants massacred. At the Peace of Westphalia in 1648, lay ownership of monastic property in protestant areas was confirmed. The first task of every surviving monastery was

---

[25] See above pp. 257–258.

to consolidate Catholicism in the surrounding district. This combination of monasticism with an active apostolate was a particular phenomenon of the Counter Reformation period.

The English Congregation, founded in 1619, was also shaped by historical circumstances. From 1558 until the first Catholic Relief Acts in 1778, Roman Catholicism in England was an underground religion proscribed by penal laws and subject, from time to time, to fierce persecution. The period was marked by extraordinary heroism, but also by unedifying squabbles, particularly between the Jesuits and their critics. These quarrels affected the english colleges abroad. In the last years of the sixteenth century some english students in Rome and Valladolid, dissatisfied with their Jesuit superiors, left to become Benedictines respectively at Montecassino, and San Benito Valladolid.[26]

Students at the english colleges took a 'Mission Oath' which bound them to labour in the English Mission when required by their superiors. Critics were soon accusing the rebel students of cowardice, of preferring the peace of the cloister to the dangers of missionary life. In fact, most of the rebels were keen to go to England—but under benedictine rather than jesuit auspices. Because of a certain disenchantment with the Jesuits at Rome, papal permission for a benedictine mission to England was given in 1602. There was now another religious order at work in England in rivalry to, and to some extent at enmity with the Jesuits. The monks, however, belonged to two different congregations—the Cassinese and the Spanish, and at the beginning the missioners were answerable to two different superiors. From the beginning there were discussions about uniting these missionaries under a single authority. Negotiations began with Rome to create an English Benedictine Congregation. Before the pope could act, a singular ceremony in London anticipated his decision.

A number of attempts to restore the religious life had been

---

[26] On the english congregation, see D. Lunn, *The English Benedictines 1540–1688* (London 1980).

made during the short-lived catholic revival under Queen
Mary Tudor (1553–1558). In 1556 a community of former
benedictine monks had taken possession of Westminster
Abbey. They lasted there for only three years before being
expelled by Queen Elizabeth. Sigbert Buckley, one of these
westminster monks, was still alive when the benedictine missionaries arrived in England. It was the opinion of Augustine
Baker, a recent convert monk and former lawyer, that the
last survivor of a corporation had all its rights vested in him.
Sigbert, 'this venerable peice [sic] of antiquity' could therefore pass on the rights and privileges of the ancient English
Benedictine Congregation.

On 21 November 1607, in his apartment in Clerkenwell,
London, this aged monk 'aggregated' two Benedictines into
the abbey of Westminster.[27] More aggregations followed in
the next few days. In this way, it was argued, the ancient Benedictine Congregation of England had been perpetuated, and
formal instruments were drawn up to this effect. The validity of
these proceedings was doubtful, among other reasons because
there had never been an English Benedictine Congregation.
The ancient abbeys of England had all been independent of
one another. It must be remembered, however, that continuity
is a very subjective concept. The seventeenth century english
monks felt, as do their successors today, that they were the true
inheritors of all the monastic traditions of their native land.

In 1619, after long negotiations, a single congregation for
all the english Benedictines received papal approval. It had
five monasteries: Douai in northern France (1606), Dieulouard in Lorraine (1608), Saint Malo in Britanny (1611), Paris
(1615), and Lambspring in the Empire in northern Germany
(1643).[28] From these houses monks were sent on the English
Mission. For Englishwomen with a monastic vocation there

---

[27] On the aggregation, see Lunn (as n. 26), 92–95; David Knowles, *The Religious
Orders in England*, 3 (Cambridge 1959) 444–455. For an older, more romantic
view of the Buckley episode, see J. C. Almond, *The History of Ampleforth
Abbey* (London 1903) 12–17.
[28] Lunn (as n. 26), 171–172; Knowles (as n. 27), 453.

were benedictine houses at Brussels (1598), Ghent (1624), Boulogne (1652), Dunkirk (1662), and Ypres (1665).[29] Most famous of all was Cambrai, founded in 1623; there Augustine Baker, the great mystic and scholar, was chaplain to the nuns from 1624–1633.[30]

In the second half of the sixteenth century France was distracted by the Wars of Religion. Only in 1593, when Henry of Navarre, the protestant leader, decided that 'Paris is worth a Mass', became a Catholic and ascended the french throne as Henry IV, was Catholicism safe. While the fighting lasted it had hardly been possible to apply the decrees of the Council of Trent. In fact, its decrees were not promulgated until 1615. The reign of Henry IV, however, saw the beginnings of a religious revival. Zealous bishops introduced the reforms of Trent in their dioceses on their own initiative. The religious orders, including the Jesuits, put aside their traditional rivalries for a time and fostered the 'devout humanism' of which Saint Francis de Sales was the most eminent exponent.[31]

Women played a prominent part in the french Catholic revival, and the restoration of discipline in benedictine houses for women came early. 'Between the years 1570 and 1670', writes Louis Brémond, 'France witnessed the birth, supremacy and death of many splendid abbesses, who in less than thirty years had re-established in every quarter of the kingdom the nearly vanished prestige of the order of Saint Benedict.' He goes on to list sixteen of them, and adds that there were 'Many more whom I pass over—in truth there are too many of them!'[32]

An early centre of reform for women religious was the benedictine abbey Montmartre, just outside Paris.[33] This house had long been very relaxed. In 1589, the future Henry IV had used Montmartre as his headquarters at the siege of

[29] Lunn (as n. 26), 198.
[30] On Cambrai and Augustine Baker, see Lunn (as n. 26), 201–219.
[31] On the religious revival in France, see L. Brémond, *A Literary History of Religious Thought in France,* 3 vols. (London 1928–1936).
[32] Ibid. 2:292.
[33] Y. Chaussy, *Les bénédictines et la réforme catholique* (Paris 1975) 21–55.

Paris and had billetted his troops in the abbey. The buildings were in ruins. The handful of nuns, having lost their revenues, were half starved.

The situation was saved by Pierre de Fresne, Henry IV's secretary of state. He rescued the abbey financially and in 1596 persuaded the king to pressure the nuns into electing a worthy superior. Pierre's choice was his own sister-in-law Marie de Beauvillier, a devout, well educated, and determined young woman of twenty-two, who had been a nun since she was a child of seven.

It took her about ten years to reform Montmartre. She decided that a literal observance of the Rule of Saint Benedict was impractical, and chose instead the milder statutes which Étienne Poncher had devised for the abbey when he was bishop of Paris (1503–1519). More important than its observances, perhaps, was the spirit of the reformed house. Marie de Beauvillier was befriended by Madame Acarie, a remarkable married woman who inspired most of the Counter Reformation initiatives in the France of her time. Through her the abbess was brought into touch with Saint Francis de Sales, who went to see her on his visit to Paris in 1602.

Montmartre was important because the hill on which it stood, the supposed site of the martyrdom of Saint Denis and his companions, was a place of pilgrimage. The reform at this ancient house therefore attracted attention, and recruits from many parts of France came to join the community. One of these was destined eventually to eclipse Marie de Beauvillier herself.

Marguerite d'Arbouze came from south-eastern France and was professed at Montmartre in 1612.[34] She had already had experience of monastic life elsewhere and in addition to being an accomplished linguist familiar with Latin, Italian, and Spanish, she had a gift of winning affection among the young. Only a year after her profession she was chosen to be prioress of La Ville l'Evêque, a property near Paris which Montmartre

---

[34] On Marguerite d'Arbouze, see ibid. 57–67.

had acquired in 1613, and where a kind of novitiate was planned.

In 1614 Marie de Beauvillier was away from Montmartre for six months while she investigated the possibility of becoming an abbess elsewhere. During all this time the nuns at Montmartre lived in a state of uncertainty. Marguerite was left as temporary superior. She did not hesitate to make major decisions. In the end, however, the abbess returned, her negotiations to take another charge having failed. She was greatly displeased with the changes which had been made in her absence. Marguerite was sent back to be prioress of La Ville l'Evêque. In 1617 the abbess visited the priory. After being publicly reprimanded, Marguerite was deposed and returned as a penitent to Montmartre.

A source of irritation for Marie de Beauvillier was Marguerite's friendship with Anne of Austria. The lonely and unhappy queen, still unfamiliar with French and neglected by her husband, had found solace at La Ville l'Evêque, where the prioress could speak Castilian. She could hardly be prevented from visiting her friend in Montmartre. In 1618 the ancient abbey of Val de Grace, or the Manger, in the countryside outside Paris, was without an abbess. Anne persuaded the king to nominate Marguerite, who left Montmartre in the following year, parting from her abbess, we are told, with dignity.

After some time Anne of Austria obtained land for the community of Val de Grace in the parisian suburb of Saint Jacques. The nuns moved there in 1621. Marguerite directed the house for six years until her death in 1627. It became the queen's favourite place of retreat. Here she came frequently to pray for an heir, and long after Marguerite's death, when her prayer had been answered, she paid for the building of the present magnificent church.

When she became abbess of Val de Grace, Marguerite found there eight nuns, of whom one was mad. She had been allowed to take two with her from Montmartre. For her, monastic reform meant an uncompromising return to Saint Benedict. She translated the Rule into French and added constitutions adapted for the use of her nuns. In the title of her book, *The True Rule of Saint Benedict, with Constitutions Adapted to it,*[35] the adjective was, no doubt, a parting shot at her former abbess. The *horarium* at Val de Grace followed Saint Benedict closely:

2 AM	Matins, followed immediately by Lauds.
	After Lauds, rest, unless any wished to pray alone in the church for half an hour.
6 AM	Prime, followed by half an hour of private prayer from which no one could be dispensed.
	Chapter, or Chapter of Faults.
	Return to cells for rest or reading.
8 AM	Terce, Conventual Mass, Sext.
	Manual labour.
10 AM	Examination of conscience, followed by dinner (on non-fast days).
	After dinner, recreation, consisting of quiet conversation in the parlour for one hour.
12 PM	Return to cells for one hour of rest.
1 PM	Nones.
	Continuation of manual labour
3 PM	Vespers.
	One hour of mental prayer.
	After this, return to cells or, the with permission of the abbess, a visit to the sick in the infirmary.
5 PM	Supper.
	After supper, recreation as after dinner.
6.30 PM	Compline.
	Examination of conscience.
8 PM	Retire to cells until the night office[36]

Marguerite's spirituality was based on the Bible, the Latin Fathers, and Saint Thomas Aquinas. During Advent and Lent

---

[35] *La vraye Règle de S. Benoist avec les constitutions accommodées a icelle . . .* (Paris 1623). Only the edition of 1676 is available to me in Scotland; see n. 36.
[36] *La Règle du bienheureux Père S. Benoist . . . avec les constitutions qui y sont accommodées par la révérende Mère Marguerite de Veni d'Arbouze . . .* (Paris 1676) 79–83.

she would propose parts of the *Summa* as meditations for her nuns. She was prepared to depart from Saint Benedict in demanding that the abbess of Val de Grace should be elected for three years only. This was the common practice of many reformed congregations, though Marguerite did allow for reelection up to four times.[37] Thanks to the patronage of the queen, abbatial elections at Val de Grace were free from interference by the civil power.[38] Reformed benedictine abbeys for women did not form part of any congregation. Each was subject to the local bishop. The superior of Val de Grace, then, was the archbishop of Paris. Without his permission no one could be professed there. Power to excommunicate the recalcitrant was his alone. Visitations were conducted by him, or by someone of whom he approved.[39]

Anne of Austria was also closely associated with the Benedictines of the Perpetual Adoration of the Blessed Sacrament. Their first house was founded in Paris in 1651, by Catherine de Bar, known in religion as Mother Mechtilde of the Holy Sacrament. The sisters combined the traditional benedictine *horarium* with perpetual adoration, day and night vigil, of the Blessed Sacrament exposed on the altar. In Paris the exposition began on 25 March 1653. A year later Anne of Austria herself, a rope around her neck and a candle in her hand, publicly made the *amende honorable* to the Sacred Host. This august example may explain the popularity of the devotion. Benedictine houses of the Perpetual Adoration were founded all over Catholic Europe, like the house founded by John Sobieski's queen at Warsaw in 1683, in thanksgiving for his victory over the Turks at Vienna.[40]

Monastic reform in France, among both men and women, was hampered by the powers of the french crown over the Church and by the system of *commendam*. The kings of France

---

[37] Ibid. 265.
[38] Ibid. 255. 'Que les Soeurs tiennent a une trés-grande grace et bénédiction de Dieu, d'avoir la liberté de choisir et élire leur Supérieure.'
[39] Ibid. 244–245, 250, 287–288.
[40] On perpetual adoration, see Schmitz (as n. 5), 7 (1956) 166–167.

had appointed to major benefices for many centuries, but their powers were formalised by the Concordat of Bologna, made in 1516 between Pope Leo X and King Francis I.[41] Canonical elections, both of bishops and of religious superiors, were suppressed. The king nominated a candidate; the pope, having satisfied himself as to the nominee's suitability, issued the bull. It was agreed that seculars should no longer be appointed as nominal abbots or abbesses of religious houses. This provision, however, was usually ignored. All too often commendatory abbots were secular clergy or even married laymen.

In theory the properties of the superior and of the community were separate. The commendator enjoyed only the superior's portion. In practice the demarcation was often unclear, and an unscrupulous commendator could encroach upon the community's property, even to the extent of taking it all, so that the monastery buildings fell into ruins and the community was reduced to two or three pensioners.

In the wake of the religious revival in the first years of the seventeenth century, however, it became unfashionable to be the proprietor of a decayed abbey. Good taste now demanded that the commendator help to reestablish the regular life. The generosity of individuals varied, but even the most sympathetic put their own interests first. Moreover, Louis XIV was extremely unwilling to lose his power of patronage. Armand de Rancé, commendatory abbot of la Trappe in Normandy, underwent a religious conversion, became a Cistercian, and lived among his monks as their 'regular' abbot. Only at the end of his life did it become clear that the king would allow a regular abbot to be elected to succeed him.[42]

These conditions mark the possibilities as well as the limitations of monastic reform in France. The earliest large

---

[41] On the concordat, see R. Aubenas, 'Le pontificat de Jules II et les débuts de Léon X (1503–17)', *Histoire de l'Église*, ed. A. Fliche et V. Martin, 15 (1951) 174–181.

[42] On commendators and their relations with reformed communities, see J. Hourlier, 'Les bénédictins', *Les ordres religieux*, ed. G. Le Bras, 1 (Paris 1979) 272–273.

monastic congregation in the kingdom was the 'Congregation of Exempts' comprising all monasteries for men which did not belong to a religious Order and were not subject to a bishop.[43] As a vehicle of reform the congregation soon ran out of steam. Its constituent houses had too little in common and as other, more successful congregations came into being, many broke away. Only eleven houses were left when the congregation was suppressed in 1770.

Effective monastic reform among the Benedictines spread into France from Lorraine.[44] This province, not yet a part of the kingdom, was coming increasingly under french cultural and political influence. The reform of monastic houses in the area began in 1598 with the visitation of the monasteries of Verdun by its bishop, Prince Erric de Vaudémont. Erric began with the abbey of Saint Vanne in that city, of which he was himself the commendatory abbot. Under pressure the monks elected as their prior Dom Didier de la Cour, who was noted for piety and humility. The monks hoped they could control him. They soon discovered their mistake. Dom Didier was assisted by his energetic bishop, who obtained for him a papal brief authorising him to use all measures to affect a reform. The monks who resisted were sent elsewhere, and from 1600 Saint Vanne began to recruit novices committed to strict observance of the Rule. Two years later the neighbouring abbey of Saint Hydulphe at Moyenmoutier was reformed, and in 1604 the congregation of Lorraine, consisting at first of only these two houses, received papal approval.

The reform soon spread throughout Lorraine. From the first the institutions of the new congregation were based on the Cassinese. This model was recommended in the papal bull of 1604. The congregation of Lorraine was governed by a chapter general consisting of the superiors and one delegate from each house. The majority of houses were held *in commendam*. The priors were the actual religious superiors. They held office

[43] On the exempts, see ibid. 264–265; Schmitz (as n. 5), 11–16.
[44] On Saint Vanne, see Hourlier (as n. 42), 266; Schmitz (as n. 5), 20–30.

for three years only. Professed monks vowed stability to the congregation and not to an individual house.

The Congregation of Lorraine was famous for the care with which novices were trained. Its handbooks for novices were translated into many languages and widely used. There was a house of studies at Pont à Mousson, the university town of Lorraine. The monks of Saint Vanne were noted for scholarship. 'An ignorant Benedictine', said Dom Didier, 'is a contradiction in terms.' He wished the new congregation to serve the public through teaching, research, and the cure of souls. The Vannists shone in the disciplines of theology, history, and natural science.

Between 1613 and 1618 a number of french monasteries joined the congregation. Foreseeing difficulties if it tried to exercise authority in France, the General Chapter at Saint Vanne advised the french superiors to form an organisation of their own. In 1618, therefore, a new french benedictine congregation came into being. It adopted as its patron Saint Maurus, the disciple of Saint Benedict who was believed to have brought the Holy Rule to Gaul. The new Congregation of Saint Maur was supported by King Louis XIII. Papal approval followed in 1621.[45]

Before a monastery could be reformed, negotiations with the commendatory abbot were necessary. Here the Maurists were helped by their connections in high places and, as time went on, their taut organisation and considerable experience. They took over a house in accordance with a written agreement between the superiors of the Congregation and the commendator. The revenues of the community and of its abbot were clearly distinguished. The monks were given complete

---

[45] For the history of the Maurists the following are useful: Schmitz (as n. 5), 30–52; Hourlier (as n. 42), 266–285; 'Maurini' DIP 5 (1973) 1082–1089 (also by Hourlier). There is much useful information in H. Leclercq, *Mabillon*, 2 vols. (Paris 1953–1957). Y. Chaussy, *Les bénédictins de St. Maur,* 1: Aperçu historique (Paris 1989), is largely prosopographical. On Maurist learning, see D. O. Hurrel, 'The Benedictines of the Congregation of St. Maur and the Church Fathers', in *The Reception of the Church Fathers in the West,* ed. I. Backus (Leiden-New York-Cologne 1997) 1009–1038.

freedom to administer their portion. The commendator surrendered all his powers as a religious superior. The community was to be ruled, in future, by its prior. There was also an agreement about the honourable treatment and accommodation of the commendator, should he wish to visit his abbey, and his rights, if he was an ecclesiastic, to preside over religious ceremonies.

There had also to be an agreement about the monks who were already resident in the abbey but who did not wish to accept the reform. These *anciens* (oldtimers) were to be given lodgings and pensions. They could elect a superior, whose office was renewable every three years, and who would represent their interests. If they wished to attend any of the services in the monastery church, they could occupy a stall according to their seniority.[46]

In 1645 there were eighty-eight maurist houses. Thirty years later the number had risen to one hundred seventy-eight. The congregation's constitutions were worked out very slowly and after much consultation. Only in 1645 was the first volume ready for printing. A chapter general of thirty- three persons held supreme power and appointed all the officers, including the conventual priors. These, and the visitors, held office for three years only and could be reappointed only once. The Superior General, on the other hand, could be reelected indefinititely. The congregation profited greatly from the accumulated experience of its early leaders who, like Dom Grégoire Tarisse (1630–1648), were elected again and again.

Maurist monasticism was notoriously austere. The monks kept perpetual abstinence. The fasts of the Rule were strictly observed. Six or seven hours a day were spent in choir. Silence was the rule outside the hours of recreation. Visits from outside, and exits from the house, required permission from the prior. The monks had their own cells, the contents of which were reduced to a minimum: a bed with a straw mattress, a

---

[46] On the experience of one of the *anciens*, see M. Ultee, *The Abbey of St. Germain des Prés in the Seventeenth Century* (Yale 1981) 133–151.

wooden table and chair, a *prie Dieu*, a tin or earthenware holy-
water stoup, an iron candlestick, a wax or tallow candle, some
devotional pictures. No fire was allowed. Even in the middle
of the winter the monks could warm themselves only in the
common recreation room. Discipline was imposed by severe
beatings or imprisonment.

Medieval monks had spent much of their time copying
manuscripts. Since the invention of printing, monastic legislators had been trying to find a suitable substitute. Dom
Tarisse found it in study and research.[47] Monks with special
gifts were encouraged to embark on particular projects. As the
work progressed they would be assigned editorial assistants,
while the whole congregation would provide copyists, proof
readers, and indexers. Not every Maurist was a scholar. It has
been estimated that, of about four thousand monks in its most
prosperous days, forty were engaged in research.[48] It was this
particular aspect, however, which marked the Maurists in their
own time and for posterity.

The headquarters of the congregation were in the ancient
abbey of Saint Germain des Prés, in a suburb of Paris. Its library
was already famous in the Middle Ages and had been open to
the public from time to time. Dom Tarisse was tireless about
enlarging the collection. At his request the library was open to
outsiders on Tuesday and Thursday afternoons. In 1647 Dom
Luc d'Achery was appointed librarian. He was a noted scholar
who corresponded with scholars and monasteries abroad. He
was also something of a perpetual invalid who inhabited the
abbey infirmary but managed, nevertheless, to reach the age
of seventy-six.

Dom Luc's first task was to catalogue the library. He also
had his own research project. The title of the series eventually
published under his name accurately defines his programme:
*Veterum aliquot scriptorum qui in Galliae bibliothecis maxime
Benedictionorum latuerant Spicilegium*—'A Gleaning from

---

[47] David Knowles, *Great Historical Enterprises* (London 1963) 35–62.
[48] Ibid. 41 n. 1.

Ancient Writings which have hitherto lain hidden in french libraries, especially benedictine ones'. This anthology of patristic and medieval texts of Dom Luc's own choosing was eventually published in thirteen volumes in 1655. The choice of extracts was inevitably arbitrary. It was clear that more material was to be found and that a more logical system was needed for it. The opportunities were to be brilliantly exploited by Jean Mabillon, a younger monk who had already done some useful research and who, in 1664, was assigned to Dom Luc as an assistant.

Mabillon was born in 1632 and became a monk at the very observant abbey of Saint Remi in Rheims in 1653. In 1663 he was transferred to the royal abbey of Saint Denis near Paris, and here began his edition of the works of Saint Bernard, on which he was engaged when he was called to Saint Germain. It was understood that he would help Dom Luc and other scholars with their editorial work while continuing his own research.

Mabillon applied cartesian logic to history. 'A true philosophy,' he wrote, 'is not halted by the authority of authors or their prejudices. It advances steadily until it has found a principle of natural light, and a truth so clear that it would be impossible to call it into doubt.'[49] Mabillon combined a clear vision of his aims with astonishing industry. He would often start work at 2 am and continue until dinner, stopping only for Mass, the Choir Office, and his own prayers.

He cut his teeth on the edition of the works of Saint Bernard, which was published in six volumes in 1667. He included spurious works along with discussions of their authenticity and their probable authors. Mabillon's remained the standard edition until 1957. The *Acta Sanctorum Ordinis Sancti Benedicti*, of which the first volume appeared in 1668, was a history of the Benedictines through the carefully edited lives of its saints, with historical notes and appendices. It was this which established Mabillon's fame. His visits to archives

---

[49] J. Mabillon, *Traité des études monastiques* 1 (Paris 1692) 377–378.

in France and abroad usually gave rise to publications in which the most interesting finds were published. The *Museum Italicum* which reported on the italian journey of 1685, contained much material on the history of liturgy, a subject on which Mabillon had already published a pioneering work: *De liturgia Gallica* (1685).

Mabillon is most famous for his *De re diplomatica* (1681) and the *Traité des études monastiques* (1691). Both were born of controversy. In 1675 the jesuit scholar Daniel Papebroeck published a treatise which cast doubt on certain diplomas attributed to Dagobert (623–639) and laid down such stringent rules for testing the authenticity of ancient diplomas that few would have survived with any credibility. In *De re diplomatica* Mabillon discussed the historical importance of administrative material. He described the materials on which diplomas were written, the methods of dating, how the subscriptions were made, and how seals were affixed. He included plates illustrating the handwriting of diplomas and an appendix of over one hundred documents. The scientific study of Diplomatics began with this pioneering treatise. It is pleasant to record that Papebroeck publicly acknowledged Mabillon as his master. The *Traité des études monastiques* was written in answer to Abbot de Rancé's contention that study was incompatible with the monastic vocation. It will be considered elsewhere.[50]

The *Réflexions sur les prisons des ordres religieux* (1694) shows Mabillon in quite another light. Brother Denis was a young and promising monk of Saint Germain des Prés in whom Mabillon possibly saw a future research assistant. In 1690, having committed some grave fault, Denis ran away from the monastery. Under the *ancien régime* leaving a monastery was a civil crime. Brother Denis went underground and 'lived rough', until he was caught by the police and returned. Perhaps at Mabillon's request he was treated with indulgence, but in 1691 he ran away again. Again he was caught and, this time, imprisoned at the abbey of Mont Saint Michel, the monastic

---

[50] See below p. 306.

Bastille. After yet another escape and capture his feet were chained.

Mabillon could not obtain permission to visit Brother Denis, but he moved heaven and earth to have the prisoner's conditions improved. He enlisted the help of an acquaintance in Normandy. He appealed for help to a cardinal in Rome. The cardinal so took the matter to heart that he wrote to the Maurist authorities even more often than he had been asked, but this only made matters worse. It was now felt that Mabillon had brought the congregation into disrepute, and he was obliged to ask for pardon.

Eventually Brother Denis escaped again, and disappears from history. It was in connection with this affair that Mabillon wrote his treatise. He remarked that while secular authorities must maintain order in society, the first priority of ecclesiastics must be the sinner's repentance. He quoted Saint Benedict's advice, 'Let the abbot show all care and solicitude towards the offending brethren'. Excommunicates were not isolated, according to the Rule, but were to be visited by senior brothers who would 'console the wavering brother . . . that he be not overwhelmed by excess of sorrow'.[51] The worst punishment envisaged in the Rule was expulsion from the monastery.[52] The Aachen statutes of 817, Mabillon went on, decreed that the monastery prison must have a fire which should be lit in the winter, and that the prisoner be given some useful work to do.[53]

Mabillon contrasted these humane provisions with the dreadful monastic dungeons of his own day. He recommended that monastic prisons should resemble the cells of the Carthusians. Each should have a garden so that the prisoner could see the daylight and have an occupation. He should be allowed books and visits from his brethren to encourage repentance. Some monks who wanted to live like hermits might also, Mabillon suggested, be assigned cells of this kind.

---

[51] RB 27.
[52] RB 28.
[53] See above p. 110.

The most eminent Maurist scholar after Mabillon was Dom Bernard Montfauçon (1655–1741). For forty years he laboured at editions of the Greek Fathers which remained standard until this century.[54] The eighteenth century, however, saw a change in the direction of Maurist research. Monasticism was being criticised, and monks were being expected to do something 'useful'. The Maurists hoped to deflect criticism by editing texts which were of national rather than of merely religious significance. Many of the great series which they began in the eighteenth century were unfinished at the Revolution and were continued in the nineteenth century by the french institutes.[55]

Among the Cistercians, one of the first to attempt a thorough monastic reform was Jean de la Barrière (1544–1600).[56] He was only twenty-one when, through family influence, he became commendatory abbot of Feuillant, an ancient cistercian abbey near Toulouse. He had not yet completed his studies. At Paris he came under the influence of a pious priest and in 1573, after many inner struggles, he decided to become a monk in his own abbey and restore its monastic observance. He found twelve worldly monks, totally resistant to his plans for reform. For a short time he went away to undergo a cistercian novitiate, make his profession, and be ordained. On his return he had no alternative but to live an austere life on his own, while his monks ignored, when they did not actually harass, him. He devoted some of his time to preaching. In 1577 the refractory monks at last agreed to leave. Two clerks and two novices stayed with their abbot. New recruits, however, soon made up for those who had left.

Apart from a brief novitiate, Jean had no experience of the cistercian life. Much of his programme anticipated that

[54] Knowles (as n. 49), 52–54.
[55] Ibid. 54–56.
[56] On Jean de la Barrière and the Feuillants, see C. Bock, *Feuillants et Feuillantines* (Paris 1961); 'Feuillants', DS 5 (1964) 274–287; 'Barrière', DHGE 6 (1931) 924–926; 'Feuillants et Feuillantines', ibid. 16 (1967) 1338–1344; 'Barrière' DIP 1 (1969) 1059–1061; 'Foglianti', ibid. 4 (1973) 93–94; L. J. Lekai, *The Cistercians. Ideals and Reality* (Kent, Ohio 1977) 134–135.

of de Rancé. It went far beyond the austerities of the early Cistercians. The reformed monks at Feuillant went barefoot at all times. They ate no meat, fish, eggs, oil, or milk products, they did not season their food even with salt, they drank no wine. Their diet consisted entirely of vegetables and coarse bread; their sole drink was water. During Advent and Lent the kitchen was closed and the community subsisted on bread and water. In the refectory there were no tables or chairs. The monks took their meals kneeling on the floor. In spite of their meagre diet they were still expected to do manual work and to preach when required.

Jean's reform received the approval of several popes. When Sixtus V issued a bull of protection in 1586, there were one hundred forty monks at Feuillant. The next year the pope referred to the abbey as a 'congregation' and allowed it to found other houses. Henry III of France offered a prestigious site in a suburb of Paris, to which a group of some sixty monks from the mother abbey walked in a spectacular month-long trek across France. A house was also founded for women. In 1602 it had fifty professed sisters.

Although the Feuillants called themselves Cistercians, they were intent on independence from Cîteaux, which viewed departures from the traditional cistercian life with a baneful eye. A chapter of Feuillant superiors met in Turin in 1589; another in Rome in 1592. The newly elected pope, Clement VIII, insisted on the elimination of the more bizarre penances. New constitutions mitigated the original dietary rules, while making no compromises about poverty, silence, prayer, and the liturgy. A papal bull removed the Feuillants completely from the jurisdiction of the cistercian Chapter General. They, like the other reformed congregations of the period, were now an independent monastic congregation, with a superior general, a centralising chapter general, and superiors elected for three years.

The chapter of 1592 was disastrous for Jean de la Barrière himself. There was opposition to his innovations, partly fuelled from Cîteaux. Most dangerous for Jean was his personal

attachment to Henry III. Strict Catholics were horrified by
the king's reported partiality for Protestants; indeed he was
almost regarded as a Protestant himself. Tainted by Henry's
friendship, Jean de la Barrière was deposed and imprisoned in
a roman monastery. Here he lived in great humility for eight
years, until Cardinal Bellarmine took an interest in his case
and proved that there had been a miscarriage of justice. Jean
did not long survive his rehabilitation. He died in 1600. Pope
Clement VIII wept at his funeral and pronounced him a *beatus*
on the spot.

The Feuillants remained a body of very strict monks until
their extinction during the French Revolution. During a controversy with Abbot de Rancé, the general of the Feuillants in
France claimed that their observance was 'sufficient to content
the strong without crushing the weak'.[57] In 1630 they were
divided into two separate congregations, one for France and
the other for Italy. Both retained the name 'Cistercian'.[58] Like
most monks of the period they combined a certain amount of
pastoral work with their austerities. They could be called upon
to preach. The monks of the parisian house were much in demand as confessors.The Feuillants also encouraged monastic
reform in general. Marguerite d'Arbouze at the Val de Grace
relied much upon the advice and support of the Feuillant
Eustache de Saint Paul.

The outstanding monastery for cistercian nuns in seventeenth century France was Port Royal. It had been founded
in the thirteenth century and was, three hundred years later,
a fairly mediocre religious house.[59] In 1599 Antoine Arnauld,
a rich parisian lawyer, sent his seven-year-old daughter there,

---

[57] A. J. Krailsheimer, *Armand-Jean de Rancé* (Oxford 1974) 113.
[58] Because the italian Feuillants called themselves 'reformed Cistercians' they
are sometimes confused with the later Trappists.
[59] From the enormous bibliography on Port Royal the following have been
found most useful: *Les moniales cisterciennes*, ed. J. de la Croix Bouton, 2
(Aiguebelle 1987) 117–130, with selected bibliography on p. 209; F. Ellen
Weaver, 'Angélique de St. Jean de Port Royal', *Cistercians in the Late Middle Ages* ed. R. Elder (Kalamazoo 1981) 90–101; 'Port Royal', *New Catholic
Encyclopaedia* 11 (1967) 597–599; 'Port Royal' DIP 7 (1973) 132–137.

promising that she would soon be its abbess. Having taken the name Angélique in religion, she succeeded as abbess in 1602, when she was eleven years old.

It is hardly surprising that she wanted to leave or that she preferred novels to pious reading. In 1608, however, she was converted by the preaching of a young Cistercian from the order's college in Paris. With his encouragement she decided to become a true religious and to reform her community. The decisive moment came on 25 September 1609, a day always remembered at Port Royal. It was the 'Day of the Grille' (*Journée du guichet*), when the abbess refused to allow her bewildered parents to enter the monastic enclosure and insisted that she could speak to them only through the grille. In time, Angélique's sisters, and eventually— after her father's death—her mother, joined the community.

The situation of Port Royal, in a valley subject to damp, was harmful to the health of the nuns. In 1624 Angélique's mother purchased a large house in a suburb of Paris and the following year the religious settled there.[60] Dissatisfied with the support she was getting from the abbot of Cîteaux, Mother Angélique obtained a papal brief allowing her to place herself under the jurisdiction of the archbishop of Paris.

In 1633 abbey took over a small house near the Louvre whose religious were dedicated to the perpetual adoration of the Blessed Sacrament. This venture failed, but in 1647 Mother Angélique renamed her abbey 'Port Royal of the Blessed Sacrament' and pledged her community to perpetual adoration. The nuns put off the black scapular of the Cistercians and replaced it with a white scapular with a large red cross embroidered on it. It looked as if they were on the way to becoming a new religious order.

So far the story of Port Royal is not untypical of many reformed religious houses for women, except that its abbess and many of the sisters were exceptionally gifted and that its

---

[60] On the site and buildings in Paris, see *Les cisterciens a Paris* (Paris: Musée Carnavalet 1986) 64–68.

position in Paris made it a natural centre for the devout. In 1621, however, Mother Angélique became acquainted with the abbé de Saint Cyran. In time he became her spiritual director, and thus involved her and her community in the jansenist controversy.

Thanks to the revival of greek studies during the Renaissance, the Greek Fathers had become familiar to western theologians. In jesuit colleges, students read Saints Gregory Nazianzen, Basil, and John Chrysostom.[61] Influenced by these writers, the theologians of the Counter Reformation took a much more optimistic view of human nature even before the infusion of divine grace than did the augustinian latin tradition. Reaction against the success of the Jesuits during the early seventeenth century, however, easily took the form of criticising their theology. It was felt, especially at the University of Louvain, that the preeminence of Saint Augustine should be restored. In 1627, Cornelius Jansen, later to be bishop of Ypres in the Spanish Netherlands, began to write his great four-volume work *Augustinus*, in which he systematically expounded Saint Augustine's much more pessimistic teachings, especially on grace. Jansenism was eventually associated with other miscellaneous opposition causes—especially anti-jesuitism, and anti-papalism.

Jansen's closest friend and correspondent in France was the abbé de Saint Cyran. The two men openly criticised the foreign policy of Cardinal Richelieu. Like most devout Catholics they felt that France, Spain, and the Empire—the three great Catholic powers—should act together to crush the protestant rebellion and restore Catholicism. Instead, Cardinal Richelieu, for reasons of state, supported the Protestants during the Thirty Years' War. As a bishop in the Spanish Netherlands, Jansen was out of Richelieu's reach, but in 1638 Saint Cyran was arrested and imprisoned at Vincennes. In 1643, shortly after the death of Richelieu he was released, but he died soon afterwards. Jansenism was now associated with opposition to

---

[61] P. Janelle, *The Catholic Reformation* (London 1971) 129–130.

the french crown. Because Saint Cyran had become a cherished spiritual director at Port Royal, the abbey came to be regarded in some quarters as a hotbed of subversion.

After the nuns had migrated to Paris, the original abbey, 'Port Royal-in-the-Fields' (*Port-Royal-des-Champs*) had been settled by friends of Saint Cyran who lived as solitaries in the abbey grange. Among them were eminent literary men and theologians. Their activities, rather than those of the nuns, gave Port Royal its jansenist reputation. By 1648 the buildings in Paris were too small for all the nuns there and some were sent back to Port Royal-in-the-Fields, Mother Angélique having obtained funds to raise the floor of the church and take other precautions to overcome the damp. She was now abbess of a large community in two locations, with about sixty nuns in Paris and thirty in the country. Religious were easily and often transferred from one house to the other.[62] In this way the ideas of the solitaries spread among the whole community of Port Royal.

The years 1625–1657 were the most fruitful in the history of the abbey. The constitutions of Port Royal, which were the work of Mother Agnès, a younger sister of the abbess, show that, in spite of having withdrawn from the jurisdiction of the abbot of Cîteaux, Port Royal remained a cistercian house. The form of the profession, the emphasis on silence, the singing of the divine office, were all taken from the rule of Saint Benedict as interpreted in cistercian tradition.

The last years of Mother Angélique were clouded by the jansenist controversy. Propositions which, it was claimed, were contained in *Augustinus* were condemned by Rome in 1653 and 1656. After the second condemnation, a formula was prepared which required the signature of all clergy and religious in France. Louis XIV had a deeply rooted dislike of Jansenists. When he came of age in 1661, he insisted that all should be forced to sign. As a preliminary, Port Royal in Paris was visited

---

[62] L. Cognet, 'Port Royal tel que l'a connu Pascal', *Pascal et Port Royal* (Paris 1962) 8–9.

by the police. The girls who were receiving their education there were sent home and the community was forbidden to receive novices. This was the situation when Mother Angélique died, in August 1661.

After numerous delays, the formula was at last presented to the nuns in 1664. A minority signed. They were allowed to remain in Paris, and their house, separated from the one in the country, was raised to the rank of abbey. The nuns who refused were denied the sacraments and sent to Port Royal-in-the-Fields, which was too small for them all, and there they lived in overcrowded conditions. The solitaries went into hiding.

Clement IX, who became pope in 1667, was conciliatory by nature and prevented matters from being pushed to extremes. The nuns were readmitted to the sacraments and Port Royal enjoyed a period of peace. The solitaries returned and resumed their activities. The abbey became a place of fashionable retreat. Madame de Sévigné considered it a new Thebaid and its religious angels on earth.[63] Louis XIV, however, was implacable. In 1701 the jansenist controversy broke out anew, and the new pope, Clement XI, found himself obliged to issue another bull of condemnation. In 1708, at the request of the king, Port Royal was suppressed by papal brief. Shortly afterwards soldiers expelled the religious and razed the buildings to the ground.

The tragic history of Port Royal is unique in monastic history. Mother Angélique's rejection of the authority of the abbot of Cîteaux, however, has many parallels. As we have already seen, Jean de la Barrière and his followers withdrew entirely from the jurisdiction of the cistercian Chapter General. Those who wished to reform the Cistercian Order frequently found an obstacle in its ancient constitution.

A general cistercian reform in France began in the last years of the sixteenth century when a number of young abbots and priors determined to observe the Rule of Saint Benedict

---

[63] Letter of 26 January 1674. *Madame de Sévigné: Correspondance*, ed. R. Duchêne (Paris 1972) Letter 365 p. 681.

'without any dispensation'.[64] This was a reference to eating meat, which had been sanctioned by a dispensation of Pope Sixtus IV in 1475. Because of their rejection of this concession, the cistercian reformers became known as 'abstinents', or the 'Strict Observance'. In fact the Maurists also observed complete abstinence from meat, as the Rule of Saint Benedict demanded. The difficulty for the Cistercians was that theirs was an international Order. No reform could be effective which ignored the opinions of monks outside France.

The devout court of Louis XIII sympathised with the abstinents. In 1622, at the king's request, the pope appointed the pious cardinal François de la Rochefoucauld as apostolic visitor of the major religious Orders in France, with powers to introduce reform. As far as the Cistercians were concerned, the cardinal was entirely under the influence of the abstinents. In 1624 he authorised them to hold their own chapter general. In 1634 he went even further. The powers of the abbot of Cîteaux and the General Chapter were suspended. The 'ancients' were refused permission to accept novices and it was made easy for the Strict Observance to take over any house in the Order. In 1637 the monks of Cîteaux itself were expelled from their own house. They took it back six years later, amidst far from edifying scenes.

A bitter pamphlet war now began. Under the leadership of the relentless Jean Jouaud, abbot of Prières in Brittany (1631–1673), the abstinents attacked their rivals, who retorted by giving their own account of the events of the last decades. The Strict Observance, which was supported by the french court, existed only in France. The strength of the Common Observance lay in Germany and eastern Europe.

When Louis XIV assumed personal power in 1661, many of the policies of the previous reign were reversed. The Common Observance was allowed to appeal to Rome, and presently a papal commission was appointed to investigate the problems of

---

[64] For an account of the movement see Lekai (as n. 56), 138–152.

the Cistercian Order.[65] Claude Vaussin, the abbot of Cîteaux, went to Rome to state the case for the Common Observance. The Abstinents were represented by two abbots, one of whom was the abbot of la Trappe. After nearly six years of weary negotiations, a papal bull to end the conflict was issued in 1666. *In suprema* was a detailed commentary on the Rule of Saint Benedict. It imposed upon both observances the common life, penitential discipline, and fulfilment of the *Opus Dei*. The only difference between the two was that houses of the Strict Observance were bound to perpetual abstinence, while those of the Common Observance were allowed meat three times a week, except during Advent and Lent. Two provinces of abstinent houses, each under a visitor appointed by the Chapter General, gave the Strict Observance a certain autonomy. The Abstinents lost their right to hold a chapter of their own, but they could appoint half the members of the Chapter General's *Diffinitorium*. *In suprema* was a compromise, but the Abstinents always regarded it as a defeat.

The negotiations at Rome from 1662–1666 brought to the fore the most famous monk of seventeenth-century France. Armand-Jean le Bouthillier, the abbé de Rancé, was born in 1626 into a wealthy family of lawyers in Paris.[66] Destined from an early age for the Church, his career as a worldly prelate was cut short at the age of thirty-one by a conversion experience. He retired into the country and devoted himself to reading and prayer. Gradually he rid himself of his many benefices. By 1663 only the decayed cistercian abbey of La Trappe in Normandy was left. Here he decided to become the regular abbot.

The buildings at la Trappe were in ruins and the few remaining monks irreformable. De Rancé began by replacing them with some monks from the abstinent abbey of Perseigne. Then he went to Perseigne himself for a year's novitiate. It

---

[65] On the negotiations in Rome, see Thomas Nguyen-Dinh-Tuyen, 'Histoire des controverses à Rome entre la commune et l'étroite observance de 1662 à 1666, *Analecta Cisterciensia* 26 (1970) 3–247.
[66] The standard biography is A. J. Krailsheimer (as n. 57).

was twice interrupted; on one occasion for three months after his health had broken down. In the summer of 1664 he was professed and became the regular abbot of la Trappe. Only a few weeks later the Strict Observance chose him as one of its two representatives in the negotiations which led to *In suprema*.

The point has often been made that de Rancé had little experience of the cistercian life at the time.[67] It is certain that he loathed Rome and returned to France in 1666, determined never to be distracted from the monastic life again. The Chapter General of 1667 was the last he ever attended. After that he concentrated his attention on la Trappe. His *Règlemens* give an exact picture of the life he instituted there.[68] He eliminated everything that was not sanctioned in the primitive cistercian documents. The monks were to live in daily expectation of the second coming of Jesus Christ.[69] Their diet was strictly vegetarian.[70] Manual labour returned to its place of honour.[71] Silence was rigorously maintained throughout the day and night.[72]

In this and much else de Rancé went a great deal further than the abbots of the Strict Observance. That was enough in itself to cause controversy. The fact that monks from other Orders left their houses to join la Trappe also caused bad blood. All this made la Trappe known. Numerous visitors came and published their impressions of it. The publicity encouraged more recruits. Eventually La Trappe became one of the largest abbeys in France.

The extent to which de Rancé was influenced by Jansenism is hard to estimate. He was always orthodox doctrinally and had

---

[67] Lekai (as n. 56), 21.

[68] *Règlemens de l'abbaye de la Trappe en forme de constitutions avec réflexions. . . .* (Paris 1718).

[69] Ibid. 33–34.

[70] Ibid. 19–23.

[71] Ibid. 64–67.

[72] Ibid. 30, 49, 67–8, 91. On silence at La Trappe, see A. J. Krailsheimer, *Rancé and the Trappist Legacy* (Kalamazoo 1985) 79–80. See also Krailsheimer's discussion of life at La Trappe ibid. 71–86.

no difficulty about signing the formula condemning the alleged errors of Jansen. 'Instead of arguing about the grace of Christ', he wrote in one famous declaration of his views, 'I should think rather of attracting it to myself and those whom it had pleased him to entrust to my charge and direction'.[73] He took stringent precautions to keep la Trappe out of any controversy, and thus avoided the fate which eventually overcame Port Royal.

On the other hand he had numerous jansenist friends. Nicholas Pavillon, the jansenist bishop of Alet, was a strong influence on him.[74] At one time he thought highly of the jansenist leader Antoine Arnauld,[75] although he later changed his mind.[76] For many years he maintained a friendship with Pasquier Quesnel, who succeeded Arnauld as the party's spokesman.[77] Robert Arnauld d'Andilly, a solitary of Port Royal, sent de Rancé his edition of the letters of Saint Cyran, which the abbot thought full of piety, grace, and light.[78] From Saint Cyran, without a doubt, came de Rancé's view that a monk might, in a spirit of penitence and with the permission of the superior, occasionally abstain from Communion.[79]

There were other influences as well. De Rancé was deeply impressed by the writings of Saint John Climacus, a seventh-century abbot of the monastery of Mount Sinai. His treatise the *Ladder of Divine Ascent* was a classic of eastern monasticism. For de Rancé John was the saint 'whom all monks should regard as their master'.[80] As far as cistercian writers were concerned, de Rancé was most influenced by *Du premier esprit de l'ordre de Cisteaux* ('On the Original Spirit of the Cistercian Order'), published in 1653 by Julien Paris, the abstinent abbot

---

[73] *Abbé de Rancé, correspondance*, ed. A. J. Krailsheimer, 2 (Paris 1993) 246–247 (#781130). The letters are quoted from this edition by volume and page number. The date/number of the letter is in brackets. Translation from *The Letters of Armand-Jean de Rancé* presented by A. J. Krailsheimer 1: 189.

[74] Krailsheimer (as n. 57), 13–15, 219.

[75] *Correspondance* (as n. 73), 1:442 (#720419).

[76] Ibid. 4:317–318 (#940902).

[77] On the friendship with Quesnel, see Krailsheimer (as n. 57), 252–255.

[78] *Correspondance* (as n. 73), 1: 433–434 (#720125a).

[79] *Règlemens* (as n. 68), 38–9.

[80] *De la Sainteté* (as n. 83), 201.

of Foucarmont (1645–1672). The book was an early attempt to write the history of the Order from the sources and explain its subsequent decadence.[81] The *Nomasticon Cisterciense*, edited by Julien Paris and published in 1664, was the first scholarly edition of the early statutes of the Order.[82]

In 1683 de Rancé published a book about monasticism. In spite of the efforts of friendly bishops to modify certain passages, *De la sainteté et des devoirs de la vie monastique* ('About the Holiness and Duties of the Monastic Life', or perhaps, 'About Holiness, and the Duties of the Monastic Life')[83] was, above all, a combative answer to la Trappe's many critics. In a famous passage de Rancé, basing himself on a chapter of Climacus, maintained that monks, even if they had led innocent lives, must consider themselves repentant criminals obliged to undertake the severest penances for their former sins.[84] He freely admitted that the austerities practised at la Trappe would shorten the monks' lives. In fact it is known that few lasted there for more than ten years.[85] To condemn this, wrote de Rancé, one would have to condemn the desert fathers. 'They preferred the sanctity of their souls to the length of their lives'.[86] It was clear to him that God approved, since he gave the saints the power to work miracles.[87]

Humiliations, wrote de Rancé, were a necessary part of the monastic *ascesis*. Every religious had need of a vigilant and charitable superior who would not hesitate even to shame him in public, if this would train him in the virtue of humility.[88]

---

[81] Chrysogonus Waddell, 'The Cistercian Dimension of the Reform of La Trappe', *Cistercians in the Late Middle Ages* (as n. 59), 111–113.

[82] *Nomasticon cisterciense seu antiquioris ordinis Cisterciensis constitutiones* (Paris 1664).

[83] Armand-Jean le Bouthillier de Rancé, *De la sainteté et des devoirs de la vie monastique* (Paris 1683).

[84] Ibid. 1:392.

[85] Cocheril, 'Les cisterciens', *Les ordres religieux* (as n. 42), 419. For a sophisticated analysis of the figures see Krailsheimer, *Trappist Legacy* (as n. 72), 85–86.

[86] *De la Sainteté* (as n. 83), 2:471–472.

[87] Ibid. 2:472–496.

[88] Ibid. 1:314.

Nothing was more controversial than de Rancé's claim that study was not a proper occupation for monks.[89] A monk, he wrote, quoting Saint Jerome, should weep not instruct. Monks should be not teachers but penitents. This part of the book brought Mabillon into the field.[90] The controversy between the two monks, conducted with courtesy on both sides, lasted nearly ten years and inspired one of Mabillon's masterpieces. The *Treatise on Monastic Study,* published in 1691, became the classic treatment of the subject.[91] Learning was necessary for religious superiors, according to Mabillon, so that they could govern properly, and for solitaries to keep them from error. Saint Bernard was in favour of it. Where learning was neglected monasticism fell into decadence. Reformers had always recommended study.

A quarrel between the two most respected monks of France shocked many. In 1693 the duchess of Guise, a friend of them both, arranged for Mabillon to visit la Trappe. He was deeply impressed by what he saw, and de Rancé was touched by his visitor's holiness and humility. The two men became friends and the controversy came to an edifying end.

Unlike Mabillon, de Rancé easily lost his head in controversy. We must never forget that *De la sainteté* was a polemical work. The actuality at la Trappe was more subtle than the book. Many of the monks were educated men. There was no need for any systematic course of advanced study.[92] Even so, reading was encouraged. Recommended books and authors were the Bible, Saint John Climacus, Cassian, the Lives of the desert fathers, the ascetic treatises of Saint Basil, the writings of Saint Ephrem, the works of Saint Bernard and other fathers.[93] At least one monk at la Trappe was engaged in research. Dom Pierre Le Nain, the subprior, published a

[89] Ibid. 2:257–308.
[90] On the controversy with Mabillon, see Leclercq, *Mabillon,* (as n. 45), 2:503–574; Krailsheimer, *De Rancé* (as n. 57), 52–53. The quotation from Saint Jerome is from *Contra Vigilantium,* chapter 15.
[91] *Traité des études monastiques* (Paris 1691).
[92] Krailsheimer (as n. 72), 77–79.
[93] *Règlemens* (as n. 68), 57.

history of the Cistercian Order in nine volumes and wrote much religious poetry. De Rancé did not stop him, though he thought little of the results. 'The hymns of Father Subprior,' he wrote to a correspondent, 'are hardly worth study by eyes as discerning as yours. They are tolerable in our rustic desert, but not elsewhere'.[94]

Visitors to La Trappe testified to the deep affection in which the abbot was held by his monks, to his concern for their spiritual and physical welfare, and to the atmosphere of peace and joy which prevailed.[95] De Rancé did not wish the infirmary to become, as it did in many monasteries, a place where monks indulged themselves on the grounds of ill health. Arrangements for the sick, nevertheless, were sensible and humane. With due safeguards, a surgeon was brought in when required.[96] Many of the austerities at la Trappe were suggested by the monks, with the abbot counselling prudence.[97] While refusing to become a fashionable director of souls, de Rancé had an enormous correspondence. Recently published in full,[98] it reveals a complex personality. His warm and sensitive letters of condolence are particularly touching.

De Rancé has never lacked critics, not least among monks of his own branch of the Cistercian Order. It may be argued that his emphasis on the penitential aspect of monasticism was excessively negative. It is certain that his criticisms of other monks were profoundly uncharitable. At different times he had the Carthusians, the Feuillants, and the Maurists— none of them laggards at asceticism—up in arms. He had little respect even for Cistercians of the Strict Observance. 'Prières is a grand monastery,' he wrote of the abbey where Jean Jouaud had been abbot. 'One lives there in abundance because of the nearness of the sea. The meals of the religious are banquets. It is a numerous community which lives according

---

[94] *Correspondance* (as n. 73), 4:44 (#900702).
[95] See Waddell (as n. 83), 122–133.
[96] *Règlemens* (as n. 70), 75–86.
[97] Waddell (as n. 81), 122–133.
[98] 4 volumes; see n. 73.

to its own rules.'[99] As for the Cistercian Order as a whole, 'the old observance has nothing but the name and the religious habit; the other, which has picked up the pieces, is becoming feebler by the day, and its downfall is at hand'.[100]

There were certainly numerous houses of the Cistercian Common Observance in France which were monasteries only in name. At a visitation of Bois-Groland in Vendée in 1683, the abbey was found to be in ruins. There were only two monks.[101] In 1687 the Order's visitor found that the community of Le Breuil-Benoît, in Eure, Normandy, consisted of a prior and four monks. They actually came from other communities and had been 'lent' to the abbey, while the two professed monks of the house lived elsewhere. The buildings were in ruins and the visitor could not be accommodated.[102]

The Cistercians were far less successful than the Maurists in negotiating with commendators. They had less influence at court and among the great. The abbots of Cîteaux themselves, though admirable men, were not outstanding personalities. The Chapter General, moreover, which met only thirteen times in the seventeenth century,[103] was bitterly divided. Nevertheless, individual houses of the Common Observance maintained a high standard. Cîteaux itself always impressed foreigners. In 1699 a visitor from Bohemia reported that the house had eighty-six professed monks. They performed manual labour twice a week, led by the abbot himself. The liturgy and the chant were noted for their beauty and dignity.[104] At the beginning of the century Clairvaux had, for a time, belonged to the Strict Observance. This changed in 1624, but the standard of observance remained exceptional. The number of professed monks seems to have remained at a steady eighty throughout the second half of the century. The

---

[99] *Correspondance* (as n. 73), 2:333 (80/3).
[100] Ibid. 1:382 (#710826a).
[101] L. J. Lekai, 'Moral and Material Status of French Cistercian Abbeys in the Seventeenth Century', *Analecta Sacri Ordinis Cisterciensis* 19 (1963) 240–241.
[102] Ibid. 244.
[103] Ibid. 215.
[104] Ibid. 229–231.

divine office was meticulously performed, the psalmody was stately and slow. It was also reported that in all houses directly subject to Clairvaux, the same high standard of discipline was maintained.[105]

Outside France the Order was divided into congregations.[106] Like those of the Benedictines, these congregations were largely organised on national lines. Chapters General assembled abbots within a particular area. Abbots or priors held office for a limited time—usually three or four years. Monks were trained in common novitiates and made a vow of stability to the congregation. Most congregations enjoyed a fairly close relationship with the secular authorities. There were not usually formal arrangements with the Chapter General at Cîteaux, though representatives from particular congregations occasionally appeared there. In Spain, Martin Vargas's Cistercian Congregation of Castile flourished, and produced in Angel Manrique (1577–1649) a notable scholar and historian. Eight other cistercian congregations came into being during the sixteenth and seventeenth centuries: Saint Bernard, for Lombardy and Tuscany (1511); Alcobaça for Portugal (1567); Poland (1580); Calabria and Lucania, for southern Italy (1605); Rome, for the papal state (1613); Aragon (1613); Bohemia (1613). The cistercian congregation of Upper Germany (1618), which included the abbeys of Switzerland, was slightly different from the others. Its abbots were elected for life, and monks vowed stability to their own house. The congregation had a formal obligation to send a delegation to every Chapter General at Cîteaux.

Far away in Poland, the abbey of Oliwa went through a period of renewal, the nature of which de Rancé would never have understood.[107] Founded in 1178, Oliwa was in the filiation of Clairvaux. It had been richly endowed with estates, privileges, and exemptions by the local polish rulers.

---

[105] Ibid. 232–233.
[106] Lekai, *The Cistercians* (as n. 56), 126–137.
[107] On Oliwa, see *Festschrift zum 750 jährigen Jubiläum des Klosters Oliwa*, ed. C. Lange (Danzig 1926); R. Stachnik, *Die katholische Kirche in Danzig* (Münster 1959); G. Nitschke, *Die Kathedrale zu Oliva* (Hildesheim 1963).

In 1308 the Teutonic Order had taken over the territory, and in 1466 the abbey had come under the rule of the kings of Poland. Oliwa became a commendatory abbey with an absentee abbot who was usually a member of the king's court. The key political and social factor, however, was its proximity to the city of Gdansk.

Gdansk (or Danzig) was largely inhabited by Germans and dominated by its wealthy german merchant families. It had accepted the Reformation and this increased the tension between the city and the very Catholic king, Stephen Bathory (1575–1586), with whom the Oliwa monks were, naturally, on terms of friendship. In February 1577, a mob from Danzig poured into the countryside and attacked the abbey, plundering and destroying its treasures and setting it on fire. A monk and a servant were shot, and two other monks dragged as prisoners into the city. After three days of mayhem, the royal army arrived and put the rioters to flight.

Danzig was put under siege, but after ten months a compromise was agreed. The city's privileges and Protestantism were confirmed, but Catholic worship was allowed within its walls. Oliwa was awarded a hefty indemnity and the work of repair was taken in hand immediately. In 1580 the abbey joined the Polish Cistercian Congregation. For the embattled Danzig Catholics the existence, a few miles from the city walls, of a great monastic community, where the liturgy was celebrated in all its splendour, and where spiritual counsel and solace were available, was of crucial importance.

The challenge was met by Oliwa's remarkable prior Philip Adler (1590–1630). Like all the Oliwa monks he came from a local german family. He had fully absorbed the spirit of the Counter Reformation. Strict cistercian discipline was reintroduced in the abbey. In addition, Prior Adler encouraged scholarship and research. A large library was collected and printing works installed, which produced devotional and theological literature in German.

Prior Adler was able to ensure the freedom of his community by negotiating an agreement which separated the estates of the abbey from those of the commendator. In 1617, he was even able to persuade the king to appoint a resident abbot. Adam Trebnitz was a man of strict life who supported the prior in every way and died in the aura of holiness in 1630. After his death Oliwa at least had residential, though not regular abbots. Appointed by the king, they were always great prelates with their own establishment. Eventually a palace was built for them next to the monastery. It still stands in its little park. The abbots had some authority over external affairs, but monastic discipline remained the sole responsibility of the prior.

The last years of Prior Adler were overshadowed by the swedish wars. In 1626 the army of Gustavus Adolphus set the abbey on fire, destroyed its treasures, and dragged seven of its monks into captivity. The rest fled and the abbey was abandoned for two years. When the monks returned the work of reconstruction had to begin again. Recovery was slow, but by the end of the seventeenth century the abbey's vigour had returned. Abbot Michael Anthony Hacki (1683–1703) was a noted theologian. He worked hard to redecorate the church after the destruction of the swedish wars. The present facade is his, as is the high altar which hides the medieval apse behind an aureole of plaster clouds, angels, and allegorical figures. Abbot Joseph Hyacinth Rybicki (1740–1782) was noted for his love of church music. He was responsible for building the abbey's two magnificent organs. In his time the monastic choir, which was capable of polyphonic and baroque music, was famed throughout the land.

Baroque monasticism, of which Oliwa is an outstanding example, was a feature of Catholic Europe from the Rhine to the borders of Russia. It was a response to the situation created by the Reformation and existed in many places where the Protestants were not far away. The abbey of Einsiedeln, for instance, seems to be set in a solidly Catholic countryside, but Protestant Zürich is a mere forty kilometres to the north. Religious wars were frequent. The Thirty Years' War (1618–1648) was the most destructive but by no means the last.

Indeed, in Switzerland the last war between Catholics and Protestants took place in 1847.

All the religious Orders learned from the Jesuits, whose sense of drama and colour pervaded Catholicism throughout this period. The Benedictines and Cistercians, however, with their great abbeys and their devotion to liturgical prayer, had something special to offer. Their houses were set in the countryside. Anyone who climbs the little hill to visit the former benedictine abbey of Saint Peter in the Black Forest sees pastures and woods in every direction. In these surroundings the baroque abbeys were citadels of the faith. Those who lived in their neighbourhood, as well as visitors, had access to experienced and learned confessors, spiritual guides, and preachers. The monks served the parish churches in the neighbourhood. Through pilgrimages, processions, and eucharistic devotions, the country people took part in the monastic life of adoration and praise. The abbeys had printing presses to produce religious literature. In spite of their music and architecture, both in the latest style, they laid great emphasis on tradition. Most of the abbeys were ancient, and the story of their foundation, their patrons, and their saints, figured prominently in the paintings which decorated the interiors of their astonishing churches.

Pilgrimages had been much ridiculed in the sixteenth century. The monks of the Counter Reformation revived them. Old cults were rejuvenated and new ones came into being. The marian pilgrimage shrine of Birnau in Swabia, Germany, had been a popular place of pilgrimage since the fourteenth century. The church was appropriated by the cistercian abbey of Salem, but stood on land belonging to the city of Überlingen, with which the abbey was often in conflict. In 1750 the abbot of Salem decided to move the miraculous image to Neu-Birnau on the shores of Lake Constance. The still-present exquisite church provided a new focus for an ancient devotion.[108]

---

[108] *Salem, 850 Jahre Reichsabtei und Schloss,* ed. R. Schneider (Constance 1984) 136.

7 Choirstalls dating to 1720 in the Benedictine Abbey of Weingarden.

In the hills above Salzburg the cult of Maria Plain began in the seventeenth century.[109] Amid the blackened ruins of a bavarian village laid waste by the Swedes during the Thirty Years' War a picture of the Virgin Mary and the divine Child was said to have been found undamaged. The picture, which passed through various hands, was for some weeks kept in Plain. Because it was much venerated, the owner had a copy made before he moved away. This copy continued to attract worshippers. The first church to house it was built in 1655; the present building was begun in 1671. Four years later the archbishop of Salzburg formally entrusted the pilgrimage to the Benedictines of Salzburg University. Under their care it became enormously popular. In 1676 the original picture, which had found its way to Augsburg, was brought to Plain amid great enthusiasm. It was at first housed in a separate chapel but in 1732 it was moved to its present position above the high altar. In 1751 it was crowned. It remained a focus of piety for the inhabitants of the land of Salzburg. From time to time the prince archbishop, accompanied by his clergy and a regiment of soldiers, made his way up the hill for magnificent ceremonies. The marian feasts were kept with special pomp. During the octave of the feast of the Assumption in 1774, the music was performed by Mozart and his father. It is likely that Mozart's *Missa Brevis* was written for the occasion.[110]

No monastery was more closely associated with a pilgrimage than Maria Einsiedeln in Switzerland.[111] The history of the benedictine abbey went back to the ninth century. In the sixteenth century it almost disappeared. The abbot resigned in 1526, and the single remaining monk left to join Zwingli's

---

[109] The entire issue of SMBO 85 (1974) is devoted to Maria Plain.

[110] It is sometimes stated that Mozart's *Coronation Mass* was written for an anniversary of the coronation of Our Lady of Plain. In fact, it has been shown that the Mass was never called the 'Coronation' Mass in Mozart's lifetime, and that it probably received its first performance in Salzburg cathedral on Easter Sunday 1779. SMBO 85 (1974) 238–239.

[111] L. Raber osb in W. Läubli, *Maria Einsiedeln* (Meiringen n.d. [c. 1945]); J. Salzgeber osb, *Die Klöster Einsiedeln und St. Gallen im Barockzeitalter* (Münster 1966); *Helvetia Sacra*, 3/1 (Bern 1986) 1:532–3:539.

protestant army. The house was saved by the cantonal authorities of Schwyz, who took possession and invited a monk of Saint Gall to become abbot. Einsiedeln thus began again with a new superior and, eventually, a new community committed to all the latest ideas about monastic reform. In 1562 Abbot Joachim Eichorn was sent, rather late in the day, to the Council of Trent as sole representative of the swiss clergy. In 1602 Einsiedeln played a leading role in the foundation of the Swiss Benedictine Congregation.

Einsiedeln can be regarded as the ideal baroque monastery. For over a century it had an unbroken line of able superiors. The best known, in his own time, was abbot Augustine Reding (1670–1692). Known, with some exaggeration, as 'a second Augustine', he was the author of forty-three books, including a commentary on the Rule of Saint Benedict. The abbey's liturgical books, which were printed in his time and remained in use until the Second Vatican Council, are witness to his zeal for the divine office. Like many of his fellow monks, he had been a professor at the benedictine university of Salzburg. Einsiedeln eagerly cultivated the tradition of monastic learning. The large library contains folio books which were purchased for the abbey from as far away as London. The abbey press, which was set up in 1664, produced 1104 books from its foundation until 1798.[112] The college run by the abbey at Bellinzona was one of the foremost educational institutions of Catholic Switzerland.

It is known that Einsiedeln was a marian pilgrimage centre in the fourteenth century, but the cult is probably much older. The monks of the baroque abbey spared no pains or expense to enhance its glory. On the patronal feasts the celebrations lasted for fourteen days, each with High Mass, sermon, and procession. Trumpeters—some hired from distant Lucerne— were stationed in the towers to blow fanfares as the clergy entered the church. Sacred dramas were staged in the open-air theatre, and for sophisticated pilgrims there were learned

---

[112] Salzgeber (as above n. 159).

disputations. The modern visitor experiences the penitential aspect of the pilgrimage most strongly in the little chapel for confession (*Beichtskirche*) which abuts the great abbey church. From a sombre crypt-like nave, dominated by the confessionals in their dark wood, the penitent takes heart as he looks into the sanctuary, twice as high as the nave and flooded with light.

The glorious baroque abbeys in the German-speaking catholic lands still hold visitors spellbound. In Switzerland and south-west Germany they were built by the *Vorarlberger*— a closely knit guild of architects from the extreme western parts of modern Austria. Their audacious structures have given international renown to such humble local names as Moosbrugger, Beer, and Thumb. In many large establishments, work was continuous from the end of the seventeenth century to the 1770s. It is a paradox that by the time these buildings stood ready, baroque monasticism and the religion it expressed were already under serious threat.

Chapter 11
THE WHIRLWIND

THE DIVISIONS WHICH WEAKENED monasticism during the eighteenth century reflected those of the whole Church. In 1713 Pope Clement XI's bull *Unigenitus* condemned the writings of Pasquier Quesnel, the jansenist leader. Some Jansenists eventually went into schism. Those who remained flooded the Church with petitions and anonymous pamphlets. The maurist congregation was so divided that for much of the eighteenth century it was practically ungovernable.[1] The Cistercians continued their own civil war with a sterile conflict between the abbot of Cîteaux and the four senior abbots.[2]

Even more serious was the challenge of the Enlightenment. In catholic countries it took a form largely hostile to the Church, and often to Christianity in general. Monasticism was severely criticised. There was no understanding for spirituality or the contemplative life. Religious who devoted themselves to prayer were considered 'lazy', 'superstitious', or 'fanatical'.

Monks often tried to head off criticism by showing how useful they really were. The eighteenth-century Maurists concentrated on editing texts relevant to the Church as a whole or to general history. After the suppression of the Jesuits in 1773, some monasteries were quick to step in and take over the socially useful task of running colleges formerly operated by the Society.[3] Teaching in monastic educational establishments was modernised. At the benedictine university of Salzburg a chair of Experimental Science was established and less emphasis

---

[1] Y. Chaussy, *Les bénédictins de Saint Maur* 1:107–234.
[2] L. J. Lekai, *The Cistercians. Ideals and Reality* (Kent, Ohio 1977) 161–165.
[3] For examples see ibid. 168–169.

than formerly was put on the thomistic method.[4] None of this deflected the general hostility. 'For the last forty years,' wrote a french observer in 1768, 'monks have been the objects of endless sarcasms and scurrilities.'[5] When the abbey of Saint Blasien in the Black Forest had to be rebuilt after a fire, the abbot suggested that in the new church the choir should be placed behind the high altar. Here the monks would be invisible, which was desirable because 'the sight of religious is intolerable to the laity'.[6] In these circumstances it is not surprising that there was a vocations crisis. There were twenty-six thousand religious in France in 1770. Nineteen years later there were sixteen thousand two hundred.[7]

The ablest attack on monasticism was the novel *La Religieuse* by the *philosophe* Denis Diderot. Although it was first conceived around 1760, Diderot never dared to publish it in his lifetime and it did not appear in print until 1796. The author showed it to his friends, however, who admired it and thought it 'a work of genius . . . of great public utility'.[8]

The novel tells the story of an illegitimate girl whose mother, not knowing what to do with her, forces her to become a nun. Her first mother superior is a sympathetic woman, but the next one takes a dislike to her and subjects her to cruel persecutions in which the rest of the community join. After an unsuccessful attempt to free herself by legal means, the hapless nun is transferred to another house. Here the lesbian mother superior is only too affectionate. In the end she escapes with the help of a dissipated monk who later rapes her. She is forced to live under an assumed name, in daily fear that she will be caught by the police.

---

[4] G. Heilingsetzer, 'Die Benediktiner im 18 Jahrhundert. Wissenschaft und Gelehrsamkeit im süddeutsch-österreichischem Raum', *Katholische Aufklärung–Aufklärung im katholischem Raum*, ed. H. Klueting (Hamburg 1993) 213–214.

[5] Quoted Chaussy (as n. 1), 238.

[6] E. Franz, *Pierre Michel d'Ixnard* (Weissenhorn 1985) 48.

[7] P. Loupès, *La vie religieuse en France au XVIIIe siècle* (Paris 1993) 160.

[8] Diderot, *Oeuvres romanesques* (Paris: Garnier 1962) 850.

It is a lurid, but credible, tale because the central character is imaginatively portrayed. Diderot was on firm moral ground when he exposed the way in which girls who, for one reason or another, were an encumbrance to their parents, were forced into convents. The novel, however, not only condemned an abuse, but went on to attack monasticism itself.

Are convents so essential for the health of the state? Did Jesus Christ institute monks and nuns? Is it impossible for the Church to do without them? What need has the spouse of all these foolish virgins? . . . The vow of poverty binds one by oath to laziness and thievery, by the vow of chastity one promises God to break the wisest and most important of his laws, by the vow of obedience one renounces liberty, the inalienable prerogative of man. To keep these vows is a crime, to break them is perjury. The life of the cloister is for fanatics and hypocrites.[9]

Inevitably governments and their servants came to be influenced by such opinions. In 1781 the emperor Joseph II (1765–1790) issued a decree closing throughout the Holy Roman Empire and its attached territories all houses of contemplative Orders which did not fulfil charitable or educational purposes.[10] Later on, active Orders were included in the suppressions. The confiscated property was to go to a 'religious fund' for the endowment of new parishes and the improvement of existing ones. Joseph's policy was particularly resented in the Austrian Netherlands. The area was in revolt at the time of the emperor's death in 1790, and his successor rescinded the more drastic enactments. Some of the condemned monasteries were thus reprieved at the last moment.

In 1766 the french government set up the *Commission des Réguliers* to report on the regular clergy.[11] Its work has

---

[9] Ibid. 310–311.
[10] *The Church in the Age of Absolutism and Enlightenment,* History of the Church, 5, edd. H. Jedin and J. Dolan (London 1981) 476–481.
[11] Philibert Schmitz, *Histoire de l'ordre de saint Benoît,* 4 (Maredsous 1948) 68–75; Chaussy (as n. 1), 208–216. On the Cistercians, see Lekai (as n. 2), 162–167.

sometimes been viewed, with hindsight, as foreshadowing the destruction of religious houses at the Revolution.[12] The commission was made up of five archbishops and five counsellors of state, with a small secretarial staff. The president, Loménie de Brienne, archbishop of Toulouse, was a career cleric whose private life was far from exemplary. 'Let us note,' writes Dom Philibert Schmitz, 'that not a single religious was a member of the commission'.[13] This was certainly a weakness, but the assumption, rightly or wrongly, was that outside help was needed to sort out the constitutional and other problems of the monasteries. There is no evidence of bias in the commission. As for Loménie de Brienne, whatever his morals or religious opinions, he carried out his duties conscientiously, and reflected, in all he did, the policies of the government.

The commission issued its decrees in 1768. The minimum age for religious profession was to be twenty-one for men and eighteen for women. No foreigners were to be professed in french religious houses. With a few exceptions, all monasteries with fewer than nine professed monks were to be closed. No Order or congregation was to have more than one house in any town or village, except for Paris, where two for each Order were allowed. The constitutions of all the Orders and congregations were to be revised at special chapters general presided over by members of the commission. Small religious Orders were to be suppressed.

It is a measure of the commission's moderation that it allowed the religious themselves to revise their constitutions, with only guidance from members of the commission. In fact, this part of the policy was the least successful. The Maurists never managed to achieve a consensus. The Cistercians, after endless delays, came up with a new constitution in 1786.

---

[12] Thus Chaussy (as n. 1), discusses it in a chapter headed 'Prodromes révolutionnaires', 201 seq.

[13] Schmitz (as n. 10), 69. On Loménie de Brienne, see P. Chevallier, *Loménie de Brienne et l'ordre monastique 1766–89*, 2 volumes (Paris 1959) especially 1: 271–281 and 2: 282–285.

Because of the French Revolution it never became operative. The closure of religious houses was inconsistent. No charterhouses or cistercian abbeys were closed at all. The Benedictines, on the other hand, lost one hundred twenty-two houses, and three small congregations, including the Exempts, were suppressed altogether.[14] In the end, the measures taken turned out to be mild. Because of special pleading and local pressures, the criteria for closures could not be rigidly enforced.

The French Revolution moved, in the course of a few years, from anti-clericalism to the persecution of Christianity. Monasticism was a prime target. In 1790 the Constituent Assembly declared religious vows null and void and abolished all religious Orders. Religious who wished to leave their houses would receive a pension; those who did not were to be assembled in *maisons de reunion*, buildings where all those who wished to observe their vows were obliged to live together, regardless of the Order to which they belonged. Nuns and congregations engaged in teaching or charitable work were, for the time being, exempt from the law. Commissioners immediately entered all religious houses of both men and women to interview each inmate about his or her intentions.[15]

The overwhelming majority of women religious declared their wish to be faithful to their vows. Among the men the answer was quite different, although there were great regional variations. There is no doubt that many chose to marry and abandon the clerical state altogether. Not all, however, went so far. Different alternatives were offered to the men and the women. Nuns who wished to remain were to be left in place. Men were given the choice of leaving their monastery or living uneasily in an artificial community with members of different Orders. Rome showed full understanding for those

[14] Schmitz (as n. 11), 72.
[15] J. Leflon, *La crise révolutionnaire, Histoire de l'Église*, 20, edd. Fliche et Martin, (Paris 1949) 54–56.

who were not attracted by the latter alternative. Dispensations from religious vows were readily granted, provided that the former religious obeyed the canonical rules applying to priests or clerks.[16]

Two years later all this was irrelevant. In 1792 all religious congregations were abolished and all religious houses closed. Former religious who did not take the oath accepting the schismatic 'Civil Constitution of the Clergy' lost their pensions and were treated as enemies of the Revolution. Many perished on the guillotine or were victims of mass drownings in the Loire or died of disease in prison hulks. Dom Chevreux, the last superior general of the Maurists, was killed during the September Massacres of 1792.[17]

The Concordat of 1801 allowed only a few congregations devoted to teaching or charity. In the meantime monasteries were closed in all territories which came under french influence. In Italy they were progressively dissolved as the french army extended its power southwards. The same happened in Germany as it came under french aegis. The left bank of the Rhine was ceded to France in 1801. Here the Concordat of 1801, which left no room for contemplative communities, was applied. Across the Rhine the Holy Roman Empire was abolished and Germany reorganised. Princes now ruled over solid blocks of territory. This replacement of the old patchwork of jurisdictions was achieved at the expense of the former ecclesiastical principalities and particularly the ancient imperial abbeys.

Only a few religious communities survived the revolutionary onslaught—some through heroism and others by sheer luck. The community of Port Royal in Paris is an example of heroic survival. The minority of nuns who had been allowed to remain there after the expulsions of 1664 lived quietly,

---

[16] Ibid. 56 n. 6.
[17] Leflon (as n. 15), 51–56; R. Aubert et al., *The Church between Revolution and Restoration,* History of the Church 7, edd. Jedin and Dolan (London 1981) 20–21; Schmitz (as n. 10), 75–83.

still observing the constitutions of Mother Agnès.[18] In the eighteenth century the house was obscure but observant. Situated in a part of Paris noted for its turbulence, it became a target for mob vandalism during the Revolution.[19] In 1790 commissioners entered to ask each nun in turn whether she wished to continue in the religious life. In spite of some bullying, especially of the youngest, each declared her intention of remaining true to her vows. Under increasing difficulties the sisters continued the regular life until September 1792. Commissioners to dissolve the community had just begun their work when one of the servants, terrified by the scenes in the streets, ran into the house. 'They're murdering everyone,' she gasped.[20] The September Massacres were under way. The confessor of Port Royal was among the victims, but at the abbey itself the commissioners had sufficient authority to protect the monastery and its inhabitants.

In order not to attract attention the nuns left the house under the cover of darkness in twos and threes. Some went to live with their families; others took up lodgings in various parts of Paris. Scattered around the city, they still considered themselves bound by their religious vows. In small groups or alone they would visit Madame de Cambise, their abbess, in her hideout to receive her orders and advice.

The fall of Robespierre in 1794 gave Catholics a momentary respite from persecution. On 20 August of that year the surviving community gathered in a church to celebrate the feast of Saint Bernard together. Under the Directory, established in 1795, persecution began again. The pensions of ex-religious were cut and the sisters were obliged to earn their living by teaching or manual work. Mother Abbess knitted baby clothes to raise money. She died in 1801. On the day after her funeral the sisters assembled to elect a successor. At last, in 1807, it proved possible to obtain premises and reunite

---

[18] See above p. 299.
[19] M. D. Séguin, 'Port Royal après Port Royal', *Cîteaux* 37 (1986) 106–123.
[20] 'On les massacre tous', *ibid.* 113.

what remained of the community and take up the regular life once more.

There was even a new community founded during the time of persecution. In 1797/1798 a number of former religious men and women formed a society to live the monastic life together secretly in Paris itself.[21] They used the constitutions of La Val Sainte, the famous community of french cistercian refugees in Switzerland. When the persecution had ceased they moved out of Paris and in 1804 finally settled at Grosbois in the forest of Senart, not far from Versailles. Here they occupied the remains of a former Camaldolese abbey—the men in one building and the women in another.

Some individuals, faithful to their religious vows during the revolutionary period, became leading figures of the monastic revival afterwards. Thérèse de Bavoz was a benedictine nun of the abbey of Saint Peter in Lyons when the Revolution broke out.[22] She was imprisoned after the house was closed and marked for execution. The fall of Robespierre in 1794 saved her life. After the Concordat she joined a group of teaching nuns at Pradines near Lyons. It was one of the 'permitted' communities, and its members had belonged to different Orders before the Revolution. In time Thérèse rose to be superior, but differences soon arose among her followers who hankered after a more contemplative life and the rest. In 1814 the archbishop of Lyons gave permission for Pradines to be transformed into a monastic house in which the Rule of Saint Benedict was observed. It was the first benedictine house founded in France since the Revolution.In 1824 it took over the monastery of La Rochette, where a number of former benedictine nuns had gathered to revive the religious life. Other foundations followed. They were formed into the Benedictine Congregation of the Sacred Heart of Mary, for which Thérèse elaborated constitutions in 1830.

---

[21] J. du Halgouët, 'Pierres d'attente' (as n. 23 below), *Cîteaux* 17 (1966) 106–107, and n. 50; C. Gaillardin (as n. 22), 258.
[22] On Thérèse de Bavoz, see Schmitz (as n. 4), vol.7 (Maredsous 1956) 195, 344.

The most famous example of monastic survival is associated with la Trappe.[23] After the death of de Rancé the community had continued much as he had intended. It cherished the memory of its founder. Four hagiographical accounts of his life were published in the eighteenth century. At the time of the Revolution la Trappe was the largest monastery in France.[24]

The community was divided in its response to the Revolution, but the novice master, Dom Augustin Lestrange, was certain that the vocations of his young charges could only be safeguarded outside France. In 1791, through the mediation of the bishop of Lausanne, himself a Cistercian, Lestrange contacted the authorities of the swiss canton of Fribourg. They granted him the buildings of La Val Sainte, a suppressed Charterhouse not far from the city, stipulating that the community was not to exceed twenty-four monks.[25]

Lestrange had the permission of the abbots of Cîteaux and Clairvaux for his move.[26] From the first the community at La Val Sainte was noted for its fervour and exceptional austerity.

> The religious . . . complained that they were not disciplined enough, not sufficiently reproved for their faults, and treated too gently. They constantly begged the reverend father to point out their slightest faults without indulgence, to impose every kind of penance upon them, and not to spare them in any way.[27]

---

[23] On abbot Lestrange and la Trappe see A. H. Laffay, *Dom Augustin de Lestrange et l'avenir du monachisme (1754–1827)* (Paris 1998); C. Gaillardin, *Les Trappistes ou l'ordre de Cîteaux au XIX siècle*, 2 vols. (Paris 1844); *Odyssée Monastique: Dom A. Lestrange et les Trappistes pendant le Révolution* (La Grande Trappe 1898); L.J. Lekai (as n. 2), 181–184. See also fifteen brilliant though disorganised articles by J. du Halgouët in *Cîteaux* 1966–1977, under the title 'Pierres d'attente pour une histoire de l'ordre dans la première moitié du XIX siècle', here cited by volume number, year of publication, and page numbers.

[24] A. J. Krailsheimer, *Armand-Jean de Rancé* (Oxford 1974) 338–40; *Rancé and the Trappist Legacy* (Kalamazoo 1985) 124–131.

[25] Laffay (as n. 23), 54–62.

[26] Ibid. 57–58.

[27] *Règlemens* (as n. 34), 1:50–51.

The asceticism of La Val Sainte far exceeded de Rancé's la Trappe. Already in 1785, Lestrange had composed for his novices a treatise which still survives in manuscript.[28] In his view, de Rancé's reforms were incomplete. Monastic reform was a continuous process. To stand still was to go backwards.[29] Some of the hardship at La Val Sainte was the result of poverty, but much was self-imposed.[30] Lestrange emphasised that everything was decided by the majority vote of the whole community. 'I saw,' he wrote, 'with the greatest satisfaction of my soul, how all my brothers were concerned about charity, so dear and precious was that virtue to us all'.[31]

From the first other French refugees, especially former religious of various orders joined the community, so that the maximum of twenty-four monks imposed by the cantonal authorities, was soon exceeded. As early as 1793, therefore, a small community was sent to Spain. In 1794 a group of Lestrange's monks settled at Westmalle near Antwerp. After the invasion of Belgium by the French they fled east, and in 1795 found a permanent home at Darfeld, near Münster in Westphalia, Germany. Meanwhile another group had crossed the Channel and, thanks to the generosity of Thomas Weld, a rich Catholic landowner, settled at Lulworth in Dorset, England. There the first monastery in the country since the Reformation came into being. Because the British Parliament had voted a pension for every refugee from revolutionary France, the Lulworth community found itself unexpectedly well endowed.[32]

A number of women religious who had fled from France to Switzerland also placed themselves under Lestrange. For them in 1796 he obtained a property at Sembrancher in the Valais, and called it, after his own motto, *La Sainte Volonté de Dieu* ('The Holy Will of God'). The women had belonged to various religious Orders and the first superior, appointed

[28] I am most grateful to Dr. A. J. Krailsheimer for this information.
[29] Laffay (as n. 23), 85–91.
[30] Ibid. 85.
[31] *Règlemens* (as n. 34), 1:49, 464.
[32] Laffay (as n. 23), 160–183.

by Lestrange, was a former Benedictine; but all voluntarily adopted the customs of La Val Sainte. The community grew rapidly. When the house opened in September 1796, there were seven religious at Sembrancher. Fifteen months later fifty-two had joined. The most eminent convert was Louise-Adelaïde de Bourbon, princesse de Condé, who took the name in religion of sister Mary Joseph. Her vivid letters describing the fortunes of the community are an important source for the history of Lestrange's movement.[33]

Anxious to demonstrate the 'usefulness' of his communities, and to silence anticlerical critics in Fribourg, Lestrange founded a 'Third Order' consisting of men and women who would devote their lives to teaching. Like the monks and nuns, they were to observe the Rule of Saint Benedict, but theirs was to be a relaxed interpretation, with all the dispensations an active ministry required.

Lestrange's monastery was called La Val Sainte de Notre Dame de la Trappe, and all its foundations had La Trappe in their title. Hence the monks and nuns soon came to be known as Trappists. In 1794 the customs of La Val Sainte were published in two volumes.[34] Two thousand copies were printed in the hope that they would be widely read.[35] As we have seen, some religious were inspired by them to form a secret trappist community in Paris.[36] In 1794 a bull of pope Pius VI raised La Val Sainte to the rank of an abbey. Its abbot was given the customary cistercian authority of a father-abbot over all daughter houses.

The first years at La Val Sainte were remembered by all Trappists with nostalgia.[37] This period ended in 1798, when Switzerland was invaded by the French. Without hesitation

---

[33] M. T. Kervingant, *Des moniales face à la Révolution française* (Paris 1989) 75–102. (English translation by Jean Holman ocso, *A Monastic Odyssey* (Kalamazoo 1999)—ed.]

[34] *Règlemens de la maison-Dieu de Notre-Dame de la Trappe par Mr. l'abbé de Rancé . . . augmentés des usages particuliers de la maison-Dieu de la Val Sainte* 2 vols. (Fribourg 1794).

[35] D'Halgouët (as n. 23); 27 (1977) 64.

[36] See above p. 324.

[37] *Règlemens* (as n. 34), 1:67.

Lestrange decided to evacuate his communities. Russia was chosen as his goal because Sister Mary Joseph, the former princesse de Condé, had a slight acquaintance with the emperor Paul. They had met in 1781, when he was still czarevich and was visiting France incognito as the 'Comte du Nord.' Lestrange encouraged her to write to him. 'I beg the charming Comte du Nord,' she wrote, 'to intercede for me with the emperor Paul'.[38]

From a handful of novices Lestrange's swiss communities had grown to some two hundred fifty-four men and women and children—sixty boys and forty girls. They were divided into small groups, each taking a different route east. Vehicles were provided for the women. The men walked. The march has become a cherished tradition of cistercian history:

> They walked from morning to midday. Then they stopped at some inn or in the bare fields, to give a meal to the children and the sick. During this halt, which lasted about two hours, they recited the different parts of the office of the day. After that they resumed the journey until sunset. This was the moment when those who were in good health could think of breaking their fast. While the meal was being prepared they sang Matins and Lauds. Throughout the journey silence was rigorously maintained. They were not even allowed to reply to the questions of a stranger, or to ask through what village or town they were passing. . . . In the evening each one wrapped himself in his coverlet. Often only bare boards or the naked earth provided a bed. On Sundays and feast days they went to a church. During the Mass they sang the litanies of the Sacred Heart and, after thanksgiving, the children sang *Salve Regina*. The caravan was an object of public curiosity. People gathered from all parts, and the spectators could not hold back their tears.[39]

---

[38] M. T. Kervingant, 'Aux origines des Cisterciens Trappistines. Un document inédit', *Cîteaux* 35 (1984) 194 and n. 10.

[39] *Odyssée Monastique* (as n. 23), 108–109. The 'Odyssey' is described in detail (with maps) in Laffay (as n. 23), 221–249, and, concentrating on the experiences of the nuns, in Kervingant (as n. 33), 109–147.

In the last months of 1799, the Trappists began to arrive in Byelorussia. The area had recently been annexed to the russian empire from Poland and contained many Catholics. A number of monasteries whose communities had become too small for their buildings were assigned to the newcomers. Nothing, however, had been properly organised. At Orscha, north of Mohilev, the trappistine nuns had to wait in their carriages in the monastery courtyard while the previous community was turned out before their eyes.[40] In the spring of 1800, before all the religious had settled in, Lestrange gave the order to leave Russia.

The reasons for this are not absolutely clear.[41] It seems that the archbishop of Mohilev, the ecclesiastical superior of the Catholics in Russia, made difficulties about granting Lestrange's communities monastic exemption. Lestrange also complained that the endowments of the monasteries which had been assigned to the Trappists were insufficient to maintain the new and larger communities. Sometimes the newcomers had to share their quarters with the previous inmates, who had nowhere else to go. There were also important political changes. In the wake of french military victories the Emperor Paul was inclined to a peaceful relationship with France. The way to this seemed open in 1799 after Napoleon Bonaparte seized power and gave France a more moderate and less revolutionary image. French emigrés, hitherto welcome in Russia, found themselves being expelled.

The changes in France worked in Lestrange's favour. In 1801 Napoleon made a concordat with the pope. The authorities in Fribourg felt safe in allowing the monks to return to La Val Sainte. Lestrange, however, was seldom there. The concordat had not allowed a restoration of contemplative communities in France, but the possibility that the law might be changed kept the abbot in Paris, where he involved

---

[40] Kervingant (as n. 33), 142–146.
[41] See the different explanations in Laffay (as n. 23), 237–245; Kervingant (as n. 33), 177; d'Halgouët (as n. 23), 28 (1977) 75–76.

himself in complicated intrigues. Meanwhile, in 1801, a group of trappistine nuns crossed the Channel and found a home at Stapehill in England. In 1802 another group of nuns obtained a site at Riedera from the Fribourg authorities. In 1803 some individual trappist monks found their way to the United States, where Lestrange had often dreamed of making a foundation, but nothing of the kind was achieved.

The period of comparative hope ended in 1809, when Napoleon invaded the Papal States and took the pope prisoner. Lestrange was unambiguous in his support of Pius VII, and even visited him in captivity. The Trappists were now proscribed. The long arm of Napoleon reached all over continental Europe. Trappist houses were everywhere closed. With the police on his tail Lestrange managed to escape from France and reached Lulworth in England, after the community, believing a rumour that he was dead, had sung a requiem Mass for him. From there he made his way to the United States. Before plans to found a monastery had been finalised, however, news came of the fall of Napoleon and the restoration of the french royal house. With his followers Lestrange returned to France. In 1815, he reclaimed La Trappe, which he had left with his small band of followers nearly a quarter of a century before.

Long before this, tensions within the trappist movement had begun to come out into the open. There can be no doubt about Lestrange's faith and heroism, but he was dictatorial, secretive, and capricious. In 1799, while still in Russia, Sister Mary Joseph, the former princesse de Condé, left the Trappists because of the excessive austerities Lestrange expected of his followers, and against which she had protested to him in vain.[42] In 1806 the monks of Darfeld, who had not been involved in the trek to Russia, revolted against the father-abbot's arbitrary government. With the support of the local clergy they declared their house, formerly a priory, to be an abbey. Darfeld's abbatial

---

[42] Kervingant (as n. 33), 156–160.

status, and its independence from Lestrange was confirmed by Rome in 1808.[43]

Had the odyssey to Russia and back, during which many died, been a gigantic folly? If so, it was only one of Lestrange's notorious 'leaps in the dark'. In the twelfth century the Cistercians had inspected the sites of proposed monasteries and made sure of endowments before actually sending out pioneer communities. Lestrange sent his followers in various directions without making any preparations beforehand. In fact, all his foundations were ephemeral. There was, moreover, considerable confusion about authority. The Cistercian Order and its Chapter General were in abeyance. Lestrange claimed that he had been given authority over the whole Order by the last abbot of Cîteaux and by Pope Pius VII in person. For these claims there was no written evidence. The abbot's only written document was the bull of Pius VI raising La Val Sainte to an abbey and giving its abbot the authority of a father-abbot over daughter houses. These powers, however, were very limited and Rome had never approved the special constitutions of La Val Sainte, which Lestrange insisted all trappist foundations must observe.

In the first years of the nineteenth century complaints about the harshness of Lestrange's régime were making themselves heard. Once again, as in de Rancé's time, we hear of deaths within the cloister.[44] When the monks of Darfeld returned to France after the fall of Napoleon, they rejected the observance of La Val Sainte and returned to that of de Rancé.[45] For decades after this the Trappists were split between 'observances': two sets of rules. Lestrange was also involved in a bitter struggle with the bishop of Séez in whose diocese La Trappe lay. Exemption, as always, was at the heart of the conflict. In 1825 the abbot went to Rome to defend himself

[43] Laffay (as n. 23), 340–341.
[44] D'Halgouët (as n. 23); 21 (1970) 44–45.
[45] Laffay (as n. 23), 409–410.

against his various critics. When he died, two years later, his tangled affairs were no nearer settlement.[46]

Shortly after his death the curia appointed Dom Antoine Saulnier provisional Superior General of the Trappists.[47] Since 1810 Dom Antoine had been superior of the monastery at Lulworth.[48] Although well content with England he had been forced to return to France with his monks in 1816, as a result of local anti-popery agitation. His community had been able to gain possession of the former cistercian abbey of Melleray in Britanny.

Essentially level headed and moderate, Dom Antoine gave the Trappists their first experience of rational government. After the fall of Napoleon the various exiled communities had returned to France. In 1827–1828 Dom Antoine conducted a visitation. There were eighteen houses—twelve following the customs of La Val Sainte, and six those of de Rancé. The visitor was authorised to mitigate the observance of the nuns, among whom there had been many deaths. He noticed that many houses were dependent on collections and that monks were sent out to beg—something which he thought incompatible with monastic discipline, but which he had sometimes to tolerate. He put an end to Lestrange's Third Order, which, he felt, could not be fitted into the life of la Trappe. For the rest, many of the trappist houses were flourishing. There were one hundred thirty-five monks at Melleray, eighty monks at Port-du-Salut in Maine (the community formerly at Darfeld), and eighty-six nuns at nearby Sainte-Catherine.[49]

For one group of religious the French Revolution came as a blessing in disguise. The eighteenth century was a lean time for the english benedictine communities on the continent. There was a considerable decline in vocations. The

---

[46] Ibid., 500–511 (bishop of Séez); 517–543 (process in Rome).

[47] D'Halgouët (as n. 23); 21 (1970) 23–32.

[48] The history of Lulworth is discussed in great detail by d'Halgouët (as n. 23); 17 (1966)–20 (1969). D. A. Bellenger, *The French Exiled Clergy* (Downside 1986) 83–90, concentrates on the unhappy reign of the first superior 1794–1802.

[49] For Dom Antoine's visitation, see d'Halgouët (as n. 23), 21 (1970) 43–46.

house at Dunkirk, for instance, which had numbered fifty to
sixty sisters at its peak, was down to eighteen choir nuns in
1777.[50] The monasteries for men trained their members for
the english mission and took them back when they retired. In
the second half of the eighteenth century, when english laws
against Catholic worship were no longer being implemented,
life on a mission could be very satisfying. There was now a
marked reluctance on the part of missioners to return to their
monasteries, the usefulness of which began to be questioned.[51]
In 1784 Benjamin Franklin suggested that the english monasteries in France should be suppressed and the funds from their
sale used to set up a college for training Catholic priests for
America.[52]

The legislation of the French Assembly closing the monasteries did not apply to foreign institutions. English religious
houses in France therefore continued as before, though they
could hardly be unaffected by the happenings around them.[53]
The situation changed in 1793, when war began between Great
Britain and revolutionary France. In October the French Convention ordered the arrest and imprisonment of all british
subjects in the Republic. At Dieulouard most of the monks
and novices had already slipped over the frontier. Prior Richard
Marsh had remained behind but was warned of his impending
arrest just before going to bed. Minutes before the officers
of the Republic burst into the house he escaped into the
night. After wandering through eastern France for some days

[50] *A History of the Benedictine Nuns of Dunkirk* (London 1958) 105.
[51] G. Scott, *Gothic Rage Undone* (Downside 1992) 24–25.
[52] T. F. McAvoy, *A History of the Catholic Church in the United States* (Notre
Dame, Indiana 1969) 46.
[53] For the english benedictine experience during the French Revolution, see
B. Green, *The English Benedictine Congregation* (London 1979) 32–67; C. Almond, *The History of Ampleforth Abbey* (London 1903) 225–299; *Stanbrook
Abbey: A Sketch of its History* (London 1925) 28–55; *A History of the Bene-
dictine Nuns of Dunkirk* (as n. 49), 105–139; L. Almond, *Downside Abbey and
School 1814–1914* (Exeter 1914) ix–xxiii; *Fr. Marsh's Escape from Dieulouard*.
St. Laurence Papers, 1, ed. A. Cramer OSB (Ampleforth 1994); A. Bellenger
OSB, ed., *The Great Return: The English Communities in Continental Europe
and their repatriation* (Downside 1994); A. Bellenger osb, 'Revolution and
Emancipations' in *Monks of England*, ed. D. Rees (London 1997) 199–212.

in disguise, he was able to find a place where it was safe to cross the Moselle and seek safely in the Empire. At Douai the community had also read the sign of the times and most of the monks had left before the war began. Prior Jerome Sharrock and a few of the monks who had stayed behind to safeguard their property were arrested and kept in prison for a year before being released in 1795.

To all the english communities abroad their own country now offered the safest place of refuge. The Catholic Relief Act of 1791 had removed the last obstacles to a free exercise of their religion. As the refugee communities arrived in England in 1793–1795, they began to look for homes. To the monks, Sir Edward Smythe, a former pupil at Douai, offered his property at Acton Burnell near Shrewsbury. Here the monks of Douai and Dieulouard lived uncomfortably together for a time. The attempt to weld them into a single community failed, and in 1795 the community of Dieulouard left. There followed a long peregrination through a number of temporary homes. In 1802 they settled down for good at Ampleforth in Yorkshire and opened a school, which, it was hoped, would provide them with a sufficient income.

The Douai monks remained at Acton Burnell. In 1811, however, their benefactor died and his heir wanted the house back. In 1814 the monks obtained the estate of Downside in Somerset. The community was installed in the manor house. A downstairs parlour served as the chapel. On feast days the singing was accompanied by a piano and two cellos. When the monarchy was restored in France, the monks, cooped up in their unsuitable quarters, thought of returning to Douai, where their buildings had survived the Revolution in tolerable repair. The decision to stay in England was passed, it seems, by only a small majority. Like their brethren in the north of England, the Downside monks opened a school to provide the revenues they needed for survival.

In Paris Prior Henry Parker of Saint Edmund's was determined to stay at his post and watch over the priory buildings and properties. He was in prison for much of the time. The community dwindled until, by 1814, he was the only one left. At the restoration of the monarchy what remained of the property was returned, but when he died in 1817 the community of Saint Edmund's was extinguished. The buildings at Douai, however, stood empty. Since the Downside monks had decided to stay where they were, some Ampleforth monks went to Douai to revive the traditions of Saint Edmund's there. A school for english boys was founded and flourished throughout the nineteenth century, since Douai became the sole beneficiary of bursaries granted by the french government in compensation for english benedictine property lost at the Revolution. As for Lambspring in the Empire, always somewhat different from the other english benedictine houses, it was efficiently suppressed when the prussian government took over the area in 1802.

October 1793 found the english benedictine sisters at Cambrai still observing the regular life in spite of the ominous events surrounding them. On the thirteenth of the month commissioners arrived to inform them that they were prisoners. For the time being they were allowed to remain in the house but five days later they were packed on to carts and began a harrowing journey, during which they were several times in danger of being lynched. On 22 October they reached Compiègne, where they were imprisoned for sixteen months. In the crowded insanitary conditions, four became ill and died. When news of their plight became known in England funds were made available for them to obtain passports and make the journey to their native land.

The Cambrai nuns arrived in England in April 1795, and, like the monks lived in temporary homes for a number of years. Hitherto theirs had been an enclosed contemplative community. In order to make ends meet they had to open a school, which many of them found uncongenial. Stanbrook Hall in Worcestershire, their final refuge, was acquired in 1838. A substantial building with extensive grounds, it answered to their needs, though some more years were to pass before all the necessary changes had been made.

October 1793 was also the critical hour for the nuns of Dunkirk. They were taken by boat to nearby Gravelines and imprisoned there for eighteen months. They might well have been guillotined, for it appears that Robespierre had their names on his list of intended victims. His fall in 1794 saved their lives but their imprisonment continued. The winter of 1795 was exceptionally cold, but they were allowed no fire. They shared their crowded prison with a number of other religious. There were numerous deaths. In April 1795, no doubt with help from England, they were able to obtain passports to leave the country. The vicar apostolic of the London district assigned them some buildings in Hammersmith in the outskirts of London. They had already been engaged in teaching at Dunkirk, and in 1796 they opened a school for girls. The community remained in Hammersmith until 1863. In the end, all the english institutions on the Continent, except for Lambspring, succeeded in transplanting themselves to the home country.

In other parts of Europe the survival of monasteries was less dramatic. When the French invaded Switzerland in 1798, they imposed a new constitution on the country which was marked by hostility to religion. All monasteries were dissolved. At Einsiedeln the monks took shelter with their families or with well-wishers in the neighbourhood. In 1801 it was safe for them to return and resume the religious life.[54]

The systematic closure of monasteries in Austria by Joseph II was halted when that monarch died in 1790. Such monasteries as had not yet been closed existed in a kind of limbo during the short reign of Leopold II (1790–1792). Under Francis II (1792–1835) their survival was confirmed. The austrian civil service, however, remained profoundly hostile. Monasteries were subject to numerous restrictions and expected to justify themselves by proving their usefulness to the state.

For the ancient abbey of Saint Peter in Salzburg the

---

[54] DIP 3 (1973) 1078.

napoleonic period was one of great uncertainty.[55] The former ecclesiastical principality of Salzburg had been secularised in 1801 and handed over to Ferdinand of Tuscany, brother of the emperor Francis II. The new ruler personally assured the monks of his good will. In 1805, however, after Napoleon's victories at Austerlitz and Pressburg, the map of Germany was altered again. The Holy Roman Empire was formally abolished. After occupation by the French and Bavarians, Salzburg was handed over to the newly formed Austrian Empire. The new authorities demanded a high price for confirmation of the abbey's survival, above all, control over the profession of novices.

Before the negotiations were complete there was more fighting. In 1809 Salzburg was occupied by the Bavarians to whom the area was presently assigned by Napoleon. The court at Munich was, at that time, pursuing an aggressively anticlerical policy. The Benedictine university of Salzburg was closed and in 1811, when the abbot of Saint Peter's died, permission to elect a successor was refused. For some years the abbey was subject to considerable harassment though the authorities relented sufficiently to allow the election of an abbot to go forward in 1816. By this time it had been agreed that Salzburg would be handed back to Austria. The imperial authorities had confirmed the abbey's future in 1805. Under Austria, then, its existence was assured, so long as it proved its usefulness to the state by running a school.

In Italy monasteries were suppressed wherever french troops were in control. There was occasional violence, as in 1799 when six cistercian monks at Casamari were shot while trying to protect the Blessed Sacrament from profanation.[56] Former monks were given pensions and found a variety of occupations. In 1814, when Pope Pius VII returned from captivity, he wanted them to return to their monasteries. Many

[55] F. K. Hermann, 'Das Kloster im Sturm des politischen Umbruchs bis 1816: Festschrift Saint Peter in Salzburg', *Studien und Mitteilungen zur Geschichte des Benediktinerordens und seiner Zweige* 93 (1982) 288–334.
[56] Lekai (as n. 2), 175.

monasteries, however, had been completely destroyed and former religious had no home to which to return. Many former monks had left the clerical state altogether and married. Others had taken up parochial duties. After the persecutions there was a shortage of clergy, and bishops were reluctant to let former religious go. Of the seven hundred parochial clergy in Venice in 1821, one hundred fifty were ex-monks.[57]

Undeterred, Pius VII made a valiant attempt to restore the monastic life, at least in the papal states. The cistercian abbey of Casamari was reopened in 1814; two houses in Rome followed three years later. By 1820 six cistercian monasteries had been restored in the papal states. They formed themselves into the Italian Congregation of Saint Bernard with a chapter general to be held every five years and a president general, whom the Holy See regarded as abbot general of all the Cistercians, including the Trappists.[58]

After fifteen years in the world, however, these monks had become unaccustomed to monastic life. Augustin Lestrange, who spent the last years of his life in Rome trying to sort out his tangled affairs, was not edified by the cistercian abbey at which he was staying. In order to observe the cistercian diet he had to dine alone in his apartment, because the community ate meat. 'I don't go to their office,' he wrote to a friend,

> because I can't keep up with them—they go so fast. I don't share their recreations because there is no silence. I only attend the *Salve Regina* if I am in the house at the time. They sing it at about 4 o'clock. Afterwards they go out to promenade in the streets. Only the youngest are obliged to have a senior with them. They come back at sunset, say Matins in the evening, and then have supper. After that they have half an hour's recreation with the Father Abbot, return to choir for prayer, and go to bed.
>
> Around 6 o'clock in the morning they say Prime. Then they hear a Low Mass. After that they take their coffee, or

---

[57] Owen Chadwick, *The Popes and European Revolution* (Oxford 1981) 592.
[58] Lekai (as n. 2), 193–194.

their chocolate if they can afford it. For nothing is held in common. They all have their own income. The house gives them so much for their clothes and other needs. Some of them have allowances from their families. . . . One of them told me that the present pope would like them to return to the common life, but that most probably he would not succeed, for their vows bind them only to the way things are now. That, my dear friend, is the state of affairs in Rome.[59]

In the restored Cassinese Congregation things were equally relaxed. Only in the middle of the nineteenth century were monks urged to make a declaration giving up their private incomes and embracing the common life in full.[60] The italian custom of eating a heavy meal late in the evening, which was expressly in violation of the Rule of Saint Benedict,[61] made it impossible to begin the night office in the small hours.[62]

The French Revolution had failed to eliminate western monasticism. The Trappists were a new and vigorous branch of the benedictine family. By the third decade of the nineteenth century they had become the principal monastic presence in France, where the Revolution had originated, and they were on the eve of spreading to England, Ireland, and America. There was also in France a flourishing congregation of benedictine women vowed to the contemplative life. There were, however, no houses for men who wished to become monks without embracing the rigours of de Rancé or Lestrange, and who were concerned to revive the venerable tradition of monastic study. Western monasticism, in all its variety, had only partly survived.

---

[59] D'Halgouët as n. 23, 26 (1975), 298–9. 50). 51). Also quoted in part by Laffay (as n. 23), 520.
[60] G. Turbessi, 'Vita monastica dell' abbazia di S. Paolo (in Roma) nel secolo XIX', *Revue Bénédictine* 83 (1973) 80.
[61] RB 41.
[62] V. Fiala, 'Die besondere Ausprägung des Benediktinischen Mönchtums in der Beuroner Kongregation', *Revue Bénédictine* 83 (1973) 200.

Chapter 12
WESTERN MONASTICISM IN THE NINETEENTH CENTURY

T HE CREATION OF A VIABLE monastic alternative to the Trappists was the work of Dom Prosper
Guéranger (1805–1875).[1] He was a native of Maine,
a french province bitterly divided between those who supported, and those who opposed, the French Revolution. Guéranger's parents were faithful to their Catholicism and accepted
the ministrations of a priest in hiding, but they were politically moderate and welcomed Napoleon's religious settlement. They felt no particular loyalty to the restored Bourbon
monarchy. Throughout his life, Guéranger's own political views
largely reflected theirs. As a young man he felt drawn to the
priesthood and entered the seminary at Le Mans in 1822. He
was ordained in 1827.

Already at school Guéranger was noted for his love of
books. As a student of theology he was impatient to get back
to the sources and was soon immersed in folio editions of the
Fathers. The level of scholarship in the seminaries at this
time was low. Raising the standard of learning among the
clergy became one of Guéranger's preoccupations. The other
was Ultramontanism, a theological position which emphasised
the importance of the pope. Gallicanism, the old alliance
of throne and altar had been found wanting. Throughout
the Catholic Church, younger clergy, like Guéranger, were

---

[1] L. Soltner, *Solesmes et Dom Guéranger 1805–75* (Solesmes 1974); A. des
Mazis, 'La vocation monastique de Dom Guéranger', *Revue Bénédictine* 83
(1973) 119–80.

rallying enthusiastically to the papacy, which had stood out uncompromisingly against the all-powerful Napoleon.

In 1826 the young Guéranger was appointed secretary to Mgr. Claude-Madeleine de la Myre-Mory, the bishop of Le Mans. Mgr. Myre was a prelate of the old school: polished, highly connected, and widely travelled. After a stroke in 1819 he ruled the diocese from his bed. In 1828 he left Le Mans, accompanied by his secretary, to consult doctors and visit his family. At the end of the year he resigned his see altogether and took up residence in Paris. Here the somewhat provincial Guéranger made friends in high society and acquired some necessary social graces. More importantly, he had ample time to pursue his studies in the rich libraries of Paris. After Mgr. Myre's death in 1829, Guéranger was called back to Le Mans by the new bishop, who promised him a post where his love of learning could be put to good use.

One of Mgr Myre's visitors in Paris had been Dom Antoine Saulnier, the trappist abbot of Melleray.[2] He was impressed by the bishop's ardent young secretary and hoped to win him for his abbey. 'I had no inclination for La Trappe,' Guéranger recalled years later, 'where I would have had to renounce study'.[3] His monastic vocation, indeed, developed slowly. In 1831 he heard that the abbey of Solesmes, not far from Le Mans, was for sale. After the Revolution it had passed into private hands. Guéranger had often gone on excursions to admire the medieval buildings. It now came to him that they could be used as a centre for priests dedicated to study. Gradually he formed the plan that they should observe the Rule of Saint Benedict.

Collections were organised to buy the building. In January 1833, after preliminary negotiations with the owners, Gueranger and some companions packed their few belongings on to a cart drawn by a single horse and made their way to Solesmes through a countryside under snow. It was only some

---

[2] See above p. 332.
[3] des Mazis (as n. 1), 138.

months later that final payments were made to complete the purchase, thanks to the generosity of Madame Swetchine, a rich russian convert to Catholicism.

The early 1830s were not a good time for starting a monastery in France. The July Revolution of 1830 had begun on a violently anticlerical note. For the sake of prudence, the community at Solesmes officially called itself 'The Regular Association formed in the diocese of Le Mans under the protection and with the approval of Monsignor the Bishop'. Dom Antoine Saulnier viewed it with a jaundiced eye. What future was there for a monastery without tradition, directed by a prior without experience? 'The poor Rule,' he wrote to Guéranger. 'You will have to take the scissors to it so many times that I doubt whether Saint Benedict would recognise it.'[4]

It was true enough that Guéranger had no personal experience of the cenobitic life. The first years at Solesmes were difficult. Of his early companions only one persevered. In time, however, new recruits replaced those who left. In 1837 Guéranger felt sufficiently secure to travel to Rome to seek papal approval. Thanks to influential friends, and the impression of his own sincerity, he was completely successful. He made his profession as a benedictine monk at the ancient abbey of Saint Paul's, without being obliged to affiliate his monastery to the Cassinese Congregation. Shortly afterwards, Pope Gregory XVI raised Solesmes to the rank of an abbey, with Guéranger as its first abbot. It was to be the nucleus of a new congregation of France.

Dom Guéranger was abbot of Solesmes for over thirty years. Under his guidance it acquired a marked character. It was to be, in his own words, 'A house of prayer and study'.[5] The monks lived out their vocation within the abbey itself and undertook no external work. They interpreted literally Saint Benedict's precept, 'Nothing is to be preferred to the Work

[4] Soltner (as n. 1), 38.
[5] Ibid., 79.

of God'.[6] The divine office and the conventual Mass were celebrated daily at the traditional times with all due solemnity. Gueranger encouraged research into the ancient plainsong of the Church. The oldest manuscripts were transcribed and deciphered. The monks sang the melodies exactly as they found them in the sources, something which had been regarded, up to that time, as impossible.

Manual labour, like gardening and cooking, was entrusted to lay brothers. The labour of the choir monks was to be chiefly intellectual. The liturgy was the abbot's passion. 'How can one remain cold when one is chanting such things?' he once exclaimed to his monks.[7] In 1841 he brought out the first volume of *L'Année Liturgique*, a vast commentary on the liturgy, which had reached its eleventh volume, and was not yet finished at his death in 1875.

Pope Gregory had recognised Solesmes as the nucleus of the 'Congregation of France'. From time to time Guéranger was involved in discussions to restore the monastic life at Cluny, Fleury, Cuxa, Lérins, and other ancient sites. All these hopes proved illusory. An attempted foundation at Paris in 1841 failed after two years. The first successful foundation was in 1853 at Ligugé, the monastery over which Saint Martin of Tours had once presided. Ten years later a small group of monks settled at Marseille. The site, in the middle of the city, with street-hawkers crying their wares outside the windows, seemed unpromising. The monks, however, developed an unique apostolate, specialising in retreats and missions to the clergy and laity. Dearest to Guéranger's heart was Sainte Cécile, a house founded in 1866 for benedictine nuns, a stone's throw from Solesmes itself. Mother Cécile, its first abbess had grown up in the neighbourhood, and as a girl had been instructed for her first communion by Guéranger himself. The phenomenal success of this house was one of the joys of the abbot's last years.

---

[6] RB 43.
[7] Soltner (as n. 1), 81.

These foundations began as dependent priories, but as soon as possible Guéranger had them raised to the status of abbeys. He wanted to return to the benedictine tradition that each house was a family, autonomous and complete in itself. He was opposed to the centralising congregations, with their chapters general, common novitiates, and superiors appointed for a limited period. All this had been borrowed from other Orders and was not, he felt, in the true benedictine tradition. He wanted abbots elected for life by each community and novices trained in their own houses. The monk's vow of stability was thus made, as Saint Benedict had intended, to a particular community and not to an Order.

In time, Solesmes was widely imitated. Yet it is worth noting that no benedictine house in the past had been quite like Guéranger's abbey. Cluny comes to mind, with its emphasis on the glory of monastic worship, but nineteenth-century monks would not have tolerated the repetitions and duplications which kept the Cluniacs in choir for hours with little time for anything else, or Cluny's domination of other houses. The life of the monks at Solesmes most resembled that of an observant maurist house in the seventeenth century. Mabillon would have felt at home there, especially in the company of Dom Jean-Baptiste Pitra, Solesmes's most distinguished scholar. On the other hand, the centralisation characteristic of the Maurists was foreign to the spirit of Solesmes. The seventeenth-century monks would have disliked the extreme papalism which marked Guéranger and his closest followers.

Guéranger's influence was soon felt in England.[8] The Benedictines who came to their native land in 1793–1795 had belonged to a missionary body, centralised after the manner of the Cassinese and other reformed congregations of the Counter Reformation. Scattered over their many missions, the majority of english Benedictines could not worship together

---

[8] B. Green, *The English Benedictine Congregation* (London 1979) 70–91; *Stanbrook Abbey, A Sketch of its History* (London 1925) 65–70; A. Clark, 'The Return to the Monasteries', in *Monks of England*, ed. D. Rees (London 1997) 213–234.

in choir. Each recited his monastic breviary office in private. In the nineteenth century, however, the nature of Catholic missionary work in England changed. Previously, Catholicism had survived in the country. In the nineteenth century the bulk of Catholics, many of them immigrants from Ireland, lived in the new industrial towns. The Benedictines played a vigorous part in founding and staffing missions in the growing urban centres, but awkward questions arose. Was life in a busy town mission really compatible with a monastic vocation?

The interpretation of the Rule at Solesmes was clearly much closer to Saint Benedict's intentions. All benedictine monasteries eventually felt challenged by Guéranger. In England his most ardent disciple was Dom Laurence Shepherd.[9] He was professed at Ampleforth in 1844. After some years of study abroad he returned to became novice-master. In 1855 he paid his first visit to Solesmes and was bowled over by the nature of the monastic life there. After that he visited Solesmes every year. He began a translation of Dom Guéranger's *Année Liturgique* and continued, volume by volume until 1875. In 1860 he even persuaded Guéranger to come to England and take part in the consecration of the new abbey church at Belmont in Herefordshire.

In 1863 Dom Shepherd became chaplain to the nuns at Stanbrook. Sainte Cécile was founded three years later and the two communities, thanks to Dom Shepherd's close contacts with Solesmes, more or less developed together. At Stanbrook a new gothic church was built, with ample space for liturgical functions. The claustral buildings were altered to make the traditional enclosure possible. From 1866 plainsong was adopted for all the offices. After some years the constitutions used at Sainte Cécile were introduced. The abbess, instead of being elected for four years, now held office for life.

Stanbrook thus became the standard bearer for Solesmes in England. There, and in the other english houses, changes were not introduced without bitter opposition. A whole way of

---

[9] Ibid., and Soltner (as n. 1), 136–137.

life dating back some two hundred years was being challenged. The changes needed in the constitutions of the english benedictine body as a whole, therefore, were opposed vigorously. It took three rescripts from Rome and two visitations to effect a transformation. Finally, in 1899, Downside, Ampleforth, and Belmont (founded 1859) became independent abbeys, each with its own novitiate. The title of president of the English Benedictine Congregation became purely honorary. The missions were divided up among the abbeys and very gradually they were handed over to the dioceses. In 1935 there were still seventy-six parishes run by Benedictines. The number had been reduced to thirty-eight by 1979.[10]

In Germany the restoration of monasteries began in Bavaria.[11] Ludwig I (king from 1825 to 1848) reacted sharply against his father's anticlericalism. His agents sought out monks in Austria and Switzerland who would populate new foundations in Bavaria. Twenty monks came from Austria in 1834 to form a benedictine community at the new abbey of Saint Stephen in Augsburg. Twelve years later the last austrian monk could leave Augsburg, where there was now a vigorous native community. Other houses founded or refounded by the king were Metten (1830, raised to the rank of abbey in 1836), Ottobeuren (1834), Scheyern (1837), and Weltenburg (1842). The abbey of Saint Boniface in Munich, founded in 1850 after Ludwig's abdication, became the ex-king's favourite project. It was his idea—revolutionary at the time—to build the church in the early christian style. Glorious with mosaics and frescoes, the huge building dominated its neighbourhood until its destruction during the Second World War.

These abbeys were planned as part of the king's educational plans for Bavaria. The monks of Saint Stephen's in Augsburg taught at three of the city's prestigious schools. Benedictine nuns, though traditionally devoted to the contemplative life,

---

[10] Figures in Green (as n. 8), 87.
[11] *Handbuch der Bayerischen Geschichte,* ed. M. Spindler, volume 4 (Munich 1975) 129–130, 922–925.

were also pressed into service. The abbey of Eichstätt (1835), the priory of Frauenchiemsee (1836), and even the cistercian abbey of Oberschönenfeld (1836) ran schools for girls. In the long run, however, this involvement with education proved burdensome. Moreover, the bishops, always short of priests, were anxious to entrust parishes to benedictines monks. In 1862 the abbot of Metten complained that his community was overwhelmed with pastoral work.[12]

A more contemplative monasticism was introduced into Germany by the brothers Rudolph and Ernst Wolter.[13] Born in Bonn in 1825 and 1828 respectively, they both entered the priesthood after their university studies. Like many of the younger german clergy they fell under the influence of Anton Günther, one of many nineteenth-century Catholic theologians who tried to reconcile traditional Catholic doctrines with the philosophy of Kant—a hopeless task which eventually defeated even the philosopher-priest Antonio Rosmini (1797–1855).

In Germany the followers of Günther were unpopular with their bishops. Life in the various dioceses was made difficult for them and it occurred to Abbot Simplicio Pappalettere of Saint Paul's in Rome that he might persuade some of them to become monks in his abbey. He was worried by Protestant propaganda in Italy. Might not learned Germans help to reduce its influence? In the event, he failed to attract the most prominent of Günther's followers. Since Günther was condemned by Rome in 1857, this was certainly providential. But the Wolter brothers entered the monastery in 1855 and 1856, taking the names Maurus (Rudolph) and Placidus (Ernst). They were not in the first rank of the theologian's followers and they showed little interest in pursuing an academic career. Instead, they were seekers after a life of perfection.

---

[12] V. E. Fiala, 'Die besondere Ausprägung des Benediktinischen Mönchtums in der Beuroner Kongregation', *Revue Bénédictine* 83 (1973) 205–206.
[13] Fiala, 'Die besondere Ausprägung . . .' (as n. 12), 181–220: V. E. Fiala, 'Ein Jahrhundert Beuroner Geschichte', *Beuron 1863–1963: Festschrift zum hundertjährigen Bestehen*, (Beuron 1963) 39–230.

From the start, then, there was a misunderstanding between the abbot of Saint Paul's and his new subjects. Abbot Pappalettere had introduced the complete communal life in 1855, but the older monks were not obliged to observe it.[14] In any case, the brothers Wolter did not at first have the opportunity of getting to know their new brethren. The cassinese novitiate was at Perugia. Here these two experienced and learned german priests were obliged to go to school with novices of fifteen and sixteen. In 1858 Pappalettere left Rome to become abbot of Monte Cassino. His successor, Angelo Pescetelli, was less interested in reform, and personally disliked the Germans in his community. He was not sorry when they left in 1860, with papal approval, to found a benedictine monastery in Prussia.

In Rome Maurus had become acquainted with the widowed countess Katharine of Hohenzollern who, after unsuccessfully trying her vocation as a Franciscan, had taken an apartment in the papal palace. She wanted to found a house for benedictine nuns in her own country, and to have a house for men, directed by Maurus Wolter, in the neighbourhood. In 1862 the countess helped the Wolters to acquire Beuron in Hohenzollern. Formerly an augustinian priory, its extensive baroque buildings had stood empty since secularisation in 1802. The countess took up residence nearby, though the hoped-for house for nuns, which she herself planned to enter, never materialised.

Thanks to the countess's influence with Pope Pius IX, Beuron's progress in its early days was rapid. In 1863 it was declared a benedictine priory independent of Saint Paul's and the Cassinese Congregation, with the right to conduct its own novitiate. In 1864 it was raised to the status of an abbey. In 1872 a daughter priory was founded at Maredsous in Belgium.

The Wolters were familiar with the discussions about the meaning and nature of monasticism which had been passionately debated in Italy. Shortly after the acquisition of Beuron,

---

[14] G. Turbessi, 'Vita monastica dell' abbazia di S. Paolo (in Roma) nel secolo xix', *Revue Bénédictine* 83 (1973) 80–81.

Maurus Wolter visited Abbot Guéranger. He stayed for three months and returned home with a clear vision. As at Solesmes, life at Beuron was to be centred on the liturgy. The superior was to be elected for life and the house was to train its own novices. The monks were not to be sent out to run distant parishes or teach in a school. On the other hand, the imitation of Solesmes was not slavish. The Wolters did not wish to give up all pastoral work. They took special care of the parish at Beuron. Its historic pilgrimage to the Mother of God was revived. The laity were encouraged to follow the offices and especially the Mass. Beuronese monks were pioneers in producing Mass-books in Latin and German for the laity. The monastic choir in their churches was so situated that the monks could be seen as well as heard. Retreats were held for the laity, missions were preached in the surrounding parishes and even further afield. Abbot Maurus also encouraged artists with a monastic vocation to enter the abbey. New side altars, an additional chapel, a shrine outside the abbey, were painted in what came to be known as the 'Beuron style'. In all this the influence of baroque monasticism, still a vivid memory in southern Germany, is obvious.

Progress was checked by Bismarck's *Kulturkampf*. The prussian government began to close religious houses. Beuron's turn came in 1874–1875. Most of the community was obliged to leave. To comply with the law, the abbey was renamed the 'palace' of Countess Katharine. Twenty caretaker monks were left behind: the superior as her 'chaplain', the others as her 'servants and lackeys'. Outside the monastic enclosure they wore livery. Every day the countess was pushed into the church in her wheel-chair to hear High Mass.

Maurus Wolter was forced to look around for homes to accommodate his exiled monks. Maredsous in Belgium provided room for some. With the help of the benedictine bishop Ullathorne of Birmingham, a site was found at Erdington in the english Midlands. In 1880 Countess Katharine's friend Cardinal Schwarzenberg, archbishop of Prague, offered the Beuronese the Emmaus monastery in that city—an ancient religious house where there was now only one remaining monk. In 1883 the austrian emperor Francis Joseph allowed the Beuronese to take over the medieval priory of Seckau. Here Maurus Wolter took up residence and founded a theological school. The nuns of Nonnenberg outside Salzburg also adopted the beuronese customs, and later sent a colony to found a house in Prague. All the new foundations attracted local recruits. The time had come to petition Rome to recognise a congregation of Beuron. The Curia, accustomed to the cassinese system of common novitiates and superiors with limited powers and terms of office, hesitated. Finally, however, abbots for life and novitiates in every house were accepted. Maurus Wolter became 'arch-abbot' of the new congregation. In 1885 it held its first chapter general. The exile from Beuron had proved a blessing in disguise.

By this time secret negotiations were in progress between Pope Leo XIII and Bismarck to end the *Kulturkampf*. In 1886–1887 conciliatory laws were passed which made a return to Beuron possible. Nevertheless, in the elections of 1887 the Catholic Centre Party opposed the government, whose concessions were purely temporary. An awkward situation arose at Beuron. The government candidate was Count Leopold of Hohenzollern, the countess's stepson. Maurus Wolter, who had returned to Beuron to make arrangements for the return of his community, openly backed the opposition candidate, who won the constituency. Countess Katharine was deeply offended. She bought herself a villa in the Black Forest and left Beuron for good. Abbot Maurus died in 1890. The countess died three years later, unreconciled to the community for which she had done so much.

Of all Beuron's foundations, none was more brilliant than Maredsous in Belgium.[15] It owed its origin to the family of Desclée. These rich industrialists from Tournai were also militant Catholics. In 1872, they acquired Maredsous, a country

---

[15] G. Ghysens, 'Fondation et essor de Maredsous 1872–1923', *Revue Bénédictine* 83 (1973) 229–257.

property near Liége. There they wished to build a little church, and contacted Maurus Wolter in the hope that he might send some Benedictines to serve it. The abbot, however, having in mind the approaching *Kulturkampf*, was thinking about a refuge for his community within reach of Germany. He therefore described to the Desclées what building a benedictine monastery would entail:

> The church of the abbey must be vast in order to accommodate a great number of altars and to permit the pomp of the liturgy . . . The abbey, with its chapter house, its cloisters, its library, its workshops, and its guest house, would be grandiose, but very expensive.

Baron Jean de Béthune, the foremost gothicist in Belgium was approached. Dom Maurus wanted a romanesque building. 'Assyro-Bavarian' growled the architect, and produced a gothic design[16] for the most complete benedictine abbey erected since the French Revolution. The church was opened for worship in 1881. When it was consecrated seven years later the massive buildings were complete.

In 1878 the Holy See raised Maredsous to the rank of abbey. Its most famous abbot was the irishman Dom Columba Marmion (1909–1923), a valued director of souls whose books on spirituality broke new ground and were appreciated by, among others, Pope Benedict XV. The abbey's internationally renowned scholars included Germain Morin, who uncovered nearly fifty previously unpublished letters of Saint Augustine,[17] and the historian Ursmer Berlière, whose most impressive monument is the *Monasticon Belge*, a systematic survey (still in progress) of all the historic monasteries of Belgium. The early history of the abbey was dominated by its energetic and almost

---

[16] P. Colman, 'L'architecture néo-Gothique en Wallonie et à Bruxelles', *Il Neogotico nel XIX e XX secolo*, 1 (Milan 1985) 94.

[17] For Germain Morin's own comments on his work, see *Sancti Caesarii Arelatensis sermones*, Corpus Christianorum Series Latina 103, ed. G. Morin, 1 (Turnhoult 1953) v.

febrile prior, Gerard van Caloën.[18] He founded an abbey school for middle-class boys on the english public school model, and launched a little review, *Le Messager des Fidèles,* which in a few years became the famed *Revue Bénédictine.* He was the moving spirit behind the foundation of a benedictine house of studies at Louvain, later to be known as the priory of Mont César. In 1894 he was sent to revive the moribund benedictine monasteries of Brazil, and in 1899, on a brief visit home, founded the priory of Saint Andrew at Bruges as a 'feeder' for them.

Associated with Maredsous was a community of sisters at Maredret. Agnès de Hemptinne, the first prioress, had made her novitiate at Sainte Cécile at Solesmes. Appropriately enough, she was known as Mother Cécile. She brought the traditions of Abbot Guéranger to Belgium. When the house achieved the status of an abbey in 1901 she was the first abbess. She held office for fifty-five years.

The progress of monastic reform in Italy was much stormier. In 1814, as we have seen,[19] former monks of the cassinese congregation had returned to the monastic life on condition that it was not too rigorous.[20] Superiors had to tolerate private incomes and possessions. Changes could only be brought about voluntarily. Towards the middle of the nineteenth century postulants were expected to give up all private property as the Rule demanded. It took longer to rearrange the *horarium* so that the offices would be celebrated somewhat nearer their traditional times.

There was one monk for whom the progress of reform was entirely too slow. Pietro Casaretto[21] was born in Ancona on

---

[18] On Dom Gerard, see G. Ghysens (as n. 15), and *Biographie nationale de Belgique* 31, Supplement 3 (Brussels 1962) 152–162.
[19] See above pp. 338–339.
[20] G. Turbessi (as n. 14); V. Fiala, 'Die besondere Ausprägung. . . .' as n. 12; G. Lunardi, 'Giovinezza e formazione di Pietro Casaretto' (as n. 21 below), especially 352–354.
[21] The whole issue of *Studia Monastica* 14 (1972) is devoted to Casaretto and the Cassinese Congregation of the primitive observance: G. M. Braso, 'Nel centenario della congregazione Sublacense' 347; G. Lunardi 'Giovinezza e

the east coast of Italy in 1810. He entered the benedictine monastery of Cesena at seventeen and was ordained in 1832. Because of his poor health his superiors sent him to various locations in the hope of improvement. In 1837 the Holy See granted him permission to live outside the monastery. He was put in charge of Portonovo, a deserted shrine of Our Lady near his native Ancona. The bracing climate, and perhaps a new sense of purpose, improved his health. His pastorate was so successful that in 1842–1843 he was moved to Pegli near Genoa. Here there was a benedictine parish with a very elderly monk in charge. The parochial work was being neglected and the archbishop was threatening to take the church back into the diocese.

Casaretto claimed that he would need a small community to help him. In January 1843, together with one companion, he took over the church. King Charles Albert of Sardinia was enlisted as a supporter. Soon a number of young recruits joined the nascent community. As early as 1844 they had outgrown their premises at Pegli and were rehoused at San Giuliano d'Albaro, a deserted charterhouse in the outskirts of Genoa. Here Casaretto added a missionary college to the novitiate. The cassinese congregation was sufficiently impressed to raise him to the rank of abbot in 1846.

As early as 1833, during a pilgrimage to Subiaco, Casaretto had written about the need for reform in the cassinese congregation. At Pegli there was particular emphasis on poverty, work, prayer, and discipline. From the first the novices shared in the pastoral work, so that the whole community was animated by a single sense of purpose. The divine office was given pride of place in the *horarium*, strict silence was observed

---

formazione di Pietro Casaretto', 349–374; G. Martinez, 'La restauracion monastica en Liguria: *Il Genovesato*' 375–403; P. Carosi, 'La provincia Sublacense (1851–67)', 405–59; D. Parry, 'The Cassinese Congregation a.p.o. (1867–72)', 461–84; W. Witters, 'La congregation Cassinaise de la primitive observance de 1872 à 1880', 485–521; G. Lunardi, 'Conclusione', 523–525. See also D. Rees, 'The Benedictine Revival in the 19th century', *Benedict's Disciples*, ed. D. H. Farmer (Leominster 1980) 297–301.

in the enclosure, and meals were accompanied by edifying reading.[22]Casaretto's policies were laid out in a memorandum of 1846.[23] Not everyone was impressed. The archbishop of Genoa thought him an impractical dreamer.[24] Maurus Wolter was later to call him a 'pitiful ignoramus in everything to do with monasticism'.[25]

Certainly, Casaretto's education in monasticism left much to be desired. Ill health had interrupted his novitiate at Cesena. To critics it seemed that he laid too much stress on externals. It must be borne in mind, however, that whereas Guéranger and Wolter were able to start their initiatives from scratch, Casaretto could never ignore the ancient cassinese congregation to which he belonged. The basis of his own spirituality can be seen in the reading he recommended for the monastic refectory: Holy Scripture, the lives of the saints, the *Imitation of Christ*, the Rule, and the cassinese constitutions.[26]

Casaretto's plans were frustrated by political developments. The revolution which forced King Charles Albert to abdicate in 1848, deprived the abbot of a powerful patron. Political unrest in Genoa obliged him to move his community to Finalpia, further from the turbulent city. In 1850 Pope Pius IX appointed him abbot of Santa Scholastica at Subiaco. Soon most of the monks from Finalpia and Albaro settled there. Three years later the Sacro Speco, the monastery at the cave where Saint Benedict himself was said to have lived, was united with Santa Scholastica.

At the Cassinese Chapter General of 1852, Casaretto, thanks to pressure from Pius IX, was elected president of the Congregation. Maurus Wolter, who became a novice at Saint Paul's in Rome at this time, was afraid that all the Cassinese would be turned into Trappists.[27] In fact, the powers of the

---

[22] Martinez (as n. 21), 378, 383–384.
[23] Ibid. 388–390.
[24] Ibid. 381.
[25] Fiala, 'Die besondere Ausprägung . . .' (as n. 12), 208.
[26] Martinez (as n. 21), 384.
[27] Fiala, 'Die besondere Ausprägung . . .' (as n. 12), 199.

president were very limited. By 1858, when his term of office came to an end, Casaretto had succeeded only in making bitter enemies of the other abbots.

More important was the creation of the province of Subiaco 'of the primitive observance' in 1851. There were still monks left at Albaro and Finalpia, and a community at Parma was in process of foundation. Pius IX united all these houses into a province which was to be directly subject to the Holy See while remaining a part of the Cassinese Congregation. The new province was, from the start, an anomaly. Cassinese provinces corresponded to the geographical and political divisions of Italy. The Subiaco province had no regional coherence. Non-Italians were readily accepted as novices, and Casaretto had every intention of making foundations abroad.

Termonde in Belgium, was incorporated into the province in 1855. It was a community of survivors from the ancient abbey of Afflighem which had been suppressed in 1796. It was facing extinction when it appealed to Casaretto. He sent some of his ablest monks. The community revived and in 1870 was able to restore Afflighem itself. In 1856 the province made a foundation at Ramsgate in England.

Subiaco's first house in France had a remarkable history.[28] Jean-Baptiste Muard, the founder of La Pierre-qui-Vire in the french department of the Yonne, was a zealous diocesan missionary who wanted to combine a life of austerity with pastoral work. He and his companions called themselves 'penitent preachers'. Their way of life was partly borrowed from the Trappists, but they also went on preaching tours. Muard himself died, worn out, in 1854, leaving to his successor, Bernard Moreau, the task of stabilising the community. Moreau visited Italy and met Casaretto. It seemed unlikely that the Holy See would approve the community's original rules. The observance of Subiaco was adopted as best suited to it.

---

[28] Carosi (as n. 21), 454–455; *Les ordres religieux,* ed. G. Le Bras, 1 (Paris 1979) 305–306.

In 1862 the ancient catalonian abbey of Montserrat joined the primitive observance. Yet as fast as it was growing abroad, the primitive observance was losing its houses in Italy. In the north an anticlerical government had taken control. After 1855 the days of the houses in the *Genovesato* were numbered. In spite of all Casaretto's efforts, Albaro and Finalpia were eventually closed. With most of its houses outside Italy, the Subiaco province was now quite unlike any other in the cassinese congregation. A separation was inevitable. In 1867, with the help of Pius IX, the province became the Cassinese Congregation of the Primitive Observance.

Casaretto owed much of his success to the support of Pius IX. The pope was irritated with the Cassinese, whom he suspected of sympathy with King Victor Emmanuel and the movement for italian political unity. Indeed some abbots had openly declared their liberal sentiments. Casaretto, on the other hand, was politically a conservative, and, where the affairs of the Church were concerned, an uncompromising papalist.

Casaretto's abrasive personality made arguments among italian Benedictines particularly bitter. Certain issues, however, divided nineteenth-century monks everywhere. Was the monastic vocation entirely contemplative? What external work, if any, was consistent with it? Could monks undertake pastoral work? Could they be active in the mission-field? A number of monks, including Casaretto himself, answered the last question in the affirmative.

Australia provides an early example of a benedictine mission.[29] During the napoleonic wars Great Britain had increased her possessions in the southern hemisphere. In 1819, after negotiations with the british government, the Holy See established an apostolic vicariate on the island of Mauritius in the Indian Ocean. It was to have jurisdiction over the Cape of Good Hope, Madagascar, Mauritius, the other islands of

---

[29] C. Butler, *The Life and Times of Bishop Ullathorne 1806–89* (London 1926) 1: 26–116.

the Indian Ocean, Australia, and New Zealand. The first three vicars apostolic were english Benedictines.[30]

As a result of the agreement of 1819, Catholic worship was permitted in Australia. Here Great Britain had two penal colonies: New South Wales, which was the area around Sydney, and the island of Tasmania, then called Van Diemen's Land. A large number of the convicts were Irish Catholics. Among these were many political prisoners who had been transported after a rebellion again Great Britain in 1798. Two Roman Catholic priests, one for each colony, were allowed in 1819. By 1832 this number had been increased to four. Each priest, however, acted independently. Divisions easily arose and there was no one to negotiate with the government on behalf of the whole Catholic community. There was a need for ecclesiastical authority, as well as for more missionaries. Bishop Morris of Mauritius naturally turned to his fellow Benedictines. Thus was born the idea of an english benedictine mission in Australia.

William Ullathorne, the Downside monk who volunteered for the mission, was destined to become one of the most outstanding of the english Catholic bishops of the nineteenth century. A bluff Yorkshireman, he had been brought up in Scarborough and as a boy had run away to sea. The lessons of this episode had turned his thoughts to religion. He became a monk at Downside in 1823 and was ordained in September 1831.

He was a young man of twenty-six when he was sent out to Australia as vicar general of the bishop on Mauritius. The seasoned and quarrelsome priests of Australia were not pleased to find themselves subordinate to a boy. He soon established his authority, however. Firmness ended the faction fighting, and his negotiations with the government were marked by courtesy and consistency. Ullathorne's main task was to minister to the

---

[30] On the unhappy experience of the first two english benedictine vicars apostolic on Mauritius, see A. Nagapen, *L'Église à Maurice 1810–41* (Port-Louis 1984).

convicts. Many had been transported for very minor offences, Many Irish had been sent to Australia for taking part in the rebellion of 1798 or for expressing sympathy with its aims. The convicts were often assigned to the free settlers as indentured labour. Since they were paid no wages they were, in fact, slaves. The slightest misdemeanour was reported to the magistrates and punished with the lash. 'This is the favourite and most frequent punishment', Ullathorne was later to write. 'For idleness the lash, for insolence the lash, for drunkenness the lash, for disobedience the lash . . . ever on the master's tongue and ever in the prisoner's ear . . . sounds the lash! the lash! the lash!'.[31] The women convicts had grievances of their own. Ullathorne wrote of a girl who was 'never safe from her master's importunities even in her kitchen, and she kept a carving-knife near at hand when he was about, to protect herself with; this knife she had to take in hand more than once'.[32]

There was a need for more priests and for a bishop nearer than Mauritius. For the episcopal office Ullathorne suggested his old novice master, John Bede Polding.[33] Rome acted quickly. In May 1834 Polding was appointed vicar apostolic with jurisdiction over all Australia. Ullathorne was to be his vicar general. The new bishop arrived in Sydney in August 1835. He shared Ullathorne's pastoral and humanitarian concerns and the two men, at first, worked together well. In 1836 it was decided that Ullathorne should be sent to Europe on a recruiting drive.

Ullathorne's journeys took him, via Rome, to England and Ireland. In 1837 he published *The Catholic Mission in Australasia*. Apart from appealing for recruits for the mission, the tract laid bare the evils of the convict system. Even more outspoken was *The Horrors of Transportation*, published in Dublin in 1838. Since a committee of the House of Commons was at that very time examining the whole convict system,

---

[31] Butler (as n. 29), 104.
[32] Ibid. 110.
[33] F. O'Donoghue, *The Bishop of Botany Bay* (Sydney 1982).

Ullathorne was summoned to give evidence. As a result of its enquiries the committee recommended the abolition of transportation. The system was phased out within a few years.

Ullathorne returned to Australia in 1838. His second sojourn there was not happy. Furious at the prospect of losing their indentured labour, the free settlers blamed him for its abolition and attacked him fiercely. Bishop Polding considered that a bishop should be above controversy, and gave his vicar general little public support. Ullathorne also saw, more clearly than his bishop, that the idea of a benedictine mission in Australia was an illusion. He left the colony for good in 1840.

Some in the English Benedictine Congregation had indulged in extravagant fantasies. On Polding's appointment as bishop the president of the Congregation wrote to him of 'the singular novelty of a new vicariate assigned to be supplied by our Congregation, a new Province probably to be erected, and yourself the first appointed Vicar Apostolic'. Another monk urged Polding to 'imitate Saint Augustine when he came to England, and secure a succession of Ministers of Religion by the establishment of one or more monasteries'.[34]

The plain fact was that the english congregation did not have the resources to send many missionaries abroad. Its monks were fully occupied with their missions in England. The priests needed in Australia came mostly from Ireland and were seculars. Between some of them and the bishop a certain amount of friction existed. In 1842 the Holy See divided Australia into dioceses and Polding became an archbishop. None of the new bishops shared the benedictine ideal.

Polding was a superb missionary. He covered his enormous diocese on horseback. No one forgot his open air sermons or his administration of the sacraments in the evening under the stars, the effect of the ceremonies heightened by his sense of drama. He was far ahead of his time in his concern for the aborigines and his appreciation of their culture. He would weep to see them wandering, bewildered, through the

---

[34] Butler (as n. 29), 21.

streets of the towns. He tirelessly argued their case with the authorities.

In sophisticated Sydney his touch was less sure. The monastery which had been established at the cathedral was a failure. Much of the opposition to him came from its midst. Because of his many journeys, Polding was seldom available for his monks. Insufficiently supervised, the members grew discontented. He was a poor administrator and a worse judge of character. His confidant Henry Gregory, whom he eventually made abbot of the cathedral establishment, was generally loathed. After Polding's death in 1877, Roger Bede Vaughan, another english Benedictine, succeeded him as archbishop. When he died in 1883, he was succeeded by a secular.

In Western Australia the Benedictines were more successful.[35] In 1845 John Brady, in charge of the Catholic mission at Perth on the Swan River, was in Rome to discuss his problems. Since his mission was three thousand miles away from Sydney, it was decided to erect a bishopric at Perth, with Brady as the first bishop. After his consecration two spanish monks, Dom Joseph Serra and Dom Rosendo Salvado, offered themselves as missionaries in the area. They were refugees from Spain, where an anticlerical government had dissolved the Congregation of Valladolid. With their new bishop they arrived in Western Australia in January 1846.

Bishop Brady was particularly concerned about the fate of the australian aborigines, who were being gradually pushed off their land by the white settlers. Dispossessed, many of them wandered around the new towns, where they fell victims to alcoholism and were subjected to the harsh punishments of a law they did not understand. Bishop Brady wanted to teach them Christianity and integrate them into european society. The two spanish monks were sent inland to begin a mission.

---

[35] G. Russo, 'Bishop Salvado and the Aborigines'. *History Today* 29 (1979) 394–414, with bibliography; H. N. Birt, *Benedictine Pioneers in Australia,* 2 (London 1911) 468–496. G. Russo, *Bishop Salvado of New Norcia* (Melbourne 1979) was not available to me.

After initial difficulties, they managed to win the confidence of some of the tribesmen. The plan was to found a model christian community. The aborigines would be taught agriculture. Settlers from Perth, particularly French and Irish, were also invited to come. With the help of the government, a large area of land was eventually assigned to the missionaries. In 1847 the foundations of a stone monastery were laid. The site was called 'New Nursia'. In 1855, after a campaign to raise money and find recruits, Salvado returned from Europe in bishop's orders. He was now bishop-abbot of New Nursia. Twelve years later the abbey was raised to the rank of *abbatia nullius*—a religious house whose superior exercised episcopal jurisdiction in the area round about it.

Salvado spent much time with the aborigines learning their traditions and languages. He sat at their camp fires, listened to their stories, studied their music, and learned about their rituals and dreams. He tolerated many of the beliefs and customs of his converts and grafted them into the Catholic life of his mission. He believed that the emerging australian civilisation must incorporate aboriginal as well as european elements. In 1848, when he applied for naturalisation as a british subject he asked that, if his application was refused, he should be considered as one of the aboriginal race.

Nineteenth-century accounts describe New Nursia's flocks of sheep, cattle, and horses—the last were exported to India for use by the army. The abbey had vineyards which produced a local wine and vegetable gardens growing produce for sale in Perth. In the fields tribesmen and monks worked side by side. Once a week the aborigines went out into the bush to hunt. They sang in the church and accompanied the services on the violin and other instruments. They recited special prayers while the monks were singing their office. There was a school on the site for the local children. At New Nursia the Spaniards had recreated the ambiance of the famous missions of Paraguay and California. Even the architecture of the abbey church is reminiscent of South America.

The first Benedictines arrived in the United States from

Germany, where Catholics were concerned about the spiritual needs of their compatriots in America.[36] In 1828 Friedrich Rese, the german vicar general of Cincinnati, had an audience with the austrian emperor which resulted in the foundation of the *Leopoldinenstiftung*—a fund to support german missionaries in America—and a decision by the Redemptorists to involve themselves in the work. In 1838 Ludwig I of Bavaria founded the *Ludwigs-Missionsverein*. Its purpose was to care for 'the preservation of the Catholic Faith and the german language and culture among german emigrants, especially german settlers in North America'.[37]

Among those who expressed an interest in the plight of Germans in the United States was Boniface Wimmer, a benedictine monk of Metten in Bavaria. He was constantly urging his superiors to involve themselves. 'All the world is ahead of us, I thought, when I heard about it', he wrote, 'Jesuits, Premonstratensians, Redemptorists! Only we stick to our "Make haste slowly"! I was ashamed. I am still ashamed to the depths of my soul.'[38]

In 1845 Wimmer published in the *Augsburger Postzeitung* an anonymous article in which he laid out his ideas about a mission among the Germans in America.[39] It was obvious, he wrote, that more priests were needed. Secular clergy were not best suited to missionary work, he went on, because missionaries needed a base to which they could return from time to time, and to which they could retire in old age. A religious order alone had the resources to fill vacant posts and lay down a policy to be followed over an entire area. Wimmer then passed in review the various religious orders already active in the United States. Few of the Jesuits spoke German. Their

[36] On the Benedictines in the United States, see B. Doppelfeld, *Mönchtum und kirchlicher Heilsdienst: Enstehung und Entwicklung des nordamerikanischen Benediktinertums in 19 Jahrhundert* (Münsterschwarzach 1974); J. Oetgen, *An American Abbot* (Washington D.C. 1997).
[37] Doppelfelt (as above), 94–95.
[38] Ibid. 56.
[39] For an english translation, see *Documents of American Catholic History*, ed. J. T. Ellis (Milwaukee 1962) 280–288.

apostolate, in any case was to run expensive schools for the rich. The Redemptorists did excellent work in the cities and in areas already thickly populated. What about the thinly populated frontier lands?

It was time the Benedictines were involved, wrote Wimmer. In the Dark Ages most of northern and eastern Europe had been converted by them. They owed their success to the fact that they were vowed to stability. They acquired land and cultivated it, thus becoming thoroughly assimilated in the regions where they had established themselves. Their way of life combined contemplation with action.

America seemed to Wimmer to resemble early medieval Europe. There were large forests, great stretches of uncultivated land, and fertile acres which could be purchased cheaply. The german settlers were scattered over large areas, with no priests or schools. A benedictine community could acquire land and in a few years turn it into a flourishing concern. It could set up printing works and establish a school. Brothers could be sent out to contact isolated families. After a time it was likely that german Catholics would settle around the monastery, just as towns had grown up around the medieval abbeys. The school would grow into a college and attract vocations to the monastic life.

The remarkable thing about Wimmer's plan is that when he arrived, at last, in the United States, he hardly needed to change it. His view of the benedictine mission in the Middle Ages was, needless to say, tinged by romanticism. It should be noted, however, that his article very accurately described the great south-german abbeys of the baroque period, with their printing presses, their schools and colleges, and their far-flung parochial work. In Bavaria the memory of these institutions was still green.

By July 1846 Wimmer had worn down opposition to his schemes and was able to set out for America with the blessing of his abbot. He took with him four ecclesiastical students and fourteen laymen who wished to embrace the monastic life in the United States. After some time spent looking for a site, he came to an agreement with Michael O'Connor, the first bishop of Pittsburgh, who offered some church land at Saint Vincent, Latrobe, in the south-west corner of Pennsylvania. It was an area where there were numerous Catholics, many of them German. Wimmer settled there with his followers, and in October 1846 clothed his eighteen companions with the monastic habit. He himself took the title of 'Father Superior of the Bavarian Benedictine Missionaries'. The theological students resumed their studies, but the whole community was involved in putting up the first buildings and setting up the farm. Wimmer set great store by agriculture. He intended it to provide the economic basis for pastoral work. He bought land wherever the opportunity offered, regardless of growing debts.

While there can be no doubt of Wimmer's energy and vision—it is said that his motto was 'Always go ahead'[40]—he owed a great deal to constant and discerning support from Bavaria. Most important were the extra volunteers who arrived from time to time to enlarge his community. The *Ludwigs-Missionsverein* was generous in its grants of money. King Ludwig followed his work with enthusiasm and supported him in Rome during the disagreements with Bishop O'Connor of Pittsburgh.

In 1846 the diocese of Pittsburgh was three years old and its institutions had hardly yet got off the ground. For the bishop the arrival of learned german Benedictines seemed a godsend. He hoped he would be able to send students for the priesthood to Saint Vincent's. Wimmer's purpose in coming to America, however, had been to meet the pastoral needs of german-speaking Catholics, and provide a german Catholic education for their children. This had also been the intention of Wimmer's bavarian backers, whose wishes he could hardly ignore. From the beginning, then, there were misunderstandings with the bishop. In 1849 another argument arose. A nephew of Wimmer had emigrated to the United States and with money borrowed from his uncle had opened a tavern and brewery.

---

[40] Rees, 'The Benedictine Revival' (as n. 21), 288.

The enterprise failed and Wimmer had been obliged to take it over. This horrified Bishop O'Connor, a follower of Father Matthew, an irish temperance preacher.Wimmer defended his actions by pointing out that for many centuries european Benedictines had been famed for brewing excellent beer.

The amount of heat generated by this quite minor matter is a measure of the tension which had built up between the two men. Soon another cause of bitterness arose. Between 1848 and 1852 Wimmer was negotiating in Rome to have his monastery erected into a canonical priory, exempt from diocesan jurisdiction. Saint Vincent's was made a priory in 1852, but because of the bishop's objections, exemption was not granted. The very next year Wimmer began a new campaign in Rome. In 1855 his efforts were at last crowned with success. At his request and in the teeth of opposition from O'Connor, Saint Vincent's was given the status of an exempt abbey, and Wimmer was made its first abbot. At the same time the Holy See created for the abbey and its dependencies the 'American Benedictine Congregation, affiliated to the Cassinese'.

Throughout the controversy Abbot Wimmer, whose temper was volcanic, had been somewhat unrestrained in his language, referring to Bishop O'Connor in one letter as 'this irish scoundrel'.[41] The bishop in his turn had suggested to the Curia that, even if Saint Vincent's were to become an abbey, Wimmer was not fit to be a religious superior. In time tempers cooled and the two men were able to do one another justice. Bishop O'Connor was an outstanding pastor with legitimate concerns. He was an essentially fair-minded man. Except at moments of extreme tension, he was ungrudging in his personal admiration for Wimmer and his achievements.[42]

In the years following his roman victory, Wimmer made his first major foundations. Saint John's, Collegeville, was founded in Minnesota from Saint Vincent's in 1856. From the beginning it was, like its founding house, an educational and pastoral

---

[41] Oetgen (as n. 36), 91.
[42] The quarrel between Wimmer and the bishop is disscussed in detail and with great fairness to both sides in Oetgen as n. 36, 114–117, 119–124, 141–153, 156.

centre. In 1858 it was recognised as an independent priory, and in 1866 was raised to the rank of an abbey. In 1857 a second foundation was made, this time in Atchison, Kansas. A priory in 1858, it became an abbey in 1876. Two other foundations were exceptions to Wimmer's vision of rural monasteries depending on their own produce. At Newark, New Jersey, a house founded in 1857, stood on an urban site and was within easy reach of New York City, thus providing his congregation with an opening on the eastern seaboard. Saint Procopius, founded in 1885 in the Pilsen district of Chicago, came into being two years before Wimmer's death to serve the pastoral needs of Czech-speaking immigrants from Bohemia.

These foundations were possible because, after the initial difficulties were overcome, vocations to the congregation were plentiful, fostered, as Wimmer had foreseen, by the monastic schools. Bishops were anxious to invite the monks into their dioceses. After his experiences with Bishop O'Connor, Wimmer laid down strict conditions: the monks must be the absolute owners of their land; in all matters of discipline they were to be subject to the abbot of Saint Vincent's; and the bishop must not oppose the quest for monastic exemption.

In the first years of the congregation the pastoral care of german Catholics was the major task. By seeking out the pioneers on isolated farms and bringing them together as a church group, the monks were actually creating new communities. In a letter to the *Ludwigs-Missionsverein* Wimmer described how the missionaries went about their work.

The priests come regularly on particular Sundays, hold services, preach, baptise, bless marriages, visit the sick, instruct the children, try to introduce the isolated to one another, make contacts and organise a formal community, distribute edifying books, introduce Catholic periodicals, attempt to counteract and ban harmful literature, and in every way labour to strengthen religious life through brotherhoods and unions.[43]

---

[43] Doppelfeld (as n. 36), 65.

Within three years of its foundation, Saint John's Collegeville was serving thirty mission stations of this kind. By 1860 the priory at Atchison had twenty-three.

Wimmer attached schools and seminaries to his monasteries so that priests for the german immigrants could be trained in America itself. These institutions were also to serve as schools for the professional classes. Unlike Jesuit schools, they were not expensive and were supported, at least in part, from the income of the monasteries themselves. German-speaking boys learned English as their first language, English-speaking boys learned German.

Wimmer's backers in the home country laid particular emphasis on the preservation of german culture. 'I shall never forget you in America,' said King Ludwig to some sisters who were leaving for the mission. 'I shall never abandon you, but stay German, German! Never become English!'[44] Just as there were French-speaking areas of Canada, it was believed, so there would be German-speaking parts of the United States. In time these illusions were dispelled. As early as 1851 Wimmer admitted that he thought of himself as a Pennsylvanian, not a Bavarian.[45] Though born in Westphalia, Alexius Edelbrock, the second abbot of Collegeville, insisted that everyone in his monastery speak English.[46]

Lacking a leader as imaginative and courageous as Boniface Wimmer, the second branch of the Benedictines to take root in America had a troubled start. In 1852 an appeal was made to the abbey of Einsiedeln in Switzerland to send volunteers to Indiana, where German-speaking priests were urgently needed. Abbot Heinrich Schmid was sympathetic, partly because anticlerical governments in Switzerland threatened the very survival of Einsiedeln itself and he hoped that America might provide a refuge for the community. Two monks were sent to Indiana to take soundings. The bishop

---

[44] Ibid. 96, n. 319.
[45] Ibid. 92.
[46] Ibid. 94.

8a   The Abbey of Einsiedeln
8b   Saint Meinrad's Archabbey

of Vincennes appointed them to a mission in the area around the town of Ferdinand.

From the start the monks exceeded their instructions by purchasing a huge tract of land. Abbot Heinrich was dissuaded from repudiating the purchase only by the urgent pleading of the bishop and his clergy. Too high a price had been paid, however, and but for help from german missionary societies, the whole venture might have collapsed. Eventually Abbot Heinrich softened sufficiently to send out six additional monks. In 1854 the community took official possession of the farm and inaugurated a monastery. It was dedicated to Saint Meinrad, the ninth-century hermit on the site of whose cell Einsiedeln had been built.

The early years brought disappointments. The monks had accepted missions over too large an area, so that there was practically no community life at Saint Meinrad's itself. There were constant changes of personel as personalities clashed. Major decisions were delayed because Abbot Heinrich insisted that all important matters must be settled at Einsiedeln by himself and the chapter. He tended, moreover, to rely for information on disgruntled monks who had returned from Indiana with contradictory excuses for their failures. Several times he was invited to Indiana to see conditions for himself, but he never came.

In 1860 he sent out one of his most trusted monks to take over as the new superior. Martin Marty was a twenty-six year old native of Schwyz and had been teaching in the school at Einsiedeln. His instructions were either to put Saint Meinrad on a firm footing or to close it down. His firmness and good sense saved the venture. He established a small permanent community at Saint Meinrad. The more distant missions were progressively abandoned. Some of the land belonging to Saint Meinrad's was sold to german Catholics who formed a supportive lay community and meanwhile provided the means to reduce the monastery's debt. The school was enlarged and in 1867 a printing press was established.

It was clear that submission to Einsiedeln was impractical

in the long run. With the advice and support of Boniface Wimmer, Marty approached the Holy See. Wimmer would have liked Saint Meinrad to join his own congregation, but this solution did not commend itself to Marty, possibly because the break with Einsiedeln would have been too painful. The bishop of Vincennes put forward the usual objections to monastic exemption. In spite of this, Rome raised Saint Meinrad to the rank of an abbey in 1870, with Marty as its first abbot. Its monks were to constitute a Swiss-American Congregation, affiliated to the Swiss Congregation from which they had come. The abbey was to be exempt, but not its parishes. Unlike Einsiedeln, therefore, Saint Meinrad never became an *abbatia nullius*.

The congregation become known for the excellence of its schools. Its other nineteenth-century foundations in the United States were Conception Abbey in Missouri (1873), New Subiaco in Arkansas (1878), Saint Joseph's in Louisiana (1889), and Saint Gall's at Devil's Lake, North Dakota (1894). In 1899, Saint Gall was moved to Richardton and changed its name to Saint Mary of the Assumption.

From 1876 Abbot Marty was involved in the missions to the Native Americans of Dakota. Three years later he was nominated vicar apostolic of the territory and resigned as abbot of Saint Meinrad the following year. His relationship with the community had been stormy. He was an autocrat, feared rather than loved. His successor was Fintan Mundwiler, who had come out to America with him in 1860. By the time he died in 1898, the present extensive buildings of the abbey, in the german romanesque style, were completed. The monks remembered their first abbot as 'the strict father', and the second as 'the kind mother'.[47]

The first benedictine sisters to set up schools for girls in America also came from Bavaria.[48] During a visit to his

---

[47] Ibid. 133.
[48] On the benedictine sisters and their disputes with Abbot Wimmer, see Oetgen (as n. 36), 196–225; J. A. K. McNamara, *Sisters in Arms* (Cambridge, Massachusetts 1996) 568–569, 605.

homeland in 1851, Wimmer had approached the nuns of Saint
Walburga's Abbey in Eichstätt, whose monastery had been
founded as a teaching institution by King Ludwig sixteen years
earlier. Sister Benedicta Riepp and two others accompanied
Wimmer back to America. They established themselves in the
german settlement of Saint Mary's, Pennsylvania, not far—
perhaps as things turned out, not far enough—from Saint
Vincent's. The sisters' school was an instant success. Soon it
was possible to expand and, since there was no lack of local
vocations, consider foundations elsewhere. By 1860 there were
fifty-one women in the sisterhood, living in five monasteries
spread over four states of the Union.

Boniface Wimmer had grandiose plans for the benedictine
sisters. All their monasteries were to be exempt and were to
form part of the American Benedictine Congregation. Somewhere there might be an abbess, but every house was to be
subject to him as head of the congregation. Unfortunately
the realities of his dictatorial manner destroyed the splendid
vision. He felt free to do as he pleased with funds sent from
Bavaria expressly for the use of the sisters. He insisted that no
nun could be professed at Saint Mary's without his permission.
Sister Benedicta Riepp claimed (though he denied) that he
had sent postulants to her community without consulting her.
Certainly Saint Vincent's was near enough Saint Mary's for
him to pay frequent and unsettling visits to the sisters. Sister
Benedicta felt that she was not free to act as superior in her
own community. Small wonder that in 1857 she left America
to place her difficulties before her patrons in Bavaria, and
ultimately to seek in Rome for definitive rulings on the limits
of Wimmer's authority.

Wimmer wrote to his bavarian patrons and to the roman
authorities in his usual vehement way. This time, however, the
decision went against him. By a decree of 1859 the american
benedictine sisters were removed from his jurisdiction. In
future each of their houses was to be subject to the authority of
the local bishop. Worn out by her many trials, Sister Benedicta
died in 1861, at the age of thirty-six. She and her sisters

had been freed from the rule of Abbot Wimmer, but in the long run the american Catholic bishops proved to be even more authoritarian, and they had no respect for the sisters' benedictine traditions.

In 1893 the Beuronese initiated the long and painful revival of the Benedictine Congregation of Brazil. Its monastic houses were on the edge of extinction, thanks to anticlerical policies followed in the time of the Emperor Pedro II. The benedictine novitiates had been closed. There were only about twenty monks left, scattered over ten houses. All were old men, some leading lives which were far from edifying.[49] In 1893 the internuncio in Brazil wrote to Abbot Placidus Wolter of Beuron asking for help.

The Beuronese sent out their stormy petrel, the volcanic Gerard van Caloën. It seemed an inspired choice. Van Caloën lacked neither energy nor ideas. Unfortunately he completely misjudged the situation. Brazil did not have the cultured middle class which would appreciate latin plainsong and provide benedictine vocations. There was, on the other hand, an intense nationalism, and a prickliness about foreigners who thought they could teach the natives. On their side the Beuronese did not disguise their contempt for the brazilian clergy. In 1903, when van Caloën took over the prestigious abbey of São Bento in Rio de Janeiro, there was a riot which had to be quelled by troops.

As abbot of Rio, van Caloën was president of the whole Brazilian Benedictine Congregation. He had himself styled arch-abbot, a title borrowed from Beuron. The papacy raised São Bento in Rio to the status of *abbatia nullius* and added to it the territory of Rio Branco on the Amazon, where the Benedictines, under van Caloën's direction, were to conduct a mission to the native american Indians. These ambitious plans were hampered, partly by van Caloën's inability to get

---

[49] J. Jongmans, 'Autour de la restauration de la congregation bénédictine brésilienne', *Revue Bénédictine* 92 (1982) 171–208; 96 (1986) 337–352; also article on van Caloën, as n. 18.

on with his subordinates, and partly by financial constraints. The arch-abbot's plans to raise money became ever more rash. Hopes of support from France and Belgium were dashed by the outbreak of the First World War. By this time the brazilian congregation was on the verge of bankruptcy. In 1915, during a visit to Rome, van Caloën was asked to resign the abbacy of Rio and the presidency of the Congregation of Brazil. He returned to Rio Branco to concentrate on the mission, but, finding himself hampered at every turn, returned to Europe for good in 1919.

In January 1930, one month before his death, he was visited by the cardinal archbishop of Rio, who wished to convey to him the thanks and appreciation of Catholic Brazil. In fact his greatest error had been to misunderstand the ecclesiastical situation. The establishment of a republic in 1889 involved a separation of church and state. The church in Brazil was now at least free to run its own affairs. In the last decade of the nineteenth century its pastorally-minded bishops were undertaking a reorganisation in close cooperation with the Holy See. They had little respect for the old religious Orders. They would have preferred to suppress them altogether and use their extensive buildings and properties for seminaries, schools, and hospitals. 'What is the use', asked a bishop on a visit to São Bento in Rio, 'of singing the divine office for hours on end? You belong to the last century'.[50]

During the baroque period the monks of central Europe had succeeded in combining the contemplative life with pastoral activity. In the troubled nineteenth century monks felt that these two ways of life were incompatible. Nowhere was the argument more impassioned than at Beuron itself, where for twelve years (1871–1883) Abbot Maurus Wolter was locked in argument with Andreas Amrhein, one of his most brilliant monks.[51] Amrhein made no secret of the fact that he wished

---

[50] Jongmans (as above), 92 (1982) 205.
[51] Fiala, 'Ein Jahrhundert . . .' (as n. 13), 112–114; H. S. Brechter 'Beurons Beitrag zur Gründung von St. Ottilien', *Beuron 1863–1963 (as n. 13)* 231–

to revive the benedictine tradition of missions, associated with Saint Augustine of Canterbury, Saint Ansgar, and many others. He was one of the monks sent out to found Maredsous in 1872, and was there again from 1876–1879. Here he made the acquaintance of Gerard van Caloën and others who were far more open than his abbot to the idea of benedictine missions.

In 1883, after numerous changes of mind, Maurus Wolter released Amrhein from his ties to Beuron. Amrhein placed himself under the jurisdiction of Propaganda Fide, the roman congregation responsible for missions throughout the world. With the help of some benefactors, he took over a ruined monastery at Reichenbach in the diocese of Regensburg. The local bishop, however, was implacably hostile. In 1887, therefore, on the invitation of the bishop of Augsburg, Amrhein moved to a property called Eming, which had been donated by a generous benefactress. Nearby was the pilgrimage shrine of Saint Ottilien, and Amrhein adopted this name for his foundation. It was a monastery and mission college combined. Lay brothers were trained in handicrafts and the special skills which a mission might need. A house was established nearby for the training of sisters. In 1887, at the request of Otto von Bismarck, the Holy See set up the Apostolic Prefecture of East Africa, and entrusted it to the Benedictines of Saint Ottilien.

The Trappists spread very rapidly after their resettlement in France.[52] The Lulworth community moved to Melleray in Britanny in 1817, taking some english and irish monks. In the following years more crossed the Channel to join the community, so that by the late 1820s many of the monks at Melleray, including the prior, the sub-prior, and the novice master, were english or irish,. After the Revolution of 1830,

267; 'Benediktiner entdecken die Mission wieder', *Mönche und Missionare*, ed. B. Doppelfeld (Münsterschwarzach 1988), 28–36.

[52] L. J. Lekai, *The Cistercians. Ideals and Reality* (Kent, Ohio 1977) 184–206; C. Friedlander, 'La filiation chez les cisterciens de la stricte observance de 1892 a 1926', *Cîteaux* 37 (1986) 242–277; 38 (1987) 59–87; J. Gell, 'The Return of the Cistercians to England', *Cîteaux* 38 (1987) 96–9; M. Cocheril, 'Les cisterciens', *Les ordres religieux* (as n. 28) 425–441.

when the government attempted to close Melleray, most of the
Anglo-Irish monks took ship for Ireland. In 1832, after some
searching, they found a site for a new monastery in county
Waterford. They called it Mount Melleray. In 1835–1836 a
site in Charnwood Forest, Leicestershire, was acquired with
help from Ambrose de Lisle Philips, a rich convert who was
anxious to see the Cistercians reestablished in England. Odilo
Woolfrey, an Englishman who had become a monk at Melleray
and then been sent as chaplain to the nuns at Stapehill, was
the first superior. A small contingent of brothers was sent from
Mount Melleray to join him. The new house was called Mount
Saint Bernard.

In 1814, Abbot Lestrange was returning to France from
America with his small following of Trappists. Their ship put in
at Halifax, Nova Scotia, and Father Vincent de Paul Merle was
sent ashore to buy provisions. He took too long and returned
to the quayside as the ship was sailing away. Was it an accident?
Stranded in Canada he worked for ten years as a missionary
among the Indians. In 1825 a small contingent of Trappists
from France joined him and they founded a monastery at
Petit Clairvaux in Nova Scotia. In 1900 they transferred to
Rhode Island in the United States, and in 1949 they moved
again to Spencer, Massachusetts. In 1848 two trappist houses
were founded in the United States—Gethsemani in Kentucky,
a daughter house of Melleray in France, and New Melleray in
Iowa, a daughter house of Mount Melleray in Ireland.

Considerable confusion existed, however, about the government of trappist monasteries. The papacy continued to
regard the president general of the Italian Cistercians as abbot
general of the whole order in all its branches. To preserve the
unity of the Cistercians, he was given the right to confirm
all abbatial elections, whatever the observance of the particular abbey. In 1869 the abbot general summoned a Chapter
General of the order, the first to be held since the French
Revolution. The trappist abbots, however, were not invited.

In fact the Trappists had largely ignored the abbot general
in Rome. A papal decree of 1834 allowed them to elect a vicar

general and hold chapters of abbots every year. It was assumed at Rome that they would amalgamate their observances. The split between those who followed the customs of Lestrange and those who were content with the reform of de Rancé, however, continued. Moreover in 1836, the belgian trappist houses formed a congregation of their own, while the italian house of Casamari, which had adopted the reform of de Rancé in its own way before the Revolution, felt no kinship with any of the existing trappist congregations.

In 1847, therefore, the Holy See resigned itself to allowing two trappist congregations, each with its vicar general: the 'New Reform', following Lestrange, and the 'Old Reform' following de Rancé. The desirability of uniting the Trappists under one set of observances and with a single vicar general was widely recognised, and several attempts at union were made in the late 1870s. Not until the last decade of the nineteenth century, however, was anything achieved.

The majority of the nineteenth-century Trappists were French-speaking. Apart from a small group in Italy, the other Cistercians, who came to be known as Cistercians of the Common Observance were, German-speaking. There is no doubt that nationalism got in the way of a reunion of the two main branches of the ancient Order. The houses which survived in the austrian empire were cramped by josephinist legislation. All ministers of religion were regarded as civil servants, carrying out government policy. Abbeys, whether benedictine or cistercian, were weighed down by the educational and parochial duties which alone guaranteed their survival. The austrian cistercian houses had no contact with the rest of the Order, and their monastic character was largely obscured.

The concordat of 1855 gave the church in Austria freedom. With the encouragement of the Holy See, Cardinal Friedrich Schwarzenberg, archbishop of Prague, undertook a visitation of cistercian monasteries in the empire and in 1859 summoned them to a provincial chapter. Statutes were passed which reestablished the daily chanting of the office, daily meditation and spiritual reading, fasting, and annual retreats. These statutes set a standard for minimum cistercian observance, but for very obscure reasons they never received the confirmation of Rome. At the ill-attended chapter general of 1869 the matter was shelved. It was agreed, however, that there should be a chapter general every ten years, at which an abbot general would be elected. He was to hold office until the next chapter general met and to be resident in Rome.

In the meantime the Common Observance had made modest advances outside Germany and Italy. In Belgium, which gained political independence from the Netherlands in 1830, some monks from the ancient cistercian house of Lieu-Saint Bernard near Antwerp acquired the buildings of a former monastery at Bornhem. The monastic life was formally resumed there in 1836. In 1840 the last surviving monk of Val-Dieu, some kilometres to the east of Liége, was able to buy the ruins of his former abbey and begin a restoration. In 1844 a cistercian community was established there. These two communities together formed a belgian vicariate of the Common Observance.

In 1855 abbé Barnouin, a devout french priest, acquired the remains of the cistercian abbey of Sénanque, near Avignon in Provence. At first the community which was founded there was affiliated to the Italian Congregation of Saint Bernard. In 1867 it was recognised as the independent Congregation of Sénanque. Three other abbeys were acquired, including Lérins off the provençal coast, the site of the most flourishing monastic community of ancient Gaul before the time of Saint Benedict. The Congregation of Sénanque was entirely contemplative but not as strict as La Trappe.

The revival of monasticism in the nineteenth century took place against a background of implacable hostility from liberal governments and of suppressions which gathered pace at the end of the century.[53] In Italy a law passed before Victor Emmanuel's entry into Rome was applied to the whole peninsula in 1873. Religious who left their communities were eligible

---

[53] DIP 8 (1973) 1764–1766, 1872–1882.

for a small pension. The rest could stay in their houses, or in those parts of them which had not been confiscated. Novitiates were abolished. When a house was down to six inmates the state could dispose of it. Works of art, libraries, and archives, were confiscated. The law could be applied to each house at the moment which seemed most convenient to the local authorities. Churches were not to be closed, but could continue to be served by some religious of the former community. The law did not apply to houses which were the headquarters of international Orders.

The italian legislators wished to proceed humanely. There was to be no sudden and harsh turning of religious into the streets. Religious susceptibilities were not to be offended by the secularisation of churches, and international complications, where foreign religious were concerned, had also to be avoided. Although very many religious houses were eventually closed, the proceedings were marked throughout by the dignity and restraint of all involved. Locally there was often a desire for compromise. In many places the expelled religious re-formed unobtrusively in smaller groups. Montecassino and the two abbeys at Subiaco were declared national monuments, with the monks as curators. At Saint Paul's in Rome, the monks argued successfully that theirs was not really a religious house. They were just canons attached to the basilica. Their case was strengthened by the abbot who made them, for the time being, the owners of the basilica and its buildings.[54]

In France the situation was different. The Third French Republic which came into being after the defeat of Napoleon III in 1871 was threatened by the monarchists who enjoyed the support of the church. The efforts of Pope Leo XIII to reconcile french Catholics to the new régime were largely unavailing. The Republicans saw in the church a major enemy, and governments followed aggressively anticlerical policies.

According to the concordat of 1801, which was still in force, only a very few named religious orders which engaged in

---

[54] Turbessi (as n. 14), 62.

teaching or charitable work were authorised. Applying the full rigour of the law to the 'unauthorised', therefore, presented no legal problems. The decrees of 1880, which ordered the enforcement of the law, resulted in the expulsion of about nine thousand men and a hundred thousand women.[55] Communities which had slipped through the net were affected by even more stringent measures passed under the premierships of Waldeck-Rousseau (1901) and Émile Combes (1902). The separation of church and state in 1905 ended the concordat and made even the 'authorised' religious Orders vulnerable.

There was considerable arbitrariness about the whole exercise. The Trappists were not touched. The worst scenes occurred at the Grande Chartreuse. Carthusians had returned to the cradle of the Order in 1816.[56] In 1903 the monks received news that their house was to be closed. They refused to move, and the army was sent in. The colonel in charge gave the necessary orders and then resigned his commission. Local people armed themselves with sticks, blockaded the roads, and lit bonfires on the hilltops. The troops arrived at the abbey at 3 o'clock in the morning and had to break down the doors with axes. The monks were arrested one by one as they were singing the night office.[57]

All monastic houses were 'unauthorised.' In 1880 some of the community of La Pierre-qui-Vire moved to Leopardstown near Dublin in Ireland, and from there to Buckfast in Devon, England.[58] The community of Solesmes was obliged to leave France in 1880. An early refuge was on the Isle of Wight in England. Here the monks presently began the building of the abbey of Quarr. Of Guéranger's foundations, Ligugé split into two groups, one settling at Santo Domingo de Silos near Burgos in Spain, the other at Chevetogne near Namur in Belgium. In spite of italian anticlerical legislation, Marseille was actually able to find refuge at Chiari, near Brescia.

---

[55] A. Dansette, *Religious History of Modern France*, 2 (London 1961) 42.
[56] G. Le Bras, 'Les chartreux', *Les ordres religieux* (as n. 28), 585.
[57] Dansette (as n. 54), 202.
[58] J. Stephan, *Buckfast Abbey* (Buckfast 1923) 57–62; Rees (as n. 21), 300.

Clervaux in Luxemburg was another community originating from Solesmes.[59] All these communities developed, in time, into independent religious houses.

In 1895 another group of exiled monks from Solesmes took over some buildings in Farnborough in the english county of Kent. Here the ex-empress Eugénie had built a church as a mausoleum for her husband, the former emperor Napoleon III, and for her son, the prince imperial. A suburban train ran from Farnborough to London, making easy a day's work in the library of the British Museum (now the British Library). The Farnborough community boasted some brilliant scholars who took full advantage of their opportunity. Fernand Michel Cabrol was a noted liturgical scholar, as was André Wilmart. Louis Gougaud interested himself in celtic christianity, and Henri Leclercq was an expert in christian antiquity. In 1907 these monk scholars published the first volume of the *Diction-naire d'archéologie chrétienne et de liturgie*, which is still, after nearly ninety years, an indispensible work of reference, and one of the most impressive monuments of benedictine scholarship. By 1922, when the monks of Solesmes were able to return to their french home, five volumes had been published and one was ready for the press.[60]

When the First World War broke out, french religious living abroad voluntarily returned to France to work as medical orderlies on the front or to serve in the ranks. When the war was over they refused to leave. Public opinion was now on their side, and they were allowed to stay.

[59] DIP 8 (1973) 1764.
[60] Ibid. 1764–1765.

Chapter 13
MONASTICISM IN THE LUTHERAN, ANGLICAN, PRESBYTERIAN, AND FREE CHURCHES

DURING THE LATER MIDDLE AGES immoral, corrupt, and greedy monks were a commonplace of satire. At the time of the Reformation, it seemed to many people that no further justification for the closure of religious houses was required. Martin Luther, however, laid little stress on monastic immorality.[1] Wicked monks, in his view, could safely be left to God's judgement. He himself had been a member of a religious house of the strictest kind. He had principled objections to monasticism iself.

It was fundamental to his teaching that Christ forgave sins without any deserts on the part of the sinner. The divine mercy was freely given and not dependent on works. Acts of penitence, long prayers, and ascetic practices could not of themselves draw down divine grace. Monastic rules had brought back the religion of the Pharisees, from which Jesus had freed his followers. Vows were contrary to the freedom which Christ had promised. All such vows, in Luther's view, should be temporary. This applied especially to vows of chastity.

---

[1] On Luther's views of monasticism, see E. Iserloh et al., *Reformation and Counter Reformation*, History of the Church, edd. Jedin and Nolan, 5 (London 1980) 85–87; Carl Volz, 'Martin Luther's Attitude towards Bernard of Clairvaux', *Studies in Medieval History presented to Jeremiah F. O'Sullivan* (Spencer 1971) 186–204; J. Halkenhäuser, *Kirche und Kommunität* (Paderborn 1978) 13–66.

Luther was opposed to the distinction, dear to late medieval canonists, between *precepta divina* and *consilia evangelica*. The former were the divine commands which all Christians must obey. The latter ('sell all you have and give to the poor') were counsels of perfection which only those with a special vocation need follow. There was no scriptural warrant for this distinction, Luther argued. All of the Gospel was for every Christian. If monks alone observed the whole Gospel, it might be concluded that they were more perfect than other Christians. Thus the Christian body would be divided against itself.

Although Luther was critical of monasticism as he knew it, he did not rule out a purged and reformed religious life. Chastity, if it could be maintained, had been approved by Saint Paul, because it set a person entirely free for the service of God (1 Cor 7:32–33). Ascetic practices such as fasting and watching perfected the inner life. Luther could envisage a small nucleus of Christians dedicated to prayer and study, living together under a special discipline and devoting their lives to preaching and the works of mercy.[2] In 1532 the Brethren of the Common Life at Herford in Westphalia, Germany, appealed to him. Although they had adopted the Reformation wholeheartedly and were noted for their piety and charity, the city council wanted to close their house. Luther championed their cause. 'If only', he wrote, 'a few such monasteries had existed, or exist today. I do not dare to hope for very many. If they were all of this kind the Church in this life would indeed be blessed.' Two years later Luther was still arguing the brethren's case, but Herford's city council dissolved the house in spite of his pleas.[3]

For most princes and nobles, the Reformation was an opportunity to seize monastic property. Luther's view that religious endowments should be used for the benefit of the christian people found an echo among a very few. Julius, duke of Brunswick and Lüneburg (1528–1589), was determined that the monasteries in his dominions would not be 'abolished or

---

[2] Halkenhäuser (as n. 1), 30, 61–63.
[3] Ibid. 65.

thrown all in a heap'.[4] A number of ducal ordinances regulated the life of the remaining religious communities. The Wolfenbüttel Ordinance of 1542 applied to houses which had been, in principle, dissolved, but where former religious had chosen to remain. The latin hours and Mass were maintained, with lutheran alterations. The main task of these institutions was now to be the education of youth. Anyone could leave for serious reasons and no novices were to be received. These communities, therefore, would eventually die out, but the schools which were founded in their buildings often survived.[5]

Some former monasteries, both for men and women, were reorganised on a more permanent basis. For each there was usually a separate ordinance, but the Wolfenbüttel Ordinance of 1569 laid down the general lines. Instead of the three vows, members made three promises. The promise of poverty bound him or her to live austerely, content with what was strictly necessary. The promise of obedience emphasised the importance of discipline in the house, under the direction of a superior. The promise of chastity involved the observation of celibacy. These promises bound members only as long as they were resident in the community. Everyone was free to leave or to marry, after obtaining permission from the prince. The main task of these lutheranised communities was to run schools for boys or girls.[6]

The ordinances for communities of women were particularly conservative. The women's task was seen as singing and praying for the welfare of the authorities, spiritual and temporal. They were to recite all the traditional offices in choir. An ordinance of 1655, renewing earlier ones, stated

> That virgins shall withdraw from the world and its distractions, and pass their lives outside matrimony in monasteries in a pure, chaste, and decent manner. That young virgins

---

[4] *Die Zisterzienser, Ordensleben zwischen Ideal und Wirklichkeit*, ed. K. Elm (Cologne 1981) 621–622.
[5] Halkenhäuser (as n. 1), 84–85.
[6] Ibid. 86–87.

and children be educated there in the fear and knowledge of God . . . to learn a quiet and withdrawn manner of living and labour as befits young women.[7]

It must be emphasised that the territory ruled by the duke of Brunswick was not extensive. The fate of the lutheranised monasteries in his dominions varied greatly. For the most part, the tasks they had been assigned were too heavy for their revenues, especially after the destruction of the Thirty Years' War. During the seventeenth century, moreover, the Lutheran *Landeskirchen*, under pressure from a Catholic revival backed by arms, insisted on uniformity. Church life was centred on the parishes. Religious houses could not be fitted into the scheme. It was a further difficulty that they were mere survivals from the past. There was no monastic theology by which their existence could be justified. Gradually discipline in the houses was relaxed and they were transformed into privileged old people's homes for the upper classes.[8]

The former cistercian abbey of Loccum was a noted exception to this general decline. It owed its survival to its outstanding abbot Gerard Wolter Molanus (1633–1722).[9] Already a noted theologian and teacher, he became abbot of the lutheran abbey in 1677. At a time when the two main denominations in Germany were at one another's throats, Molanus maintained ecumenical contacts with Catholics. His correspondents included Bishop Bossuet, the noted court preacher of Louis XIV.

Loccum had adopted lutheran teaching in 1593. Molanus studied the abbey's traditions and was determined to revitalise them in a lutheran context. His views are to be found in a sermon, the text of which is preserved in manuscript in the Loccum archives. In abolishing all monasticism he felt that the reformers had gone too far. It would have been wiser to

---

[7] Ibid. 99–104.
[8] Ibid. 87–90, 103–104.
[9] On Molanus, see Halkenhäuser (as n. 1), 92–96; *Die Zisterzienser* (as n. 4), 622–626. H. W. Weidemann *Gerard Wolter Molanus, Abt zu L'occum, eine Biographie,* 2 vols. (Göttingen 1925 and 1929) was not available to me.

observe the ancient maxim, *Tollatur abusus, maneat usus.*[10] 'Monachatus sine regula,'[11] observed Molanus, in his curious latinised German, 'is a *contradictio in adjecto.*[12] It can survive without a *regula*[13] as little as a *res publica civilis*[14] without laws or an army without articles of war.'[15] As far as the conventuals at Loccum were concerned, Molanus expected them to observe the Rule of Saint Benedict according to the statutes of the Cistercian Order and the particular statutes of Loccum. 'However this is to be understood *in quantum Regula S. Benedicti et statuta Cisterciensia*[16] are not superseded or changed by our evangelical religion.'[17]

In 1669 Molanus issued statutes for the school at Loccum. The curriculum was based on the Bible, Luther's Catechism, and the Church canticles. The boys' education ended with their Confirmation, which was seen as the culmination of their studies.[18] Statutes for the abbey's *hospitium* were made in 1677. Since 1593 it had been the custom to admit as guests three or four young unmarried graduate theologians. Molanus laid down that they were to pursue their studies, join in the singing of the hours, and help the pastoral work in the parishes which, since before the Reformation, had been committed to the abbey's care.[19] Loccum survives to this day as a lutheran religious community under an abbot, and remains a notable centre for theological research.

Further south, the dukes of Würtemberg took care to make the former monastic endowments available to their new *Landeskirche*. The monasteries were mostly turned into schools. The presiding cleric retained the title of abbot. Teachers and scholars were expected to take part in liturgical worship every

---

[10] 'Preserve the use, abolish the misuse'. Halkenhauser (as n. 1), 95 n. 60.

[11] 'Monasticism without a rule'.

[12] 'Contradiction in terms'.

[13] 'Rule'.

[14] 'Civil government'.

[15] Halkenhäuser (as n. 1), 93.

[16] 'In so far as the Rule of Saint Benedict and the cistercian statutes. . . .'

[17] Manuscript at Loccum, quotations in Halkenhäuser (as n. 1), 93–94.

[18] *Die Zisterzienser* (as n. 4), 624–625.

[19] Ibid., 626, 629.

morning. This consisted of two or three psalms, followed by
a seasonal antiphon. A chapter from the Old Testament was
read, after which the *Benedictus* or Athanasian creed was sung.
A prayer ended the service.[20]

The most famous of these south-german school-monas-
teries was Maulbronn, a cistercian abbey lutheranised in 1534.
Under Valentin Vannius, its first lutheran abbot (1558–1567)
and formerly a monk there, the school quickly achieved distinction. New statutes in 1556 marked it out as an academy
for the training of clergy. Among its former scholars were
the astronomer Johannes Kepler, and two prominent writers:
Friedrich Hölderlin and Hermann Hesse who was a student
there in 1891–1892. It is because of their use as a school that
all the medieval buildings of the former cistercian abbey have
been preserved.[21]

While traditional communities declined or disappeared in
protestant areas during the eighteenth century, monastic or
quasi-monastic communities came into being on the fringes
of the official churches—or altogether independently of them.
Gisbert Voetius (1588–1676) formed a group of 'awakened
Christians' in the Netherlands. The men separated from the
women, and all devoted their lives to prayer and an intense
study of the Bible.[22] They remained attached to the Reformed
Church of the Netherlands. Jean de Labadie (1610–74), however, left the church with his followers. On a remote farm in
western Frisia the Labadists developed a form of the common life. They could marry and live in separate houses, but
property and profits from their work were administered by the
community as a whole. In the last decades of the seventeenth
century their society was said to number between three and
four thousand members and in 1684 a party of them emigrated
to settle on Bohemia Farm in northern Maryland. By the

[20] Ibid. 256.
[21] Ibid. 256, 627.
[22] Halkenhäuser (as n. 1), 115–117.

middle of the eighteenth century, however, there were few Labadists left.[23]

An attractive local religious leader was Gerhard Tersteegen (1697–1769). A minor landowner, he had property at Otterbeck in what is now the Ruhr in western Germany. Gerhard had a conversion experience in 1724 and began to read the Bible, the *Imitation of Christ*, and other works of the *Devotio Moderna*. Eight others joined him in the 'pilgrim's hut' which he built on his estate. They earned their living by weaving. Much of their time was given to silent prayer and study. Their labours included visiting the sick and the troubled, preaching, and writing books. They had an impressive library of writers on mysticism, which included the standard Catholic authors. Gerhard himself was sympathetic to the traditions of medieval monasticism. He wrote poetry and translated mystical writings from Dutch into German.[24]

Gerhard Tersteegen's appeal lies in the intimate, almost domestic nature of his ministry. Count Nicholas Zinzendorf (1700–1760), on the other hand, was an aristocrat with cosmopolitan connections, who planned generously and had a genius for organisation.[25] He was partly inspired by Luther's vision of small christian communities within the Church devoted especially to prayer and charity. The time for these, he believed, had now come. From 1722 Moravian Brethren and other Protestants who did not belong to the official Lutheran Church, settled on his estate in Upper Lusatia, which he renamed *Herrenhut*, 'The Watch of the Lord'.

Here and subsequently elsewhere, model christian communities were established. Zinzendorf believed that interaction with others was essential for christian perfection. Although he never intended to leave the Lutheran Church, his organisation eventually developed into a world-wide communion and, as such, it falls outside the scope of this study. It

---

[23] Ibid. 118.

[24] Ibid. 120–122.

[25] For an introduction to the work of Zinzendorf and his followers, with ample bibliography, see 'Brüderunität/Brüdergemeinde', TRE 7 (Berlin 1981) 225–233. See also Halkenhäuser (as n. 1), 128–134.

is worth noting, however, that after 1736 the community at Herrenhut was divided into 'choirs'—groups of persons of the same sex and status—men, women, widows, widowers, bachelors, unmarried girls, craftsmen, even children. All the choirs assembled for the common services, in which they played an important part, but they also met separately for daily worship. After 1739 separate 'choir houses' were built at Herrenhut. The houses for the unmarried young became centres of intense spiritual activity. In accordance with Luther's teaching, members were not bound by vows but were free to leave and to marry.

Known as 'Moravians' in the English-speaking world, Herrenhut communities spread to America during Zinzendorf's lifetime. Other religious nonconformists from Germany had already taken the same route. In 1694 Johann Kelpius (1673–1708) emigrated to Pennsylvania with forty of his followers. They lived in log cabins awaiting the end of the world, and in anticipation of it they renounced marriage. Kelpius wrote a treatise on mystical prayer, and tried to unite all the protestant churches.[26]

The Christian Order of the Brothers of Ephrata was founded by Johann Christian Beissel (1690–1768), a refugee from religious persecution. With a group of followers he settled in Pennsylvania in 1720 and instituted a way of life based, as far as possible, on the example of the Desert Fathers. He eventually attracted three hundred men and women, all of whom took a vow of celibacy. Separate buildings at Ephrata housed the different sexes. Each member had his or her own room. All assembled together in a large building for common worship. From their printing works they produced books on mysticism and prayer. A daughter foundation, known as 'Snow Hill Nunnery' flourished throughout the nineteenth century. The Order has died out, but the buildings at Ephrata are well preserved and serve today as a museum.[27]

---

[26] Halkenhäuser (as n. 1), 139–140.
[27] Ibid. 140–143.

The most distinctive of the many quasi-monastic communities in America came from England. The so-called Shakers began in 1747 as a breakaway branch of the Quakers in Bolton, Lancashire. After some years leadership of the group was taken over by Ann Lee, a dynamic visionary from Liverpool. In 1774 she led a small group of her followers to America. They settled near Albany, in New York state, and, thanks to Ann's magnetic personality, the number of adherents grew rapidly.

Mother Ann, as she came to be known, died in 1784. Her followers proclaimed her to be the second incarnation of the Holy Spirit, revealing the female, as Jesus had revealed the male aspect of the Godhead. An able group of elders now framed rules for the new Church and regulated the ritual dance from which its members derived their popular name. The Church called itself the United Society of Believers in Christ's Second Coming and held that the millennial promises of the Bible must be believed quite literally. Mother Ann had regarded sexual intercourse as the source of all evil, and since the end of the world was thought to be close at hand, her followers believed that it was necessary for Christians to be gathered in celibate communities, holding, like the apostles, 'all things in common.' Before joining, converts had to confess all the sins of their past life to the elders. By the middle of the nineteenth century there were some six thousand Shakers in about twenty communities. They were strictly disciplined and noted for the plainness of their food and their unostentatious clothing. Many believed themselves to be in direct contact with spirits and some of the manifestations at their services were so bizarre that the public had to be kept away. In the later part of the century the elders clamped down on undisciplined enthusiasm. The Shakers' industriousness and mechanical ingenuity brought prosperity to their communities but also a decline in new recruits. Today the Church has all but died out, having made a conscious decision not to accept new members. In several places its buildings are lovingly preserved—a Roman Catholic Benedictine monastery inhabits one former Shaker village—and the well crafted and simple Shaker furniture is prized by collectors.[28]

In Germany the secularisation which followed the abolition of the Holy Roman Empire affected the lutheran as well as the catholic religious houses. Loccum barely escaped, the rest were abolished. Lutheran religious life, however, was revived by two remarkable theologians who were exact contemporaries—J. H. Wichern (1808–1891) and Wilhelm Lohe (1802–1872). Unencumbered by any survivals from the past, they could start afresh and provide the theological basis of which a monasticism in the spirit of the Reformation was greatly in need.

As a young prussian officer in the catholic Rhineland, Wichern had been impressed by the catholic religious Orders.[29] 'It is a frightful loss,' he wrote, 'that the Reformation threw out the Orders instead of reforming them in an evangelical spirit'.[30] In the ordinances which he composed for his foundations in 1858, Wichern insisted on absolute loyalty to the Lutheran Church and an avoidance of all sectarianism. Indeed, he insisted that his 'diaconic brotherhoods' existed for the service of the Church. He realised that charitable action is most effective when performed by groups, but that action must always be based on sound doctrine and anchored in contemplation and prayer. Members of the Brotherhoods therefore spent a part of every day in common worship and serious study of the Bible. The two houses founded by Wichern were 'Das Rauhe Haus' in Hamburg (1843/4) and 'Das evangelische Johannesstift' in Berlin (1858).

Wilhelm Lohe[31] was a lutheran pastor in Middle Franconia, a mixed area of Catholics and Protestants. Catholic nursing sisters were particularly active, and Lohe did not hesitate to

---

[28] S. J. Stein, *The Shaker Experience in America: A History of the United Society of Believers* (New Haven 1992); R. J. Handy, *A History of the Churches in the United States and Canada* (Oxford 1976) 221–222.
[29] Halkenhäuser (as n. 1), 145–152.
[30] Ibid. 146.
[31] Ibid. 156–166.

learn from them. In the last two decades of his life he concerned himself with the organisation of lutheran deaconesses who would devote themselves to caring for and visiting the sick and the troubled. A mother house for their training was founded in 1853. Lohe emphasised the importance of a common spirit based on the teaching of Saint Paul, and expected the deaconesses to make three promises: of chastity, obedience and poverty. In the spirit of Luther they took no vows and were free to marry if they left the institution. Lohe emphasised, however, that chastity had a special importance. While insisting on the dignity of marriage, he maintained that denigrating virginity had impoverished the Church. There would always be some who were called to give themselves absolutely to the Gospel. This 'inner freedom' to be open to the Lord's call must once again be available to all Christians.[32]

During the English Reformation, the monasteries were suppressed in two stages. The smaller ones went in 1536, the larger houses in 1538–1539.[33] Since King Henry VIII would countenance no changes in Catholic doctrine or practice other than a repudiation of the pope, the suppressions received no theological justification. The pretext was immorality and disorder in the houses, or sympathy with the pope, according to information supplied by Henry VIII's commisioners of enquiry, the notorious doctors Legh and Layton. The aristocracy and the rising merchant class were encouraged to enrich themselves from monastic property.

In former cathedral monasteries like Canterbury and Worcester, however, there were few changes of personnel. The prior and the monks were now renamed the dean and the prebendaries. For the rest, life continued much as before. This was true also of large monasteries which became cathedrals, like Peterborough and Gloucester. The liturgical *horarium* was maintained. Except that prayers for the pope were omitted

---

[32] Ibid. 162.
[33] For a detailed discussion of the suppression see M. D. Knowles, *The Religious Orders in England,* 3 (Cambridge 1959) 268–359.

from the Mass, the latin liturgy continued to be used unaltered until the far more radical religious changes which followed the death of Henry VIII in 1547.

Once the Church of England was more firmly established some clergy voiced moral doubts about Henry VIII's actions. Lancelot Andrews (1555–1626) was of the opinion that monasticism had been of great benefit to the Church and that Henry VIII had only wanted to abolish those houses which had fallen from their original purity.[34] George Herbert (1593–1632) advised the english country parson to consider carefully whether he was called to marry or to remain single. Herbert was in no doubt that 'virginity is a higher state than matrimony'. The unmarried country parson should spend his days in fasting and prayer, adding extra fasts and vigils to those enjoined by the Church.

> He often readeth the lives of the primitive monks, hermits, and virgins, and wondreth not so much at their patient suffering and cheerful dying under persecuting emperors . . . as at their daily temperance, abstinence, watchings, and constant prayers.[35]

Similarly, in his treatise on *Holy Living* (1650) Jeremy Taylor (1613–1667) gave a positive assessment of the state of virginity.

> Virgins must remember, that the virginity of the body is only excellent in order to the purity of the soul; who therefore must consider, that since they are in some measure in a condition like that of angels, it is their duty to spend much of their time in angelical employment; for in the same degree that virgins live more spiritually than other persons, in the same degree is their virginity a more excellent state.[36]

---

[34] A. M. Allchin, *The Silent Rebellion* (London 1958) 16–18.

[35] George Herbert, *A Priest to the Temple or, The Country Parson*, chapter 9; *The Works of George Herbert*, ed. F. E. Hutchinson (Oxford 1972) 237.

[36] Jeremy Taylor, *The Rule and Exercises of Holy Living and Dying*, Section 3: Of Chastity—Acts of Virginal Chastity, from *Taylor's holy Living and Dying* (London 1850) 64.

There was some support, then, for the idea that an individual, following the Fathers of the Desert, might embrace a life of celibacy and asceticism. Jeremy Taylor, at least, does not appear to have ruled out some kind of private vow. No one, however, dared to advocate religious houses. One receives the impression that, on this matter, theologians dared not say all they thought.

This necessary caution may explain some of the ambiguities in the career of Nicholas Ferrar (1592–1637).[37] He was born in 1592 to a wealthy merchant family of London. After some years at Cambridge he travelled extensively in Italy, France, and Spain. He was a gifted linguist, but although the spirituality of the Counter-Reformation made a certain impression upon him, we are told that 'he returned from his travels as he went, eminent for his obedience to his mother, the Church of England'.[38]

From 1619 Nicholas played an active part in the affairs of the Virginia Company, of which he was elected Deputy Treasurer in 1622. Two years later, after complex political intrigues, the company was dissolved by King James I. It was a serious blow to Nicholas and his family, who had all been deeply involved in its affairs. The crisis hastened Nicholas's resolve, made some years earlier, to retire from public life.[39]

The community which settled around him at Little Gidding in Huntingdonshire consisted, essentially, of his family. As long as she lived, his widowed mother exercised a certain authority. Other members of the community were Nicholas's elder brother John, who came with his second wife Bathsheba. Two of their children were born at Little Gidding. Equally important was John Collett, who had married Nicholas's elder sister Susannah. The Colletts had many children. Some were already adults at the time of the move to Little Gidding, but

---

[37] Allchin (as n. 34), 20–23; A. L. Maycock, *Nicholas Ferrar of Little Gidding* (London 1963).
[38] Izaak Walton, *The Life of Mr. George Herbert* (London 1895) 218.
[39] Maycock (as n. 37), 104.

seven were brought up there. Eventually some of the Collett grandchildren also came to live at Little Gidding. According to Izaak Walton, the community grew to number about thirty persons.[40] Nicholas had taken a vow of virginity, and so had the two older daughters of John Collett. The younger Collett girls eventually married and left, though it appears that Nicholas wished them to marry clergymen and was seriously displeased when one of them married outside clerical circles.[41] Least contented was Bathsheba, John Ferrar's second wife. Alone of those living at Little Gidding, she did not feel the appeal of the religious life and clearly resented Nicholas's ascendancy over her husband.

The manor had been bought by the family in 1624. Extensive repairs were needed to the manor house and the church, which had fallen out of use. It took several years to bring everything into order. Because there were small children in the community, a schoolhouse was built and three resident schoolmasters employed to educate the young Ferrars and Colletts. The school was thrown open to local children. The family undertook extensive charities in the area. Because of the community's heterogeneous nature and the variety of its activities, several years passed before a way of life suitable to it took shape.

It is unlikely that there was ever a formal rule. Nicholas Ferrar always indignantly denied that the community was a 'nunnery', as its many puritan critics claimed. One may ask, however, whether he would have gone further had he dared? For our knowledge of the way of life at Little Gidding we depend on Nicholas's own letters, and on various descriptions, some made retrospectively a generation after his death. These sources are inconsistent in some details, although the main lines can be reconstructed.[42]

---

[40] Izaak Walton (as n. 38), 219.
[41] Maycock (as n. 37), 285–286.
[42] Ibid. 197–226. On the sources, see ibid. 313–314. See also Walton (as n. 38), 219–220.

The whole family attended church three times daily—for Matins, the Litany, and Evensong. In the Great Chamber of the house, a short office lasting fifteen minutes was recited at every hour of the day from six in the morning to eight in the evening. It consisted of a hymn, a psalm, and a reading from the Gospels. For the maintenance of this round of prayer the family was divided into groups of three or four, each taking part in turns. Psalms were also recited every hour of the night from nine in the evening until one in the morning, at which time it was usual for Nicholas himself to rise and take over. These night watches were kept in two oratories, one for men and the other for women. Participation was voluntary and things were so arranged that no one was involved more than once a week. Thus the whole psalter was recited at Little Gidding each day. Nicholas, who was in deacon's orders, presided over the offices in church on weekdays. The parson, who also held the neighbouring benefice of Steeple Gidding, came over on Sundays to preach, and, once a month, to celebrate the Eucharist.

Certain monastic practices were adopted. After 1631 the women dressed alike. Meals were taken in silence and accompanied by reading. The most exacting labour for the adults was the making of Bible concordances. School took up much of the children's time. Nicholas took time in the morning to interview anyone from the neighbourhood who required his help. 'The whole land was better for their sanctity', wrote an admirer of the family a generation later.[43]

It was not a view shared by all in Nicholas Ferrar's time. The household at Little Gidding was bitterly criticised as a crypto-papist nunnery. Nicholas did not live to see the Civil War which tore England apart in the years 1642–1648. Some years after his death the family had to abandon the house, and in 1646 it was sacked and destroyed. Only the little church survives.

---

[43] Quoted Allchin (as n. 34), 22.

How the community would have developed had England remained peaceful is impossible to say, nor can we be sure what Nicholas would have done if puritan hostility had not imposed caution. Little Gidding owed almost nothing to Saint Benedict. The greatest influence came from early christian practice and there never was a religious community quite like this one. It united men and women, old and young, the celibate and the married. They all shared the same vision, but participation in the work and worship of the house varied according to the circumstances of each member. Here Nicholas anticipated the aims of many religious communities of the present time.

In the eighteenth century the most eloquent plea for a revival of monastic life in the Church of England was made by William Law in his *Serious Call to a Devout and Holy Life* (1728). He contrasted the lives of fashionable people in his day with the life of a woman who spent the minimum of her fortune upon herself and devoted all she could spare to help the poor and the unfortunate.[44] It would be possible to go even further than this, he continued.

> Ever since the beginning of Christianity there have been two orders, or ranks of people, amongst good Christians. The one that feared and served God in the common offices and business of a secular worldly life. The other, renouncing the common business, and common enjoyments of life, as riches, marriage, honours, and pleasures, devoted themselves to voluntary poverty, virginity, devotion, and retirement, that by this means they might live wholly unto God, in the daily exercise of a Divine and heavenly life.[45]

Law went on to quote the evidence of Eusebius in the fourth century, and continued:

> If, therefore, persons of either sex . . . should unite themselves into little societies, professing voluntary poverty,

---

[44] William Law, *A Serious Call to a Devout and Holy Life*, Chapter 8 (London 1955) 75–84.
[45] Ibid. 95.

virginity, retirement, and devotion, living upon bare necessities, that some might be relieved by their charities, and all be
blessed with their prayers, and benefited by their example . . .
such persons would be so far from being chargeable with any
superstition, or blind devotion, that they might be justly said
to restore that piety which was the boast and glory of the
Church, when its greatest saints were alive.[46]

William Law here expressed the longing, which had also
been felt by many Anglicans during the seventeenth century,
for the contemplative life. During the nineteenth century
anglican religious societies were at last able to come into being,
but would-be monks and nuns had to struggle, not only against
their numerous Protestant-minded opponents, but also against
misunderstandings among their friends, especially those few
bishops who felt able to support them. Only a small number
of bishops were prepared to countenance religious societies
whose members bound themselves to celibacy and a common
discipline and who made more or less explicit commitments
to those ends. Such societies, however, had to justify their
existence to the rest of the Church by works of charity or by
active participation in pastoral work. Until the very end of
the nineteenth century no anglican bishop would have dared
to approve a contemplative community. The situation is well
illustrated by a dramatic incident in the history of the american
order of the Holy Cross. The very bishop who braved the
disapproval of his colleagues by supporting its early struggles
for survival some years later repudiated it when it began to
develop in a contemplative direction.[47]

The very idea of a religious order had to be accepted first.
The struggle to achieve this took up most of the second half
of the nineteenth century. In England the beginnings came
in the 1840s. Marion Hughes, the first Anglican to become a
nun, took her vows in 1841. She lived her dedicated life alone.

---

[46] Ibid. 96.
[47] A. D. McCoy OHC, *Holy Cross: A Century of Anglican Monasticism* (Wilton,
CT 1987) 39–43, 91–92.

The first religious community in the Church of England was founded in 1845 at Park Villas West, near Regent's Park in London. Lydia Sellon started another community in the slums of Devonport in 1848. At Wantage a community dedicated to Saint Mary the Virgin had its modest beginnings in the same year. A society of women formed to help prostitutes began its work at Clewer in Oxfordshire in 1849.[48]

Closely involved with the arduous beginnings of anglican religious life was Edward Pusey (1800–1882), Regius Professor of Hebrew at the University of Oxford, who succeeded as unofficial leader of the tractarian or catholic movement after John Henry Newman left the Church of England. Marion Hughes made her vows privately in his presence. Pusey was also closely associated with the community at Park Villas. It was planned as a memorial to Robert Southey, the Poet Laureate who had died in 1843 and who had frequently regretted the fact that the Church of England had no Sisters of Mercy. A committee to bring an anglican community into being was formed. Its eminent members were all men. Pusey drew up the rules, borrowed, in part, from the Visitation Order of Saint Francis de Sales. Two religious moved into Park Villas in the spring of 1845. More joined later in the year.

In January 1848, Henry Phillpotts, bishop of Exeter, published a newspaper article in which he described the spiritual and material degradation in the slums of Devonport. In this thickly populated area there were no churches and no public money was available to check disease and ignorance. Help came from an unexpected quarter when Lydia Sellon, a young woman of twenty-seven, put herself at the bishop's disposal.

Priscilla Lydia Sellon was the daughter of a retired naval commander. After the death of her mother, her father had married a second time, and she owed her gift with children to the experience of looking after her eleven half-brothers

---

[48] On anglican religious orders, see Peter F. Anson, *The Call of the Cloister* (London 1955); A. M. Allchin, *The Silent Rebellion* (as n. 34); T. J. William's *Priscilla Lydia Sellon* (London 1965).

and sisters. Later on she won the loyalty of the slum boys at Devonport because 'she spoke to them as if they were her own little brothers'.[49]

In her twenties she had become interested in the catholic movement in the Church of England. She visited the community at Park Villas and there met Dr Pusey. It was Pusey who wrote a letter of introduction for her to a clergyman at Devonport, who was to become one of her loyal supporters. As for the bishop of Exeter, it is a measure of his desperation that he accepted help from this quite unknown and inexperienced young woman. No other offer had been made. It was an advantage that he was the only bishop at that time sympathetic to the catholic movement within the English Church.

Lydia Sellon began by taking over an unsuccessful school for girls. Soon she had persuaded their brothers to come to school as well. A relentless but just disciplinarian, she fearlessly faced down rebellions. She took care to visit the children's parents. Most were unbaptised and quite ignorant of religion. Gradually volunteers joined her. Pusey advised the formation of a sisterhood, and in August 1848 Bishop Phillpotts gave his consent and assumed the office of visitor. When, in 1849, a cholera epidemic broke out in Devonport Lydia and the sisters won universal praise for the way they cared for the victims.

In 1852 Bishop Phillpotts listed the institutions founded and run by 'The Church of England Sisterhood of Mercy of Devonport and Plymouth':

An orphan's home for 27 girls.
A college for sailor boys, with 27 pupils.
A House of Peace, where 12 girls were trained for domestic work.
A Home for Old Sailors, housing three men and one couple.
An Industrial School, where 120 young women were trained to be self-supporting.
Seven model lodging houses for poor families, with schools for the children.

---

[49] Williams (as n. 48), 15.

Five ragged schools attended by children living at home.

Night schools for boys and girls working in the docks.

Evening schools for adults.

Homes for very young destitute children.

Soup kitchens where 80–100 persons were fed on soup and bread. Those who attended church got a pudding on Sundays.[50]

Lydia had no time for the dull misery associated with much victorian religion. At the college for sailor boys the inmates danced to a fiddle at recreation time, and in the evening a sister told bedtime stories. Once a month Lydia organised a tea for local children. This function was really intended for their mothers. The sisters played with the children whilst the mothers, unencumbered for the time being, enjoyed a delicious meal.[51]

Bishop Phillpotts blessed two new sisters at a ceremony in October 1848.[52] In the early 1850s the community was still fairly small—five or six professed sisters, eight novices, and a number of 'ladies in residence', including one of Lydia's half-sisters.[53] All were free to leave and, if they had brought any property with them, it, or its value, was returned. Regular leave was also given to visit parents. In 1851 the society was large enough to justify Lydia into composing a more formal rule. She called it 'The Seven Great Rules'. The society was divided into three orders: the Sisters of Mercy of the Holy Communion who were chiefly engaged in active work, the contemplative Sisters of the Sacred Heart, and the Sisters of Charity who were associates, many of them married, and gave a portion of their time to helping with the charitable work.[54]

In 1850 Lydia moved her headquarters to a new and elaborate building at Abbeymere on the outskirts of Plymouth. After 1851 she called herself abbess, and Pusey planned that

---

[50] Williams (as n. 48), 102, Anson (as n. 48), 263.

[51] Williams (as n. 48), 70–71.

[52] Ibid. 23.

[53] Ibid. 66.

[54] Ibid. 74–75.

she should become the mother superior of all anglican communities of women.[55] The Crimean War was a turning point in the development of her sisterhood. A group of anglican sisters drawn partly from Devonport and partly from the Park Villas community accompanied Florence Nightingale to Scutari. These anglican religious were led by Sister Emma, who had been superior at Park Villas. She was made a member of the Devonport community before she left, and while she was away Lydia set up her headquarters in London and gradually absorbed the Park Villas community into her own.

Throughout her life Lydia Sellon was involved in controversy. The very idea of an anglican sisterhood offended those in the 'protestant' wing of the Church of England and the story of the pamphlet and newspaper war conducted against her is a dismal one. In 1852 Bishop Phillpotts, until then her doughty champion, thought it politic to withdraw his public support, though he continued to praise her in private. Even more distressing were criticisms and departures within her own sisterhood. Some former members of the Park Villas community resented her authority and joined with malcontents from her own community who thought her increasing emphasis on monastic discipline a departure from the early days at Devonport. Even clergy in the catholic wing of the Church regarded her with suspicion.

It is not easy to assess her character. She was either uncritically loved or hated. She was in bad health for most of her life. In Devonport and Plymouth she was wheeled from one of her institutions to another in a chair. She could not stand or even sit upright for long, and reclined on a mattress even in church.[56] She did not believe much in consultation. She made all the decisions and expected unquestioning obedience. On the other hand, she had a unique understanding of the social problems of victorian England. Her work in the slums of Devonport and Plymouth, and later in London, went far

---

[55] Ibid. 90.
[56] Ibid. 67.

beyond fashionable charity. She instructed her sisters that the poor were not to be 'talked down to' but should always be treated with respect. The best was to be taken for granted in them, failings were to be met with indulgence, and sisters must not shrink from dirt.[57] The Church of England's remarkable record of social concern owes much to her.

In her last years her society was overstretched and most of its charitable institutions had either to be closed or handed over to others. It was decided to concentrate on the care of orphans and convalescent patients. In 1864 Lydia agreed to send missionary sisters to open a school in Hawaii, and, although almost incapacitated by a stroke, travelled there to supervise the early stages. At the end of her life she lived mostly at Ascot, where a priory of contemplative nuns was opened in 1863. She died there in 1876.

The community at Wantage began modestly.[58] This Berkshire parish was much in need of regeneration when William Butler, a young clergyman of tractarian views, took it over in 1847. It seemed to him that some devoted sisters could help with parish visiting and running schools, and he asked the advice of his friend Henry Manning, then archdeacon of Chichester. Manning recommended two ladies—Elizabeth Lockhart and Mary Reid. In 1848 they came to Wantage and rented two cottages and began to teach the children. A young woman called Harriet Day joined as a postulant, and there were two servants who, it was hoped, would eventually join the community also. From the first the community recited the Office regularly from english translations of the medieval Sarum rite, as well as attending the parish church for Matins and Evensong.

Within two years Elizabeth Lockhart and Mary Reid had left the Church of England, followed a short time later by Archdeacon Manning himself. Harriet Day, who had only two years experience as a religious behind her, succeeded as supe-

---

[57] Ibid. 69–70.
[58] Allchin (as n. 34), 85–95; Anson (as n. 48), 242–259.

rior. Without the guidance of William Butler the venture might have failed. He insisted on absolute loyalty to the Church of England. He had little sympathy for ritualism; the services of the community and the decorations of the chapel remained simple. Within this anglican framework Butler was able to accommodate his wide knowledge of continental religious houses and their rules, and adapt them to the rule he himself composed. The other mainstay of Wantage was Samuel Wilberforce, bishop of Oxford. He insisted that there should be no vows, that the dress worn by the religious should not be 'monastic', and that the influence of Dr Pusey should be completely excluded. On these conditions, which Butler loyally accepted, the bishop wholeheartedly supported this, and the other young anglican communities in his diocese.

The community, whose official title is the Community of Saint Mary the Virgin, began to expand in the last years of the nineteenth century. An establishment for training young women as teachers opened at Wantage in 1864. A girls' boarding school was begun in 1873. A new school in Plymouth was founded in 1907, and in 1925 a hostel for women students at Oxford. Wantage itself became a centre for liturgical studies. The Sarum books were translated from Latin into English, and the text adapted to the original plainchant.

The Community of Saint John the Baptist at Clewer began a year after Wantage.[59] The Reverend Thomas Carter, rector of Clewer, was anxious to reclaim the prostitutes and abandoned women who inhabited a part of his parish. One of his parishioners began the work by taking some of them into her own home. In 1851 she was forced to retire because of ill health, and her work was taken over by Mrs Harriet Monsell, widow of a recently deceased clergyman.

Other volunteers joined in the work. Both Carter and Mrs Monsell were influenced by the Tractarians, and they decided to form the little group of volunteers into a sisterhood. 'We did not found a sisterhood and look for work for it,'

---

[59] Allchin (as n. 34), 69–84; Anson (as n. 48), 304–317.

Carter was later to write. 'But the work came first and the sisterhood followed.'[60] Pusey, who was Mrs Monsell's director, was asked for advice. Carter also approached Bishop Samuel Wilberforce.

As at Wantage, the bishop made a number of demands. The influence of Pusey was to be eliminated. The sisters were not to take vows. Both Carter and Mrs Monsell had doubts about these conditions, but their loyalty to the Church of England was absolute. The bishop, for his part, gave positive encouragement to the young community and helped it through the early stages. From the beginning its mission was directed towards the underprivileged. In the 1860s houses were established in the poorer parts of London. In 1870 the community expanded to America, and in 1881 to India.

Mother Harriet was noted for her common sense and her useful connections. She was related to Archibald Tait (1811–1882), successively bishop of London and archbishop of Canterbury. Tait was no friend of Tractarians in general, but he made an exception of Mother Harriet. Queen Victoria, another critic of the catholic movement in the Church of England, was won over, and paid a private visit to Clewer in 1864.

Admired by some Anglicans, the burgeoning religious communities were detested by others. The question of anglican sisterhoods first came before the Convocation of Canterbury in 1861.[61] No action was taken, but guided by Bishops Wilberforce and Tait, the other bishops were moderately supportive, although there was strong opposition to religious vows. In 1875 Convocation drew up a report on sisterhoods and brotherhoods in the Church. It was, on the whole favourable, and estimated that there were about seven hundred sisters in the Church of England. Religious communities finally received the approval of Convocation in 1891. By then opposition to vows was weakening. William Stubbs (1825–1901), the

---

[60] Allchin (as n. 34), 71.
[61] On anglican religious communities and Convocation, see Allchin (as n. 34), 157–180.

medievalist bishop of Oxford, and Edward King (1829–1910), the very anglo-catholic bishop of Lincoln, both defended them and they were therefore tacitly allowed.

Considerable progress had been made in the Church of England with religious communities for women before anything was organised for men. During the 1840s life in anglo-catholic clergy houses was sometimes very strict. The priests of Saint Barnabas in Pimlico, a deprived area of London, for instance, lived a quasi-monastic life in common.[62]

The Church of England's oldest successful community for men was founded by Richard Meux Benson (1824–1915).[63] As a student at Oxford he came under the influence of Pusey. His wide reading, especially of the Fathers, gave him a feeling for the religious life when he was quite young. In 1843–1844 he visited Rome, made friends with some Jesuits, and extended his travels to Monte Cassino. He took his degree at Oxford in 1848, and two years later was presented to the living of Cowley in Oxfordshire. He quickly made his reputation as a conductor of retreats, which were then almost unknown in the Church of England. He became a highly valued spiritual guide, but it was not until after the death of his Protestant-minded mother in 1859 that he dared to consider the foundation of a religious community. He first conceived the idea of a missionary society in India. Bishop Wilberforce, however, begged him to stay in England and to continue to care for the poor of Oxfordshire.

In August 1865, when Charles Grafton, an american episcopalian clergyman, joined Benson in a little house behind Cowley's iron church, the Society of Saint John the Evangelist came into being. A little later Oliver Prescott, another American, joined them. Each of the three took vows of celibacy, poverty, and obedience in the presence of the other two. In this case Bishop Wilberforce seems to have accepted a *fait accompli*, since Benson's loyalty to the Church of England

---

[62] Allchin (as n. 34), 186–187.
[63] Allchin (as n. 34), 183–204; Anson (as n.48), 72–86.

was known to be rock-like. He was no ritualist and had no difficulty about using *The Book of Common Prayer*, the approved service book of the Church. There was nothing sensual about the iron church at Cowley or the community's cramped house chapel.

Benson saw the work of his society as largely intellectual. He wanted to combat the growing religious scepticism of the middle classes. A base in London was therefore very desirable, and the Society's first house there was acquired in 1898. Long before this the Society had spread outside England—in 1870 Benson himself went to the United States to start a community there. In 1874 a house was founded in India, and in 1883 another in South Africa.

The society's apostolate was partly exercised through the written word, but the Cowley Fathers, as they were known, also conducted missions and retreats. Benson's profound understanding of the religious life gave the society a quality of its own. He insisted that the effectiveness of the society's work depended on the sanctification of its members. For him theology was never an abstract study, but a knowledge of the living God.

The Community of the Resurrection[64] was founded by Charles Gore (1853–1932) in 1892. At the time he was Principal Librarian of Pusey House, an institution at Oxford founded to preserve the library and keep alive the spirit of the great leader of the Oxford Movement. Life at Pusey House was quasi-monastic. The librarians were committed to celibacy and a regular round of prayer in the chapel. The foundation of a formal religious community was under discussion from 1890. Two years later six priests, including Gore, formed themselves into the Community of the Resurrection. Theirs was to be a missionary society and members were to devote their spare time to the study of theology. Gore was the first superior. In 1893 the community moved to Radley, a village five miles from Oxford, where Gore had recently been appointed vicar.

---

[64] Allchin (as n. 34), 240–243; Anson (as n. 48), 122–139. There is also a full-scale history of the community: A. Wilkinson, *The Community of the Resurrection—A Centenary History* (London 1992).

The most eminent anglican theologian of his time, Gore was too brilliant and too sophisticated to settle down for long in a country parish. In 1894 he was appointed a prebendary of Westminster Abbey. Some of the community went with him, and there was a little chapel of the Society in the abbey cloisters. The rest of the community remained at Radley. It is likely that Gore rather lost interest in the community during his London years, for he resigned from it in 1902, on becoming bishop of Worcester.

As a society of missionaries, the Community of the Resurrection had to differentiate itself from the Cowley Fathers. Although he had not been a satisfactory superior, Gore decisively influenced the community's spirit. He insisted upon a democratic constitution. He wished the superior to be called the 'senior' and to be elected for only three years. Decisions were made by the society collectively after free discussion. Above all, the Community of the Resurrection inherited Gore's Christian Socialism. This was the motive for the move, in 1897, to Mirfield, an industrial town in the North of England. The religious life was to be lived in future amidst chimneys and smoke, and pastoral methods were adapted accordingly. The occasional open-air services in Mirfield Quarry differed little from revivalist meetings. The Fathers did not hesitate to involve themselves in politics. Many were active members of the British Labour Party. The tradition was maintained when foundations were made abroad. In our own time Trevor Huddlestone, a Mirfield Father, acquired world renown as one of the most notable opponents of apartheid in South Africa.

By the end of the nineteenth century a large number of anglican religious communities had come into being. As in the case of Little Gidding, one is forced to ask, how far would the founders have gone had they been free? One wing of the Church remained resolutely opposed. Even sympathetic bishops like Samuel Wilberforce inhibited any developments which might cause controversy. Those like Lydia Sellon and Richard Benson, who had a real understanding of the contemplative life, allowed themselves to be held back. For some of their followers, however, the frustrations were intolerable. Since it was inevitable that much of the spirituality which sustained the religious life came from the Continent, conversions to Rome were understandable. Their effect was naturally unsettling, and they seemed to confirm the fears of evangelicals. The establishment of purely contemplative communities within the Church of England was thus bound to be hazardous. The difficult personalities of those who first made the attempt did not help.

As a young clergyman in Plymouth, Joseph Leycester Lyne (1837–1908)[65] came to know Lydia Sellon and shared with her his dream of restoring the full monastic life in England. With her encouragement he declared himself a monk and publicly donned a monastic habit which she had designed. He became curate of a mission church in London, where his fiery preaching and monastic appearance drew large crowds. A visit to Belmont Priory introduced him to the Rule of Saint Benedict. He now declared himself a Benedictine, calling himself, with characteristic inconsistency, Brother Ignatius after the founder of the Jesuits. In 1863 he resigned his curacy and with a handful of followers set out to found a benedictine monastery.

Lyne loved drama and had a flair for publicity. A pamphlet he wrote about the revival of benedictine life in England was widely circulated and earned him an invitation to install his community in part of a large rectory in Norfolk. Here Lyne and two companions began to live out the Rule of Saint Benedict as they understood it, devoting their spare time to teaching in the village school. Lyne's sermons drew the usual crowds, but there was also strong local opposition, sometimes leading to violence. In the end the community was forced to leave. For some years it was on the move. In 1869, with the help of a benefactor, it acquired land at Llanthony in the Black Mountains of South Wales.

Life at Llanthony was eclectic. To the Rule of Saint Benedict were added any other details which caught Lyne's fancy.

---

[65] Anson (as n. 48), 51–72.

He was often away, leaving his community without guidance while he addressed packed meetings all over Britain, the United States, and Canada. He was certainly a celebrity. His causes included Welsh Nationalism, British Israel, and the Flat Earth. Above all he conducted a fierce war against religious scepticism and the higher criticism of the Bible. He was indignant when Charles Gore supported some aspects of modern scriptural scholarship. On one occasion in 1893, when Gore was addressing a meeting, Lyne rose repeatedly and shouted, 'In the name of Jesus, he has no right to speak!' 'Funny old thing', was Gore's comment.[66] In 1898 Lyne left the Church of England altogether. A 'British Catholic Church' was planned but came to nothing. Llanthony was abandoned after his death in 1908.

Benjamin Carlyle (1874–1955) became interested in Anglo-Catholicism and the monastic life while a medical student at Saint Bartholomew's Hospital in London.[67] He frequented Roman Catholic monasteries, particularly Buckfast in Devon, and for a time thought of becoming a Roman Catholic himself. In 1896 he rented a small house in a deprived part of the London East End and, with one companion, began to live as a Benedictine, calling himself Brother Aelred.

At the end of the nineteenth century many more anglican bishops were favourable to monasticism. Brother Aelred had the support of the archbishop of Canterbury. Finding a suitable home for the growing community proved more difficult. In 1901, after various moves, the community settled at Painsthorpe Hall near York. The monks had now found a generous patron in Lord Halifax, the unofficial lay leader of the Anglo-Catholics. At Painsthorpe Aelred was elected as abbot, with the approval of the archbishop of York. With the archbishop's permission he travelled to the United States to

---

[66] Wilkinson (as n. 63), 28.
[67] Anson (as n. 48), 164–181. There is a biography of Carlyle by Peter Anson, *Abbot Extraordinary—A Memoir of Aelred Carlyle* (London 1958). See also P. Anson, 'The "Caldey Conversions" of 1913', *Church Quarterly Review* 164 (1963) 322–331.

be ordained a priest. This meant that, as far as the Church of England was concerned, he was a 'priest in colonial orders' with permission to minister only to his own community.

In 1906 the community acquired the island of Caldey off the southern coast of Wales. The island was 'extra-diocesan'. The anglican bishop of Saint David's had no jurisdiction there. Dom Aelred regarded himself, in effect, as bishop as well as abbot. Prudence was never a part of his character, nor, it must be added, had he Richard Benson's profound understanding of the essentials of the religious life. Buckfast Abbey was Dom Aelred's ideal and he set about creating an anglican model of it on Caldey Island. All the offices and Mass were celebrated in Latin from books brought in from the Continent. Eucharistic devotions were borrowed wholesale from Roman Catholicism and included Reservation, Benediction, and Exposition of the Blessed Sacrament. All these were practices of which the anglican bishops, even the most anglo-catholic ones, disapproved.

There were persistent rumours that the Caldey monks were 'going over to Rome'. Abbot Aelred felt that his position in the Church of England should be regularised. In 1911 he appealed to the archbishop of Canterbury, who referred him to Charles Gore, now bishop of Oxford. It was suggested that Gore might become visitor of the Caldey community. He was a prominent Anglo-Catholic, an eminent theologian, and himself the founder of a religious community.

Gore made a number of conditions: Caldey Island should be the property of the Church of England and not (as it was then) the private property of an unaccountable trust; priests of the community should make the usual oath of obedience to the local bishop, and in future use *The Book of Common Prayer* for the Communion Service, and for Morning and Evening Prayer; the feasts of the Assumption and the Immaculate Conception of the Blessed Virgin should not be celebrated; Exposition and Benediction of the Blessed Sacrament should be abandoned.[68]

---

[68] Anson, 'The "Caldey Conversions"' (as above), 323–329.

The abbot felt these conditions to be intolerable. He and twenty-two of his monks left the Church of England and made a collective submission to Rome. In the opinion of Lord Halifax and others, Bishop Gore's rigidity had driven them to take this extreme step.[69] More recently it has been pointed out that Gore's conditions were not unreasonable, and that, as a bishop of the Church of England, he could hardly have taken a different stance.[70]

One member of the Caldey community remained faithful to the Church of England. With the support of Lord Halifax a home was found for the handful who still wanted to live as Benedictines within the Anglican Communion.[71] In 1914, with the encouragement of the bishop of Worcester, they settled at Pershore, under the shadow of an ancient medieval abbey church. The First World War brought more strains, but the small community began to flourish under Denys Prideaux, its second abbot. Abbot Denys was a noted scholar and attracted learned recruits. The community retained its latin liturgy and most of its distinctive devotions. In 1926 it moved to more spacious premises at Nashdom, near London. Here it flourished, under the patronage of successive anglo-catholic bishops of London. In 1987 the monks moved to Elmore in Berkshire.

The first anglican monastery for benedictine sisters was at West Malling in Kent, amid extensive remains of a nuns' abbey founded by Saint Gundulf, William the Conqueror's bishop of Rochester (1077–1108). In 1893 the buildings were handed over to a community of women who had originally adopted the Benedictine Rule under the influence of Joseph Leycester Lyne, but who, finding his erratic rule intolerable, had broken with him. At the beginning of the twentieth century they had begun to conform their customs to those of benedictine sisters on the continent, but the attraction of Rome grew with the adoption of its norms. It was a condition of the trust

---

[69] Anson (as n. 48), 184.
[70] Anson, 'The "Caldey Conversions"', (as n. 66).
[71] Anson (as n. 48), 183–192.

which owned the buildings that any community using them should belong to the Church of England. In 1911, therefore, the sisters felt obliged to move while they considered their allegiance. The buildings were vacant until 1916 when another group of anglican nuns moved into West Malling. Originally engaged in charitable work in a London suburb, they had felt drawn to a more contemplative life. In the 1960s the erection of an impressive but very simple conventual church brought the abbey a brief moment of fame in the architectural world, but for the rest, the nuns of West Malling have followed the same outwardly uneventful life of prayer and recollection characteristic of all benedictine houses for women .[72]

Many of the new anglican institutes spread to the United States. As we have seen, two Americans joined Richard Benson in the very early days of the Society of Saint John the Evangelist. In 1870 Benson himself crossed the Atlantic with a companion to found a community in Boston, Massachusetts.[73] In 1871 the recently founded Boston Children's Hospital was in difficulties. A group of Episcopalians appealed for help to the Sisters of Saint Margaret in East Grinstead,[74] a society of nursing sisters which had been founded by John Mason Neale in 1855. Mother Alice, the superior, came out to Boston with Sister Theresa, one of her novices. After a short stay she returned, leaving Sister Theresa in charge. The young woman was an immediate success. After eighteen months she travelled to East Grinstead to be professed, and then returned to Boston with two more sisters. These three formed the nucleus of a community which eventually flourished and established branches in other cities of the United States.

The Episcopal Church in the United States had its own Catholic traditions. After the American Revolution bishops of the Church of England refused to consecrate bishops for the american church and the former colonists turned to the

---

[72] Anson (as n. 48), 418–420, 424–428, 462–466.
[73] Anson (as n. 48), 81, 531.
[74] *Doing the Impossible—A Short Historical Sketch of Saint Margaret's Convent, East Grinstead* (East Grinstead: privately printed 1984) 38–39.

Scottish Episcopal Church, whose bishops in 1784 consecrated Samuel Seabury as the first american bishop. The scottish bishops were 'non-Jurors', whose predecessors had refused to recognise the 'Glorious Revolution' of 1688 which had displaced the Catholic king James II with the Protestant William of Orange. Theirs was not, therefore, an established Church, and through them there were links with the anglican 'high church' of the seventeenth century. In the new american republic, the Episcopal Church was untramelled by any links with government or the law, and the Oxford Movement later found many adherents there. In fact, attempts to found Anglican religious communities for men predated similar moves in England. In 1840 a small group of missionaries in what is now the state of Wisconsin lived together for some years as a religious community, holding their property in common, engaged in communal labour, and regularly worshipping together in their little chapel.[75] In 1847 Bishop Ives of North Carolina recruited the first five members of the missionary Society of the Holy Cross which he had founded.[76] They were to be anglican Jesuits. He settled them in a valley in Tennessee which he called Valle Crucis. The community was heavily criticised by the evangelical wing of the Episcopal Church, and most of the brothers left after some years.

The first successful religious community in the American Episcopal Church was the Order of the Holy Cross.[77] It started around the mission of the Holy Cross in New York's Lower East Side. Dedicated to the Holy Cross, this mission was inaugurated in 1874 when sisters of the Community of Saint John the Baptist moved into the area. In 1881 they invited to help them three clergymen who had recently decided to form a religious order. It was from the mission that the new Order derived its name. The area to be evangelised was one of the most deprived in the city. Small wonder that, of the three

---

[75] Anson (as n. 48), 532–535.
[76] Ibid. 535–540.
[77] For a history of the Order, see McCoy (as n. 47).

pioneers of the order, two left. James Otis Huntington, son of
the bishop of Central New York carried on for a time alone.
In 1884 he made a public monastic profession before three
bishops, including his father. The act was fiercely denounced
by the more Protestant-minded in the Church, including many
bishops, but around this time the tide seemed to be turning.
The first recruit came to join the order, and the mission had
made sufficient progress to justify the building of a spacious
church. Faced with the poverty and deprivation around him,
Father Huntington did not hesitate to advocate social reform
in his sermons. To some he seemed a dangerous radical. In
the end the mission work in this part of New York proved
too much for two people, especially since Father Huntington
was increasingly invited to preach elsewhere. In 1892 the two
monks moved to Westminster in the diocese of Maryland.

In semi-rural surroundings, the monastic character of the
order received new emphasis. Recruits began to join. Father
Huntington and his companions were in constant demand
all over the United States to conduct missions and retreats.
Paradoxically, because of the hostility of the local bishop, they
were able to do very little in the diocese of Maryland itself.
In 1904, therefore, they moved again. They established their
new headquarters at West Park in New York state, overlooking
the Hudson river. From here they developed their unique
apostolate, combining a structured life of worship in their
monasteries with preaching and conducting retreats when one
of them was called out for this purpose.

One of the best known religious communities of modern times came into being within the Reformed Churches of
Switzerland and France.[78] Roger Louis Schutz-Marsauche was
born in 1915. He is the son of a swiss protestant pastor and was
brought up in the Swiss Jura. He was a student of theology at
Lausanne during the Second World War. All Roger's relations

---

[78] K. Spink, *A Universal Heart* (London 1986); D. O. Hicks, 'The Taizé Community: Fifty Years of Prayer and Action', *Journal of Ecumenical Studies* 29
(1992) 202–214.

on his mother's side were French. After the fall of France in 1940 he felt that he could not stand aside in neutral Switzerland. In September 1940 he acquired a farmhouse at Taizé, a small, somewhat run-down village not far from the ruins of the ancient abbey of Cluny. The village was near the border between German-occupied France and the area controlled by the Vichy régime. Jews and others escaping from the Germans and trying to make for Switzerland often came that way.

Roger was joined at Taizé by some student friends from Lausanne. They began to organise themselves into a community. A number of fugitives were helped to make their way to Switzerland, but the authorities became suspicious. In November 1942, when Roger was in Switzerland raising money for his venture, he was warned that he had been denounced and that he should not return. Shortly afterwards the Germans occupied the part of France allocated to Vichy. For the rest of the war Roger and his community lived in Geneva.

They returned to Taizé in 1944 after the liberation. The community began to grow. In 1949 the brothers took the traditional three vows of chastity, poverty, and obedience. From the first they strove for good relations with the local Roman Catholics. Cardinal Gerlier, the archbishop of Lyons, was very supportive of the community in its early days. He visited Taizé several times and encouraged the brothers in their devotion to the Virgin Mary. It was on the cardinal's suggestion that Roger paid two visits to pope Pius XII to persuade him to take a more positive view of ecumenism. Although little was achieved, Roger made numerous contacts in Rome. His friendship with Mgr. Montini, the future pope Paul VI, was particularly important. These visits to Rome, however, were offensive to Pastor Boegner, president of the Federation of Protestant Churches in France.

After the death of Pius XII in 1958 the situation changed. As a former papal nuncio in France, Pope John XXIII already knew and admired brother Roger and in 1962 invited him to be an observer at the Second Vatican Council. Contacts were also made with the Orthodox after a personal visit to Patriarch

Athenagoras of Constantinople. Carson Blake, president of the World Council of Churches, invited Roger to address the Council at Uppsala in 1968. Eventually even Pastor Boegner was won over.

Taizé has been in the forefront of the movement for christian unity. It is best known, perhaps, for its work with youth. Ever since young people began to converge on the community in large numbers, Brother Roger has concerned himself with their problems. The youth congresses organised by the community have acquired world renown. The first was held in 1974 and others in different parts of the world have followed at intervals of a few years. The brothers have also tried to give help in deprived areas. Their policy is to send out a small team to a particular place for a few years; just long enough to create a structure which can be maintained locally. In 1976 Brother Roger and some of his community spent time in Calcutta cooperating with Mother Theresa. They compiled a joint letter about suffering in the world, and about the shame of christian divisions. In Rome during Holy Week in 1984 Brother Roger and Mother Theresa together led the meditations on the Way of the Cross.

The first rule of Taizé was worked out in 1941. Brother Roger wished the brothers to be so aware of God that, even after their formal prayer had ended, all their other activities would be a continuation of it. They were to preserve an inner silence in all things, so that they could dwell in Christ. 'Be filled with the spirit of the beatitudes,' he wrote, 'The joy that is afforded by Christian freedom and the promises of the Gospel, mercy in a world of mounting hatred, and simplicity in your way of life and in your most profound attitude, the kind of simplicity which strives for a renunciation of the self'.[79]

In any history of the early days of religious orders within the churches of the Reformation, those who opposed religious life are, perhaps inevitably, cast in a negative light. While it is true that the language some used was unjustifiably abusive, it should

---

[79] Spink (as above), 47.

be remembered that not all those who objected were ignorant or bigoted. They sincerely valued and vigorously defended their Protestant heritage. No completely satisfactory answer to their objections has been found. Among Lutherans, religious communities have gained most acceptance, because they have been careful to remain within certain limits and never to overstep the bounds set by Martin Luther himself. Among Anglicans, however, religious orders, while no longer under threat, are cherished only by those belonging to the more 'catholic' wing of the Church. Anglicans of more protestant or modernist tendencies still see no use in religious societies bound by vows, especially those that favour the contemplative life. Here then, a proper synthesis within the Church has yet to be achieved.

Chapter 14
THE TWENTIETH CENTURY

THE GREAT POPE LEO XIII (1878–1903), held the
Benedictines in high esteem, but the bewildering profusion of overlapping congregations troubled his logical mind. No doubt he would have liked a single Benedictine
Order, but the monks feared for the traditional independence
of their monasteries. After discussions at a congress of abbots,
a confederation of congregations was agreed and formally
inaugurated by the decree *Summum Semper* of July 1893.
An abbot-primate was elected whose functions were largely
honorary. He was to preside over periodical congresses of
abbots. His place of residence was fixed in the college of Saint
Anselm on the Aventine. This institution had originally been
run from the abbey of Saint Paul in Rome. Reformed in 1867,
the college was moved to its present site in 1893 and became
a veritable benedictine university.[1]

With the encouragement of the pope some unity was restored to the Cistercians. In 1892 three of the four branches of
the Trappists[2] united as an independent Order under an abbot
general.[3] Its monks were now known officially as Reformed
Cistercians, or Cistercians of the Strict Observance. About
this time it became known that the buildings of the former
abbey of Cîteaux, which had undergone various vicissitudes
since the Revolution, were for sale. With help from a generous
benefactress the newly united Order purchased the property

---

[1] *Beuron 1863–1963* (Beuron 1963) 140; J. Hourlier, 'Les bénédictins', *Les ordres religieux* 1, ed. G. Le Bras (Paris 1979) 320.
[2] See above p. 337.
[3] P. Vernet, 'Les moines sont de retour', *Pour une histoire monumentale de l'abbaye de Cîteaux 1098–1998*, ed. M. Plouvier and A. Saint Denis (Dijon-Vitreux 1998) 311–328.

and in 1898 the first monks arrived to take possession. In the following year the community of Cîteaux elected the superior general of the Strict Observance as their abbot. The administrative headquarters continued to be at Rome but from 1899 the annual Chapter General could again take place, as tradition demanded, at Cîteaux.

The abbey of Casamari stood aloof from these developments. The Sacred Order of Cîteaux—often, though not officially, known as the Common Observance—continued as a federation of congregations. Within each congregation individual houses enjoyed considerable autonomy. The ethos of this branch of the Cistercians was shaped by their historical experience. The conditions of the Counter Reformation had made it necessary for many of them to undertake pastoral work. Governments in the period of the Enlightenment had forced them to justify their existence by running schools and academies. As a result there was an emphasis on intellectual distinction, especially in those houses to which colleges were attached.[4]

After the First World War it was impossible for the belgian Benedictines to remain in the congregation of Beuron, in Germany. In 1920 therefore the belgian abbeys were formed into the congregation of the Annunciation.[5] In England the anglican monks of Caldey who had submitted to Rome were received into the Subiaco congregation and settled at Prinknash in Gloucestershire.[6] In 1943, the Prinknash community was offered the estate of Pluscarden in Scotland and the extensive ruins of the medieval abbey which stood there. The offer was accepted and the first community set out in 1948 to begin the laborious work of restoration.[7]

---

[4] See above pp. 309–311; 317–318. On the Cistercians of the Common Observance, see L. J. Lekai, *The Cistercians, Ideals and Reality* (Kent, Ohio, 1977) 193–206.

[5] *Beuron* (as n.1), 196–197.

[6] S. Ortiger 'Benedictines today', *Benedict's Disciples*, ed. D. H. Farmer (Leominster 1980) 330.

[7] Anonymous [Peter Anson], *The Story of Pluscarden Priory* (Pluscarden 1948); R. Hamilton, *The Pluscarden Story* (Pluscarden 1988).

Throughout the twentieth century vocations to the monastic life have fluctuated. A period of expansion began after the First World War. Scourmont, a cistercian abbey of the Strict Observance in Belgium, for instance, increased from about eighty to one hundred two religious in the inter-war years.[8] Even more spectacular was the increase at Cîteaux itself. In his first seven years as superior Dom Godefroid Bellorgey (1932–1952) took ninety-nine postulants into the noviciate. In the year 1936 alone he took in twenty-four—two a month. By no means all of them persevered. Nevertheless, at the outbreak of the Second World War, there were eighty-eight religious at Cîteaux. In 1932 there had been thirty-seven.[9]

The flow was interrupted by the Second World War and then resumed at an accelerated pace. At Gethsemani, a cistercian abbey of the Strict Observance in the United States, there were seventy novices when the community celebrated its centenary in 1948. In the mid-1950s it had one hundred fifty novices and a total of two hundred seventy religious.[10] The surge in benedictine and cistercian vocations in America and western Europe lasted until the early 1960s. Throughout this period many candidates for the monastic life were ex-servicemen. The religious revival after the Second World War, which affected all countries except those which had fallen to Communism, probably accounts for this monastic renaissance. It should be emphasised, however, that at present no systematic statistical analysis of the monastic expansions after the world wars exists, and it is probably too early for one to be made. Until we have one, all generalisations about the phenomenon must be tentative.

Inevitably this impetus could not last, and at the end of the twentieth century the situation looks less promising. The decline in religious belief and the reluctance of young people to make lifelong commitments has adversely affected

---

[8] A. le Bail and C. Bock, *Scourmont* (Forges-lez-Chimay 1950) 57.
[9] P. Vernet (as n. 3), 321–324.
[10] Monica Furlong, *Merton: A Biography* (London 1980) 165, 202.

religious houses. Even so, the situation is patchy. Some religious houses have closed whereas others have flourishing
noviciates. In France the religious Orders have recently made
modest advances. In 1969 the Cistercians of the Common
Observance felt obliged to abandon the twelfth-century abbey
of Sénanque and for nearly twenty years the buildings were
used as a cultural centre. In 1988 the monks were able to
return and to restore the cistercian life for which the abbey had
been built. In 1970 cistercian nuns of the Strict Observance
established themselves at Anduze in the Cevennes. This was an
area of France noted for fierce antagonism between Catholics
and Protestants. The sisters made it their special task, through
prayer and example, to bring about inter-denominational rec-
onciliation. Four small benedictine houses for men have been
founded in France within the last thirty years: Flavigny (1972),
Lepuix-Guy (1980), Randol (1971), and Triors (1984). A new
Charterhouse was founded at Benonces in 1971.[11]

A striking development in the twentieth century has been
the expansion of benedictine and cistercian houses into Africa,
Asia, and South America.[12] To further this end, two missionary congregations of benedictine sisters were founded in
1921: the Congregation of Mary, Queen of the Apostles, at
Bethanie, near Bruges in Belgium, and the Congregation of
Sainte Bathilde at Vanves, just outside Paris.[13] Among benedictine monks, the Congregation of Saint Ottilien spread into
east and southern Africa, Korea, and Venezuela. The Belgian Congregation opened houses in Zaïre. La Pierre-qui-
Vire made foundations in Vietnam, Cambodia, Madagascar,
and Morocco.[14] As may be expected from a house that originated from Solesmes, the abbey of Kerr Moussa in Senegal
has become noteworthy for the way it has introduced african
senegalese music into the liturgy.[15]

---

[11] Colinon, *Guide* (as n. 43), 46, 61–62, 98, 100–101, 113, 167, 210–211.

[12] S. Ortiger (as n. 6), 333–334.

[13] Hourlier (as n. 1), 315, 322.

[14] Ortiger (as n. 6), 334

[15] Report in *The Tablet* 249, No.8091 (2 September 1995) 1104–1105.

The expansion out of Europe and the United States of the Cistercians of the Strict Observance has been equally impressive. The first house in China was founded in 1883. A daughter house was founded in 1926, by which time the Order had also spread into Japan.[16] French abbeys were responsible for foundations in 'francophone' Africa, whilst communities in Zaïre were founded from Belgium.[17] American houses made foundations in 'anglophone' Africa and also turned their attention to fostering cistercian monasticism in South America. American Cistercians have also been instrumental in bringing their Order back to Norway, from which it was banished at the Reformation. In 1999, american and norwegian nuns settled at Tautra in the Trondheim fjord. Within walking distance of their house are the remains of an historic abbey of white monks, the northernmost house of the Order in the Middle Ages.

Although monks renounce the world, their stability depends to some extent on external political circumstances. The war in Vietnam, the civil disorders in various african countries, inevitably disrupted religious life. The sufferings of the monks from the two cistercian abbeys in China after the communist takeover of the country have been documented in detail.[18] In Europe monasticism was dealt cruel blows by the spread of Communism. Twenty-three benedictine monks of Montserrat in Spain were murdered in 1936–1937.[19] After 1945, monasteries in communist-dominated eastern Europe were closed wholesale and the monks were driven into exile or imprisoned. With the collapse of Communism the religious life revived. Very recently, for instance, the Benedictines returned to the abbey of Brevnov outside Prague in the Czech Republic.[20]

The Second Vatican Council concerned itself with the religious life in October 1965.[21] The Council Fathers' justifi-

---

[16] P. B. Quattrocchi, *Monaci nella tormenta* (Cîteaux 1991) 21–79.

[17] M. Cocheril, 'Les cisterciens', *Les ordres religieux* (as n. 1), 558–561.

[18] Quattrocchi (as n. 16).

[19] A. M. Albareda, *Historia de Monsterrat* (Montserrat 1977) 113.

[20] *Das Kloster Brevnov*, ed. Z. Dragoun, P. Preiss, and P. Sommer, (Prague 1992) 32.

[21] *Decrees of the Ecumenical Councils*, 2, ed. N. P. Tanner, BIB 939–47.

9 The Community of our Lady of the Mississippi Abbey, with the
Bishop-prelate of Trondheim.

cation for the religious life has a particular interest for anyone
who bears in mind Luther's criticisms of monasticism.[22] The
council does not maintain that life in the cloister is more
perfect than life in the world. Instead it states that the Church's
beauty is revealed through the different gifts of her children,
like a bride adorned for her husband.[23] So it is that, from the
beginnings of the Church, there have been men and women
'striving, through the practice of the Gospel counsels, to follow
Christ more freely and imitate him more exactly'.[24] Inspired
by the Holy Spirit, some lived as solitaries, others founded

---

[22] See above pp. 383–384.
[23] *Decrees* (as n. 21), 939: 'Variis donis filiorum suorum decorata appareat sicut
sponsa ornata viro suo.'
[24] Ibid.: 'Inde ab exordiis quidem ecclesiae fuerunt viri ac mulieres qui per
praxim consiliorum evangelicorum Christum maiore cum libertate sequi pres-
siusque imitari intenderunt.'

religious communities which were welcomed and approved by the Church.[25]

The Council Fathers therefore saw the religious life within the context of christian freedom. Some men and women will be drawn to live out the gospel counsels quite literally. The Council defended their right to imitate Jesus in this way, and it is significant that it saw in religious vocations a direct inspiration of the Holy Spirit. The conciliar language about the contemplative life was carefully chosen. Religious had traditionally applied to themselves the incident of Martha and Mary in Saint Luke's Gospel.[26] While Martha busied herself about the house, Mary sat at the feet of Jesus and listened to his words. Contemplatives saw themselves in Mary and noted that Jesus had said, in the Vulgate version, that she had taken *optimam partem*—'the best option'.[27] The Council Fathers, echoing this passage, subtly altered it. Contemplatives, they stated, had taken *praeclaram partem*—'an outstanding option'.[28]

The Council decreed that each Order, remaining true to the original spirit of its founder, should renew itself according to contemporary norms. Constitutions and rules were to be thoroughly examined, obsolete enactments suppressed, and revised texts were to accord with the decrees of the Council.[29] Chapters General, which should genuinely represent the wishes of all members of the Order,[30] were the proper organs to carry out these provisions, and sufficient time should be allowed for discussions among all those concerned.[31] The duty of religious obedience was stressed, but superiors were urged to consult their subjects and listen to them.[32]

The relationship of religious to the rest of the Church has always been complex. Saint Anthony was strictly orthodox

---

[25] Ibid.
[26] Luke 10:38–42.
[27] Lk 10:42.
[28] *Decrees* (as n. 21), 941.
[29] Ibid. 940.
[30] Ibid. 945.
[31] Ibid. 940–941.
[32] Ibid. 945.

and Saint Athanasius owed much to his support. On the other hand, the Fathers in the egyptian desert were seeking solitude and a life of hardship at the very time when the Church was beginning to enjoy the patronage of the state and bishops were exercising influence at the imperial court. From the beginnings, then, there were differences of attitude and the ancient demand for monastic exemption, however galling for the ecclesiastical authorities, could be justified by the need of monks to have their special needs and character respected. The greatest difficulties in this regard have been experienced by anglican religious. During most of the nineteenth century the majority of bishops opposed their very existence. Their few episcopal friends could not allow them to develop as they would have wished, especially if they were drawn to the contemplative life. As late as 1952 a Catholic-minded anglican bishop could still state—with some exaggeration—that there was not a single contemplative community for men in the Church of England.[33]

The value of the contemplative life has always been an important element of Catholic belief. This has been confirmed several times by popes, not least by Pius XI in his apostolic constitution of 1924, *Umbratilem*. 'By the inward holiness of those who lead the solitary life in the silence of the cloister', wrote the pontiff, in the somewhat cloudy curial Latin of the time, 'and by their most intimate union with God, is kept brightly shining the halo of that holiness which the spotless bride of Jesus Christ holds up to the admiration and imitation of all'.[34] It might have been thought, then, that religious would flourish under the authority of the Roman See, yet here, too, there have been difficulties. The centralisation of church government since the thirteenth century has hampered charismatic leaders. In the twelfth century it was still possible for a holy man or holy woman to go into a desert place, gather disciples, and work out a rule of life. Provided the group was known to be orthodox,

---

[33] Peter Anson, *The Call of the Cloister* (London 1955) 215.
[34] Pius XI, *Umbratilem* (Parkminster 1933) 8–10.

it would eventually, if it flourished, receive papal approval and encouragement.

In more modern times, down to the Second Vatican Council, this freedom was severely curtailed. As far as religious institutes which existed in more than one diocese were concerned, new rules or constitutions, and even major alterations to those that already existed, required the approval of the Holy See. This meant, in fact, the approval of the Congregation of Religious,[35] a commission of the Curia consisting of cardinals and other experts, which had all the bureaucratic faults of slowness of procedure and lack of imagination. An appeal for the intervention of the pope himself was useless, for it was the Congregation which briefed the pope. It was a weakness of Dom Augustine Lestrange's position that the constitutions of La Val Sainte had never received the necessary papal approval. Here Rome may have been wiser than the abbot. On other occasions the Curia's proceedings have been more difficult to defend. A notorious case in the twentieth century was that of Mother Suzanne Aubert, a dynamic New Zealand nun, much admired in her own country. At the age of seventy-seven, she was obliged to travel to Rome to clarify the status of the religious Order she had founded. There she languished from 1913 to 1919. Ultimately her cause triumphed, but for a time everything came to a halt because all the papers had been mislaid.[36]

Contemplata tradere—handing on the fruits of contemplation—has always been a tradition of western monasticism. Catholic spirituality, indeed, comes largely from monks and religious. Their intervention in the affairs of the Church was constantly demanded because it was felt that they had something very special to contribute. Monks and hermits like Peter

---

[35] The Congregation has had various titles and terms of reference. Throughout the nineteenth century it was the Congregation of Bishops and Regulars. In 1908 the two sections were separated and a special Congregation of Religious was established. Since 1967 its title has been the Congregation for Institutes of the Consecrated Life and Societies of the Apostolic Life.

[36] Jessie Munro, *The Story of Suzanne Aubert* (Auckland 1997) 339–368.

10 Abbot Cuthbert Butler and the Benedictine Community of Downside, 1914.

Damian and Saint John Gualbert were at the heart of the church reform of the eleventh century. In the twelfth, Saint Bernard and Saint Hildegard were venerated as prophets. No monks were more strictly enclosed than the Carthusians in the late Middle Ages, but they spoke eloquently to their contemporaries through the books of which they themselves were the authors and the works of spirituality written by others which they copied and distributed.

Twentieth century monks have continued the tradition. In his writings and in practice, Dom Ildefons Herwegen, abbot of Maria Laach in the Rhineland during a tragic time (1913–1946), anticipated many of the liturgical reforms of the Second Vatican Council.[37] Reacting against what he considered to be the excessive individualism of much contemporary spirituality, Abbot Herwegen emphasised that the Church continued the incarnation of Christ in the flesh, and that the faithful shared his life through their participation in the divine mysteries of the liturgy. The fervent community at Maria Laach exemplified the abbot's theology and was seen as a focus of renewal in the whole Church.

A contemporary of Dom Ildefons was Dom Lambert Beaudouin (1873–1960).[38] In 1906, after some years as a secular priest, he entered the benedictine abbey of Mont César in Louvain, Belgium. From there he edited a number of periodicals and organised conferences aimed at liturgical renewal. In 1921 he went to Rome for a period of study at Sant' Anselmo. There he became interested in the traditions of the ancient eastern churches, and he returned to Belgium with a plan for reunion between east and west—an idea which, in his time, was revolutionary. He wished neither for more 'uniate' churches nor for individual conversions. True union, in his view, must

---

[37] On Abbot Herwegen, see A. Olivar, 'Warum ich mein erstes Buch der Laachener Klostergemeinde gewidmet habe' and A. Häussling, 'Die Gabendarbringung', in *Ecclesia Lacensis: Beiträge aus Anlass der Wiederbesiedlung der Abtei Maria Laach . . .* , ed. E. von Severus (Münster 1993) 264–271, 272–302.
[38] Biographies: L. Bouyer, *Dom Lambert Beaudouin, un homme d'Église* (Paris 1964); S. A. Quitslund, *Beaudouin, A Prophet Vindicated* (New York 1973).

be based on genuine discussions between the leaders of the churches. For this a growth in mutual understanding would be necessary.

In 1925 Dom Lambert founded a benedictine monastery at Amay where these principles were to be put into practice. There was a single community, but two chapels so that the eastern and western liturgies could both be celebrated. In 1939 the community moved into more ample quarters at Chevetogne, near Namur. The monastery was to host discussions between eastern and western Christians, and serve as a study centre for those who wanted to learn about eastern Christendom. In 1928 Dom Lambert started a periodical, *Irenikon*, in which the matters under discussion could be aired in a scholarly and eirenic way. The Second Vatican Council's decree on ecumenism owes much to his pioneering work.

In England the work done at Amay-Chevetogne inspired the Benedictine Dom Bede Winslow.(1888–1959).[39] Whereas Dom Lambert in Belgium had a prestigious institution at his back, however, Dom Bede stood alone. He brought forward the work of christian unity first and foremost through personal contacts. No doubt only someone with his self-effacing manner and modesty could have pursued ecumenism in the bleak inter-Church atmosphere of the time. He had numerous anglican and methodist friends, but above all he cultivated his relations with the Orthodox. For the *Eastern Churches Quarterly*, which he founded and edited, he attracted articles on the liturgy, history, and current situation of the Christian East by leading scholars of all denominations. Dom Bede maintained high editorial standards, while the binding, typography, and quality illustrations reflected in a unique way his aesthetic sensibility and love of order. The collapse of the *Eastern Churches Quarterly* soon after his death has been a tragedy for scholarship and for east-west ecumenism.

---

[39] For a memorial of the life of Dom Bede Winslow see, *Rediscovering Eastern Christendom: Essays in Memory of Dom Bede Winslow*, ed. E. L. B. Fry and A. H. Armstrong (London 1963) 1–10.

Without doubt the best known monk of the twentieth century was Thomas Merton (1915–1968).[40] He was born in Prades, in France. His mother was an American, his father an artist from New Zealand. Both his parents died when he was very young. His spent a peripatetic youth, sometimes in New York with his maternal grandparents, sometimes in France, sometimes in England. In 1935 he moved to America and became a student in Columbia University. Here he discovered his gift for writing and began to take an interest in religion. He became a Roman Catholic in 1938. In 1941 he joined the community of the Cistercian Strict Observance at Gethsemani Abbey in Kentucky.

The authorities at Gethsemani encouraged him to write. In his first years as a monk he wrote the biographies of some cistercian saints. But it was his autobiography, *The Seven Storey Mountain,* published in New York in 1948, which made him, and the Trappists, famous. The book became a best-seller. In his brilliant way Merton was describing a spiritual odyssey in which, however they might differ from him, readers could recognise their own modern predicament. He also made graphic the very austere and unfamiliar cistercian way of life in a way that could be understood from the inside. By the time Merton became novice master at Gethsemani in 1955, quite a number of the young men in the noviciate had been attracted to the monastic life by his book.[41]

In the journal which he published under the title *The Sign of Jonas* (New York 1948), he was ready to take a more nuanced view of the monastic life and its problems. In *Seeds of Contemplation* (New York 1949), he distilled into one hundred ninety-eight octavo pages the traditional teaching of the Fathers about prayer, and enriched the discussion with illuminating comments from his own experience. A large quantity of publications now followed. In all of them he brought

---

[40] There is a vast literature on Thomas Merton. Monica Furlong's biography (as n. 10), and Michael Mott, *The Seven Mountains of Thomas Merton* (Boston 1984) may serve as introductions.
[41] Furlong (as n. 10), 218.

the public's attention to the importance of the contemplative life.

That a monk who had sought prayerful solitude at Gethsemani was now a celebrity with extensive fan-mail created difficulties for Merton and for his community. In the 1960s the emphasis of his writings changed. He involved himself in campaigns of protest against nuclear weapons, and in the agitation against the war in Vietnam. His ecumenism embraced not only other Christians, but also Buddhists, whose rich monastic tradition he particularly appreciated. He also helped, at some cost to himself, to bring about a relaxation of the more negative restrictions on cistercian life inherited, in part, from de Rancé and Lestrange. In December 1968, while attending a conference at Bangkok, he was accidentally electrocuted.

Most monasteries nowadays share their insights with seculars by opening the doors of their guesthouses to retreatants who, for a few days, can attend the regular choir offices, find opportunities to pray and meditate in solitude, and discuss their problems with an experienced spiritual guide. At Easter 1999 more than three hundred people were on retreat at the benedictine abbey of Worth in Sussex, England.[42] In 1977 the 'francophone' religious houses of France, Belgium, and Luxemburg cooperated in the production of a guide which publicised the facilities available for individual or group retreats at each house. This guide has now gone into its tenth edition.[43] Among over four hundred religious houses, one hundred fifty-one monasteries are listed: thirty-five benedictine houses for men of various congregations and sixty-two for women, twenty-two cistercian houses of the Strict Observance for men and twelve for women, three cistercian houses of the Common Observance for men and eight for women, three houses of

---

[42] *The [London] Times* 31 March 1999, //3.
[43] M. Colinon, *Guide des Monastères: France, Belgique, Luxembourg* (Paris 1990).

the cistercian 'congregation of Esquermes' for women, four charterhouses for men and two for women.[44]

The guide was compiled by sending round a questionnaire. To the question, 'Do you accept guests in your monastery?' one superior answered, 'No.' A few days later she sent a letter of explanation. 'I am afraid you might have misunderstood us,' she wrote. 'We certainly do not refuse to open our doors. But we have only three small rooms, and they are so bare that we could not offer them to anyone who had not, like ourselves, taken a vow of poverty'.[45]

Monks, writes de Rancé, live in their cloisters:

> Within sight, in the expectation, as well as the faith of the second coming of Jesus Christ, just as the holy fathers in Limbo sighed endlessly for it. We have an advantage and a comfort, however, which they did not have. We already enjoy his presence, according to the promise which he made to us when his Father removed him from the world, that he would be with us until the very end of the ages.[46]

Not only monks but all men and women need something of this vision as we enter, with mixed feelings, upon the Second Millennium.

---

[44] Ibid. 17–19. The cistercian sisters of Esquermes combine teaching with the contemplative life. In evaluating the figures it should be noted that not all religious houses in the area chose to be included in the *Guide*.

[45] Ibid. 8.

[46] *Règlemens de l'abbaye de la Trappe en forme de constitutions avec des réflexions* (Paris 1718) 33–34.

SELECT BIBLIOGRAPHY

PRINTED SOURCES

Abbé de Rancé: Correspondance, ed. A. J. Krailsheimer, 4 vols. Lonrai 1993.

Acta Sanctorum Ordinis S. Benedicti ed. L. d'Achery and J. Mabillon, 9 vols. Paris 1668–1701.

Adomnan's Life of Columba, text, trans., commentary by A. O. and M. O. Anderson. London 1961.

Annales Cistercienses ed. A. Manrique, 4 vols. Lyons 1642–1659.

Annales ordinis Cartusiensis ab anno 1084, ed. C. Le Couteulx, 8 vols. Montreuil 1887–1891.

Athanasius:

    Vie d'Antoine, text, trans. (French), commentary, J. G. M. Bartelink. Paris 1994.

    Vita S. Antonii, trans. and introd. R. C. Gregg. New York 1980

    Werke, ed. H. G. Opitz, 2 vols. Berlin-Leipzig 1935.

Athenagoras, ed. W. R. Schoedal. Oxford 1972.

Augustine of Hippo:

    Confessions, ed. and trans. R. S. Oine-Coffin. London 1961.

    La Règle de saint Augustin, ed. L. Verheijen, 2 vols. Paris 1967.

Basili Regula a Rufino Latine versa, ed. K. Zelzer. Vienna.

Bede: The Ecclesiastical History of the English Nation, trans. J. Stevens. London 1952.

Benedict of Nursia:

    La Règle de St. Benoît, text, trans. (French), commentary, A. de Vogüé and J. Neufville, 7 vols. Paris 1972–1977.

    Règle de St. Benoît, édition du centenaire, text. trans. (French), commentary, E. Manning and H.Rochais. Rochefort 1980.

    The Rule of Saint Benedict. A Doctrinal and Spiritual Commentary by A. de Vogüé. Kalamazoo 1983.

    The Rule, ed. and trans. T. Fry and I. Baker. Collegeville 1981

The Rule, ed. and trans. J. McCann. London 1952.

The Rule, trans. A. C. Meisel and M. L. del Mastro. New York 1975.

Benoît XII, lettres closes et patentes intéressant les pays autres que la France, ed. J. M. Vidal and G. Mollat. Paris 1950.

Bernard of Clairvaux:

> *Apologia to Abbot William*, ed. and trans. M. Casey. Kalamazoo 1970.
>
> *Sancti Bernardi Opera*, ed. J. Leclercq, C. H. Talbot, and H. M. Rochais, 8 vols. Rome 1957–1977.
>
> *Opera*, ed. J. Mabillon, 6 vols. Paris 1839.
>
> *The Letters of St. Bernard of Clairvaux*, trans. B. Scott James. London 1953; rpt. Stroud-Kalamazoo 1998.

Biografie di Giovanni Gualberto a confronto, ed. P. di Re. Rome 1974.

Βίος καὶ Πολιτεία τοῦ ὁσίου Πατρός ἡμῶν Νείλου τοῦ νέου (Vios kai politeia tou hosiou patros himon Neilou tou neou), ed. G. Giovanelli. Grottaferrata 1972.

Bridget of Sweden:

> *Acta et Processus canonizacionis sancte Birgitte*, ed. I. Collijn. Uppsala 1924–1.
>
> *Den heliga Birgittas Revelaciones Extravagantes*, ed. L. Hollman. Uppsala 1956
>
> *Den heliga Birgittas Revelaciones Bok VII*, ed. B. Bergh. Uppsala 1967.
>
> *Sancta Birgitta, opera minora* 1–Regula Salvatoris, ed. S. Eklund. Stockholm 1975.

Cassian:

> *Conférences*, text, trans. (French), commentary, E. Pichery, 3 vols. Paris 1955–1959.
>
> *Conferences*, introd. O. Chadwick, trans. C. Luibheid. New York 1985.
>
> *Institutions Cénobitiques*, text, trans. (French), commentary, J. C. Guy. Paris 1965.
>
> see also *The Nicene and Post-Nicene Fathers*.

Césaire d'Arles, oeuvres monastiques, text, trans. (French), commentary, A. de Vogüé and J. Courreau, 2 vols. Paris 1994.

Chartes et Documents concernant l'abbaye de Cîteaux, ed. J. Marilier. Rome 1961.

Columbani Opera, ed. G. S. M. Walter. Dublin 1957.

Consuetudines Monasticae, ed. P. B. Albers, 5 vols. Stuttgart, Vienna, Monte Cassino, 1900–1912.

Corpus Consuetudinum Monasticarum:
1). *Initia Consuetudinis Benedictinae: consuetudines saeculi octavi et noni*, ed. K. Hallinger et al. Siegburg 1963.
6). *Consuetudines Benedictinae variae*, ed. G. Constable et al. Siegburg 1975.
7). *Consuetudinum saeculi x/xi/xii/ monumenta* pars i–introductiones ed. K. Hallinger. Siegburg 1984; pars ii–*consuetudines Cluniacensium antiquiores cum redactoribus derivatis* ed. K. Hallinger. Siegburg 1983; pars iii–*consuetudinum saeculi x/xi/xii/ monumenta non-Cluniacensia*, ed. K. Hallinger. Siegburg 1984.

Decrees of the Ecumenical Councils, ed. N. Tanner, 2 vols. Georgetown 1990.

Die Regeln der Väter, ed. M. Puzicka. Münsterschwarzach 1990.

Evagrius: the Praktikos and chapters on Prayer, ed. and trans. J. E. Bamberger. Kalamazoo 1981.

Ferrerii Historia Abbatum de Kynloss una cum vita Thomae Chrystalli abbatis, ed. J. P. Muirhead. Edinburgh 1839.

Geoffrey Chaucer: The Canterbury Tales, trans. N. Coghill. London 1985.

Gertrude of Helfta:
Oeuvres Spirituelles, text, trans. (French), commentary, J. Hourlier et al., 5 vols. Paris 1967–86.
The Herald of God's Loving Kindness, Books 1–2. ed. and trans. A. Barratt. Kalamazoo 1991.
The Herald of God's Loving Kindness, Book 3, ed. and trans. A. Barratt. Kalamazoo 1999.
The Spiritual Exercises, ed. and trans. G. J. and J. Lewis. Kalamazoo 1989.

Gregory the Great:
  Dialogues, text, trans. (French), commentary, A. de Vogüé,
     3 vols. Paris 1978–1980.
  Life and Miracles of St. Benedict, ed. and trans., O. J. Zimmer-
     mann and B. R. Avery. Collegeville 1949.
  Registre des Lettres, ed. P. Minard. 1991 (in progress).
Hildegard of Bingen:
  Lieder, text (with music), trans. (German), commentary,
     P. Barth, M. I. Ritscher, and J. Schmidt-Gorg. Salzburg
     1969.
  Scivias, ed. A. Führkotter and A. Carlevaris, 2 vols. Turnhout
     1978.
Historia sive Notitiae Episcopatus Daventriensis, ed. J. Lindeborn.
  Cologne 1670.
Jerome:
  Lettres, ed. J. Labourt, 8 vols. Paris 1949–1963.
  Select Letters, trans. F. A. Wright. London 1975.
*La Règle du bienheureux pere S. Benoist. . . . . .avec les constitutions
  qui y sont esté accommodées par la reverende mère Marguerite
  Veni d'Arbouze*. Paris 1676.
Les Codifications cisterciennes de 1237 et de 1257, ed. B. Lucet.
  Paris 1977.
Les 'Ecclesiastica Officia' cisterciens du XIIe siècle, ed. D. Choisselet
  and P. Vernet. Reiningue 1989.
Les plus anciens textes de Cîteaux, ed. J. C. Bouton and
  J. B. van Damme. Achel 1974.
Les Règles des Pères, text, trans. (French), commentary, A. de
  Vogüé, 2 vols. Paris 1982.
Lettres des premiers Chartreux, text, trans (French), commentary,
  by a Carthusian. Paris 1967.
Luther's Works, ed. J. Pelikan and H. T. Lehmann, 55 vols. Saint
  Louis, MO, 1958–1986.
Madame de Sévigné: correspondance, ed. R. Duchêne, 3 vols. Paris
  1972.
Medieval Latin Lyrics, ed. and trans. H. Waddell. London 1948.
Mise Pádraig, ed. and trans., L. MacPhilibín. Dublin 1961.

Nomasticon cisterciense seu antiquiores ordinis cisterciensis constitutiones, ed. J. Paris. Paris 1664.

Pachomian Koinonia, ed. and trans., A. Veilleux, 3 vols. Kalamazoo 1980–1982.

Peter Damian

> *De Gallica Profectione*, PL 145:865–880.

> *De ordine eremitarum et facultatibus eremi Fontis Avellani*, PL 145:327–336.

> *De suae congregationis institutis ad Stephanum monachum*, PL 145:335–364.

Pius XI, *Umbratilem*, ('The Power of Contemplation'). Parkminster 1933.

Règlemens de l'abbaye de la Trappe en forme de constitutions avec des reflexions. Paris 1718.

Règlemens de la maison-Dieu de la Trappe par Mr. l'abbé de Rancé. . . . .augmentés des usages particuliers de la maison-Dieu de la Val Sainte. . . . . . en Suisse, 2 vols. Fribourg 1794.

Regula cuiusdam patris, PL 66:987–994.

Regula Monastica Communis, PL 87: 1111–1130.

Regularis Concordia, ed. T. Symons. London 1953.

Sancti Fructuosi Regula Monachorum, PL 87:1099–1110.

Sancti Isidori Regula Monachorum, PL 83:867–904.

Sancti Leandri Regula Monachorum, PL 72:873–894.

Statuta Capitulorum Generalium ordinis Cisterciensis, ed. J. M. Canivez, 8 vols. Louvain 1933–1941.

'Statuten von Generalkapiteln ausserhalb Cîteaux: Wien 1393 und Heilsbronn 1398', ed. B. Griesser. *Cistercienser Chronik*, NF 33/4 (1955), 65–83.

Sulpicius Severus, see *The Nicene and Post-Nicene Fathers.*

Symeonis monachi opera omnia, ed. T. Arnold, 2 vols. London 1882.

The Book of St. Gilbert, ed. R. Foreville and G. Keir. Oxford 1987.

The Celtic Monk, trans. U. Ó Maidin. Kalamazoo 1996.

The Cloud of Unknowing and related treatises, ed. P. Hodgson. Salzburg 1982.

The Decameron of Giovanni Boccaccio, trans. J. M. Rigg, 2 vols. London 1930.

The Historia Occidentalis of Jacques de Vitry, ed. J. F. Hinnebusch. Fribourg 1972.

The Letters of Armand-Jean de Rancé, ed. and trans., A. J. Krailsheimer, 2 vols. Kalamazoo 1984.

The Letters of Peter the Venerable, text, trans., commentary, Giles Constable, 2 vols. Cambridge Mass., 1967.

The Life of Beatrice of Nazareth, ed. and trans. R. de Ganck with J. B. Hasbrouck. Kalamazoo 1991.

The Life of Blessed Henry Suso, trans,. T. F. Knox. London 1913.

The Life of Catherine of Siena by Raymond of Capua, ed. and trans. C. Kerans. Dublin 1980.

The Monastic Constitutions of Lanfranc, text, trans., commentary, D. Knowles. London 1951.

The Nicene and Post-Nicene Fathers, 2nd Ser., ed. P. Schaff and H. Wace, vol. 11. Grand Rapids 1978 (repr.): Sulpicius Severus 1–122; Vincent of Lérins 131–156; Cassian, Institutes 201–290; Conferences 295–545.

The Oxford Book of Medieval Verse, ed. F. J. E. Raby. Oxford 1959.

The Paraclete Statutes: Institutiones Nostrae, ed. and trans., C. Waddell. Kalamazoo 1987.

The Rule of the Master:
  La Règle du Maître, text, trans. (French), commentary, A. de Vogüé et al., 3 vols. Paris 1964–1965.
  The Rule of the Master, trans. L. Eberle, introd. A. de Vogüé. Kalamazoo 1977.

The Sayings of the Desert Fathers, ed. and trans., B. Ward. Oxford-Kalamazoo 1975, 1983.

The Twelfth Century Cistercian Hymnal, ed. C. Waddell. Gethsemani–Kalamazoo 1984.

Thomas à Kempis:
  The Imitation of Christ, ed. and trans., L. Sherley-Price. London 1952.
  Thomae Hemerken a Kempis opera omnia–2, De Imitatione Christi, ed. M. J. Pohl. Freiburg-im-Breisgau, 1904.

Three Byzantine Saints, ed. and trans., E. Dawes and N. H. Baynes. Oxford 1977.

'Un plaidoyer du XIVe siècle en faveur des cisterciens', ed. N. Valois, *Bibliothèque de l'école des chartes* 69 (1908) 352–68.

Vie des Pères du Jura, text, trans. (French), commentary, F. Martine. Paris 1968.

Vincent of Lérins, see *The Nicene and Post-Nicene Fathers*.

DICTIONARIES AND ENCYCLOPAEDIAS

Biographie nationale de Belgique, 44 vols. Brussels 1866–1986.

Dictionnaire d'Archéologie Chrétienne et de Liturgie, 15 vols. Paris 1907–1953.

Dictionnaire des Auteurs Cisterciens, 3 vols. Rochefort 1975–1978

Dictionnaire de Spiritualité, 17 vols. Paris 1937–1995.

Dictionnaire de Théologie Catholique, 15 vols. Paris 1909–1950; Tables générales, 3 vols. Paris 1951–1972.

Dictionnaire d'Histoire et de Géographie Ecclésiastiques. Paris 1912—(in progress).

Dizionario biografico degli Italiani. Rome 1960—(in progress).

Dizionario degli Istituti di Perfezione. Rome 1974—(in progress).

Encyclopaedia of Early Christianity. Chicago-London 1990.

Encyclopaedia of the Early Church, 2 vols. Cambridge 1992.

Lexikon des Mittelalters. Aachen 1980—(in progress).

The New Catholic Encyclopaedia. 17 vols. Washington D. C. 1967–1979.

Theologische Realenzyklopädie. Berlin 1977—(in progress).

BOOKS AND ARTICLES

A History of the County of Lancaster, 2, ed. W. Farrer and J. Brownhill. London 1908.

A History of the County of Middlesex, 1, ed. J. S. Cockburn, H. P. F. King, and K. G. T. McDonnell. Oxford 1969.

Alamo, M.'Cisneros (Garcia ou Garzias de)', DS 2/1 (1953) 910–921.

Albareda, A. M.*Historia de Montserrat*. Montserrat 1977.

Albers, B.'Une nouvelle édition des *consuetudines Sublacenses*', *Revue Bénédictine* 19 (1902) 183–204.

Allchin, A. M. *The Silent Rebellion*. London 1958.

Almond, J. C. *The History of Ampleforth Abbey*. London 1903.

Almond, L. *Downside Abbey and its School 1814–1914.* Exeter 1914.

Angerer, J. *Die liturgisch-musikalische Erneuerung der Melker Reform,* Österreichische Akademie der Wissenschaften: Philosophisch-Historische Klasse 287. Vienna 1974

Anonymous. *A History of the Benedictine Nuns of Dunkirk.* London 1958.

Anonymous. *Odyssée monastique: Dom A. Lestrange et les Trappistes pendant la Révolution.* La Grande Trappe 1898.

Anonymous. *Stanbrook Abbey: A Sketch of its History.* London 1925.

Anson, Peter. *Abbot Extraordinary. A Memoir of Aelred Carlyle.* London 1958.

———. 'The "Caldey Conversions" of 1913', *Church Quarterly Review* 164 (1963) 322–331.

———. *The Call of the Cloister.* London 1955.

———. *The Story of Pluscarden Priory.* Pluscarden 1948.

Auberger, J. B. *L'unanimité cistercienne primitive.* Citeaux: Commentarii Cistercienses. Achel 1986.

Aubert, R. 'La restauration monastique dans l'Europe occidentale du XIXe siècle', *Revue Bénédictine* 83 (1973) 8–32.

Axters, S. *The Spirituality of the Old Low Countries.* London 1954.

Barrow, G. W. S. *The Kingdom of the Scots.* London 1973.

Bayer, A. 'Griechen im Westen im 10 und 11 Jahrhundert: Simeon von Trier und Simeon von Reichenau', *Kaiserin Theophanu,* 1:335–341. Ed. A. von Eeuw and P. Schreiner. Cologne 1991.

Beaunier, J. M. Besse, J. Laurent, F. Claudon, J. Becquet, *Abbayes et prieurés de l'ancienne France,* vols. 1–12, 1905- (in progress).

Bellenger, D. A. *The French Exiled Clergy.* Downside 1986.

Becker, A. *Papst Urban II.* Stuttgart 1964.

'Benediktineruniversität Salzburg', SMBO 83 (1972).

Berlière, U., 'Le cardinal Matthieu d'Albano', *Revue Bénédictine* 18 (1901) 113–140, 281–303.

———. 'Les collèges bénédictins aux universités du moyen âge', *Revue Bénédictine* 10 (1893) 130–153.

———. 'Les monastères doubles aux XIIe et XIIIe siècles',

Académie royale de Belgique, classe des lettres et des sciences morales et politiques 18/3 (1923).

Bernardus Magister, ed. J. R. Sommerfeldt. Kalamazoo 1990.

Beuron 1863–1963: Festschrift zum hundertjährigen Bestehen. Beuron 1963.

Bieler, Ludwig. *Ireland, Harbinger of the Middle Ages.* London 1963.

Bienvenu, J. M. *L'étonnant fondateur de Fontrevaud, Robert d'Arbrissel.* Paris 1981.

Birt, H. N. *Benedictine Pioneers in Australia*, 2 vols. London 1911.

Bligny, B. *L'Église et les ordres religieux dans le royaume de Bourgogne aux XI et XII siècles.* Grenoble 1960.

Bodenstedt, M. I. *The Vita Christi of Ludolphus the Carthusian.* Washington DC 1944.

Bloch, H., *Monte Cassino in the Middle Ages* 1. Cambridge, Massachusetts 1986.

Bock, C. *Feuillants et Feuillantines.* Paris 1961.

Bouyer, L. *Dom Lambert Beaudouin, un homme d'Église.* Paris 1964.

Bredero, Adriaan. *Bernard of Clairvaux between Cult and History.* Grand Rapids 1996.

———. 'Cluny et Cîteaux au XIIe siecle; les origines de la controverse', *Studi Medievali* ser 3, 12 (1971) 135–175.

———. 'Le "dialogus duorum monachorum"—un rebondissement de la polémique entre cisterciens et clunsiens', *Studi Medievali* 22 (1981) 501–585.

Brémond, L. A *Literary History of Religious Thought in France*, 3 vols. London 1928–1936.

Brown, Peter. *Augustine of Hippo.* London 1990

Butler, Cuthbert. *The Life and Times of Bishop Ullathorne 1806–89*, 2 vols. London 1926.

Canivez, J. M. 'Barrière (Dom Jean de la)', DHGE 6 (1931) 924–6.

———. 'Cîteaux (ordre)', DHGE 12 (1951) 852–997.

———L'ordre de Cîteaux en Belgique. Scourmont 1926.

Carbonara, G. *Iussu Desiderii.* Rome 1979.

Carosi, P. 'La provincia Sublacense (1851–1867)', *Studia Monastica* 14 (1972) 405–459.

Catalogo dos Bispos, Gerais, Provinciais, Abades e mais cargos de ordem de São Bento do Brasil 1582–1975, ed. D. José Lohr-Endres. Salvador-Bahia 1976.

Ceglar, Stanley. 'The Chapter of Soissons (autumn 1132) and the authorship of the *Reply of the Benedictine Abbots of Cardinal Matthew*', *Studies in Medieval Cistercian History* 2, ed. J. R. Sommerfeldt. Kalamazoo 1976. Pp. 92–105.

———. 'William of St Thierry and his Leading Role at the First Chapters of the Benedictine Abbots', *William Abbot of Saint Thierry*. A colloquium at the abbey of Saint Thierry. Kalamazoo 1987. Pp. 34–49.

Chadwick, Owen. *John Cassian.* Cambridge 1968.

———. *Priscillian of Avila.* Oxford 1976.

———. *The Popes and European Revolution.* Oxford 1981.

Chaussy, Y. *Les Bénédictines et la reforme catholique.* Paris 1975.

———. *Les Bénédictins de Saint Maur*, 1: aperçu historique de la congrégation. Paris 1989.

Chevallier, P. *Loménie de Brienne et l'ordre monastique 1766–89*, 2 vols. Paris 1959.

Chitty, D. W. *The Desert a City.* Oxford-Crestwood, New York 1966.

Christian Spirituality, ed. Bernard McGinn, John Meyendorf, and Jill Raitt, 2 vols. New York-London 1986–1987.

Clanchy, M. *Abelard: A Medieval Life.* Oxford 1997.

Cognet, L. *La reforme de Port-Royal.* Paris 1950.

———. 'Port Royal tel que l'a connu Pascal', *Pascal et Port Royal*, Paris 1962. Pp. 7–12.

Colinon, M. *Guide des Monastéres: France, Belgique, Luxembourg.* Paris 1990.

Collett, B. *Italian Benedictine Scholars and the Reformation.* Oxford 1985.

Colman, P. 'L'architecture néo-Gothique en Wallonie et a Bruxelles', *Il Neogotico nel XIX e XX secolo*, 1:91–99. Milan 1985.

Conant, K. J. *Carolingian and Romanesque Architecture.* London 1959.

Constable, Giles. 'Aelred of Rievaulx and the Nun of Watton', *Medieval Women,* ed. D. Baker. Oxford 1978. Pp. 205–226.

————. *Cluniac Studies.* London 1980.

Cowan, I. B. and D. E. Easson. *Medieval Religious Houses: Scotland.* London 1976.

Cowdrey, H. E. J. *The Age of Abbot Desiderius.* Oxford 1983.

————. *The Cluniacs and the Gregorian Reform.* Oxford 1970.

————. 'Quidam frater Stephanus anglicus natione', *Revue Bénédictine* 101 (1991) 322–340. Rpt. In *The New Monastery*, ed. E. R. Elder. Kalamazoo 1998. Pp. 57–77.

Crouzel, H. *Origen.* Edinburgh 1989.

Dalarun, J. *L'impossible sainteté: la vie retrouvé de Robert d'Arbrissel.* Paris 1985.

————. *Robert d'Arbrissel, fondateur de Fontrevaud.* Paris 1986.

Daly, W. M. 'Caesarius of Arles, A Precursor of Medieval Christendom', *Traditio*, 26 (1970) 1–28.

Dansette, A. *Religious History of Modern France,* 2 vols. Edinburgh-London 1961.

De Bascher, J. 'La "Vita" de St. Bernard d'Abbeville, abbé de Saint-Cyprien de Poitiers et de Tiron', *Revue Mabillon* 59 (1979) 411–416.

De Ganck, Roger. *Beatrice of Nazareth in her Context.* 2 vols. Kalamazoo 1991.

De Jong, M. 'Carolingian Monasticism: The Power of Prayer', *The New Cambridge Medieval History* (q.v.), 622–653.

De Mazis, A. 'La vocation monastique de Dom Guéranger', *Revue Bénédictine* 83 (1973) 119–180.

De Puniet, P. 'Blois (Louis de)', DS 1 (1937) 1730–1738.

De Rancé, Armand-Jean le Bouthillier, *De la sainteté et des devoirs de la vie monastique.* Paris 1683.

Dereine, C. 'Ermites, reclus et recluses dans l'ancien diocèse de Cambrai entre Scarpe et Haine (1075- 1125)', *Revue Bénédictine*, 97 (1987) 289–313.

De Vogüé, A. 'The Master and Benedict: A Reply to Marilyn Dunne', *English Historical Review* 107 (1992) 95–103.

D'Haenens, 'Gerard de Brogne à l'abbaye de St. Ghislain', *Revue Bénédictine* 70 (1960) 101–118.

Diderot, D., *Oeuvres romanesques.* Paris 1962.

Die Cistercienser: Geschichte, Geist, Kunst, ed. A. Schneider. Cologne 1974.

Die Zisterzienser: Ordensleben zwischen Ideal und Wirklichkeit, ed. K. Elm, P. Joerissen, H. J. Roth. Cologne 1981.

Di Re, P. *Giovanni Gualberto nelle Fonti dei Secoli XI-XII.* Rome 1974.

Documents of American Catholic History, ed. J. T. Ellis. Milwaukee 1962.

Doing the Impossible—A Short Historical Sketch of St. Margaret's Convent, East Grinstead. Privately printed, East Grinstead 1984.

Doppelfeld, B. *Mönchtum und Missionare.* Münsterschwarzach 1988.

———. *Mönchtum und kirchlicher Heilsdienst: Entstehung und Entwicklung des nordamerikanischen Benediktinertums im 19. Jahrhundert.* Münsterschwarzach 1974.

Dragoun, Z. *Das Kloster Brevnov.* Prague 1992.

Dressler, F. *Petrus Damiani: Leben und Werk.* Rome 1954.

Dubois, J. 'Les ordres religieux au XIIe siècle, selon la Curie romaine', *Revue Bénédictine* 78 (1968) 283–309.

Du Halgouët, J. 'Pierres d'attente pour une histoire de l'ordre dans la première moitié du XIXe siècle', *Cîteaux,* 17 (1966)–28 (1977) *passim.*

Dunn, M., 'Eastern Influence on Western Monasticism in the Eleventh and Twelfth Centuries', *Byzantium and the West.* Proceedings of the 17th Spring Symposium of Byzantine Studies, Oxford . . . 1984. Amsterdam 1988. Pp. 245–259.

———. 'Mastering Benedict: Monastic Rrules and their Authors in the Early Medieval West', *English Historical Review* 105 (1990). Pp. 567–594.

———. 'The Master and Benedict: A Rejoinder', *English Historical Review* 107 (1992) 104–111.

Duvernay, D. R. 'Cîteaux, Vallombreuse et Étienne Harding', *Analecta Sacri Ordinis Cisterciensis* 8 (1952) 379–494.

Ecclesia Lacensis: Beiträge aus Anlass der Wiederbesiedlung der Abtei Maria Laach . . . ed. E. von Severus. Münster 1993.

Elkins, Sharon K. *Holy Women of Twelfth Century England.* Chapel Hill, North Carolina 1988.

Ellis, R. *The Spirituality of the English Bridgettines.* Salzburg 1984.

Engelbert, P. 'Bursfelder Kongregation', LM 2 (1983) 1108–1110.

———. 'Die Bursfelder Benediktinerkongregation', *Historisches Jahrbuch* 103 (1983) 35–55.

Evans, G. R. *The Mind of Saint Bernard of Clairvaux.* Oxford 1983.

Farmer, D. H., ed. *Benedict's Disciples.* Leominster 1980.

Feige, P., 'Filiation und Landeshoheit—die Entstehung der Zisterzienserkongregation auf der iberischen Halbinsel', *Zisterzienserstudien* 1 (1975) 37–76.

Ferrando, L. 'Feuillants et Feuillantines', DHGE 16 (1967) 1338–1344.

'Festschrift St. Peter in Salzburg', SMBO 93 (1982).

Festschrift zum 750 jährigen Jubilaum des Klosters Oliwa, ed. C. Lange. Danzig 1926.

Fiala, V., 'Die besondere Ausprägung des Benediktinischen Mönchtums in der Beuroner Kongregation', *Revue Bénédictine* 83 (1973) 181–228.

Finnegan, M. J. *The Women of Helfta.* Athens, Georgia 1991.

Fliche, A. and V. Martin. *Histoire de l'Église*, vol. 15: Le pontificat de Jules II et les debuts de Léon X (1503–17). Paris 1951; vol. 20: La crise révolutionnaire. Paris 1949.

Fox, R. L. *Pagans and Christians in the Mediterranean World from the Second Century AD to the Conversion of Constantine.* London 1988.

Franz, E. *Pierre Michel d'Ixnard.* Weissenhorn 1985.

Frend, W. H. C. *The Rise of Christianity.* London 1984.

———. 'Paulinus of Nola and the Last Century of the Western Empire', *Journal of Roman Studies* 59 (1969) 1–11.

Friedlander, C. 'La filiation chez les cisterciens de la stricte observance de 1892 à 1926', *Cîteaux* 37 (1986) 242–277; 38 (1987) 59–87.

———. 'La revision des constitutions après le code de droit canonique de 1917', *Cîteaux* 38 (1987) 309–325.

Furlong, Monica. *Merton. A Biography.* New York-London 1980.

Gaillardin, C. *Les Trappistes ou l'ordre de Cîteaux au XIXe siècle*, 2 vols. Paris 1844.

Gell, J. 'The Return of the Cistercians to England', *Cîteaux* 38 (1987) 96–99.

Ghysens, G. 'Fondation et essor de Maredssous 1872–1923', *Revue Bénédictine* 83 (1973) 230–257.

Gibbon, E. *The Decline and Fall of the Roman Empire*, 7 vols. London 1910

Gilson, Etienne. *The Mystical Theology of Saint Bernard*. London 1955; rpt. Kalamazoo 1990.

Golding, Brian. *Gilbert of Sempringham and the Gilbertine Order*. Oxford 1995.

Green, B. *The English Benedictine Congregation*. London 1979.

Gribomont, J. 'Gerolamo', DIP 4 (1973) 1106–1107.

———. 'Le monachisme au sein de l'eglise en Syrie et en Cappadoce', *Studia Monastica* 7 (1965) 7–24.

Griffe, E. *La Gaule Chrétienne à l'Époque Romaine*, 3 vols. Paris 1964–1966.

Grundmann, H. 'Eremiti in Germania dal X al XII secolo: "Einsiedler" e "Klausner"', *L'eremitismo in Occidente* (q.v.) 311–329.

———. *Religiöse Bewegungen im Mittelalter*. Berlin 1935. Translated by Steven Rowan, *Religious Movements in the Middle Ages*. Notre Dame-London 1995.

Guillon, A. 'Il monachesimo greco in Italia meridionale e in Sicilia nel medioevo', *L'Eremitismo in Occidente* (q.v.) 355–379.

Guy, J. C. 'Jean Cassien, historien du monachisme egyptien?', *Studia Patristica* 8 (1966) 363–371.

Gwynn, A. and R. N. Hadcock. *Medieval Religious Houses: Ireland*. London 1970.

Halkenhäuser, J. *Kirche und Kommunität*. Paderborn 1978.

Hallinger, K. *Gorze-Kluny*. Rome 1950.

Hamilton, Bernard. 'The Monastic Revival in Tenth Century Rome', *Studia Monastica* 4 (1962) 35–68.

Hamilton B. and P. McNulty., '*Orientale lumen et magistra latinitas*: Greek Influences on Western Monasticism (900–1100)', *Le*

Millénaire de Mont Athos 963–1963. Chevetogne 1963. Pp. 181–216.

Hamilton, R. *The Pluscarden Story*. Pluscarden 1988.

Handbuch der Kirchengeschichte, 3, ed. H. Jedin et al. Freiburg 1973.

Handy, R. T. *A History of the Churches in the United States and Canada*. Oxford 1976.

Harper-Bill, C. 'Herluin Abbot of Bec and his Biographer', *Religious Motivation: Biographical and Sociological Problems for the Church Historian*. Studies in Church History 15. Oxford 1978. Pp. 15–25.

Harvey, B. *Living and Dying in England 1100–1540*. Oxford 1993.

Heilingsetzer, G. 'Die Benediktiner im 18. Jahrhundert. Wissenschaft und Gelehrsamkeit im süddeutsch österrreichischem Raum', *Katholische Aufklärung—Aufklärung im katholischen Deutschland*. Hamburg 1993. Pp. 208–224.

Helvetia Sacra 3/1: Benediktiner und Benediktinerinnen, 3 vols. Bern 1986.

Hicks, D. O. 'The Taizé Community: Fifty Years of Prayer and Action', *Journal of Ecumenical Studies* 29 (1992) 202–214.

Hillgarth, J. N. 'Popular Religion in Visigothic Spain', *Visigothic Spain—New Approaches*, ed. E. James. Oxford 1980. Pp. xi–xiii, 3–60.

Histoire de la Bretagne, ed. J. Delumeau. Toulouse 1969.

Holdsworth, C. J. 'The Early Writings of Bernard of Clairvaux', *Cîteaux* 45 (1994) 21–60.

Horn, W. and E. Born. *The Plan of Saint Gall*, 3 vols. Berkeley 1979.

Hourlier, J., 'Maurini', DIP 5 (1973) 1082–1089.

Hughes, K. *The Church in Early Irish Society*. London 1966.

———.'Irish Monks and Learning', *Los monjes y los estudios*, IV semaña de estudios monásticos. Poblet 1963.

Hunt, Noreen. *Cluny under Saint Hugh*. London 1967.

———, ed. *Cluniac Monasticism in the Central Middle Ages*. London 1971.

Hurel, D. O. 'The Benedictines of the Congregation of St. Maur and the Church Fathers', *The Reception of the Church Fathers in the West*, ed. I. Backus. Volume 2:1009–1038. Leiden 1997.

Huyghebaert, N. 'Le moine face au monde du XIXe siècle', *Revue Bénédictine* 83 (1973) 258–277.

Jacob, E. F. 'Gerard Groote and the Beginnings of the "New Devotion" in the Low Countries', *Journal of Ecclesiastical History* 3 (1952) 40–57.

Jakobs, H. *Die Hirsauer.* Cologne-Graz 1961.

Janelle, P. *The Catholic Reformation.* London 1971.

Jedin, H. *Handbuch der Kirchengeschichte* 3: *Die mittelalterliche Kirche.* Freiburg 1973.

Jedin, H., and J. Dolan. *History of the Church,* 5: *Reformation and Counter Reformation.* London 1980; 6: *The Church in the Age of Absolutism and Enlightenment.* London 1981; 7: *The Church between Revolution and Restoration.* London 1981.

Jenal, G. 'Grégoire le Grand et la vie monastique dans l'Italie de son temps', *Colloques internationaux du CRNS: Grégoire le Grand.* Paris 1986. Pp. 147–157.

John, E. '"Secularium Prioritas" and the Rule of St. Benedict', *Revue Bénédictine* 75 (1965) 212–238.

Johnson, Penelope D. *Equal in Monastic Profession.* Chicago 1991.

Jongmans, J. 'Autour de la restauration de la congrégation bénédictine brésilienne', *Revue Bénédictine* 92 (1982) 171–208; 96 (1986) 337–352.

Judge, E. A. 'The earliest use of *monachus* for "monk" (P. Coll. Youtie 77) and the origins of monasticism', *Jahrbuch for Antike und Christentum* 20 (1977) 72–89.

Kervingant, Marie de la Trinité, 'Aux origines des Cisterciennes Trappistines. Un document inédit', *Cîteaux* 35 (1984) 185–214.

———. *Des moniales face à la Révolution française.* Paris 1989. [English trans. by Jean Holman, *A Monastic Odyssey.* Kalamazoo 1999.]

King, A. A. *Cîteaux and her Elder Daughters.* London 1954.

King, Peter. 'Attendance at the Cistercian Chapter General during the 14th Century', *Festskrift til Troels Dahlerup.* Aarhus 1981. Pp. 55–63.

———. *The Finances of the Cistercian Order in the Fourteenth Century.* Kalamazoo 1985.

Klewitz, H. 'Das Ende des Reformpapstums', *Deutsches Archiv* 3 (1939) 372–412.

Klingshirn, W. E. *Caesarius of Arles*. Cambridge 1994.

Knowles, David. *Great Historical Enterprises*. London 1963.

———. *The Monastic Order in England*. Cambridge 1950.

———. 'The Regula Magistri and the Rule of St. Benedict', *Problems in Monastic History*. London 1963 Pp. 139–195.

———. *The Religious Orders in England*, 3 vols. Cambridge 1950–1959.

Knowles D., and R. N. Hadcock. *Medieval Religious Houses: England and Wales*. London 1971.

Koch, A. C. F. 'Gerard de Brogne et le maladie du comte Arnoul I de Flandre', *Revue Bénédictine*, 70 (1960) 119–126.

Krailsheimer, A. J. *Armand-Jean de Rancé*. Oxford 1974.

———. *Rancé and the Trappist Legacy*. Kalamazoo 1985.

L'abbaye de Gorze au Xe siècle, ed. M. Parisse and O. G. Oexle. Nancy 1993.

Laffay, A. H. D*om Augustin de Lestrange et l'avenir du monachisme*. Paris 1998.

Laporte, J. 'Fleury', DHGE 17 (1971) 441–476.

Läubli, W. *Maria Einsiedeln*. Meiringen n.d. [c. 1945].

Law, William. *A Serious Call to a Devout and Holy Life*. London 1955.

Lawless, G. *Augustine of Hippo and his Monastic Rule*. Oxford 1987.

Lawrence, C. H. *Medieval Monasticism*. London 1989.

Le Bail A. and C. Bock. *Scourmont*. Forges-les-Chimay 1950.

Lecler, J. *Vienne*, Histoire des conciles écumeniques, 8. Paris 1964.

Leclercq, H., *Mabillon*, 2 vols. Paris 1953–1957.

———. 'Radegonde', DACL 14 (1948) 2044–2055.

Leclercq, Jean. *St. Bernard of Clairvaux and the Cistercian Spirit*. Kalamazoo 1976.

———. 'S. Romuald et le monachisme missionaire', *Revue Bénédictine* 72 (1962) 307–323.

———. *The Love of Learning and the Desire for God*. New York 1982.

————. *Un maître de la vie spirituell au XIe siécle: Jean de Fécamp*. Paris 1946.

Lekai, Louis J. 'Moral and material status of French Cistercian abbeys in the seventeenth century', *Analecta Sacri Ordinis Cisterciensis* 19 (1963) 199–266.

————. *The Cistercians: Ideals and Reality*. Kent, Ohio 1977.

L'eremitismo in Occidente nei secoli XI e XII, Miscellanea del centro di studi Medioevale, 4. Milan, 1962.

Les moniales cisterciennes, ed. J. C. Bouton, 4 vols. 1986–1989.

Les Ordres Religieux, ed. G. Le Bras, 2 vols. Paris 1979, 1980.

Leyser, Henrietta. *Hermits and the New Monasticism*. London 1984.

Lietzmann, H. *The Era of the Church Fathers*. New York 1951.

Linage Conde, A. *Los origines del monacato benedictino en la peninsula iberica*, 1. Leon 1973.

Lohse, B. *Mönchtum und Reformation*. Göttingen 1963.

Lorenz, R. 'Die Anfänge des abendländischen Mönchtums im 4 Jahrhundert', *Zeitschrift fur Kirchengeschichte*, 77 (1966) 1–61.

Loupès, R. *La vie religieuse en France au XVIIIe siècle*. Paris 1993.

Luchs, A. 'Alive and Well in Florence', *Cîteaux* 30 (1979) 109–124.

Lugano, P. 'Inizi e primi sviluppi dell' istituzione di Monte Oliveto 1313–48', *Benedictina* 1 (1947) 43–81.

Lunardi, G. 'Giovinezza e formazione de Pietro Casaretto (1810–1843)', *Studia Monastica* 14 (1972) 349–374.

Lunn, D. 'Benedictine Reform Movements in the Later Middle Ages', *Downside Review* 91 (1973) 275–297.

————. *The English Benedictines 1540–1688*. London 1980.

Lynch, Joseph H. *Simoniacal Entry into Religious Life 1000–1260*. Columbus, Ohio 1976.

Mabillon, Jean. *Traité des études monastiques. 2 volumes*. Paris 1692.

McAvoy, T. F. *A History of the Catholic Church in the United States*. Notre Dame, Indiana 1969.

McCoy, A. D. *Holy Cross. A Century of Anglican Monasticism*. Wilton, CT 1987.

McDonnell, E. W. *The Beguines and Beghards in Medieval Culture*. New Brunswick, New Jersey 1954.

McHugh, M. P. 'Eugippius', *Encyclopaedia of Early Christianity* [q.v.], 324–325.

McNamara, J. A. 'Muffled Voices', *Distant Echoes [See Medieval Religious Women]*, 11–29.

———. 'Living Sermons', *Peace Weavers [See Medieval Religious Women]*, 19–37.

———. *Sisters in Arms*. Cambridge, Massachusetts 1996.

Mahn, J. B. *L'ordre cistercien et son gouvernement des origines au milieu du XIIIe siècle*. Paris 1951.

———. *Le pape Benoît XII et les cisterciens*. Paris 1949.

Maier, P. 'Ursprung und Ausbreitung der Kastler Reformbewegung', SMBO 102 (1991) 75–204.

'Maria Plain', SMBO 85 (1974).

Marsh, R. *Fr. Marsh's Escape from Dieulouard. His Own Account Written in 1794*, St Laurence Papers, 1, ed. A. Cramer OSB. Ampleforth 1994.

Martinez, G. 'La restauración monástica en Liguria: il Genovesato', *Studia Monastica* 14 (1972) 375–403.

Maycock, A. L. *Nicholas Ferrar of Little Gidding*. London 1963.

Medieval Religious Women, ed. L. T. Shank and J. A. Nichols, 1: *Distant Echoes*. Kalamazoo 1984; 2: *Peace Weavers*. Kalamazoo 1987.

Mollat, G. *The Popes at Avignon*. London 1949.

Monastische Reformen im 9. und 10. Jahrhundert, ed. R. Kottje and H. Maurer. Sigmaringen 1989.

Monks of England, ed. D. Rees. London 1997.

Moorman, J. R. H. *A History of the Franciscan Order*. Oxford 1968.

Mott, M. *The Seven Mountains of Thomas Merton*. Boston 1984.

Müller, G., 'Der Fleischggenuss im Orden', *Cistercienser Chronik* 18 (1906) *passim*.

Munro, J. *The Story of Suzanne Aubert*. Auckland 1997.

Muschiol, G. *Famula Dei*. Munster 1994.

Musset, L. *Normandie Romane*, 2 vols. La Pierre-qui-Vire 1974–1975.

Nagapen, A. *L'église à Maurice 1810–41*. Port-Louis 1984.

Nguyen-Dinh-Tuyen, 'Histoire des controverses à Rome entre la commune et l'étroite observance de 1662 à 1666', *Analecta Cisterciensia* 26 (1970) 3–247.

Nitschke, G. *Die Kathedrale zu Oliva.* Hildesheim 1963.

O'Donnell, J. J. *Cassiodorus.* Berkeley 1979.

O'Donoghue, F. *The Bishop of Botany Bay.* Sydney 1982.

Oetgen, J. *An American Abbot: Boniface Wimmer OSB, 1809–1887.* Washington DC 1997.

Orlandis, J. *Estudios sobre instituciones monásticas medievales.* Pamplona 1971.

Patricia, Sister, o ss s. 'Birgitta Birgersdotter', *Studies in St. Birgitta and the Brigittine Order,* 1 (1993) 7–28.

Pantoni, A. 'Congregazione benedettina Cassinese', DIP 2 (1975) 1477–1485.

Parry, D. 'The Cassinese Congregation A.P.O. (1867–1872)', *Studia Monastica* 14 (1972) 461–484.

Pavan, V. 'Eugippius', *Encyclopaedia of the Early Church* [q.v.] 1:296.

Penco, G. *Storia del monachesimo in Italia.* Rome 1961.

Pepi, R. 'Sta Giustina', DIP 8 (1988) 693–702.

Picasso, G. 'Gregorio VII e la disciplina canonica: clero e vita monastica', *Studi Gregoriani* 13 (1989) 151–166.

Picasso, G. M. 'Aspetti e problemi della storia della congregazione benedettina di Monte Oliveto', *Studia Monastica* 3 (1961) 383–408.

Platt, Colin. *The Abbeys and Priories of Medieval England.* London 1984.

Post, R. R. *The Modern Devotion.* Leiden 1968.

Pour une histoire monumentale de l'abbaye de Cîteaux 1098–1998, ed. M. Plouvier and A. Saint Denis. Dijon-Vitreux 1998.

Pratesi, R. 'Ludovico Barbo', *Dizionario biografico degli Italiani,* 6 (1964) 244–249.

Quattrotrochi, P. B. *Monaci nella tormenta.* Cîteaux 1991.

Quitslund S. A. *Beaudouin, A Prophet Vindicated.* New York 1973.

Quivy, P., 'Robert de Tombelaine et son commentaire sur le cantique des cantiques', *Millénaire monastique de Mont Saint-Michel,* ed. R. Foreville, 2. Paris 1967. Pp. 347–356.

Raison, L. and R. Niderst. 'Le mouvement érémetique dans l'ouest de la France à la fin du XIe siècle et au début du XIIe', *Annales de Bretagne* 55 (1948) 2–45.

Rediscovering Eastern Christendom: Essays in Memory of Dom Bede Winslow, ed. E. L. B. Fry and A. H. Armstrong. London 1963.

Reformbemühungen und Observanzbestrebungen im spätmittelalterlichen Ordenswesen, ed. K. Elm. Berlin 1989.

Reform von Kirche und Reich zur Zeit der Konzilien von Konstanz und Basel, ed. J. Hlavácek and R. Patschovsky. Constance 1996.

Reynolds, R. E. 'The Organisation, Law, and Liturgy of the Western Church 700–900', *The Cambridge Medieval History* [q.v.]. Pp. 587–621.

Robinson, J. A. *Gilbert Crispin, Abbot of Westminster.* Cambridge 1911.

Roisin, Simone. *L'hagiographie cistercienne dans le diocèse de Liège au XIIIe siècle.* Louvain 1947.

Rorimer, J. J. *The Cloisters: The Buildings and the Collection of Medieval Art in Fort Tryon Park.* New York 1963.

Rousseau, P. *Ascetics, Authority, and the Church.* Oxford 1978.

———. *Basil of Caesarea.* Berkeley 1994.

———. *Pachomius.* Berkeley 1985.

Ruppert, F. *Das Pachomianische Mönchtum und die Anfänge klösterlichen Gehorsams.* Münsterschwarzach 1971.

Russo, G. 'Bishop Salvado and the Aborigines', *History Today* (1979) 394–414.

Rüthing, H., 'Die Kartäuser und die spätmittelalterlichen Ordensreformen', *Reformbemühungen* [q.v.]. Pp. 35–58.

Ryan, J. *Irish Monasticism.* Dublin 1931.

Sainsaulieu, J. 'Ermites', DHGE 15 (1963) 766–787.

St. Bernard of Clairvaux: Studies Commemorating the Eighth Centenary of his Canonization, ed. M. B. Pennington. Kalamazoo 1977.

St. Peter in Salzburg, Dommuseum zu Salzburg, Sonderschein 7. Salzburg 1982.

Salem, 850 Jahre Reichsabtei und Schloss, ed. R. Schneider. Constance 1984.

Salzgeber, J. *Die Klöster Einsiedeln und St. Gallen im Barockzeitalter.* Münster 1967.

Schimmelpfennig, B. 'Das Papstum und die Reform des Zisterzienserordens im späten Mittelalter', *Reformbemühungen* [q.v.]. Pp. 399–430.

——. 'Zisterzienserideal und Kirchenreform—Benedikt XII (1334–42) als Reformpapst', *Zisterzienserstudien* 3 (1976) 11–43.

Schmitz, P. *Histoire de l'ordre de St. Benoît,* 7 vols. Maredsous 1948–1956.

Scott, G. *Gothic Rage Undone.* Downside 1992.

Seguin, M. D. 'Port Royal après Port Royal', *Cîteaux* 37 (1986) 106–124.

Seibrich, W. *Gegenreformation als Restauration.* Münster 1991.

Semmler, J. 'Die Beschlüsse des Aachener Konzils im Jahre 816', *Zeitschrift fur Kirchengeschichte* 74 (1963) 15–82.

Skinner, Mary. 'Benedictine Life for Women in Central France— A Feminist Revival', *Distant Echoes* 87–113. See *Medieval Religious Women.*

Silvestre, H. 'Heloïse', DHGE 23 (1990) 946–958.

Soltner, L. *Solesmes et Dom Guéranger.* Solesmes 1974.

Southern, R. W. *St. Anselm and his Biographer.* Cambridge 1963.

Spindler, M. *Handbuch der Bayerischen Geschichte.* Munich 1975.

Spink, K. *A Universal Heart.* London 1986.

Stachnik, R. *Die katholische Kirche in Danzig.* Münster 1959.

Stancliffe, C. *St. Martin and his Biographer.* Oxford 1983.

Standaert, M., 'Feuillants (congrégation des)' DS 5 (1964) 274–287.

Stein, S. J. *The Shaker Experience in America: A History of the United Society of Believers.* New Haven 1992.

Stephan, J. *Buckfast Abbey.* Buckfast 1923.

Suarez Fernandez, L. *Historia General de España y America,* 19 vols. Madrid 1985–1987.

Tabacco, G. 'Romualdo di Ravenna e gli inizi dell' eremitismo camaldoense', *L'eremitismo in Occidente* (q.v.). Pp. 73–119.

Tasso, I. *Ludovico Barbo (1381–1443).* Rome 1952.

Taylor, Jeremy, *Holy Living and Holy Dying.* London 1850.

Tenth Century Studies, ed. D. Parsons. Chichester 1975.

The Cambridge History of Latin America, 1. ed. L. Bethell. Cambridge 1984.

The Great Return: The English Communities in Continental Europe and Their Repatriation 1793–94, ed. A. Bellenger. Downside 1994.

The Influence of St. Bernard: Anglican Essays, ed. B. Ward. Oxford 1976.

The New Cambridge Medieval History, 2, ed. R. McKitterick. Cambridge 1995.

The Reception of the Church Fathers in the West, ed. I. Backus. 2 vols. Leiden-New York-Cologne 1997.

The Spirituality of the Middle Ages, edd. J. Leclercq, F. Vandenbroucke, and L. Bouyer. London 1968.

The Works of George Herbert, ed. F. E. Hutchinson. Oxford 1972.

Thoma, F. X. 'Petrus von Rosenheim osb', SMBO 45 (1927) 94–222.

Thompson, Sally. *Women Religious: The Founding of English Nunneries after the Conquest*. Oxford 1991.

Turbessi, G. 'Vita monastica dell' abbazia di San Paolo nel secolo XIX', *Revue Bénédictine* 83 (1973) 49–118.

Ultee, M. *The Abbey of St. Germain des Prés in the Seventeenth Century*. New Haven 1981.

Vacandard, E. *Vie de St. Bernard*, 2 vols. Paris 1927.

Van Damme, J. B. 'Le prologue de la charte de charité', *Cîteaux* 36 (1985) 115–128.

———. 'Les textes cisterciennes de 1119', *Cîteaux* 34 (1983) 92–110.

Van der Meer, F. *Atlas de l'ordre cistercien*. Paris-Brussels 1965.

Van Engen, John. 'The "Crisis of Cenobitism" Reconsidered: Benedictine Monasticism in the Years 1050–1150', *Speculum* 61 (1986) 269–304.

Van Meter, D. C. 'Count Baldwin IV, Richard of St. Vanne, and the Inception of Monastic Reform in Eleventh-century Flanders', *Revue Bénédictine* 107 (1997) 131–148.

Van Moolenbroek, J. *Vital l'ermite prédicateur itinérant, fondateur de l'abbaye normande de Savigny*. Maastricht 1990.

Vaughn, S., *The Abbey of Bec and the Anglo-Norman State, 1034–1136*. Woodbridge 1981.

Veilleux, Armand. *La Liturgie dans le Cénobitisme Pachômien au quatrième siècle*. Rome 1968.

Verdon, J. 'Les moniales dans la France de l'ouest aux XIe et XIIe siècles: étude d'histoire sociale', *Cahiers de Civilisation médiévale*, 19 (1976) 247–264.

————. 'Recherches sur les monastères f'éminins dans la France du Sud aux IXe aux XIe siècles', *Annales du Midi* 88 (1976) 117–138.

Viti, G. 'Barrière, Jean Baptiste de la', DIP 1 (1969) 1059–1061.

————. 'Foglianti, Fogliantine', DIP 4 (1973) 94–95.

Vogel, C., 'Deux conséquences de l'eschatologie grégorienne: la multiplication des messes privées et les moines-prêtres', *Colloques internationaux du CNRS—Grégoire le Grand*. Paris 1986. Pp. 267–276.

Volz, Carl. 'Martin Luther's Attitude towards Bernard of Clairvaux', *Studies in Medieval History presented to Jeremiah F. O'Sullivan*. Spencer-Kalamazoo 1971. Pp. 186–204.

Von Falkenhausen, V. 'Il monachesimo Italo-Greco e i suoi rapporti con il monachesimo Benedettino', *L'Esperienzia Monastica e la Puglia*, ed. C.D. Fonseca. Bari 1983. 1:119–135.

Waddell, Chrysogonus. 'The Cistercian Dimension of the Reform of La Trappe', *Cistercians in the Late Middle Ages*, ed. E. R. Elder. Kalamazoo 1981. Pp. 102–161.

Wallace-Hadrill, J. *The Frankish Church*. Oxford 1983.

Walton, Izaak. *The Lives of Doctor John Donne, Sir Henry Wotton, Mr. Richard Hooker, Mr. George Herbert, and Doctor Robert Sanderson*. London 1895.

Weaver, F. Ellen. 'Angélique de St. Jean de Port Royal', *Cistercians in the Late Middle Ages*, ed. E. R. Elder. Kalamazoo 1981. Pp. 90–101.

Wemple, S. F. 'Female Spirituality and Mysticism in Frankish Monasticism: Radegund, Balthild, and Aldegund', Peace Weavers 39–53. See *Medieval Religious Women*.

Whale, J.M. 'St. Bartholomew of Grottaferrata', *Eastern Churches Quarterly* 11 (1956) 202–214.

Wilkinson, A. *The community of the Resurrection—a centenary history*, London 1992.

Williams, T.J. *Priscilla Lydia Sellon*, London 1965.

Williams, W. *St. Bernard of Clairvaux*, Manchester 1935.

Wisplinghoff, E. ' Die Benediktinerklöster des Niederrheins', *Festschrift H. Heimpel*, (Veröffentlichungen des Max-Planck-Instituts fur Geschichte 36, ii), Göttingen 1972, 277–291.

Witters, W. 'La congrégation cassinaise de la primitive observance de 1872 a 1880', *Studia Monastica* 14 (1972), 485–521.

Wollasch, J. 'Gerard von Brogne unde seine Klostergründung', *Revue Bénédictine*, 70 (1960), 62–82.

Yanez, D. 'Los primeros usos de la congregacion de Castilla', *Cîteaux* 32 (1981), 1–16.

INDEX OF PERSONS

Peter von Rosenheim, see
  Rosenheim, Peter von.
Petronax, monk of Monte
  Cassino: 122.
Petronilla, abbess of Fontrevaut:
  204.
Philagathos, John, see John
  Philagathos.
Philips, Ambrose de Lisle: 376.
Philpotts, Henry, bishop of
  Exeter: 400, 401, 402.
Pitra, Jean-Baptiste, monk of
  Solesmes: 345.
Pius V, pope: 276.
Pius VI, pope: 327.
Pius VII, pope: 330, 331, 337,
  338.
Pius IX, pope: 349, 355, 356, 357.
Pius XI, pope: 428.
Pius XII, pope: 417.
Polding, John, Bede, archbishop
  of Sydney: 360–361.
Poncher, bishop of Paris: 282.
Pons of Melgueil, abbot of Cluny:
  186.
Pontician: 50.
Poppo, archbishop of trier: 155.
Prescott, Oliver, religious of
  Cowley: 407.
Prideaux, Denis, abbot of
  Nashdom: 413.
Priscillian: 54, 55, 64.
Prosper of Aquitaine: 150.
Pusey, Edward, 400, 401, 402,
  405, 406.

Quesnel, Pasquier: 304, 317.

Rabanus Maurus, abbot of Fulda:
  117.
Radegund, nun of Poitiers: 62–64,
  195.
Ramwold, abbot of Trier: 119.

Rancé, Armand de, abbot of La
  Trappe: 286, 292, 295, 296,
  302–307, 325, 331, 332, 339,
  377, 434, 435.
Raoul de la Futaye, abbot of Saint
  Sulpice-la-Forêt: 166, 201.
Raymund of Capua: 230.
Reding, Augustine, abbot of
  Einsiedeln: 315.
Reid, Mary: 404.
Rese, Friedrich, vicar general of
  Cincinnati: 363.
Richard, abbot of Saint Vanne:
  137, 155.
Richard of Saint Victor: 260.
Richard II, duke of Normandy:
  137.
Richelieu, Armand Jean du
  Plessis de, cardinal bishop of
  Luçon: 298.
Riepp, Benedicta, superior of
  SaintMary's Pennsylvania:
  372.
Robert of Arbrissel, master of
  Fontrevaut: 166, 201–204.
Robert, hermit of Tombelaine:
  145.
Robert, nephew of Saint Bernard:
  187.
Robert, abbot of Molesme:
  168–169, 170, 181.
Robespierre, Maximilien: 323,
  324, 336.
Rochefoucault, François de la,
  cardinal: 301.
Rode Johannes, abbot of Saint
  Matthias: 257.
Rodolfo, abbot of Vallombrosa:
  164.
Roger (Roger Louis Schutz-
  Marsauche): 416–418.
Romanus, abbot of Condat: 49.
Romanus IV, emperor: 135.

INDEX OF PLACES

CISTERCIAN PUBLICATIONS
Texts and Studies in the Monastic Tradition

TEXTS IN ENGLISH TRANSLATION

THE CISTERCIAN MONASTIC TRADITION

Aelred of Rievaulx

* Dialogue on the Soul
* The Historical Works
* Liturgical Sermons, I
* The Lives of the Northern Saints
* Spiritual Friendship
* Treatises I: Jesus at the Age of Twelve; Rule for a Recluse; Pastoral Prayer
* Walter Daniel: The Life of Aelred of Rievaulx

Bernard of Clairvaux

* Apologia to Abbot William (Cistercians and Cluniacs)
* Five Books on Consideration: Advice to a Pope
* Homilies in Praise of the Blessed Virgin Mary
* In Praise of the New Knighthood
* Letters
* Life and Death of Saint Malachy the Irishman
* On Baptism and the Office of Bishops
* On Grace and Free Choice
* On Loving God
* Parables and Sentences
* Sermons for the Summer Season
* Sermons on Conversion
* Sermons on the Song of Songs, I-IV
* The Steps of Humility and Pride

Gertude the Great of Helfta

* Spiritual Exercises
* The Herald of God's Loving-Kindness, Books 1 and 2
* The Herald of God's Loving-Kindness, Book 3

William of Saint Thierry

* The Enigma of Faith
* Exposition on the Epistle to the Romans
* Exposition on the Song of Songs
* The Golden Epistle
* The Mirror of Faith
* The Nature and Dignity of Love
* On Contemplating God, Prayer, Meditations

Gilbert of Hoyland

* Sermons on the Song of Songs, I-III
* Treatises, Sermons, and Epistles

John of Ford

* Sermons on the Final Verses of the Song of Songs, I-VII

Other Cistercian Writers

* Adam of Perseigne, Letters, I
* Alan of Lille: The Art of Preaching
* Amadeus of Lausanne: Homilies in Praise of Blessed Mary
* Baldwin of Ford: Commendation of Faith
* Geoffrey of Auxerre: On the Apocalypse
* Guerric of Igny: Liturgical Sermones, I-II
* Helinand of Froidmont: Verses on Death
* Idung of Prüfening: Cistercians and Cluniacs. The Case of Cîteaux
* In The School of Love. An Anthology of Early Cistercian Texts
* Isaac of Stella: Sermons on the Christian Year, I-[II]
* The Letters of Armand-Jean de Rancé, Abbot of la Trappe
* The Life of Beatrice of Nazareth
* Mary Most Holy: Meditating with the Early Cistercians
* Ogier of Locedio: Homilies [on Mary and the Last Supper]
* Serlo of Wilton & Serlo of Savigny: Seven Unpublished Works (Latin-English)
* Sky-blue the Sapphire, Crimson the Rose: The Spirituality of John of Ford
* Stephen of Lexington: Letters from Ireland
* Stephen of Sawley: Treatises
* Three Treatises on Man: A Cistercian Anthropology / Bernard McGinn

EARLY AND EASTERN MONASTICISM

* Besa: The Life of Shenoute of Atripe
* Cyril of Scythopolis: The Lives of the Monks of Palestine
* Dorotheos of Gaza: Discourses and Sayings
* Evagrius Ponticus: Praktikos and Chapters on Prayer
* Handmaids of the Lord: Lives of Holy Women in Late Antiquity and the Early Middle Ages / Joan Petersen
* Harlots of the Desert. A Study of Repentance / Benedicta Ward
* Isaiah of Scete: Ascetic Discourses

CISTERCIAN PUBLICATIONS Titles Listing

- John Moschos: The Spiritual Meadow
- The Life of Antony (translated from Coptic and Greek)
- The Lives of the Desert Fathers. The *Historia monachorum in Aegypto*
- The Spiritually Beneficial Tales of Paul, Bishop of Monembasia
- Symeon the New Theologian: The Practical and Theological Chapters, and The Three Theological Discourses
- Theodoret of Cyrrhus: A History of the Monks of Syria
- Stewards of the Poor. [Three biographies from fifth-century Edessa]
- The Syriac Book of Steps *[Liber graduum]*
- The Syriac Fathers on Prayer and the Spiritual Life / Sebastian Brock

LATIN MONASTICISM

- Achard of Saint Victor: Works
- Anselm of Canterbury: Letters, I–III
- Bede the Venerable: Commentary on the Acts of the Apostles
- Bede the Venerable: Commentary on the Seven Catholic Epistles
- Bede the Venerable: Homilies on the Gospels, I–II
- Bede the Venerable: Excerpts from the Works of Saint Augustine on the Letters of the Blessed Apostle Paul
- The Celtic Monk [An Anthology]
- Gregory the Great: Forty Gospel Homilies
- Guigo II: The Ladder of Monks and Twelve Meditations / Colledge, Walsh edd.
- Halfway to Heaven
- The Life of the Jura Fathers
- The Maxims of Stephen of Muret
- Peter of Celle: Selected Works
- The Letters of Armand-Jean de Rancé, I–II
- The Rule of the Master
- The Rule of Saint Augustine
- Saint Mary of Egypt. Three Medieval Lives in Verse

STUDIES IN MONASTICISM / CISTERCIAN STUDIES

Cistercian Studies and Reflections

- Aelred of Rievaulx. A Study / Aelred Squire
- Athirst for God. Spiritual Desire in Bernard of Clairvaux's Sermons on the Song of Songs / Michael Casey
- Beatrice of Nazareth in her Context, I–II: Towards Unification with God / Roger DeGanck
- Bernard of Clairvaux. Man. Monk. Mystic / Michael Casey
- The Cistercian Way / André Louf
- Dom Gabriel Sortais. An Amazing Abbot in Turbulent Times / Guy Oury
- The Finances of the Cistercian Order in the Fourteenth Century / Peter King
- Fountains Abbey and Its Benefactors / Joan Wardrop
- A Gathering of Friends. Learning and Spirituality in John of Ford
- Hidden Springs: Cistercian Monastic Women, 2 volumes
- Image of Likeness. The Augustinian Spirituality of William of St Thierry / D. N. Bell
- Index of Authors and Works in Cistercian Libraries in Great Britain / D. N. Bell

- Index of Cistercian Authors and Works in Medieval Library catalogues in Great Britain / D. N. Bell
- The Mystical Theology of Saint Bernard / Etienne Gilson
- The New Monastery. Texts and Studies on the Earliest Cistercians
- Monastic Odyssey [Cistercian Nuns & the French Revolution]
- Nicolas Cotheret's Annals of Cîteaux / Louis J. Lekai
- Pater Bernhardus. Martin Luther and Bernard of Clairvaux / Franz Posset
- Rancé and the Trappist Legacy / A. J. Krailsheimer
- A Second Look at Saint Bernard / Jean Leclercq
- The Spiritual Teachings of St Bernard of Clairvaux / John R. Sommerfeldt
- Studies in Medieval Cistercian History
- Three Founders of Cîteaux / Jean-Baptiste Van Damme
- Understanding Rancé. Spirituality of the Abbot of La Trappe in Context / D. N. Bell
- William, Abbot of Saint Thierry
- Women and Saint Bernard of Clairvaux / Jean Leclercq

Cistercian Art, Architecture, and Music

- Cistercian Abbeys of Britain [illustrated]
- Cistercian Europe / Terryl N. Kinder
- Cistercians in Medieval Art / James France
- SS. Vincenzo e Anastasio at Tre Fontane Near Rome / J. Barclay Lloyd
- Studies in Medieval Art and Architecture, II–VI / Meredith P. Lillich, ed.
- Treasures Old and New. Nine Centuries on Cistercian Music [CD, cassette]
- Cistercian Chants for the Feast of the Visitation [CD]

Monastic Heritage

- Community and Abbot in the Rule of St Benedict, I–II / Adalbert de Vogüé
- Distant Echoes: Medieval Religious Women, I / Shank, Nichols, edd.
- The Freedom of Obedience / A Carthusian
- Halfway to Heaven [The Carthusian Tradition] / Robin Lockhart
- The Hermit Monks of Grandmont / Carole A. Hutchison
- A Life Pleasing to God: Saint Basil's Monastic Rules / Augustine Holmes
- Manjava Skete [Ruthenian tradition] / Sophia Seynk
- Monastic Practices / Charles Cummings
- Peace Weavers. Medieval Religious Women, II / Shank, Nichols, edd.
- Reading Saint Benedict / Adalbert de Vogüé
- The Rule of St Benedict. A Doctrinal and Spiritual Commentary / Adalbert de Vogüé
- Stones Laid Before the Lord [Monastic Architecture] / Anselme Dimier
- What Nuns Read [Libraries of Medieval English Nunneries] / D. N. Bell

Monastic Liturgy

- From Advent to Pentecost / A Carthusian
- The Hymn Collection from the Abbey of the Paraclete, 2 volumes
- The Molesme Summer Season Breviary, 4 volumes
- The Old French Ordinary and Breviary of the Abbey of the Paraclete, 5 volumes
- The Paraclete Statutes: *Institutiones nostrae*
- The Twelfth Century Cistercian Hymnal, 2 volumes
- The Twelfth Century Cistercian Psalter [NYP]
- Two Early Cistercian *Libelli Missarum*

MODERN MONASTICISM

Thomas Merton

- Cassian and the Fathers: Initiation into the Monastic Tradition
- The Climate of Monastic Prayer
- The Legacy of Thomas Merton
- The Message of Thomas Merton
- The Monastic Journey of Thomas Merton
- Thomas Merton Monk
- Thomas Merton on Saint Bernard
- Thomas Merton: Prophet of Renewal / John Eudes Bamberger
- Toward An Integrated Humanity [Essays on Thomas Merton]

Contemporary Monastics

- Centered on Christ. A Guide to Monastic Profession / Augustine Roberts
- Inside the Psalms. Reflections for Novices / Maureen McCabe
- Passing from Self to God. A Cistercian Retreat / Robert Thomas
- Pathway of Peace. Cistercian Wisdom according to Saint Bernard / Charles Dumont
- Poor Therefore Rich / A Carthusian
- The Way of Silent Love / A Carthusian

CHRISTIAN SPIRITUALITY PAST AND PRESENT

Past

- A Cloud of Witnesses. The Development of Christian Doctrine [to 500] / D. N. Bell
- Eros and Allegory: Medieval Exegesis of the Song of Songs / Denys Turner
- High King of Heaven. Aspects of Early English Spirituality / Benedicta Ward
- In the Unity of the Holy Spirit. Conference on the Rule of Benedict
- The Life of St Mary Magdalene and of Her Sister St Martha [Magdalene legend]
- The Luminous Eye. The Spiritual World Vision of St Ephrem / Sebastian Brock
- Many Mansions. Medieval Theological Development East and West / D. N. Bell
- The Name of Jesus / Irénée Hausherr
- Penthos. The Doctrine of Compunction in the Christian East / Irénée Hausherr

CISTERCIAN PUBLICATIONS Titles Listing

EDITORIAL OFFICES

Cistercian Publications • WMU Station
1903 West Michigan Avenue
Kalamazoo, MI 49008-5415   USA
tel 269 387 8920   fax 269 387 8390
e-mail cistpub@wmich.edu

CUSTOMER SERVICE—NORTH AMERICA: USA AND CANADA

Cistercian Publications at Liturgical Press
Saint John's Abbey
Collegeville, MN 56321-7500 USA
tel 800 436 8431   fax 320 363 3299
e-mail sales@litpress.org

CUSTOMER SERVICE—EUROPE: UK, IRELAND, AND EUROPE

Cistercian Publications at Columba Book Service
55A Spruce Avenue
Stillorgan Industrial Park
Blackrock, Co. Dublin, Ireland
tel 353 1 294 2560   fax 353 1 294 2564
e-mail sales@columba.ie

WEBSITE
www.cistercianpublications.org

Cistercian Publications is a non-profit corporation.